Theodore Dreiser

Letters to Women

NEW LETTERS, VOLUME II

THE DREISER EDITION

Sponsored at
the University of Connecticut
by
the Department of English,
the Thomas J. Dodd Research Center,
the College of Liberal Arts and Sciences, and
the University Research Foundations
and by
the University of Pennsylvania Library

Thomas P. Riggio

General Editor

Theodore Dreiser

Letters to Women

NEW LETTERS

VOLUME II

Edited by

THOMAS P. RIGGIO

University of Illinois Press
Urbana and Chicago

Frontispiece, Theodore Dreiser, 1928
Portrait by Wayman Adams.

Photos on pages i, xvi, 8, 35, 46, 53, 76, 81, 121, 150, 155, 229, 261, 308, 353, 364, 373, and 375 from the Theodore Dreiser Papers, Annenberg Rare Book and Manuscript Library, University of Pennsylvania. Photo on page 57 reprinted courtesy of the Sheaffer-O'Neill Collection, Connecticut College. Photo on page 129 reprinted courtesy of Robert Craig. Photo on page 213 reprinted by permission of the Collection of the International Institute of Social History, Amsterdam.

Manufactured in the United States of America
c 5 4 3 2 1

Research for this publication was supported by a grant from the National Endowment of the Humanities. The NEH is not responsible for the views expressed in this book.

∞ This book is printed on acid-free paper.

Library of Congress Cataloging-in-Publication Data
Dreiser, Theodore, 1871–1945.
Letters to women / Theodore Dreiser ;
edited by Thomas P. Riggio.
p. cm. — (New letters ; v. 2) (The Dreiser edition)
Includes bibliographical information
ISBN 978-0-252-03376-6 (alk. paper)
1. Dreiser, Theodore, 1871–1945—Correspondence.
2. Authors, American—20th century—Correspondence.
I. Riggio, Thomas P. II. Title.
III. Series: Dreiser, Theodore, 1871-1945.
Selections. 1988.
PS3507.R55Z483 2008
813'.52—dc22 [B] 2008033688

For the four New Women in my life:

Annabelle Margaret Rosen

Isadora Dahlia Carolyn Brink

Josephine Lia Rosen

Sophia Mercedes Iris Brink

CONTENTS

List of Illustrations x
Preface xi
Acknowledgments xiv
Introduction xv
Editorial Note xxxiii
LETTERS 1
Index 377

ILLUSTRATIONS

Theodore Dreiser portrait
by Wayman Adams, frontispiece

Dreiser, late 1910s xvi

Dreiser in the 1890s 8

Sara White Dreiser and Dreiser 35

Dreiser, ca. 1905 46

Thelma Cudlipp 53

Edna Kenton 57

Dreiser, ca. 1912 76

Kirah Markham 81

Dreiser to May Calvert Baker,
15 February 1917 121

May Calvert 129

Sallie Kusell 150

Helen Richardson 155

Emma Goldman 213

Marguerite Tjader 229

Clara Clark 261

Esther McCoy 308

Dreiser in 1944 353

Vera Dreiser 364

Louise Campbell 373

Hazel Godwin 375

PREFACE

Theodore Dreiser wrote an estimated 20,000 letters over the span of a half-century. Only some 1,300 of these have been previously published, mainly in Robert H. Elias, *Letters of Theodore Dreiser* (1959); Louise Campbell, *Letters to Louise* (1960); and Thomas P. Riggio, *Dreiser-Mencken Letters* (1986). As the first collection devoted exclusively to Dreiser's letters to women, this volume makes available a neglected portion of the general correspondence. The letters reveal intimate aspects of Dreiser's life and also provide a full and immediate record of his ideas, beliefs, and activities. Like his diaries, Dreiser's letters present a picture of the writer that complements the one he created in autobiographies such as *Dawn* and *Newspaper Days*. Of course, as is the case with any collection of personal documents, it is good to remember that the self-portraits that appear are determined by the character of the author and his correspondents, not to mention the editorial decisions made during the selection process.

Dreiser's correspondence with women—even the most private, such as his courtship letters to his first wife, Sara O. White—often went beyond the purely personal and contain reflections on his current writing and reading, and on the historical events of the day. Dreiser addressed such letters to lovers, relatives, former teachers, writers, artists, and political figures with whom he often maintained both personal and professional relationships. In direct and in oblique ways, the correspondence addresses many of the social and cultural changes in the status of women in the period between 1893 and 1945.

The provenance of the documents has been noted at the head of each letter. The Dreiser Papers at the University of Pennsylvania's Annenberg Rare Book and Manuscript Library include many letters placed there by women who were aware of the historical value of the correspondence. This edition also draws on letters housed in archives throughout the United States, as well as those in private collections. Previous gatherings of Dreiser letters were understandably restricted by consideration for persons alive at the time. Today, over sixty years after Dreiser's death, this concern no longer obtains.

Because Dreiser did not write these letters for publication, the edition has been prepared in conformity with widely accepted principles governing the editing of private documents. As with other private papers published in the Dreiser Edition, the holograph letters have been edited diplomatically, with an eye towards preserving the preliminary, personal nature of the original texts, to the extent that this is possible in a typeset medium. Accordingly, nearly all original misspellings, grammatical mistakes, slips of the pen, and other idiosyncrasies are retained and presented in a clear text. Most of the letters to women are handwritten, and the few typed by secretaries contain no typographical errors. These editorial practices are more fully discussed in the "Editorial Note." In addition, the editor's introduction offers a general account of Dreiser's career in relation to his correspondence. The headnotes provide historical, personal, and thematic context to the letters, including biographical data about Dreiser's correspondents. Historical annotations identify significant figures and references in the texts.

The decision to devote the present volume to Dreiser's exchanges with women derives largely from the number, variety, and special nature of the correspondence. The distinctive combination of intimate and professional concerns in these letters is the major reason for presenting them apart from other types of correspondence. The editor has chosen for inclusion only a fraction of the thousands of extant letters to women. An epistolary treasure chest of this sort creates problems of its own. Among other things, the sheer volume of material is a luxury that results in the exclusion of many extraordinary letters.

The principles of selection have been established largely by two factors: the quality of the letters and the degree to which they represent the range of Dreiser's interests, ideas, and emotions. The scope of the letters (1893–1945) has determined the format of the volume. They have been ordered chronologically rather than in discrete units devoted to individual women. A chronological ordering preserves the important historical continuum that otherwise would be lost to the reader. The letters were written over a period of five decades, during which Dreiser's thought and personality naturally evolved. Much of the pleasure in reading the letters derives from observing Dreiser respond to the pressures of shifting historical events, as well as changes in his own thought and circumstances. Moreover, some women received hundreds of letters over decades; letters to others are limited to a handful written in a restricted period of time. A chronological presentation reflects these distinctions and preserves the integrity of the life story at the heart of the letters.

* * *

This edition of Dreiser's correspondence is part of an ongoing series in the Dreiser Edition. It continues the Dreiser Edition's tradition of publishing texts that are not easily accessible, even to the specialist. Such an undertaking would be unimaginable without the sponsorship of two institutions: the University of Connecticut and the library of the University of Pennsylvania.

Several individuals at the University of Connecticut deserve special mention for their initiatives and continuing generous support of this project: Janet Greger, vice provost and dean of the Graduate School; Ross D. MacKinnon, dean of the College of Liberal Arts and Sciences; Robert Tilton, head of the English Department; Thomas P. Wilsted, director of the Thomas J. Dodd Research Center. Linda Perrone, director of external relations for the Connecticut university libraries, has expertly mediated between the two sponsoring institutions to facilitate the complex administrative aspects of this project. The goodwill and special training of the staff at the University of Pennsylvania's Annenberg Rare Book and Manuscript Library have been essential to the progress of the Dreiser Edition. Director Michael T. Ryan has generously devoted his own time and the resources of his staff to facilitating the work of the Dreiser Edition. Curator of manuscripts Nancy M. Shawcross continues to contribute her expertise and special service to the project. John Pollack has consistently and untiringly assisted Dreiser Edition editors in their work. Finally, Dr. Willis Regier, the director of the University of Illinois Press, continues against high odds to provide imaginative guidance and commitment to the project.

Thomas P. Riggio
General Editor
The Dreiser Edition

ACKNOWLEDGMENTS

I am indebted to the trustees of the University of Pennsylvania for permission to publish the Dreiser letters and to quote from other correspondence and manuscripts at the Annenberg Rare Book and Manuscript Library.

A generous grant from the National Endowment for the Humanities freed me from teaching duties during a critical stage in my research.

No book is completed alone. Special thanks go to many friends and colleagues for their support and encouragement of this project: John Abbott, Renate von Bardeleben, the late Harriet Bissell, Jude Davies, Lee Ann Draud, Clare Eby, Yvette Eastman, Robert H. Elias, Tedi Dreiser Godard, Larry Hussman, the late Clara Clark Jaeger, Fred Jaeger, Judith Kucharski, Richard Lingeman, Jerome Loving, Ross Miller, Keith Newlin, Miles Orvell, Donald Pizer, George Pozderec, John Reynolds, Milla Riggio, Dorothy Ruddick, Nancy M. Shawcross, Maggie and Mark Walker, James L. W. West III. In various degrees and combinations, they shared their knowledge with me, provided scholarly and editorial advice, read the manuscript, and willingly listened to and exchanged ideas on numerous topics related to the letters. My former student and research assistant, Anthony R. Vecchiarelli, became himself a staunch Dreiserian as he diligently and enthusiastically checked and double-checked transcriptions, notes, formatting—and saved me from more embarrassments of error than I can count.

INTRODUCTION

A decade after winning the first National Book Award in fiction for *The Man with the Golden Arm* (1949), Nelson Algren reviewed Robert H. Elias's landmark publication of Theodore Dreiser's correspondence. Algren praised the three-volume edition for casting light on Dreiser's ideas, but he was unhappy with Elias's decision to exclude "all matter that does not reveal 'a point of view that shaped Dreiser's books.' The first to get the bounce, of course, are the love letters, apparently upon the assumption that a man whose life was one perpetual emotional storm was able to keep his work afloat in a dead calm." Perhaps sensitized by his widely publicized affair with Simone de Beauvoir, Algren put his finger on an aspect of Dreiser's correspondence that has remained neglected to this day. What Algren could not guess was how much Dreiser's intimate letters reveal about his writing, or the extent to which his erotic preoccupations were entangled with his social, political, and philosophical ideas. The correspondence gathered in the present volume—by no means limited to "love letters"—shows how the ongoing discourse Dreiser carried on with women for decades was a vital part of his public life and central to "the point of view that shaped his books."

Born in 1871 and living into his seventies, Dreiser is among the last prolific letter writers in America. As his diaries reveal, on any given day he could respond to or initiate a dozen or more letters. Even if an editor were to include only the surviving letters to the women represented in this book, the complete correspondence would easily fill a multi-volume series of "Letters to Women." The more than 350 letters to the talented actress, painter, and designer Kirah Markham, of which forty appear here, would themselves fill a book of substantial size. Similarly numerous are the letters to Helen Richardson, Sara O. White, Louise Campbell, Hazel Godwin, Harriet Bissell, Ruth Kennell, and Yvette Szekely. Many of these exchanges began with love letters, but the correspondence frequently continued years after the affairs had evolved into friendships. Often the working relationships remained, with the women continuing to conduct research, edit his writing, consult on political matters, and even occasionally serve as co-authors for magazine ephemera. Besides his lovers, Dreiser wrote frequently to women who were teachers, authors, political activists, family members, critics—and in his various editorial posts he sought out other women to write articles on the social changes affecting their lives during the half-century before World War II.

Dreiser in His Tenth St. Greenwich Village Apartment, late 1910s.

The survival of letters is fortuitous. The earliest courtship letters to Sara O. White are lost, and even among those later letters that survive there are occasional signs of tampering, likely by family members. Clara Clark burned over one hundred letters in what she called a "fit of conscience"—an act she later lamented. The letters to Kirah Markham did not come to light until 2005. Doubtless other caches will surface in the future. Some collections remain under wraps in family estates. Fortunately, many of Dreiser's correspondents realized the historical value of his letters and placed them among the Dreiser Papers at the University of Pennsylvania. In addition, his letters served as aide-mémoire for books by Helen Richardson Dreiser, Clara Clark Jaeger, Marguerite Tjader, Yvette Szekely, Ruth Kennell, Louise Campbell, Vera Dreiser, and Dorothy Dudley, who wrote the first and still valuable Dreiser biography. These and other women such as Emma Goldman, Edna Kenton, Lena Goldschmidt, Thelma Cudlipp, and Esther McCoy had significant careers of their own, and Dreiser letters can be found among their papers.

Unhappily, many of the letters *to* Dreiser have vanished, often making the surviving correspondence one-sided. Where both sides exist, I have tried to give a sense of the exchange by providing excerpts in notes. The "bunch of files—letters from women" that Louise Campbell says were an integral part of Dreiser's records are largely missing from the scores of letters housed among his papers (Louise Campbell to Evelyn Light, 29 October 1931). Those who knew him recalled how much he liked to receive letters, a fact on display here as well as in his diaries, where he habitually reflected on them and then stashed many away between the diary pages. This was not merely a sentimental or narcissistic gesture; the letters often became the raw stuff of his fiction. It is dismaying, then, to consider the disappearance of records such as the "four letter files full of your letters" that Dreiser told Kirah Markham he kept after they had separated (19 April 1917). The scarcity of such correspondence is something of a mystery, since Dreiser usually held on to almost every letter sent to him, however slight. Perhaps Helen Richardson Dreiser, who had charge of the final disposition of his papers (and who had for years bitterly resented the letters he received from women), purged these files. Moreover, in his late years Dreiser was disposed to excise certain information from the record. Biographer Robert Elias recalls coming upon an early letter from Sara White Dreiser, discussing her editing of the novel *Jennie Gerhardt*. When shown to Dreiser, it was abruptly snatched from Elias's hand, carried off and never seen again.

* * *

Written over more than five decades, Dreiser's letters to women begin in the days of the steam train and end just months after nuclear bombs fell on Hiroshima and Nagasaki. They follow the curve of his entire career, from his financially strapped midwestern origins to the well-known literary icon of his late years. The concerns of these letters mirror those of his general correspondence, but the intimacies Dreiser developed with women allowed him a freedom to dwell on details of his personal history not found elsewhere. Notoriously secretive in all his affairs, he was curiously unguarded when writing to women. Because the letters often possess the intensity of confidential attachments, we witness numerous instances of personal exposure and a vulnerability that, not surprisingly, seems to have been one of his appeals for women. Stories about his impoverished youth, his errant siblings, his ungainly physical presence, his moods, ambitions, loneliness, joys, depressions, late-life fears, insecurities about his work—all were easier for him to express to women than to even his closest male friends.

In these letters Dreiser appears in many capacities and with a startling variety of voices: the obscure and itinerant newspaperman in his early twenties, the ambitious editor and freelance writer of his first years in New York City, the dapper editor-in-chief of prestigious national magazines, the impecunious but rising literary star of his forties, the rebel with many cultural causes, the social activist, the amateur scientist hell-bent on proving the existence of God, and the world-famous celebrity caught up in global politics. Throughout, whether in romantic affairs or public and family relationships, there is a constant pull and tug between his desire to write and the equally strong need for female companionship. He regularly would combine the two, bringing manuscripts to the bedroom for alternating sessions of editing and lovemaking. It is a rare letter that doesn't contain, often amid effusive sentiments of passion, reflections on his work at hand.

Dreiser played many roles in the lives of the women he knew. He was a rake, an author who identified with and portrayed the fate of women who had defied convention, a lonely man in endless need of affection, a literary power-broker to aspiring artists, a seductive father figure, a personal confessor on matters of the flesh and spirit, a penitent eager to confess his own transgressions, a writer who furtively managed a stable of adoring female editors and researchers, a champion of radical feminists, a devoted brother, a lover constitutionally unable to commit himself to one person and yet capable of maintaining loyal friendships after the sex had ended. In short, Dreiser's relations with women were always complex and full of contradictions. The letters challenge the reductive portrait of a callous Lothario that W. A. Swanberg's *Dreiser* (1965) etched deeply into the hardwood of American literary history. Swanberg correctly portrayed a man of large and seemingly insatiable sexual appetites, but on this point he missed an important facet of Dreiser's story—one that was best understood by his only female biographer. In preparing her 1932 book, Dorothy Dudley anticipated the part, unmatched among American writers, that women would come to play in the assessment of Dreiser's career. At one point she asked him to send her a "catalogue" of his relationships, knowing that her biography "would be one-sided unless it suggested the scope of his life with women. They were half of the legend surrounding him" (138). He denied the request, but the letters gathered here provide readers with a small portion of what Dudley needed to draw a more fully rounded picture of Dreiser.

The earliest letters, those written in the 1890s to Emma Rector and Sara White, present an idealistic, introspective, seemingly conservative young man in his twenties aspiring to master the rhetoric of middle-class respectability. His ideas about marriage and a woman's place in society were far from progressive, even for the time. To Emma Rector he exclaimed, "Girls of much egotism in regard to the exquisitely womanly things of their character, like me, for I adore the womanly traits, when confined, and not roughened by the world. If you can lecture 40 minutes on Greek history, or have a weakness for discussion, you cannot possibly hope to get along with me" (1 March 1894).

His courtship letters to Sara White were nearly as conventional. For a fervent suitor with a literary bent there was nothing exceptional in the vivid mixture of the erotic and religious in his exchanges with her. These letters support Peter Gay's argument, in his monumental history of the senses in the nineteenth century, that genuine (and often illicit) passion permeated life among the Victorian bourgeoisie. (Even as late as the 1910s, in Dreiser's abortive flirtation with Thelma Cudlipp and his passionate affair with Kirah Markham, there are verbal echoes of his early romanticism and its sources in the imagery of nineteenth-century writers and painters.) Furthermore, in the letters to his fiancée Sara White he drew the only pictures we have of his daily activities as the editor of *Ev'ry Month*, as well as recording the sights and people he encountered in his travels as a prolific freelance writer. Also on view in letters from the 1890s are sides of Dreiser that he sought to downplay in later memoirs, particularly the intensely charged nature of his initial relationship to Sara White and the early, highly self-conscious awakening of his literary ambitions.

In the 1900s he appears first as editor at the *Delineator*, an international magazine specializing in women's fashion designs. His letters to Edna Kenton give a good idea of his editorial practice, his social interests, and his business dealings with women. Kenton did more than contribute articles. She reviewed his books and assisted him in the other major pursuit of this period, the critical rehabilitation of his first novel. Dreiser asked her to intercede for him in obtaining an endorsement from the respected novelist Henry Blake Fuller for the 1907 Dodge republication of *Sister Carrie*. This is the first example of a request that would be repeated for decades with women who were more than willing to help him in his struggles with publishers, publicists, and various stage and film producers.

As editor, whether assigning articles on Chicago's high society or on prominent figures such as Jane Addams, he paid special attention to the place of women in modern society. Even when he attempted to have Theodore Roosevelt write for the *Delineator* on "Patriotism," he wanted the article written "particularly from the women's point of view, the American wives and daughters of the Civil War, the Spanish American War and other significant stages of American history" (Dreiser to Richard V. Oulahan, 11 July 1907). He wanted, that is, to hear about the effects of war, not only on the soldiers but also on the lives of their wives, mothers, and daughters. This was not simply a good editor's sense of what was hot in the marketplace. It stemmed from the same basic impulse that twenty years later led him to ask Ruth Kennell to provide, for his book on Russia, data on four topics of special interest to him, one of which was "The Woman Question—(that is morals, marriage-divorce)" (24 February 1928).

In 1910 Dreiser left his editorial chair and made a second attempt to support himself entirely with his pen. He had considerable success. By 1917, his writing had earned him a national reputation among his peers, if not with general readers. His output was as large as his reputation. In seven years he wrote four big novels, two equally long travel books, numerous plays, short stories, and articles published in magazines as diverse as *Masses*, *Cosmopolitan*, *the Seven Arts*, and the *Saturday Evening Post*. He completed *Dawn*, a hefty autobiography that remained unpublished until 1931, and kept working on a pet project, *The Bulwark*, his novel about modern Quakers that would take three decades to finish. In the years immediately before he published *An American Tragedy* (1925), he added volumes of philosophical essays and poems and a memoir of his newspaper days. To the published books must be added manuscripts discussed in the letters that either were discarded or remain in fragments among his papers. For editorial advice he regularly turned to women when men such as H. L. Mencken and Floyd Dell became disenchanted with his increasingly experimental writing. By 1924 he more readily wrote to Helen Richardson and Sallie Kusell about his struggles in composing *An American Tragedy* than to any of the key members of the literary brotherhood.

The letters after 1910 reflect the changes in Dreiser's circumstances and thought. They are more sophisticated, assertive, philosophical, devious, and playful, whether they are addressed to his former teacher May Calvert Baker, Louise Campbell's mother, Emma Goldman, or any of his sexual partners. Fame gave him a wider range of acquaintances. No longer limited to the journalist's distant view of a William Jennings Bryan or William Dean Howells, he could write about personal contacts with prominent contemporaries—including H. L. Mencken, Hamlin Garland, Lillian Russell, Bertha Kalish, Eugene O'Neill, Edgar Lee Masters, Isadora Duncan, and John Cowper Powys. Put another way, these are unmistakably the letters of the historical Dreiser, increasingly aware of his place in the pantheon of American writers. An immensely curious man, he was always eager to express his opinions on anything that crossed his path. As a result, the letters are a rich source of information on the people he knew, his ideas, books, reading, and habits of composition.

Success brought its own problems. Because his income depended solely on his writing, he worked hard to make ends meet. Constant deadlines induced bouts of melancholy and somatic symptoms. There was a nomadic quality about his life. Before 1919, the letters show him sporadically sharing an apartment with his estranged wife Sara, living with his sisters, taking brief trips south and west to settle his nerves, and counting dollars and cents whenever he rented a place of his own. Train rides for trysts with lovers in Chicago or Ann Arbor were put off to pay utility bills. A month after meeting Helen Richardson in 1919, he was on his way to sun-drenched Los Angeles, where he found relief for his chronic bronchitis but got little writing done. Three years later he returned to his peripatetic ways in New York, there managing to devote himself single-mindedly to the arduous task of composing *An American Tragedy*.

With publishers he picked up where he had left off with *Sister Carrie* and the Doubleday fiasco: the Century Company cut *A Traveler at Forty* by half; the prestigious but conservative Harper's scrapped *The Titan* without forewarning after printing ten thousand unbound copies. "This is all so much like the Sister Carrie incident of 1900," Dreiser immediately wrote to Kirah Markham (18 February 1914). A historical cause célèbre followed upon the John Lane Company's refusal to distribute *The "Genius"* (1915) when the New York Society for the Suppression of Vice declared the novel obscene. With the support of H. L. Mencken and the League of American Writers, the book became the centerpiece of a highly publicized assault on the bastions of "puritanical" censorship. In letters Dreiser readily connected his struggles against the puritans with those of women oppressed by the same mindset. His name was now synonymous with freedom of expression, and he became required reading for progressives of all stripes. As Waldo Frank later wrote, "In the good old days before the War [World War I], Dreiser was the one American novelist whom a self-respecting American radical could take time to read. And there was none beside him" (159).

Battles with publishers and censors made him a cult figure for the younger generation. If not wealth, this sort of fame brought one reward Dreiser had dreamed of as a young reporter. He was a magnet for newly liberated women, often of considerable talent, who offered him immediate relief from the isolation and pressures of authorship. Affairs often began with letters praising his writing. And, as in the case of Helen Richardson, many a knock on his door led to quick intimacies. Before 1919 he lived in or near lower Manhattan among the artists and intellectuals who constituted the avant-garde of the era, and he partook of the lifestyle suggested by the title of Floyd Dell's memoir *Love in Greenwich Village* (1926). He was a literary star in the age of Chaplin, Djuna Barnes, Picasso, Edna St. Vincent Millay, Anaïs Nin, John Reed, Willa Cather, Gertrude Stein, and Margaret Mead—that is, in a period of open sexual experimentation and new freedoms, especially for women. Dreiser reveled in this setting, though he could never quite forget that his celebrity allowed him indulgences that he otherwise would not have enjoyed—a sore spot that comes up in diverse ways in these letters. Nevertheless, by 1912 he had forever put behind him the forlorn figure in the self-portrait of his 1903 diary: "Being homely and awkward, with no art of impressing women, I have always suffered on the side of my affections. Some men have had so much. I have had so little" (14 February 1903).

Other diversions lured him from his writing desk. At Polly's Restaurant and at the Liberal Club, he gathered with like-minded neighbors to debate politics, free love, repressive bourgeois values, corporate abuses, the plight of workers, the new psychology, the latest advances in the arts, labor relations, communism, and socialism. This sort of activity had taken place a generation before in the beer halls, cafes, and salons of Western Europe and the Scandinavian countries. Like their old world predecessors, American bohemians came largely from the middle classes, and most had better formal educations than Dreiser. They read Marx, Nietzsche, George Sand, Strindberg, Havelock Ellis, Ibsen, Oscar Wilde, Lenin, Trotsky, Freud, Jung and, above all, themselves. Visual artists were attempting to digest the recent innovations in cubism and Dadaism and to decode the radical futurist manifestos of F. T. Marinetti. Dreiser took it all in, addressed the Playwright's Club, hobnobbed with painters in their studios, and participated in productions of his own expressionist plays. His letters are replete with thoughts about the new work of Eugene O'Neill, the phenomenon of the Little Theater movement, the imported symbolic naturalism of the German director Emanuel Reicker, the experimental art exhibited at the 1913 New York Armory Show. There was also less heady fare to be had at local vaudeville shows, new jazz clubs, dancehalls, and occasional excursions to Gatsby-like parties, such as the one Dreiser describes at W. C. Fields's summer hideaway on Long Island (Dreiser to Helen Richardson, 26 May 1924).

Dreiser was especially interested in the women he met in these venues. Encounters with actresses and artists fill the letters, to be sure, but there also appear figures whose influence on him would surface in later years. He absorbed the radical labor and anti-war positions of Emma Goldman, supported Margaret Sanger's program for birth control, inspected jails with the philanthropist and prison reformer Alma Clayburgh, discussed the new Russia with Louise Bryant, and listened attentively to the views of feminists such as Henrietta Rodman, the redoubtable schoolteacher whose advocacy of free love and social reform for women, including the right to decide when and if to have children, greatly upset orthodox members of the New York City Board of Education. One catches an occasional glimpse of Dreiser marching in a suffragette parade, but mainly he was an onlooker at organized protests. The letters, however, reveal the more elusive ways he internalized the ideas preached at the meeting places within walking distance of his West Tenth Street flat. He might, for instance, take pains to detail the wretched living conditions and street-tough talk of an immigrant housekeeper. Or to tell how he suddenly halted his all-consuming work on *The Titan* to visit the site of the 1913 Patterson Silk Strike for data to use in a play. Or to describe his time in the courthouse with Cecile Greil, a physician arrested for performing an abortion—a dramatic story, as he tells it, and a reminder of the legal penalties facing doctors and their patients before Roe v. Wade.

Dreiser thought of the women who intrigued him as representative types of his day. In his writing he presented them as an emerging class—the offspring of a half-century of industrialization, of the movement from small towns and farmlands to big cities, of new educational opportunities, and of rapid transformations of moral and social codes. He seems to have traveled light years from the sentiments expressed in the letters to Emma Rector. He responded strongly to the many changes described by the social historian Carroll Smith-Rosenberg: "The years immediately preceding and following the First World War saw women's greatest professional visibility and political activism. The number of women receiving advanced degrees and entering the professions reached a peak not to be equaled again until the late 1970s. Neither before nor since have women been so political—and so politically successful. They battled for peace, suffrage, child labor and protective labor legislation, for birth control and sexual liberation. They encouraged women's participation and leadership in the trade-union movement. They helped to found the NAACP and fought lynching. Flamboyantly, they not only supported but reported the Bolshevik revolutions in Russia, in Germany, and in Hungary" (34). Dreiser wrote of and to such women. But being the writer he was, he also depicted the darker fates of those—such as Jennie Gerhardt, Angela Blue, and Roberta Alden—who had no access to such liberties.

Such unhappy characters were not products of incurable pessimism. Dreiser understood that cultural and social biases kept all but well-placed or uniquely talented women out of many careers. When asked by a Turkish journalist to compare the basic nature of men and women, he responded, "I believe there is no difference between the intelligence of men and women. To date psychologists have offered no convincing data that women are less brilliant than men and vice versa. There have, however, been notable instances of women geniuses. I cannot think of a field in which they would not accomplish as much as men. However, whether they will ever be equal with men in this sense, I question. Firstly, the ingrown prejudices of centuries would have to be overcome. Secondly, women seem happier in the subordinate role which they almost naturally pick for themselves. I think it is perfectly true that more and more women are likely to take a hand in ruling the world. This is because silly prejudices and silly tripe are being overcome" (Dreiser to Nazife Osman Pasha, 21 November 1931). However one interprets this line of reasoning, Dreiser was clearly not an essentialist in his thinking about gender.

Dreiser is a classic case of a writer well matched with his historical moment. From the start his readers sensed, not always approvingly, the way empathy and curiosity mixed with sexual attraction in his writing. Women, at least as much as men, responded to these undercurrents and identified not only with the characters in his fiction but often with the figure he portrayed of himself. They identified, that is, with Dreiser's impulse to defy the social order, to cast off traditional marital bonds, and to free himself from sexual taboos engendered by the dictates of organized religion. His self-portraits, in letters as in books about himself, conveyed a sense of common needs, fantasies, frustrations, and triumphs. In public battles, he turned out to share common enemies with progressive women. Anthony Comstock's New York Society for the Suppression of Vice promoted anti-abortion legislation as rigorously and successfully as it suppressed literature and the arts. In the same year that Comstock's successor John Sumner forced *The "Genius"* off the bookshelves, the society compelled Margaret Sanger to flee New York for England or face a stiff jail term for distribution of abortion and birth control pamphlets.

The identification was reciprocal. Although he was not always above the prevailing gender stereotyping of the day, Dreiser's early experiences of social marginality made him deeply sympathetic towards the life stories of women. One woman in particular had long been an essential character in his imaginative landscape. Memories of his mother's hard life and the social ostracism that scarred her days are sources for the story of his childhood that he repeated to many women. Mother-love, in a variety of forms, is a motif that runs through these letters, and Dreiser often sought maternal comforts in romantic affairs. Whatever the origin of his fascination with women's lives, as Marguerite Tjader observed, "Women's characters and experiences interested Dreiser endlessly. He loved to question them about themselves, their impressions, their reactions to this and that. He was never tired of studying the likes and dislikes that made up what was to him the mystery of feminine behavior" (12). In his diaries he often mentions asking a woman to write her life story ("a history of myself," he called it) for him to read.

His fiction derived much of its energy from the histories of women found in his letters. The youthful rebellions of his sisters Emma and Mame inspired *Sister Carrie* and *Jennie Gerhardt*. His third completed novel, *The "Genius,"* drawing from his relationship with Thelma Cudlipp and from his life with Sara Dreiser, explores the complexities of modern marriage with more insight than he brought to his somewhat epigonous genius, Eugene Witla. The story of "Chains" grew out of long discussions with Louise Campbell. The germ of his novel about Quakers in the modern world, *The Bulwark*, began with Anna Tatum's stories about her family—and the investigation continued in his liaisons with Clara Clark and Hazel Godwin, among other women whose Quaker backgrounds quickly engaged his energies. Anna Tatum appears in the "This Madness" series, as do Lillian Rosenthal and Kirah Markham—and Markham also served as the model for Stephanie Platow in *The Titan*.

The women in Dreiser's life were mainly white, middle class, and most often well educated. In a period of "newisms"—New Realism, New Drama, New Hedonism, New Technology—none was better known than the New Woman. As Clare Eby has noted in her edition of *The Genius of 1911*, Dreiser in manuscript had "in fact used the phrase 'New Woman,' defining her as one who sought 'to smash the traditions in regard to women's place in the universe.' . . . [Eugene Witla] pines for what the text calls the 'newer order of femininity, eager to get out in the world and follow some individual line of self-development and interest.' In other words, Eugene favors New Women, the self-directed, independent women who emerged on the American scene in the 1880s and 1890s" (766). By the 1920s, when Dreiser began writing the two volumes of quasi-biographical sketches that appeared as *A Gallery of Women* (1929), his interest in the "Woman Question" had become a fixed element of his writing. During 1927 and 1928 several American newspapers published a series of syndicated articles by Dreiser called "Dreiser Analyzes Rebellion of Women," under the general heading of "Love, Women, and Marriage." He asked Louise Campbell to edit them for him, noting that, "It's on the restlessness of women these days" and he added, as an aside, "You ought to know" (28 October 1927). The *New York Times* review of *A Gallery of Women* appeared as "Theodore Dreiser in the Maze of Feminine Psychology." He had as he outlined to his Russian editor and translator, Sergei Dinamov, a rationale for doing a companion book to the earlier *Twelve Men*: "For added to character analysis—a clinic of temperaments, I might say—is the color of chemic attraction between the sexes—a striving to capture the elusiveness of the feminine temperament, which of course as all men know, is much more difficult, and therefore more interesting than a study of men by men" (14 March 1927).

As in his public writing, Dreiser encouraged women in letters to move beyond fixed societal boundaries, to express themselves artistically and professionally. There was a self-serving side to this, of course, and at times his appeals and tributes take on a formulaic quality. But there was also sincere conviction behind his support, or so the women felt, which didn't stop with pep talks and flattery but continued with genuine admiration and concrete support for their careers. As Louise Campbell wrote to W. A. Swanberg after reading his biography, "I think, looking back, I was influenced by a quality Dreiser had that partly explains his attraction for women—he made one feel important and *capable* of realizing one's dreams and ambitions, even though one never really did. And then there was the fun and excitement of it all—never a dull moment" (Campbell to Swanberg, 22 April 1965). Many of Dreiser's correspondents did in fact realize their dreams, as writers of fiction, actresses, biographers, painters, singers, architectural historians, psychologists, illustrators, social activists, and editors.

Dreiser's life changed after the financial success of *An American Tragedy*. For six years after 1925 he lived for the first time without having to count dollars and cents. He took a plush apartment near Carnegie Hall on Fifty-seventh Street and built a country home he called "Iroki" at Mount Kisco, New York. He regularly entertained at both places in grand style. The tone and content of the letters changed noticeably in 1928 after he returned from an extended tour of Russia. En route home he remarked in his diary (13 January 1928) that his last words to his expatriated guide Ruth Kennell were, "I'd rather die in the United States than live here" (276). Back in New York, however, he wrote her of a new fact of American life that significantly altered his analysis of Russia: "Learning that there were bread lines here—the first since 1910—I became furious because there is too much wealth wasted here to endure it. Hence, while I am going to stick to what I saw favorable and unfavorable [in his book on Russia] I am going to contrast it with the waste and extravagance and social indifference here" (24 February 1928). In this lies the germ of Dreiser's activism for years to come. The backdrop to the letters after 1929 is Dreiser's reaction to the collective disruptions brought on by the Great Depression and the onset of World War II. In these years he came to rely more heavily on politically active women, such as Ruth Kennell, Esther McCoy, Harriet Bissell, and Marguerite Tjader, who continued to prod him into action on a number of fronts.

The attention paid to Dreiser's pronouncements and activities was a result of his belated acceptance as a world-class writer. The author of *An American Tragedy* was often introduced as the foremost writer of the day. As such, he took on another high-profile editorial post—this time as co-editor with Eugene O'Neill, Ernest Boyd, James Branch Cabell, and George Jean

Nathan of the *American Spectator*. He tapped the women he knew for contributions, and was practically alone among his associates in his insistence that the journal replace "literary" articles with broad social commentary. What he did and said now made news. The author inspired by the Patterson Strike to write his first play now led a committee to investigate the treatment of workers in Kentucky's notorious Harlan County mines. The concerned neighbor who had accompanied the jailed Dr. Griel to her 1913 abortion appeal appears only in his letters; the famous author publicly defending Tom Mooney and the Scottsboro Boys against wrongful imprisonment appeared in headlines across the country. In 1931, he was elected to chair the National Committee for the Defense of Political Prisoners. Though still personally skeptical of doctrinaire politics, he now openly embraced many of the causes sponsored by communist and socialist groups, supported anti-fascist causes, and was placed on the list of subversives kept by the FBI, then headed by a devotee of Anthony Comstock, J. Edgar Hoover.

He found a sympathetic audience among women for his anti-war sentiments and his radical domestic politics. He often tested out ideas in correspondence before they appeared in polemical essays or public statements. Letters describing his trips abroad to speak at international peace conferences contain firsthand news about the divided political positions among various leftist groups. To Helen Richardson and Harriet Bissell he reported on the gruesome details of daily life during the Nazi bombing of Barcelona, scenes that world events today have made all too familiar. He was urged by Spanish leaders and Ruth Kennell to approach President Roosevelt (which he did) to petition for aid to the civilian victims of the Spanish Civil War. He loved to, as he put it, "roast the British beef" whenever the occasion arose. At times he came close to being scorched himself, as when in 1942 he and Hazel Godwin found themselves literally on the run from Toronto after he openly lashed out against what he considered the colonizing and imperialistic ambitions of the British ruling class.

The confusions of the 1930s—over such key issues as the Soviet-Nazi Pact, the British concessions at Munich, the aims of the German war machine—are evident in these letters. Dreiser's pacifist views on the war, his often blind espousal of the Soviet system, and his intemperate anti-English bias look today, with the 20/20 vision of hindsight, more eccentric than they did at the time. Dreiser himself had to recant some of the views he published in *America Is Worth Saving* (1941), as events quickly proved him wrong. The letters are valuable, however, in displaying the genuine uncertainties facing concerned and thoughtful citizens at the time. As Dreiser wrote to Ruth Kennell in reaction to Neville Chamberlain's 1938 Munich agreement to partition Czechoslovakia with Germany, France, and Italy, "I myself do not know what to make of the European situation. It is seemingly too complicated to follow. My personal deduction, at first, was that Hitler had truly split with England & France and that Russia has come to some workable understanding with Hitler that would permit of both going ahead on a social-democratic base. But when I heard that Poland (its executives) would not allow the Russian Army to aid the Poles, I began to doubt. I had not forgotten Hitler's share in the destruction of Democratic Spain—nor England's. Nor France's. Nor Italy's" (31 October 1939). Kennell urged him to discriminate more sharply between the goals of Hitler's Germany and those of Soviet Russia, advice he belatedly took.

Despite all these new causes, Dreiser had not undergone a complete metamorphosis. He continued his jousting with publishers and added a new set of bêtes noires: the film companies and censors with whom he dickered over the use of and rights to his novels. Once again a bevy of women came to his aid, this time as intermediaries between him and radio or movie executives. He resumed correspondence with Thelma Cudlipp, counseled her on her unhappy marriage, and eagerly examined her diary with an eye toward a story or screenplay. Brother Paul Dresser reappeared in a script Dreiser co-wrote with Helen Richardson that was produced as *My Gal Sal* (1942), a biographically unreliable and badly made film. His sexual adventures continued with Hazel Godwin, who was thirty years his junior. With Elizabeth Coakley and Marguerite Tjader he shared, as he had with women before them, both companionship and writing projects. His curiosity never abated. The young Dreiser reported on the etiology of tuberculosis to Sara White and exclaimed to Kirah Markham that he'd worked out philosophically the existence of God. In his sixties and seventies he pursued these interests on a grand scale. He seriously, if vainly, began constructing a philosophical-scientific treatise on the nature of things, "The Formula Called Man," that led him to posit the existence of what he called "My Creator." Visiting laboratories in New England and California, he befriended scientists and attempted to absorb the latest biochemical knowledge of the day. He not only shared with women friends his discoveries, but as in former times, put them to work on research for the project.

The late letters possess an elegiac tone. They display a nostalgia for longstanding relationships without ever completely losing the worldly and seductive nuances of his middle years. Into his seventies he still required the attention of many women, and in that pre-Viagra era, his capacity for sexual high jinks remained prodigious. Although often physically rundown and compulsively concerned about impotence following prostate surgery (neither of which he had), he attempted, with mixed results, to stimulate himself back to the rigors of his youth in liaisons with younger women. In his last decade he was equally as willful about his writing. Although his fiction fell off in quality from the work he had done before his sixties, the letters allow us to observe the doggedness with which he gathered himself to complete his final two novels, *The Bulwark* and *The Stoic*. He still found solace in writing, though time and illness exhausted what at one time had seemed like boundless energy to combine work and play. In his courtship letters to Sara White, he had lamented his moodiness, physical weaknesses, depressions, nervousness, and insomnia. He still sought comfort from women for such frailties, though the symptoms no longer seemed odd or called for much explanation.

* * *

Dreiser's association with women took on a life of its own after his death in December 1945. The subject increasingly gained importance in critical and biographical studies. In part, the numerous (and largely sympathetic) memoirs written by women who had known him stimulated this interest. Dreiser has been the subject of more personal accounts by women than any other American writer. In the last four decades, mainly under the influence of feminist criticism, attention has shifted to more theoretical considerations of Dreiser's treatment of gender, sexuality, and class. Although there has not been a systematic book length study devoted to the subject, important essays and sections of books devoted to these issues have been written by, among others, Nancy Warner Barrineau, Stephen C. Brennan, Clare Virginia Eby, Shelley Fischer Fishkin, Irene Gammel, Blanche H. Gelfant, Laura Hapke, Lawrence E. Hussman, Carol A. Nathanson, Caren J. Town, and Susan Wolstenholme. As might be expected, there is a considerable range of interpretation among these critics. Putting aside the subtleties and biases of individual arguments, they tend to agree on two main ideas: As a man of his time, Dreiser shares with the culture at large uncertainties about the nature of social interactions between men and women, and the complexity of Dreiser's expression of these relations makes it difficult to categorically assess his beliefs.

Beyond the desire to provide pleasure in reading the unique letters of a major writer, the aim of this edition is to offer the necessary texts on which to base future analyses. It is a basic critical assumption that evidence must precede interpretation, but too often judgments are made without the benefit of primary documents. If the correspondence gathered here provides such material and encourages readers to explore the subject beyond the selections of a single volume, this book will have achieved its ends.

* * *

Works and Authors Cited in the Introduction

All letters quoted are from the Dreiser Papers Collection in the Annenberg Rare Book and Manuscript Library at the University of Pennsylvania.

Algren, Nelson. "Dreiser Hedged Out," *The Nation* 188 (6 May 1959): 18.
Anonymous. "Theodore Dreiser: In the Maze of Feminine Psychology," *New York Times* (1 December 1929), 64.
Barrineau, Nancy Warner. "Recontextualizing Dreiser: Gender, Class, and Sexuality in *Jennie Gerhardt*," in *Theodore Dreiser: Beyond Naturalism*, ed. Miriam Gogol (New York: New York University Press, 1995), 55–76.
Brennan, Stephen C. "This Sex Which Is One Language and the Masculine Self in *Jennie Gerhardt*," in *Theodore Dreiser and American Culture: New Readings*, ed. Yoshinobu Hakutani (Newark: University of Delaware Press, 2000), 138–57.
Dreiser, Theodore. *The American Diaries, 1902–1926*, ed. Thomas P. Riggio (Philadelphia: University of Pennsylvania Press, 1982).
———. *The Genius of 1911*, ed. Clare Virginia Eby (Urbana: University of Illinois Press, 2006).
———. *Letters of Theodore Dreiser: A Selection*, 3 vols., ed. Robert H. Elias (Philadelphia: University of Pennsylvania Press, 1959).
———. *Dreiser's Russian Diary*, ed. Thomas P. Riggio and James L. W. West III (Philadelphia: University of Pennsylvania Press, 1996).
Dudley, Dorothy. *Forgotten Frontiers: Dreiser and the Land of the Free* (New York: Harrison Smith and Robert Haas, 1932).
Eby, Clare Virginia. "Dreiser and Women," in *The Cambridge Companion to Theodore Dreiser*, ed. Leonard Cassuto and Clare Virginia Eby (Cambridge: University of Cambridge Press, 2004), 142–59.
Fishkin, Shelley Fisher. "Dreiser and the Discourse of Gender," in *Theodore Dreiser: Beyond Naturalism*, ed. Miriam Gogol (New York: New York University Press, 1995).
Frank, Waldo. *Time Exposures* (New York: Boni and Liveright, 1926).
Gammel, Irene. *Sexualizing Power in Naturalism: Theodore Dreiser and Frederick Philip Grove* (Calgary: University of Calgary Press, 1994).
———. "Sexualizing the Female Body: Dreiser, Feminism, and Foucault," in *Theodore Dreiser: Beyond Naturalism*, ed. Miriam Gogol (New York: New York University Press, 1995), 31–51.
Gay, Peter. *The Bourgeois Experience: Victoria to Freud: Education of the Senses*, vol. 1 (New York: Oxford University Press, 1984).
———. *The Bourgeois Experience: Victoria to Freud: The Tender Passion*, vol. 2 (New York: Oxford University Press, 1986).
Gelfant, Blanche H. "What More Can Carrie Want? Naturalistic Ways of Consuming Women," in *The Cambridge Companion to American Realism and Naturalism*, ed. Donald Pizer (Cambridge: Cambridge University Press, 1995), 178–210.
Hapke, Laura. "Men Strike, Women Sew: Gendered Labor Worlds in Dreiser's Social Protest Art," in *Theodore Dreiser and American Culture*, ed. Yoshinobu Hakutani (Newark: University of Delaware Press, 2000), 104–14.
Nathanson, Carol A. "Anne Estelle Rice and 'Ellen Adams Wrynn': Dreiser's Per-

spectives on Gender and Gendered Perspectives on Art," in *Dreiser Studies* 32, no. 1 (Spring 2001): 3–35.

Smith-Rosenberg, Carroll. *Disorderly Conduct: Visions of Gender in Victorian America* (New York: A. A. Knopf, 1985).

Swanberg, W. A. *Dreiser* (New York: Charles Scribner's Sons, 1965).

Tjader, Marguerite. *Theodore Dreiser: A New Dimension* (Norwalk, Conn.: Silvermine Publishers, 1965).

———. *Love That Will Not Let Me Go: My Time with Theodore Dreiser*, ed. Lawrence E. Hussman (New York: Peter Lang, 1998).

Town, Caren J. "Gender," in Keith Newlin, ed., *A Theodore Dreiser Encyclopedia* (Westport, Conn.: Greenwood Press, 2003), 158–60.

Wolstenholme, Susan. "Brother Theodore, Hell on Women," in Fritz Fleischmann, ed., *American Novelists Revisited: Essays in Feminist Criticism* (Boston: G. K. Hall, 1982), 243–64.

EDITORIAL NOTE

This book gathers a portion of Dreiser's known correspondence between 1893 and 1945. The letters are presented chronologically by year, month, and (with few exceptions) day. The total count of letters is 208, nearly all "new" in the sense of being published for the first time. The only exceptions are the four letters to Emma Rector edited by Richard Dowell and published in *American Literary Realism, 1870–1910*, vol. 3, no. 3 (Summer 1970), 259–70. They are re-edited from the originals to make them available to a general audience in more convenient form. In addition, there are ten letters that have previously been printed in truncated form. One letter to Louise Campbell and four letters to Harriet Bissell are in Robert H. Elias's *Letters of Theodore Dreiser: A Selection* (1959). They are included here because Elias admittedly excised portions of their contents that are personal in nature. The same altered presentation of letters is found in Louise Campbell's *Letters to Louise* (1959), from which five are presented here in their original state. All other letters, including many to Campbell and Bissell, appear here for the first time. The letters to Kirah Markham and Clara Clark had not been housed in archives and are new even to specialists.

All but a small number of Dreiser's letters to women are handwritten. A few, mainly those sent in his capacity as editor of the *Delineator* and the *American Spectator*, were typewritten by secretaries. For this edition the guiding principle for holograph and typed letters is to maintain their integrity as private documents. They consequently are printed as they were received. The chief exceptions to this rule come in the positioning of the place of origin, the date, and the complimentary close, all of which are regularized. In the matter of end punctuation, Dreiser was consistently careless in omitting the period, which has been silently added as a convenience to the reader. His equally consistent use of periods in place of question marks, however, has been retained. There are no typographical errors in the few letters typed by secretaries. Dreiser's letterheads from magazines, hotels, and other public places have been silently shortened after their first appearance.

Readers should experience no difficulty with this format. Dreiser tended to be consistent in his peculiarities of punctuation and spelling. For example, one soon begins to adjust to and even anticipate such idiosyncrasies as *your* in place of *you're*, *its* for *it's*, and easily identifiable misspellings such as *opourtunity*, *thousend*, and *accross*. As often as not he reversed the correct positions of i's and e's, used British forms of words such as *colour* and *labour*, and used dashes and commas interchangeably. Errors of fact or dating are corrected in the notes. Whenever words were inserted above lines, they are included in the text without comment. Notes record all marginalia. Illegible cancellations and slips of the pen are omitted, but legible cancellations that have substantial value are cited in the notes. Words underlined by Dreiser are underscored. When a handwritten word is impossible to decipher, "word unintelligible" has been placed in brackets. Words carelessly or intentionally omitted—or rare instances of pages missing—are noted in each instance.

Notes at the ends of letters identify people, events, allusions, titles of books, plays, films, special activities, and historical facts needed to understand Dreiser's references and ideas. When appropriate, citations from the letters of Dreiser's correspondents (or from Dreiser letters not in this book) are included in the notes and headnotes. The headnotes provide historical context to the letters and identify the recipients of the correspondence. Data initially supplied in notes are afterwards cross-referenced to earlier endnotes or headnotes. If there is no information known about a person or subject, it is noted as unidentified. Certain prominent and frequently used names (such as H. L. Mencken and Walt Whitman) are cited only on first mention, but a complete list of persons and works appears in the index.

The following abbreviations on the top right-hand side of each letter describe the physical nature of the document:

H	Holograph letter
HP	Photostat of holograph
TC	Typewritten unsigned carbon
TS	Typewritten signed ribbon copy

In the same place, the following abbreviations identify the location of each letter:

CU	Columbia University
DPUP	Dreiser Papers, Dreiser Collection, Annenberg Rare Book and Manuscript Library, University of Pennsylvania
HRHUT	Harry Ransom Humanities Research Center, University of Texas, Austin
LLIU	Lilly Library, Indiana University
RIG	Personal possession of Thomas P. Riggio
SCHR	Schlesinger Library, Radcliffe
UCLA	University of California, Los Angeles, Library
UV	University of Virginia Library

A work of this sort relies on countless sources for general historical data, from obituaries to specialized reference books, too numerous to list separately. Two reference works, however, deserve special mention: *A Theodore*

Dreiser Encyclopedia, edited by Keith Newlin (Westport, Conn.: Greenwood Press, 2003) and *Theodore Dreiser: A Primary and Secondary Bibliography*, 2nd edition, edited by Donald Pizer, Richard W. Dowell, and Frederic E. Rusch (Boston: G. K. Hall, 1991).

The following are abbreviations used for works cited in the editor's notes:

Bardeleben, *Traveler at Forty*: Theodore Dreiser, *A Traveler at Forty*, ed. Renate von Bardeleben, Dreiser Edition (Urbana: University of Illinois Press, 2004).

Barrineau, *Ev'ry Month*: *Theodore Dreiser's Ev'ry Month*, ed. Nancy Warner Barrineau (Athens: University of Georgia Press, 1996).

Campbell, *Letters to Louise*: *Letters to Louise: Theodore Dreiser's Letters to Louise Campbell*, ed. Louise Campbell (Philadelphia: University of Pennsylvania Press, 1959).

Conn, *Pearl Buck*: Peter Conn, *Pearl S. Buck: A Cultural Biography* (Cambridge: Cambridge University Press, 1996).

Dawn: Theodore Dreiser, *Dawn* (New York: Horace Liveright, 1931).

Dreiser, *The "Genius"*: Theodore Dreiser, *The "Genius"* (New York: John Lane Company, 1915).

Dreiser, *The Genius*: Theodore Dreiser, *The 1911 Genius*, ed. Clare Virginia Eby, Dreiser Edition (Urbana: University of Illinois Press, 2006).

Dreiser, *My Life with Dreiser*: Helen Dreiser, *My life with Dreiser* (New York: World Publishing Company, 1951).

Dreiser, *Sister Carrie* (1900): Theodore Dreiser, *Sister Carrie* (1900): Norton Critical Edition, Donald Pizer, ed., 3rd edition (New York: W. W. Norton, 2006).

Dreiser, *Sister Carrie*: Theodore Dreiser, *Sister Carrie*, ed. John C. Berkey, Alice M. Winters, James L. W. West III, and Neda M. Westlake, Dreiser Edition (Philadelphia: University of Pennsylvania Press, 1981).

Elias, *Letters*: *Letters of Theodore Dreiser: A Selection*, ed. Robert H. Elias, 3 vols. (Pennsylvania: University of Pennsylvania Press, 1959).

Hakutani, *Selected Magazine Articles*: *The Selected Magazine Articles of Theodore Dreiser*, ed. Yoshinobu Hakutani, 2 vols. (London: Associated University Presses, 1985; 1987).

Henderson, *On the Banks of the Wabash*: Clayton W. Henderson, *On the Banks of the Wabash: The Life and Music of Paul Dresser* (Indianapolis: Indiana Historical Society Press, 2003).

Hoosier Holiday: Theodore Dreiser, *A Hoosier Holiday* (New York: John Lane Company, 1916).

Lingeman, *American Journey*: Richard Lingeman, *Theodore Dreiser, An American Journey, 1908–1945* (New York: G. P. Putnam's Sons, 1990).

Martin, *In Defense of Marion*: Edward A. Martin, ed., *In Defense of Marion: The Love of Marion Bloom and H. L. Mencken* (Athens: University of Georgia, 1996).

May and Metzger: *Oxford Annotated Bible*: Herbert G. May and Bruce M. Metzger, eds., *The New Oxford Annotated Bible with the Apocrypha* (New York: Oxford University Press, 1962; 1977).

Newlin and Rusch, *Collected Plays*: *The Collected Plays of Theodore Dreiser*, ed. Keith Newlin and Frederic E. Rusch (Albany, N.Y.: Whitston Publishing Company, 2000).

Pizer, *New Letters*: *New Letters of Theodore Dreiser*, vol. 1, ed. Donald Pizer, Dreiser Edition (Urbana: University of Illinois Press, 2008).

Pizer, *Novels of Theodore Dreiser*: Donald Pizer, *The Novels of Theodore Dreiser: A Critical Study* (Minneapolis: University of Minnesota Press, 1976).

Riggio, *American Diaries*: *Theodore Dreiser, The American Diaries, 1902–1926*, ed. Thomas P. Riggio, Dreiser Edition (Philadelphia: University of Pennsylvania Press, 1982).

Riggio, *Dreiser-Mencken Letters*: *Dreiser-Mencken Letters: The Correspondence of Theodore Dreiser and H. L. Mencken, 1907–1945*, 2 vols., ed. Thomas P. Riggio (Philadelphia: University of Pennsylvania Press, 1986).

Riggio and West, *Russian Diary*: *Dreiser's Russian Diary*, ed. Thomas P. Riggio and James L. W. West III (Philadelphia: University of Pennsylvania Press, 1996).

Salzman, *Critical Reception*: Jack Salzman, ed., *Theodore Dreiser: The Critical Reception* (New York: David Lewis, 1972).

Swanberg, *Dreiser*: W. A. Swanberg, *Dreiser* (New York: Charles Scribner's Sons, 1965).

Tjader, *Love*: Marguerite Tjader, *Love That Will Not Let Me Go: My Time with Theodore Dreiser*, Lawrence E. Hussman, ed. (New York: Peter Lang, 1998).

Theodore Dreiser

Letters to Women

NEW LETTERS, VOLUME II

1893

To Emma Rector [H-LLIU]

Dreiser was a twenty-two year old newspaperman on the St. Louis Republic *when he wrote to Emma Rector, who was then a schoolteacher in Linton, Indiana. During their various periods of residence in Sullivan, Indiana, the Dreisers had been friends of the more prosperous Rectors. They had provided farm work for Dreiser's older brother Paul during hard times when it was difficult to find employment. Dreiser had left Sullivan when he was eleven, but memories of visits to the Rector farm provided an incentive for him to undertake with Miss Rector the sort of distantly flirtatious exchange that might be expected of someone his age.*

Office-Night.

St Louis, Dec. 13th 93.

My Dear Miss Rector,

Your answer[1]—despaired of—came today and I address you with more of that bon homme freedom than you grant me, "My dear Miss." Of course I will say right here that I was pleased to hear from you and to think that my letter had not been so egregiously flat after all as to have discouraged you at the very outset. Now let us both hope that the exchange will be, say, of mutual benefit. I know that I shall be improved and I can only hope that you will. Do you know you write exactly like someone else that I know. You would be astonished to see how much they look alike. The other person has not the charm of diction that your latest missive shows. You delight do you in recieving letters from persons once held near and dear. What a pity it was that I didnt remain near and dear—then you wouldnt have cause to write me and recieve my answers in the mood retrospective. But thats neither here nor there. To be candid I remember ever so faintly a few particulars about our old acquaintanceship. I remember that I was given to considering you a jolly playmate and a good fellow generally but I cant remember just how pretty you were. Ill wager a goodly sum that you have grown graceful and pretty with dark brown hair and large lustreful eyes to match. I cant say now why but I imagine you must have. You see I'm reckoning without a picture. Your in Linton now. Somehow I know something about Linton. I had a friend once by the name of Brandon who either lived in Linton or had a young lady friend on whom he doted and who resided there. I'm talking about college days now at Bloomington.[2] Another person, I cant exactly call a friend for I never did like him, one William Yakey[3] either lived in Linton or called there as did Brandon. Yakey was of the stripe belligerent, entirely too enthusiastic and very passé to say the least. I feel as though I care very little to hear anything about him. I heard very recently again of Miss Maggie and Miss Jennies[4] visit to Chicago. I erred when I thought that you had been there. Chicago is an ideal city, very swift, very new and very satisfying. I enjoyed working there but now that I am away I really believe that it will be years, if ever, before I return to it. I despised St. Louis at first, then learned to tolerate it and now I like it. Ive picked up a number of acquaintances here—ever such agreeable acquaintances and so Im content in a measure. Im thinking seriously of going east though. New York is my objective point and probably in time to come I'll reach there. New Yorks the place for special writers and literary effusions are my strong "fast ball" as our Indiana friends often say, so that I think that I must go. Not now however. I'm a newspaper man at present with all the untoward instincts of one and not until I have achieved a certain status of perfection will I be able to throw off the shell as they say and spring out into that other much desired sphere. Do you know that often I look back over the years of labor that I have endured and cast into the mold of my making with a feeling akin to sorrow, almost disgust. I long at times to be young again and to appreciate the beauties of life again with the vivid fancy and fascination of a child. Your house and yourself are connected with a few of these happier moments and if you knew just how dear they are to me you would feel too that they are sacred. One of the happiest mornings of my existence I spent on your fathers farm near Dugger while on a visit there.[5] I remember seeing the gorgeous sun rising over one of the neighboring hill crests bathed with that early dew which is pearly and casting its molten arrows aslant the meadow and the stream that ran near your house. I went fishing that morning in that dainty little rivulet whose waters were no deeper than a knee and as clear as crystal. You came with me I believe and we improvised tackle of plane tree branches, twine and pins, fishing more excellently with the same. I used to see the sun rise very frequently then, but now I must confess I have not seen the sun rise in a year or more. I never get up until 10 a.m.

I believe that I'm leading you into these dry newspaper facts and fancys of my life that are of no interest. I'm writing away here until I positively feel that this letter is becoming outrageously extensive and a burden. You will have no objection then to my drawing these opinions of mine to a close and awaiting another opourtunity. I hope that now I address you at Linton you will not be long in answering. I know I shall be delighted to hear from you and besides very soon I have a favor to ask of you which will be facilitated by a better understanding.

Will you kindly give my regards to your relatives—those who remember me, and allow me to remain

Sincerely your friend,
Theodore Dreiser

c/o Republic

1. Dreiser first wrote to Rector on 28 November 1893. He expressed the "hope of renewing what I remember as a pleasant childish acquaintance" (LLIU).

2. Dreiser spent two semesters at Indiana University (1889–90) where he met the classmates he mentions in this letter, including Brandon, who has not otherwise been identified.

3. William Yakey was Dreiser's freshman year roommate at Indiana University. In *Dawn* (1931) Dreiser recalls that Yakey (whom he there calls William Levitt) "was clever as well as practical in the social sense of the word, also liberal and good-natured, a fighter for the love of fighting and the glory of it. In sum, his was a light-hearted swashbuckling nature of that western day and world, fair at his studies, and genial as a companion. More, he was possessed of many popular or college charms—looks, strength, grace, means, which made him a hero and idol" (384). Despite Yakey's attempt to befriend him, Dreiser felt him to be superficial and condescending.

4. Emma Rector's younger sisters.

5. The Rector farm was located in Dugger, Indiana, which was about eight miles from the town of Sullivan.

1894

To Emma Rector [H-LLIU]

Republic

Saturday, Feb. 18th 1894

Miss Emma Rector,
My Dear Friend:

Your curt little note, filled with righteous indignation came today, or rather late last night. It was a revelation to me for it brought me the knowledge that I have recieved a letter from you and had been ungentlemanly enough not to answer. I know that before your note, I had been wondering why you didnt write, and had concluded that my last letter, away back in December sometime, had proved distasteful. Now comes your letter and rebukes for not answering something I never recieved. Its really embarrassing to me and I'm lost for an explanation. Surely Miss Emma you would not accuse me of deliberately neglecting a correspondence that was begun at my own solicitation and with the most pleasurable sensations. I dont believe you do, else you never would have written your inquiry. You must have imagined the letter went astray or something and took this method of informing me; or am I too sanguine in my explanation. Anyhow I'm sorry—I'm awfully sorry. I would give a great deal to get the letter even now, and a great deal more to make you understand just how I feel upon the subject of your accusation.

How could you think that your inquiry would be offensive? Hereafter you must pin your faith to the gentlemanly instincts of your old acquaintance and never doubt once that he would show the slightest irregularity that might in anyway irritably affect a young lady—and a pretty young lady at that.

You say, "Why have I not heard from you"? How shall I tell you? Part of the time since I wrote you last (and maybe just at the time your letter came) I was out of the city. I've been away, once two weeks, once five days and a third time three days. A half dozen times I've been away one or two days at a time. It must have failed to reach the Republic or if it came it may have got mixed with the counting room or the typographical department mail. Several times in the past I have missed letters and found them dust covered and forsaken lying upstairs, belonging supposedly to some errant printer, who had come and gone like a thousand others. Such mishaps are rare though and its just my luck to have the very identical letter I most long for go astray and fail to reach me. I've instituted a search. The two departments shall be rummaged and if that letter comes to light I'll answer it, even at this late day. Meanwhile wont you write me? Tell me the news of your pleasant house and the college boys I once knew. If your other letter had come I had intended asking (begging) you in this for your picture. I believe I told you that I had something to ask you—a great, great, great favor. I want to see "who you are" anyway and to revive my recollection of such a dear old playmate as you once were. If you think not—if I'm too bold or its not exactly proper, why then I'll forego my wish and try to look demure, and just as though I didn't want it at all;—but I do. I'll do, or say, or give most anything in my poverty-stricken possession to get it and if you have one, for the sake of old family acquaintanceship give it to me.

But maybe your angry? Maybe your disgusted with the miserable trend events have taken and intend, as soon as your wounded pride is allayed, to stop writing and count the explanation sufficient: Dont do it! Answer again just as though nothing had happened and I promise that barring mishap my answers will always come soon and as neat as I can make them. Then if I dont hear from you for a long time I'll take it for granted that the letters gone astray and write you anyhow. Now, how is that?

Mr. Paul was here week before last in the Danger Signal.[1] He had a lot of lovely new songs he's composing to sing to me and lots of very droll stories to tell. He inquired whether I ever heard anything of the Rector family and I mournfully told him, no. He said he expected, maybe, that next summer he would pay a visit to southern Indiana and to his dear old friend Jesse Rector,[2] especially. Have you recieved any word from Chicago? Who all writes to you?

I hope that you have become mollified now and that you aren't a bit angry. I hope too that youve decided to write me a nice long letter telling me that I'm forgiven and that I'm going to recieve a picture of you. Then I'll smoke right up and be ever so grateful and happy and we'll get along after the fashion of "ye ancient fairy tale" very happily ever afterwards.

With the kindest wishes and a whole heart full of regrets I'm

Faithfully yours,
Theodore Dreiser

c/o Republic

1. Dreiser's brother, the songwriter and actor Paul Dresser (1858–1906) was part of a road company then playing in Henry DeMille's farce, *The Danger Signal*.
2. Her father.

To Emma Rector [H-LLIU]

Republic

Thursday Mch 1st, 94

My dear Miss Rector,

Today has been so fair and cool, so brilliant in the glory of all its sunshine and blue sky, that I have felt much more like writing you an answer in rhyme, than in this dull prose strain. Surely March has entered like a lamb, soft and meek. Let us hope, you and I, that it remains so and does not retire the ferocious, proverbial lion, all changed as though the worlds iniquities had transformed it.

And by the way, I often feel as though the world were making a lion of me in temperament, so wearied am I, at times, and so disgusted; and that sometime, I too shall retire snarling, a cynic and a dissembler—but this is no conversation for so fair a day. Your letter came this A.M; a part of the delight of the day to me. It began with a delightful little odour of vindictiveness that read as though you were still uncertain whether you had not best punish me for my not receiving your letter anyhow; and wound up with mellowed kindnesses, that charmed me beyond measure. How pleased I shall be to have your picture! and how sure I am that I shall prize it very highly! If mine be of any interest to you, why certainly you will have one. I shall proceed forthwith to have some new ones taken. Still that will require two to three weeks you know. Before then I hope to have yours.

Your letter has been found. I have it. It is very pleasant, but not so good as the one I just received. In writing this I answer both. So my friend Brandon sends his regards.[1] I thank him. I liked Brandon. Rather a frank, unassuming fellow, I thought; open and generous. Will you kindly remember me to him, and hope that he will be all well in the future. As for Mr. Yakey, he was not so much of a friend. I remember him as a boisterous, hair-brained athletic fellow, with unbalanced ideas and a warm heart, sadly offset however by a belligerent attitude on all questions, and a dominant desire to rule. I never imagined for an instant that he liked me, or would remember me at all. Since my memory is not defiled, I surely ought to be grateful, and am. For all of his mentioned generosity, please return my regards. It is my thanks—nothing more. These gentlemen would not think much of me now as I am. The worldly experience of mine has shattered the ideals that were reflected in my eyes those days. Still ambitious, until my very heart aches, and filled with the knowledge of the endless good about, I am modified in temperament and void of that wild enthusiasm, that in those dear old college days made every silvery cloud a fairy legend; and every song birds voice, a poem, sung by the great Master of All. I dream now of lesser conquests and my visions have narrowed down. Perhaps though all this is for the best and I am to be happier in the end. If I did not trust beyond my heart however, I should not believe it. But I weary you. I was thinking this morning what would be the end of this correspondence; friendship, or the sorrowful knowledge that we had met just one more person in the world, whom we could not like. You know how such things go: First curiosity—a continued desire to know of the life and environment of the newcomer; then satisfaction and pleasure, or dissatisfaction and weariness; and lastly a bonded feeling and sentiment, or a most discouraging remembrance, that you would much prefer not to have at all. You do not know me, nor I you. I cannot even imagine from your words, how you look. Perhaps when I see your picture, I shall discover a physiological tracing of thought upon your countenance, that I could not like—then I should wish to cease writing. When you look at mine, you will see egotism written in every lineament; a strong presentment of self love in every expression. I have a semi-Roman nose, a high forehead and an Austrian lip, with the edges of my teeth always showing. I wear my hair long, and part it in the middle, only to brush it roughly back from the temples. Then I'm six feet tall, but never look it, and very frail of physique. I always feel ill, and people say I look cold and distant. I dislike companionship, as far as numbers go, and care only for a few friends, who like what I like. I prefer writing to reading, and would rather see for myself, than hear or read all the knowledge of the world. You will not like me, Im sure. Here is another fact. Girls of strong personality invariably dislike me. Girls of much egotism in regard to the exquisitely womanly things of their character, like me, for I adore the womanly traits, when confined, and not roughened by the world. If you can lecture 40 minutes on Greek history, or have a weakness for discussion, you cannot possibly hope to get along with me. I never discuss, and yet am thoroughly self-opinionated. Above all I am of a gloomy disposition, and a dreamer, to whom everything romantic appeals, and everything (in fact nothing but the) natural in real action, satisfys. Can you imagine now? However I must close this outrageously extensive letter. Write me a long letter. Tell me about Emma Rector alone. If ever I pass near Linton I shall visit you.

Faithfully yours,
Theodore Dreiser

Use same size envelope each time. I shall save your letters.

T. D.

1. For Brandon (and Yakey in this paragraph), see Dreiser to Emma Rector, 13 December 1893, n. 2 and n. 3.

Dreiser as a young reporter (ca. 1894).

To Emma Rector [H-LLIU]

Boody House

Toledo, O., Wed. Apr. 4th 1894

My Dear Miss Rector,

I will wager ever so much that you are angry with me, in daring to drift along so monotonously and not answer your delightful letter, which I recieved in St. Louis sometime since. Well I am out on the road. I have been to Detroit and Cincinnati very recently and once I must have passed within 60 miles of Linton, anyhow for I came from St. Louis to Toledo, over the Clover Leaf route. That passes Kokomo Ind. and ever so many other towns but I cant recall their names now. Tonight I leave for Cleveland Ohio, and have reason to believe I shall be in Buffalo N.Y. by Sunday. If not I shall be in Cleveland. From there I shall travel even farther east, perhaps Pittsburg and Philadelphia. If you answer you had best address me care of the Cleveland Plain Dealer, editorial rooms. No—I'll take that back. You had better address me care of Arthur Henry,[1] city editor of the Blade, here in Toledo, and he will forward it to me wherever I may be. Since March has gone lovely weather has prevailed here. There has been ever so much of warm flooding sunshine and pleasant spring breeze. I traveled up the beautiful Maumee river here, for 30 miles of its winding course and never saw fairer hillsides, nor more beautiful farm lands. The water of the river is not deep, but wide spread, and hurrys along over the coolest and mossiest of all stones. I was pleased beyond measure and felt ever so rested. If I come west shortly, and I do so much want to run back to St. Louis I am coming to Linton, to see you. I shall pass near you, and instead of doing so I will climb down and run over. Will I be at all welcome after this long delay? Well if you were I, and found yourself brushed around from place to place, you would forgive yourself for not writing letters, and so I trust my country school ma'am will forgive her erratic friend and condone one of the most apparent flagrant faults of the profession—poor letter writing. I sincerely trust that a letter will come soon and relieve me upon this score. I owe you a picture.[2] Shortly you shall have it.

Faithfully yours,
Theo. Dreiser

1. Arthur Henry (1867–1934), journalist, editor, novelist, and memoirist. Making the rounds of midwestern newspapers, Dreiser had met Henry in March 1894. Then city editor of the *Toledo Blade*, Henry could offer Dreiser little work, but the two men became immediate and fast friends. They discovered that they shared the dream of becoming famous novelists; later they teamed up in New York as freelance

writers and wrote fiction in their spare time. Henry provided Dreiser with encouragement (and editorial assistance) in writing his first novel, *Sister Carrie* (1900). See Maggie Walker and Mark Walker, *Dreiser's 'Other Self': The Life of Arthur Henry* (McKinleyville, Calif.: Fithian Press, 2005).

2. The photograph is among the Rector papers at the Lilly Library (IU).

1896

To Sara O. White [H-LLIU]

Between 1894 and 1898 Dreiser wrote many letters to his wife-to-be Sara O. White (1869–1942). Born in the village of Danville, Missouri, Sara White was a schoolteacher in a suburb of St. Louis when she met Dreiser on a Chicago-bound train to the 1893 World's Columbian Exposition. A reporter on the St. Louis Republic, *Dreiser had been assigned to cover the activities of the winners of a contest for teachers sponsored by the newspaper. Sara White was among the group given a free five-day trip (July 17–22) to the fair. Dreiser was attracted by her intelligence and calm demeanor, as well as her trim figure, abundant auburn hair, and almond-shaped eyes. A courtship of over four years followed before they married in 1898. During this time Dreiser was trying to establish his career as a journalist in St. Louis, Pittsburgh, and New York—and then as an editor and freelance writer in New York. He wrote often, but the earliest surviving letters are those dating from 1896 when he was in New York City employed as the editor of* Ev'ry Month. *His brother the songwriter Paul Dresser had a working partnership with Howley, Haviland & Company, the music firm that published the magazine. During a visit to Miss White in April 1896 they became officially engaged. His letter reflects the pain of separation that followed their leave-taking.*

New York, May 2nd '96

My Very Own Honey Girl:—

Tho' I sent you a letter last night and tho' one, a beautiful letter, came from you today,[1] I cannot rest until I have written you again. You know I love you; you know it better than anything else you have ever learned in this world. Let me say this and then I will go on. You pictured that long, miserable first day, but oh! my honey, you could not see me then, for if you could have your love would have been satisfied. It rained on the way to St. Louis and some broad-shouldered Missouri lawyer grew poetic and said to another fellow with him that everyone had their troubles and that into each life some rain must fall. Then I thought of how it applied to me and somehow I hated the sight of all those in the car because I fancied that to such as they such suffering as mine could never come. I imagined that we, you and I, are superlatively sensitive and then I longed for you as you long for me, no more, no less. All the scenery seemed only to speak of you. The landscape, towers and structures were bare and dismal without you. It seemed at some moments, as tho' I could not possibly bear the strain longer and the only relief was the imaginary one, the one born of the fanciful thought that the rapidly moving train was dragging me away from my own consciousness—my own hopeless misery. They say here, that I am a perverted cynic. Ah! honey, why shouldn't I be, I who wrung my hands in almost fainting misery as I passed through Forrest Park[2] and looked upon the spot—green and fair in the noontime sun (for it cleared), and who shut my eyes, praying that sentiment might be torn from my heart if its only fruit was to be the horror of parting. I exclaimed against God and the world, and the awful law that can bind two hearts so closely as to bring pain with every shadow of separation. If I could have wept it would have been a relief. As it was I could only moan and I did.

If heaven is earned by suffering surely I may claim it, tho' I would willingly exchange all hope for a score of years with such love as yours ever filling the blissful moments of my days.

Oh, my own Jug! What a lover you are. You are Sapphic[3] in your fire. You love as I never dreamed a woman could, before I met you. You have widened my heart and life. It seems now as tho' nothing [here a part of the letter is torn away][4] for sweetheart sounds weak. You are all in all to me. I will never be happy until I see you again and I love you, love you love you, as only you know and can understand. I kiss you, dearie. I fold you close in my arms and sigh to you, in spirit at least, and I am ever to be

Lovingly,
Theodore.

To my own darling Jug.

1. None of Sara White's letters to Dreiser from this period have survived.

2. The chronology of Dreiser's itinerary can be a bit confusing here. He had seen Sara off on a train from Chicago, after which he traveled alone to St. Louis to see old newspaper friends. There he visited Forrest Park, the scene of an earlier rendezvous with Sara, and experienced the emotions he describes here. He then returned to Chicago on business before returning to New York.

3. Dreiser is associating Sara with the erotic intensity of the Greek lyric poet Sappho (ca. 615 BC–ca. 570 BC), not with her sexual preferences. Dreiser's knowledge of Sappho seems to have been imprecise, as the uncertain reference to "Madame Sappho" in Chapter VII of *Sister Carrie* suggests.

4. In a few letters, parts of pages have been cut out or words scratched out and marked over. Whether this had been done by Sara White at the time or later—or by other hands—is not known, but the excisions appear to come at places where Dreiser's language is about to become openly passionate.

To Sara O. White [H-LLIU]

Sara wrote to Dreiser from Mexico, Missouri, where she had been vacationing, and apparently took the opportunity to remind him that there was at least one other suitor waiting in the wings. His response suggests that her message had succeeded in rekindling his desire for her.

EV'RY MONTH

Edited and arranged
by Theodore Dreiser

HOWLEY, HAVILAND CO.
Publishers
4 East 20th Street
(Bet. Broadway and 5th Ave.)

A MONTHLY MAGAZINE
DEVOTED TO
Popular Music and Literature.

New York, May 21–1896

My Own Honey-Girl:—

A little note came from Mexico this morning, and it wasn't any too soon for I was just beginning to wonder what had happened my love,—no letter in six days. I'm glad tho' that your enthusiasm has modified sufficient to permit you to rest so long, partially free of the destroying anguish of love. Incessant and gnawing thoughts compel us to write often sometimes, and it is best when they cease and give one an opourtunity to recover. You need it Honey-girl and sincerely, I am glad.

What you said of Mr. Rodgers is quite true.[1] He is admirable in many respects but of a phlegmatic turn of mind. I couldn't be that way. Restless sentiments and passions fill my nature. These are so strong that I am always moving, seeking to be nearer and more in touch with my ideals. You are one of them, quite the most dominant tho', but still one. I could not rest long away from you. If I did, it would be as now, at the bitter expense of my own heart. Loving you as I do, I should always want to be near you.

I was thinking only this morning what a blissful thing (condition) it would be, if we were only nicely located in a hotel, or up on Riverside drive, where I could come home and spend an hour with you before lunch, and then the evening, afterwards. Tuesday night the same thought came to me as I walked about the outer confines of Madison Square Park.[2] It was so beautiful that evening. A little while before it had rained, but the clouds had parted and drifted away and the yellow light in the low west made the sky all thru serene, not quite blue and not quite violet. And as I walked along the Eastern edge of the Park, I looked beneath the leaves of the thick trees which were all the more soft and odourous because they were wet, and over the carpet of close grass, and there on the west walk were lined the brilliantly lighted windows of Delmonicos, the Hoffman House, the Fifth Avenue hotel,[3] and all the many bright shops of flowers, candies and Knick-knacks that make Madison Square a blaze of fire, by night, whose lights glimmered like floral patches of fire, most exquisite because framed in emerald of grass and leaves. Beyond still glowed the yellow sky, and overhead was the soft blue, and I said, "Oh, if I might only walk here with Jug, or sit with her by one of these windows of the mansions that look out upon it all, and just hold her hand, how complete it would be."

I wanted you, dearie, because every such beautiful vista wakens to stronger charms when I am at your side. They are beautiful in themselves of course, but for me they lack that last touch of completeness, which is you. It seems as tho' you must be added to make it all perfect—to take from it the last vestige of longing.

Do you really understand how consuming my love for you is? Do you ever dream how you walk before me, the very air and spirit of all things fair and good. Why the very essence of charm which settles like a twilight of peace about my weary heart is that which reminds me of you, my own precious love! You are here, you are everywhere, though I sigh that I cannot make you real, and I am happy, for all my longing.

Lovingly, Your Theo.

1. Robert Rogers was a childhood friend living in Mexico, Missouri, who showed a romantic interest in Sara.

2. Originally the site of a pauper's burying ground, Madison Square Park was opened in 1847 and named after President Madison. In 1891, architect Charles F. McKim rebuilt the Madison Square Garden. Located then between Fifth and Madison Avenues and Twenty-third and Twenty-sixth, it was one of the jewels of the Manhattan park system.

3. Dreiser is describing some of the luxury establishments in the old Madison Square district: Delmonico's Restaurant at Fifth Avenue and Twenty-sixth Street; the Hoffman House Hotel, whose bar was the most popular in the city, between Twenty-fourth and Twenty-fifth Streets; and the Fifth Avenue Hotel at Fifth Avenue and Twenty-third Street.

To Sara O. White [H-LLIU]

Dreiser's letters at this time harken back to their last meeting in Sara White's hometown of Danville, Missouri, seen as the idyllic country site of their official engagement. They also look forward to their future as a married couple in the great city.

Ev'ry Month
New York, Friday, July 10th 1896

My own Baby,

Another lovely letter from you today and I am as happy in reading it as I well can be. Quite a lot of letters have come from you since I came east again from Danville and they are all mixed up but under lock and key in my desk. I am going to sort them out this P.M. and arrange them in their order and of course some of my time will be spent in reading them. Then I'll love you very, very much, and grow recklessly passionate as I always do when I read what you say to me.

All of the literary people I meet here tell me I'm the most easy going editor in town, and I think I must be. Here in my office I do more thinking about you than I do about my various duties and frequently I abandon all details and announce myself "out" to all comers, just so I may have an hour's peace in which to write you. It's by hook and crook that I shift along and yet somehow I get along and get things around in time. Like Dinah's meals in Uncle Tom's Cabin, "Ev'ry Month" comes out of chaos all ok.[1] By the way, did you receive the July no. I put your name on the cover as usual. Your the books mascot.[2]

Since yesterday I have been feeling utterly exhausted, and for no cause. I go about yawning and constantly feeling as though I could not go one step further, but must sit down and rest. I used to feel that way almost all the time in St. Louis. You mentioned visiting a consumptive woman out there. Do you know, my precious, that consumption is contagious—quite as much so as other fevers.[3] The tubercles of phthisis never die. Such microbes which are in the consumptives phlegm never die. The matter she expectorates dries and becomes fine dust, which, when the room is swept others are liable to inhale and so contract the awful disease. Such sweepings rise and settle as dust on window-sills and door top, and picture frames. Months and even years after, when the consumptive patient is no more, if this dust be examined the microbes that engender this disease will be found in it, and if the dust be inhaled consumptions will start up in nine cases out of ten. There is no explaining the subtle workings of these deadly germs and half the people do not know what risk they run in associating with and lingering near consumptive persons.

I tell you this because I am anxious that you should be fully aware of the danger of visiting such patients. You are not strong Baby, and that climate is a resort of those afflicted by this disease. You must be very careful. The strongest people fall a prey to this dread disease, and all because they do not know of the contagion. It is not hereditary. Weak lungs will not engender these eating germs. They always come from some outside source and weak lungs nourish them quickest.

It is disagreeable to indulge such medical explanations, but really my love, you must be very, very careful. Don't visit these poor persons and never linger over them, or long in their chamber, if you come upon them. Life is too precious to risk for so small a thing as sympathetic charity, and besides your life is linked with mine now, and by endangering yourself you endanger my happiness and future hopes. I know, if I could picture truly, any one single misery that would some day accrue to me from the loss of you, you would exercise every precaution. All I can say now is that I love you, and to be worthy of great love you must retain your physical strength. So great care of yourself becomes a duty.

After this lecture I feel like saying, "now run along, little girl, and be good."

Your fancy for rapid streams is different from mine, for I love the still, peaceful currents, where clear water flows silently over yellow sand, or long green grass. When a very young boy I used to lie beside the banks of the Tippicanoe, in Indiana and watch the little fishes hurrying here and there, after their own eccentric fashion.[4] The long green blades of water grass stretching out with the current and waving as the water changed its flow from side to side, always impressed me. Clouds mirrored themselves in the glassy depth and sailing birds cast their silent reflection as they floated by overhead. I always imagined that should some overwhelming sorrow take from life its natural delight I would love to seek that quiet nook and lie down to rest in that crystal sepulcher and pillow my head upon the grass and shining sand. There would be peace at last, for the flesh. There would be quiet and beauty unmarred by sorrow and wearisome longing. Even now, sometimes I fancy such a nook would prove a haven of rest, indeed.

But I'm not gloomy, Baby. I've you now and my days have been turned into interesting periods which I fill with earnest thought for your sake. I want no peaceful stream in which to sink to death. Rather, I want a little quarter of our own, with you and pretty furniture in it to make it lovely. I want money to buy you rich dresses and soft luxurious lingerie and best of all I want you with me, in warm, voluptuous embrace for nights and nights, unending. Such is my ambition and I want you completely reserved to me as I am to you, and then we shall be precious to each other and always happy. I shall be your attentive lover and you will be mine to fondle and caress, my little Venus, whom I shall fold warm and breathless in my arms, whose life I shall smother with burning kisses.

That is better than cold lands of scenery and quiet streams. Don't you feel the wide difference? Do you understand now why passion is typified by a "red, red rose" and purity by a cold, white lily? Give me the rose of passion, the warm color of delicious nights in which our arms shall enfold each other and our lips be sealed in one long passionate kiss. When

> "your little shoes and my big boots
> Are under the bed together"[5]

Lovingly, Your Theo.

1. In Harriet Beecher Stowe's novel, Dinah is the head cook in the household of Augustine St. Clare. Stowe devotes several pages of Chapter 18 to a description of the chaos of Dinah's kitchen, out of which sublime meals emerge, and suggests that her tendency toward disorder is characteristic of her natural genius. The chaos surrounding the publication of *Ev'ry Month* included the large number of tasks Dreiser had to do himself, often writing a good number of the reviews and columns under various pseudonyms.
2. Dreiser slipped into the magazine Sara's initials (she preferred the more anonymous "S. J. W.") in any way he could, sometimes writing an article himself under the name "S. J. White," with the "J." signifying "Jug," her family nickname.
3. Dreiser's "lecture" on tuberculosis incorporates the period's most recent research on the subject.
4. Dreiser is referring to the Tippecanoe River near Warsaw, Indiana, where he lived between 1884 and 1886. For his boyhood activities there, see *Dawn*, 180, 187, 196, 252, 266.
5. Dreiser is quoting a portion of a traditional toast:

> Here's to the wings of love
> May they never moult a feather
> Till your little shoes and my big boots
> Are under the bed together.

To Sara O. White [H-LLIU]

EV'RY MONTH
New York, Aug. 14th '96

Dearest Jug,

Everything has been so much Bryan[1] here during the last two days that my head has quite been turned. His progress to New York was heralded so loudly as to make everyone wildly desireous to see him. I staid in town Wednesday and went to Madison Sq. Garden where he spoke. You can never imagine what that night was like. Howley, Morse,[2] and I were almost crushed to death getting in. Never, I believe, was there such wild anxiety to see a man. Fully 15,000 people crowded into the Garden and waited patiently. Governor Stone[3] spoke but you couldn't hear him. I expected that Bryan would rise and make the hall ring with his eloquence, for I was there to be thrilled; but he didn't do it. Instead, he read his manuscript, and while his speech was powerful it was argumentative and logical and without rhetorical flourishes.

You didn't know I am a silver advocate and enthusiast, did you? Well I am, only Bryan didn't make me so. I was before he came and I waited for his coming with positive thrills of delight and even now I consider him a wonderful man. He disappointed me, however. He should have seized his opportunity and caused that throng to become a mob of frenzied enthusiasts. He could have done it. I believe he still can do it and I only hope he does not leave the east until he has met Cochran[4] and vanquished him.

I saw him again, Wednesday night, as he addressed a vast throng at Broadway & 23rd St. from the balcony of the Bartholdi Hotel. Oh it was a glorious sight. He looked just as I longed to see an orator look. His face was bright, his hair disheveled, his whole figure vigorous and erect and he harangued the crowd until it yelled with delight. There was the wildest kind of applause and everyone thought him wonderful, but alas, he didn't move the 15,000 that way. It is really too bad.

However, you must forgive me this enthusiasm. It doesn't concern us particularly and you have a right to reject a Bryan letter from a lovers standpoint. However, I can't help it. I had to vent my feelings some way or other and you happen to be the other.

Several blessings have befallen lately. One, in the guise of a letter from you, the other in the form of cooler weather, it having rained all day. Both have done me a world of good and I would feel fine tonight if I hadn't studied all day long and simply wearied myself and superinduced a headache.[5] Now, instead of feeling fine I am yawning and so I'm going to close this. Next summer, please God, I will have you to take care of me, and believe me, my love, I need you badly. Not my need, but my heart calls to you dearie, however, and I would not sacrifice you to my own needs, if I could.

Lovingly, Theodore.

1. William Jennings Bryan (1860–1925), political leader whose spellbinding oratory was legendary. Bryan was the most prominent advocate of the movement for the unlimited coinage of silver, for which he argued most famously in his "Cross of Gold" speech at the 1896 Democratic National Convention.

2. Patrick J. Howley (1847–1918), one of the principals in the Howley, Haviland Company, the publisher of *Ev'ry Month*.

Theodore F. Morse (1873–1924), popular songwriter of the day who at this time was the staff composer at Howley, Haviland.

3. William Joel Stone (1848–1918), governor of Missouri from 1893 to 1897.

4. W. Bourne Cochran (1854–1923), businessman and legislator from New York who was a power in the Democratic Party. A skillful orator, he used his talents to

persuade Democrats to vote against Bryan and the silver platform. He convinced many in his party to vote for the Republican McKinley by portraying Bryan as part of a Populist conspiracy to further the causes of anarchy and socialism.

5. Dreiser was not taking a formal course of studies. He had, however, devised a program of reading that he adhered to diligently.

To Sara O. White [H-LLIU]

New York, Oct. 11th 96

My Own Honey Girl:—

It's Sunday night again and blowing a perfect gale outside. Its raining and sleeting—a fair indication no doubt that the winter is on in good earnest. I have left Morse and Ed[1] downstairs in the main office to come up here into my own retreat and let you know what has taken place during the week. I can't recall so very much of importance unless it be that I saw Woolson Morse's new opera "Lost, Strayed or Stolen"[2] and "Evangeline"[3] during the week. Morse and I saw both and reaped a certain amount of enjoyment. "Lost, Strayed—" wasn't so very good and so we paced up and down the foyer between acts, telling each other how much better we could arrange it if we took it in hand. One scene made us laugh heartily enough to repay for all the dullness—and so we noted it fair. By the way I sent you Morse's latest composition "Dreaming" a song without words which you ought to learn. It certainly is dreamy and much more delightful than I can prove to you, by merely saying so.

This morning I went to breakfast at 9:30 and came way from the café at 12:30 so you can imagine how long we talked over the rolls and tea. I take all my meals at the Continental and as the café windows look out into Broadway it makes it very comfortable. The crowd, street cars, vehicles and pedestrians all tend to dispel gloomy moments and so I love to lounge at table and look out. On a day such as this when it's cold, and the rain is driving along in chilly sheets, it is particularly comfortable, because of the warmth and excellent service inside. Its getting to be a source of idleness, this dining.

Some things I did during the week was to get measured for a winter coat, to have several drawings by Archie Gunn and Chas. Howard Johnson[4] framed for my office and to buy several of Darwins works, preparatory to a course of heavy reading during the winter. From now on I shall settle down to extra hard work and as each added day brings the cold and cheerless days I shall congratulate myself on being so comfortably situated.

By the way, Honey Girl, you spoke of getting large writing paper. If you will postpone it a few days I am having some private editorial paper prepared—Baronial style,[5] with "Editorial" only in small blue letters (the paper will be a rich shade of cream or yellow)—and you can use that. We will have it for our private correspondence.

Ev'ry Month is going fine. A number of the leading papers reproduce our photos and matter and we receive splendid notices in every part of the country. There is no question about the future. It is assured.

I'm glad your father[6] liked the last number. I don't see just how he figured out that I pronounced for Bryan.[7] I am a Bryanite, if there be one at all, but I didn't mention him. It isn't policy and would only create enemies among those who favored the other side, but I shall vote for Bryan, and in private I never fail to defend the cause of silver. If it should be defeated my faith will remain unshaken. I am well grounded in the belief, and did not change from gold without weighing the evidence.

I don't imagine you will like this letter but I am going to add a page about sentiment right here. I went into Central Park Friday afternoon seeking relief from a miserable headache and spent several hours looking at the vari-colored leaves and the grass, still fresh and green. My eyes fairly ached when I settled down but contemplation of the wide lawn, the surrounding groves, and the broken sunlight as it fell through the branches overhead and checkered the sod, brought them rest. It was delightfully still. Some pretty women rode along a neighboring road on bicycles, and some school girls tripped along as light hearted as only school-girls can be—talking Algebra.

I sat there—a sort of invalid some would say, and admired four stalwart park policemen in gray uniforms who came swinging along, reminding me, in comparison with ordinary citizens, of the difference between immense Norman horses and thin racers. They were very heavy, very red faced, very huge in their motions and as they drew near I seemed even more frail and worthless, sitting there straining for rest and fresh air.

Then I thought of how different you are to some of the splendid and portly dames who attract attention on the thoroughfares here, how little and how sentimental. Some of these well fed social lights are stout and imposing, like those huge policemen, compared to others, and they look at one with an "eye askance," making me realize that I am not much. But they don't impress me favorably, for all their silks, pug dogs and coaches, and I would prefer one minute of your sentimental conversation to hours of their blasé smiles. In fact I'm tired of affectation and just as I longed for that little outing in the Park, so do I long for another hour with you. That day books and papers made me ill. Tonight, and all time this unbroken atmosphere of prosaic effort palls on me and I would give, ah anything I have, to share an evening with you. I should like to draw up my chair and talk with you once more, to hold your hand in mine and just rest. Do you realize what that means to me. Why, dearest, its like a day in the woods and

fields—no special thought, no care, no special desire for anything except a continuance
[THE REMAINDER OF THIS LETTER IS MISSING.]

1. Theodore F. Morse. See Dreiser to Sara O. White, 14 August 1896, n. 2. Ed is Dreiser's younger brother Edward Minerod Dreiser (1873–1958).

2. Woolson Morse (1858–97) was a composer whose musical comedy, *Lost, Strayed, or Stolen* opened at the Fifth Avenue Theatre on 31 August 1896.

3. *Evangeline* by Edward Rice (1858–96) is a musical comedy loosely based on Henry Wadsworth Longfellow's poem "Evangeline." The play opened on 31 August 1896 at the Garden Theatre on Twenty-seventh Street and Madison Avenue.

4. Archie Gunn (1863–1930), a London-born artist best known for his theatrical posters, was then working on the staff of the New York *World*.

Charles Howard Johnson (1858–96) was an illustrator from Kansas City who at this time was connected with several New York newspapers and magazines.

5. Baronial, a style of paper and envelope which comes in a wide range of sizes and paper stock, used as social and personal stationery for a more formal and elegant look than the business stationery of *Ev'ry Month*.

6. Sara's father: Archibald Herndon White (1831–1902), a prosperous farmer who was politically active in Democratic circles in Missouri. See Dreiser's portrait of him as "A True Patriarch" in *Twelve Men* (1919). He also appears as Jotham Blue in *The "Genius"* and in a more fictional (and less favorable) portrait in "Rella," a sketch in *A Gallery of Women* (1929) thought to be based on Sara White's sister Rose.

7. William Jennings Bryan. See Dreiser to Sara O. White, 14 August 1896, n. 1.

To Sara O. White [H-LLIU]

New York, Nov. 4th. 96

My Own Baby:—

Give my regards to your father and tell him I'm sorry New York didn't answer for Bryan as Missouri did.[1] I'm glad I cast a losing vote in so good a cause.

By the by, between you and I, I have just finished a chapter of Darwin at this late hour (11 P.M.) relating to probable reasons why in nature, the male courts the female. You would [word missing] care for such study I suppose, seeing you don't believe in Evolution, but your lover is firmly grounded in the belief and gains as much satisfaction from observing the truth of it, as some would in observing the nearness of a novelistic fiction to actual life. I set aside my book however placing the magazine in the front rank. At the same time I would not willingly injure anyone unjustly.[2]

I hope your family have not died of grief. Tell them to consider me, here among plutocrats and cantankerous goldites. Each member of the firm is strongly opposed to my convictions but still bows to my judgment. I stand quite alone, but unterrified. Here's a goodnight caress for you, Mme. Recamier.[3] If you look as sweet as she did sitting before your mirror undoing your hair you can imagine how the sight of you will thus someday ravish my eyes. I will abandon myself to the maddest love at that time and wrap you close about so that through all the sweet hours you will have scarce a chance to breathe.

Moral—breathe now, while you may

Lovingly
Theodore.

1. Bryan: see Dreiser to Sara O. White, 14 August 1896, n. 1.
Sara's father: see Dreiser to Sara O. White, 11 October 1896, n. 6.

2. The logic of this statement is difficult to see. Perhaps Dreiser is referring to the idea of "survival of the fittest" that became associated with Charles Darwin's ideas by way of Herbert Spencer's formulation.

3. Jeanne Francoise Julie Adelaide Recamier (1777–1849), a celebrated French beauty who made her home a meeting place for intellectuals and artists. Dreiser may have been recalling the portrait of Madame Recamier painted by Jacques-Louis David in 1800.

To Sara O. White [H-LLIU]

[26 December 1896]

Ev'ry Month.
Editorial.

My Dearest Honey Girl:—

In this letter I am going to make up, if possible, for the long time that has elapsed since I wrote you last (—a week, I think!) Until today (Sat. P.M.) I have not had many moments to myself, free of interruptions. Now, however, everything is so dull and quiet as though it were a holiday instead of the day after one. I spent Christmas up at my sister's[1] and ate everything from candy to imported plum pudding. Her children had a Christmas-tree and I officiated at the evening illumination of the same, while Paul and Ed[2] created as much unholy noise as possible. We had quite a family reunion, Mr. and Mrs. Brennan,[3] and Tillie[4] having come in from Chicago. Ed happens to be here these two weeks, Paul and I, and two other sisters[5] being residents. It was quite a house full and for once I enjoyed the day thoroughly. It was quite cold, but clear and bright, with about 5 inches of snow on the ground.

Brennan took sick in the evening and is now confined to his room at the hotel, but there is no special cause for alarm. He is subject to all the ailments that come to one because of high living and will not live over long I believe. He does not exercise judgment nor control in the matter of eating and drinking—principally the latter, and constantly depends on his wife and the Lord to pull him through. She is more of a nurse than anything else, now-a-days.

I'm waiting patiently for a long Christmas letter from you, because I am anxious to hear how you spent your time. I have to wait for Christmas to come before you tell me anything about the rest of your family. About that time you usually mention them in connection with something and then I learn that they are all alive. How is Mrs. Rogers?[6] You haven't spoken of her for months. And Rose? She also has been relegated to oblivion, so far as I am concerned.[7]

You don't tell me half about yourself. I read your letters and to the meagre details I add whatever general setting I desire, which causes me to exaggerate, a very bad quality. For it, you are to blame. You never tell me how you look, or feel or what you do. I guess, that is all.

You hear enough about me. I write almost everything I know and you get the magazine which shows you what I do, so that you really have plenty of information.

And by the way, why didn't you read the second paragraph in the Dec. number? It was written because I was longing for you at the time and took that way of expressing my sentiment.[8]

I received a letter from Hutchinson,[9] yesterday, the first in a year, I think. You remember "Hutch." I introduced him to you on a Market Street car one day in St. Louis and as you were interested in our venture at Grand Rapids, you will probably enjoy the enclosed letter. He mentions Mrs. Dreiser but unfortunately that party is single, though much loved, at that.

I sent you a glass present and the Express Co. stamped the reciept "not responsible," but they are and if anything arrived injured, I want to know it. I received all I need in the way of presents, having been presented with a pair of engraved gold link-buttons, a silver collar button, a jewel scarf pin, a half dozen neck ties and several practical bits of "gents furnishings." I only hope you were good enough to substitute some little frill from your own costume, for the thing (whatever it was) you contemplated purchasing for me. I would appreciate the first much more, as you certainly must know, and would have the pleasure of being able to preserve it intact. Anything practical always involves use and I do not like to think of practical things and my love in the same breath. If I could only make you understand you wouldn't ever send me useful things. What I do need is some reminder of you and the more effective it is, the better. I am keeping all my presents from you, and I have quite a collection. I wish you would give me a glove and slipper, because they belong among the things I already have. If you will send me the measure of each I'll send a pair (both gloves & slippers) & then you can break an old pair to gratify my wish. Do this for me, deary and you will reward me much more than I deserve. Send the measure right away.

I had you well in mind yesterday, especially as I sat before the grate after the festivities were over and contemplated the departed pleasure, quite alone. It is a mingled pleasure, that of sitting before a fire Christmas night and revolving your various experiences over. All the pleasant hours I had ever had seemed more pleasant as I looked back on them, so that I wished I might live them over again, although I know that at the time of their being, I thought I was not as happy as I might be. I recalled all the girls I ever knew and particularly those in whom I had been interested and then I thought of you and compared each one to you, or you with each one. I do not know whether it was because when I met you I was older, or because of your more fascinating qualities, or both together, but my experiences with you seem to have been by far the most delightful. I said to myself they might seem so because of their recent occurrence and the unchanging love which I bear you, but after impartially remembering or recalling certain details, I concluded, that after all, your love has been more to me—has contributed more to my general happiness and welfare than anything else. The others and particularly one, gave me great pleasure, but none ever stirred the desire in me to be something, and to do everything possible for my welfare.

That was left for you and that is why I am so sure your love has been and is best, and why I fail to change in the slightest detail of my feeling for you. I continue to glow with love's fire because you have bound me to you by kindness and extreme good-nature, over and above all passion and affection. You have made your-self indispensible to my welfare although so far I have postponed sharing it fully with you. You will perhaps forgive the long delayed marriage when I have begun to atone in all the ways I know how. This I hope to do soon, and until then I know you will continue to love me.

Ever
Theodore

1. Emma Wilhelmina Dreiser (1863–1937), Dreiser's sister; he would fictionalize one of her romantic affairs in *Sister Carrie* (1900).

2. His brothers Paul Dresser and Ed Dreiser.

3. Austin Brennan (1861–1928) and Dreiser's sister, Mary Frances Dreiser, called "Mame" (1861–1944); their early life together would be one of the models for the relationship between Jennie and Lester Kane in *Jennie Gerhardt* (1911).

4. Clara Cothilde Dreiser (1869–98), called "Tillie" or "Claire."

5. Mary Teresa Dreiser (1864–97) and Cecilia Sylvia Dreiser, called "Syl" or "Sylvia" (1866–1945).

6. Unidentified. Perhaps a relative of Robert Rogers, a suitor of Sara in Missouri. See Dreiser to Sara O. White, 21 May 1896, n. 1.

7. Rose White, Sara's sister. Dreiser's reference to her being "relegated to oblivion" may be a disguised allusion to his flirtations with her. See the semi-fictional sketch "Rella" in *A Gallery of Women* (1929) and the character of Marietta Blue in *The "Genius"* (1915) for various treatments of his relationship to Rose.

8. Perhaps a reference to the second paragraph of his "Reflections" column in the December 1896 number of *Ev'ry Month*, in which he speaks of "Christmas feeling" being absent without "brighter fires, more genial home plans, more affectionate greetings and givings among friends and relatives" (Barrineau, *Theodore Dreiser's Ev'ry Month*, 209).

9. Winfield Hutchinson was Dreiser's friend from his newspaper days on the *St. Louis Dispatch*. At one point in 1894, Hutchinson had proposed that they attempt to run a country newspaper near his family home in Grand Rapids, Ohio. Although Dreiser visited the area with Hutchinson and investigated the possibility, nothing came of the plan.

1897

To Sara O. White [H-LLIU]

[20 January 1897]

Ev'ry Month.
Editorial

Dearest Honey Girl:—

You will begin to think I am forsaking you entirely if I do not manage to write more often and at greater length. But I havent, in any sense. Only last night, being particularly troubled with restlessness I endeavored to fix my mind (according to instructions) upon some one particular object, and not to permit a variety of subjects to distract my attention. This is supposed to be good inducement to sleep. I tried a number of distinct subjects without avail. Finally I fixed my mind on you, never removing my mental gaze for one moment and then my restlessness departed and sleep came. It struck me as rather wonderful when I awoke this morning, and I certainly have you to thank dearie, as I have for many another blessing.

You mustn't worry over me. I'm not going to perish for some time. Life owes me at least a few years of peace in your loving arms and I mean to possess them. Anyhow I'm somewhat better.

I have to interrupt here with the announcement of the arrival of your photo. You certainly are a sensitive girl. The mere fact of my comparing you to Cleo de Merode[1] induces you to have a photo taken to prove it. Well you do, and this photo shows it more clearly than I would have thought. But, oh my! What a trial it is to look at you as this photo shows you, and not be able to take you in my arms. I would be delighted if I might. Your little circlet wouldn't set long upon your forehead, I'm afraid, nor would your hair hang so graceful and smooth. I'd just hug you to death, that's all and banish all the saintliness out of your face. I think you look simply out of sight or exquisitely beautiful. It makes me feel all my blood to know that you love me and are willing in your love, to yield yourself up to me. You are all there is in life—its greatest bliss for me is involved in your beauty. If I may not reap the delight of possessing you completely, then there is nothing. But you are mine and I will possess you and be perfectly happy, I am sure.

What is the central letter of the initials on this little leather case? I recognize S and D but the middle one seems to be either simply H. or W and J combined. I hope its only H.[2] I'd prefer to think you had let my name go on the case for the two of us, seeing that you are to be mine anyhow. I could then—but I won't surmise until you tell me what the middle letter is. I was offered the editorial chair of a new magazine in three colors, which H. C. Jones[3] is going to start. However I think I have had enough of new magazines. Another one would kill me, sure.

Well my love, I'm going to stop here. I shall look at this latest photo and long for you Oh! inexpressibly much. One of these days I'll come along and get you and then you'll suffer the penalty of beauty at the hands of the beast.

Lovingly
Theodore.

1. Cléo de Merode (1873–1966) was a celebrated Parisian dancer renowned for her beauty and luxurious hair. Dreiser had in an earlier letter attached a photo of de Merode, hinting that Sara was her "look-alike." Sara's willingness to accept the association suggests a freedom from sensual restraint that Dreiser later tended to downplay. De Merode was as well known for her flamboyant lifestyle as for her dancing. In 1896 the gossip of an alleged affair between her and Leopold II, King of Belgium, so outraged de Merode that she left Paris to dance in other European capitals and in New York.

2. A lover's question: Dreiser is asking whether Sara used his initial "H" for Herman (his first name at birth), along with her initial "S," or she had simply written her initials "J" and "W."

3. H. C. Jones, publisher of such successful magazines as *The Monthly Illustrator* and *Home and Country*.

1898

To Sara O. White [H-LLIU]

Dreiser's letters to Sara between April 1897 and January 1898 have not survived. During this period, he had become dissatisfied at Ev'ry Month *with his meager salary and lack of editorial independence, and he had left the magazine after issuing the September 1897 number. Even before his departure, he had begun writing for the popular magazines, and by this time he was making a good living as a freelance writer. He had recently joined the Salmagundi Club at 14 West Twelfth Street, which had been founded in 1871 as the home of a sketch class; in the 1890s its members included artists and writers interested in the arts.*

SALMAGUNDI CLUB

New York, Feb. 16–98.

My Dearest Jug:—

If you have been abusing me mentally for not writing before now you must take it back, for I have been hard at work on three separate magazine articles the past week—one for the Cosmopolitan, one the Metropolitan and one Success—and I have had little or no time for anything else.[1] I notice you plead company and other such things as valid excuses every now and again and think them valid and sufficient, although I am afraid a similar excuse coming from me would receive a hearty protest from you. The present excuse is well-grounded in fact as you will discover soon enough after marriage, when I am compelled to leave you for three and four days, and even a week at a stretch to execute magazine commissions. I couldn't take you along because you would not be able to see me but the least portion of the day, and to be frank, would only be in the way. Then you will realize that one can be busy beyond the possibility of writing letters or caring for wives, or anything else in fact, except the matter in hand.

I am not sure how you will take this, but forewarned is forearmed, and you have time to steel yourself. I have one such commission now for June or July, which takes me to Hartford, Cambridge, Concord and John Borroughs house on the Hudson.[2] It means a week of "hurry-up" and you are sure to be left alone. How now, Honey-girl?

In accordance with your suggestion I looked up the place of mailing of the letter which I thought had been opened, which was Montgomery. No doubt it was opened, but it is not so effulgent in contents as some of the others—rather mild indeed so you neednt worry. Use your stamp better and mail them on the train when they are too luxurious and we will be safe.

About the last letter I wrote, I cannot say now. It was at a time when we were exchanging rather lurid thoughts of the future and may have been very warm. I remember telling you of your peculiarly artistic and yet sensuous mouth, and of its kissableness, but cannot recall more. If the clerk you mention read it he must now be eating himself with envy and the thought of his own deprivation at not having some one thus to so love and be near to—for no one the possessor of a beautiful woman's affection would be morbid enough to pry into the love-letters of others. Only those who pine distraught for a love affair of their own think of such things, I am sure.

About the place of wedding, make it Annapolis.[3] "Oh, how that would be nize" as the little Jap lady said.[4] We could knock around there awhile and then explore nearby historic points and run over to Brandywine and Valley Forge. Do that if you can. It would really be a boon to me for I know how I shall feel in Danville among your relatives, as in St. Louis where I will run slap-bang into a score of people who know me. Make it Annapolis if you can and you will see how deliciously it will all pan out.

I once asked you when we were together how much you thought you could run a house or flat on per month, but I've forgotten your maiden estimate. I should like to hear your opinion on the matter of personal expenses and all that. I have been having consultations with my friend Gray[5] here, who is a wise boy having had several experiences with maidens of different temperaments and is now dwelling comfortably in furnished rooms. We have discussed all sides of the question without much result and now I want to hear from you. To simplify matters I might as well take Grays proposition which he puts in the form of a question "can a married couple live on $100 a month in New York." From this we figured out a determinate negative several times, applying the sum to a hotel, a furnished suite, and a flat successively. However he figures less than I do.

In studying the question you need not limit yourself to that but only give an honest opinion covering the nearest reasonable sum. I want to know for our own good. It will indicate how energetic I shall have to be for the rest of my days.

Lord, how I wish I were a millionaire and money had nothing to do with love and marriage. We would be happy then sure enough.

In looking over Rossetti's "The Streams Secret,"[6] I find these lines, so near to me, who have you.

> "Oh sweet her bending grace
> Then when I kneel beside her feet;
> And sweet her eyes o'er hanging heaven; and sweet
> The gathering folds of her embrace;

And her fall'n hair at last shed round my face
When breaths and tears shall meet,
+
Beneath her sheltering hair,
In the warm silence near her breast,
Our kisses and our sobs shall sink to rest;
As in some still trance made aware
That day and night have wrought to fullness there
And love has built our nest
Till tenderest words found vain
Draw back to wonder mute and deep,
And closed lip in closed arms a silence keep."

In another place he says so beautifully

"Afresh, endures love's endless drouth
Sweet hands, sweet hair, sweet cheeks,
Sweet eyes, sweet mouth,
Each singly wooed and won."

And this:—

"Oh passing sweet and dear
Then when the worshiped form and face
Are felt at length, in darkling close embrace."

Read this Jug slowly and think how it will be with us.

"Therefore, when breast and cheek
Now part, *from long embraces free,*—
Each on the other gazing shall but see
A self that has no need to speak:
All things unsought, yet nothing more to seek,
One love in unity."

———

So it will be with us Baby, "each on the other gazing," and never a need to speak,-hot lips uniting to answer every thought.

Lovingly
Theo

1. For examples of Dreiser's free-lance magazine writing, see Hakutani, *Selected Magazine Articles of Theodore Dreiser*, vols. I and II.

2. Dreiser's visit to the naturalist John Burroughs (1837–1921), known as "The

Apostle of Plain Living and High Thinking," resulted in an article first published as "Fame Found in Quiet Nooks," in *Success* (1 September 1898), 5; repub. Hakutani, *Selected Magazine Articles*, vol. I, 50–56.

3. Dreiser and Sara were married in Washington, DC, on 28 December 1898. Also present were Sara's sister Rose and her brother Richard Drace White, who was then a midshipman at Annapolis. When they returned to New York they took an apartment at 6 West 102nd Street.

4. A line from *Madame Butterfly* (1898), a story by John Luther Long (1861–1927) which appeared in the January 1898 issue of *Century Illustrated Magazine*. David Belasco dramatized it and Giacomo Puccini used it as the basis of his opera.

5. Charles N. Gray, a businessman and acquaintance of Dreiser and his brother Ed.

6. Here Dreiser quotes selectively and accurately from "The Stream's Secret" (1870), a poem by Dante Gabriel Rossetti (1828–82) consisting of thirty-nine six-line stanzas. In places Dreiser underlines words for emphasis.

To Sara O. White [H-LLIU]

SALMAGUNDI CLUB

N.Y. Feb. 23rd. 98

My Dearest Baby:—

Your long letter explains much that I wanted to know and interested me on the side of the future. I cannot help noticing though, how the miserable matter-of-fact details exclude rapturous expression of love. The two will not keep company even in a letter, and where finances and housekeeping need to be discussed the lighter and more airy side of love seems out of place. Poor lovers! Life certainly was not made for them and their pleasures. What do you think.

What you say about St. Louis applies equally well to New York. There is a fashionable section here (or used to be) which is very small and exclusive within which any kind of quarters rent at 150^{00} per month, but only millionaires occupy it. The remainder of the population, who have a few hundred thousand each are scattered almost indifferently in all directions. We could get a nice four or five room flat for \$35^{00} here, and even less. Outside of Fifth Ave, where prices are exclusive, the average price of six and seven room flats in N.Y. is \$35^{00}. Some acquaintances of mine have a lovely little flat in West 21st St, overlooking a Seminary campus—5 rooms I think—for which they pay only \$25^{00} on the 2nd floor. New York flats are different from those in any other city. Houses here are only 22 feet wide (frontage, they call it) and the flat rooms are usually very small. You will be astonished when you come to look, but several million people seem to exist in them.

I thought that we would get married, and on coming back to New York stay at a hotel or take a large room in one of the private houses for awhile. Then we could talk over the flat idea and carry it out more at leisure. I know furniture costs a great deal if you fit up a flat and settle for it spot cash. I am not inclined to venture that until I know more, but my friend Gray[1] advises me to have the place fitted up on credit, and should it work all right, settle for it. If not, there would be no loss, whatever. Or I can rent a furnished flat, which is about the same thing, except that you pay all to a landlord, where in the other case you pay both landlord and furniture dealer.

I should not have a study in the house, since I have an office in the Bible House, and the reading room at the Club.[2] As for the room for my brothers—you need not fit one up for them. Paul will never put in an appearance. A New York rounder of his character could not live outside a hotel.[3] We would want separate sleeping rooms however, so that in case of individual indisposition of any kind, (or a disagreement!) we could rest calmly apart.

As for your clothes, I have no comment to make. You know I want to dress you according to your own good taste, and shall, as long as ever I am able. I am perfectly free as to time now. All my work is purely literary and my relations are with the magazines exclusively. There is no more uncertainty about my income than there is about that of a broker in stocks or a painter, and there is no less, either. With my present standing and ability my income ought to average $5,000 a year. Judging from monthly returns so far, now that I am regaining my health, it will eventually come to that. It is all a matter of contacts and I have an easy pen, but you might as well marry an artist, for all the certainty there is to income. Of late I have being laying aside for a rainy day but you know me well enough to know that I am not much of a hand at that. I rather thought that I would get you to do it and then I would never need to worry.

To give you a rough idea, I counted up tonight and find that four magazines are indebted to me to the extent of $670^{00}, all of which I will collect by June 1st. Of this $270^{00} represents expenses so that my work will really net me $400^{00}. This four hundred represents nearly 6 weeks labor, so you can see how my income runs at present. I figure that during the coming year I will do ever so much better and of course will live accordingly.

In arranging my work for the summer I find that for this year at least, I am going to be compelled to travel a great deal. There are four trips arranged for now, the longest covering ten days, and I see no way of taking you along. In fact I couldnt. You wouldnt be able to stand the jumping round from point to point and while I would not let you owing to the unsatisfactory character of such travel, you would still only be in the way. The amount of work I have to do will make a wretched thing of the whole business, and I look at the approach of this hot New York summer with some nervous apprehension.

From what you said of your dress making, and your fear of remaining alone, together with the present indications of the work that I shall need to do, makes me want to postpone the wedding until Fall. I could have things straightened out then and we could spend the winter after the honey-moon uninterruptedly in the city. I have my fears as to the agreeableness of the present arrangement and I think after you consider it, you will come to the same conclusion. If we do not it will be an interrupted honeymoon, which will be distasteful to both of us. In the fall and winter I remain right here and there would be no occasion for separation. Probably by the summer following I could arrange to do my work in a more leisurely manner and so take you along, or you would have become hardened to the idea of living alone. As things stand now this seems the only reasonable thing to do.

As for Annapolis, I wish it could be arranged. I should love to have you run-a-way and meet me not only for the fun of it, but because of all the nervousness and misery it will save me. I don't believe in your ill-luck theory.

However I shan't say more than I have already on that. If my Baby don't do something strikingly original in keeping with her past record I shall be surprised. However I wouldn't want much risk to rest on you. If I thought running away were not perfectly feasible and interesting for both, I would prefer that you did not do it.

Write me a love letter Honey-girl after you answer this one seriously.

Lovingly,
Theodore

1. See Dreiser to Sara O. White, 16 February 1898, n. 5.

2. Dreiser's magazine writing included articles for *Success*, a magazine founded by Orison Swett Marden and George H. Sandison, the editor of the *Christian Herald*. He was given desk space to complete his assignments at the *Success* office in the Bible House, the home of the *Christian Herald*. The "Club" is the Salmagundi Club.

3. For a later personal portrait of Paul Dresser, see "My Brother Paul" in *Twelve Men* (1919).

To Sara O. White

[H-LLIU]

SALMAGUNDI CLUB.
14 WEST 12Th ST.

May 15th. 98.

Dear Lord was there ever such weather?

You are not the dear Lord, tho' are you? So you cannot say. If it's as bad in Danville as it is in New York, you have a right to complain, Honey-girl, for it's miserable here. It rains every day or at best every other day. At present it is drizzling, having changed to this from a heavy down-pour which began in the early hours of the morning. Being alone I have had more or less depressed thoughts, as becomes foul weather.

Your letter has a tonic effect however. You have a sunny disposition which will not change for all your troubles. I wish I were similarly constituted, for I am a self-torturer of the first order. A strain of German blood gives me a naturally gloomy disposition out of which it is very hard for me to recover myself. This with a long since shattered constitution forms a poor fend against bad weather. My only relief is in work and much of that I am not able to endure.

Since I wrote you I have had more insomnia—in fact a great deal. On Saturday the 7th I quite fainted from sheer exhaustion and Sunday the 8th my friend Gray[1] called in a doctor, who prescribed for me. That night I slept, but since then my rest has been indifferent—partially dozing and partially waking. Tonight I hope for rest, and think maybe I will get it. We shall see.

Yes, dearie, I wrote the words as I said of "On the Banks of the Wabash."[2] There was no "Mary" in my life.[3] That idea is merely introduced for effect, nothing more. Poetic license I suppose. Therefore you can store your hate for some other purpose. Perhaps the next live girl I get.

You did not know I had turned poet did you. I know you never thought much of such verse of mine as you have seen. However I have seriously taken to it, and my poems are appearing right and left in the magazines. One of them—Exordium, appeared in the New York Journal, May 3rd—the day after Dewey's[4] victory, and has since been copied widely. Another "Resignation," which appeared in Demorests,[5] has been widely copied also. A number are under way, particularly with Munseys and the Cosmopolitan, where they will appear shortly. I am sending you a copy of the Journal, of May 3rd, where you can read the poem and I will enclose "Resignation" here, for your special edification. You wont be able to hold me when my book of poems comes out—as it will next winter.[6]

Sara White Dreiser and Dreiser.

About what you say concerning September, I am treasuring it all up and you may be sure that, whatever I may do it will not be for want of love. I cannot say more now, for it is not possible.

Your last words in the letter "don't wait a whole week to write again" make me feel quite in error again, but I have not been in such condition of mind as permitted writing. Consequently I must be forgiven. My intentions are always good, but I am not always able to fulfill them.

I am glad your mother is better. She ought to live a long while yet, and I hope she does for your sake. You cannot always have her, but evil postponed is always better. So I hope my girl will have no worry on that score, until at least I may be near enough to kiss away the tears that must of necessity be. Then perhaps, some resignation will come, as it should eventually, and you will accept the world and its ills without complaint.

Concerning the cooking, I will have three helpings of chicken please, two cups of tea and many biscuits, and I will take them quick, thank you—for I am hungry.

Lovingly
Theodore.

Do you like a funny story. Here is one that appeared in a country paper out your way.

"Once upon a time there was a poor young man who fell deeply in love with a wealthy young heiress whose mother kept a candy store. Being too poor to ask for the hand of the rich old candy-lady's daughter the young man was about to commit suicide, when he was approached by a vile tempter who offered him twenty-five dollars if he would become a drunkard.

The young man not knowing what to do started for the nearest saloon, but at the door he turned and said, 'No, I will not become a drunkard, not even for great riches.' On the way home the young man found a pocket-book containing a million dollars in gold. Thereupon he was accepted by the daughter of the old candy-shop lady. They had a beautiful wedding and the next day had twins. Thus virtue was duly rewarded."

How is that for luck.

TD.

1. See Dresier to Sara O. White, 16 February 1898, n. 5.

2. Dreiser often said that he suggested to Paul the idea of writing a song about the Wabash River in the manner of Stephen Foster's song about the Sewanee. He also maintained that with Paul's encouragement he "scribbled in the most tentative manner imaginable the first verse and chorus of that song almost as it was published" ("My Brother Paul," in *Twelve Men* [1919], 100). Dreiser notes that Paul subsequently finished the lyrics of "On the Banks of the Wabash, Far Away" in about an hour and wrote the music in not much more time. He later recounts this episode in a similar fashion in his introduction to *The Songs of Paul Dresser* (1927); however, in his account of the incident in *Metropolitan Magazine* ("Birth and Growth of a Popular Song" 8 [November 1898], 497–502), he does not mention having a role in the writing of the song. The cases for and against Dreiser's contribution to the

song are summarized by Paul Dresser's biographer Clayton W. Henderson, *On the Banks of the Wabash*, 201–6.

3. For the second verse of the song, Paul Dresser added the story of a man's unrequited love for a young sweetheart named Mary: "Many years have passed since I strolled by the river, / Arm in arm, with sweetheart Mary by my side." Although Dresser later dedicated the song to Mary South, the daughter of a friend from his early Indiana days, he told Dr. Thomas Moorhead that "this personage was fictitious in the extreme . . . and was written merely for rhythmical purposes" (quoted in Henderson, *On the Banks of the Wabash*, 206).

4. Dreiser is referring to Commodore George Dewey (1837–1917), the commander of the U.S. Asiatic Squadron. On the morning of 1 May 1898, Dewey, commanding six United States war vessels, destroyed the Spanish fleet in the Battle of Manila Bay, which was the first hostile engagement of the Spanish-American War.

5. Dreiser published a good number of poems in this period, including the patriotic "Exordium" on the theme of the Spanish-American War and "Resignation," which appeared in *Demorest's* a month before this letter.

6. Although no such book has survived, Dreiser did collect a manuscript of his poems, which he sent to the poet Edmund Clarence Stedman and perhaps to William Dean Howells. Moreover, Dreiser's scrapbook contains newspaper notices of a book of his poems to be published by the Dodd, Mead Company; there is also mention of Dreiser as "Author, Studies of Contemporary Celebrities, Poems" in the 1899 edition of *Who's Who*. It is likely that Dodd, Mead had made some arrangements to publish a book of Dreiser's poetry, though there is no record of the transaction or its outcome.

To Sara O. White [H-LLIU]

Although he used his New York letterhead, Dreiser wrote this letter in Chicago, where he was interviewing eminent businessmen for Success *articles. Before arriving in Chicago he had visited St. Louis, where he and Sara White had rendezvoused.*

SALMAGUNDI CLUB

June 2, 1898.

My Baby-girl.—

How are you by now? I have been anxious to write for two nights but each evening has been so late in winding up my local business that I have not had time. Not for the want of inclination or love, though. Oh, I wish I could see you just one more time before I go east. It does seem so hard to go back without one more kiss. I just cannot get over my longing, try as I will.

I have had an excellent week here. Have had talks with Armour and Field.[1] The famous Dr. Gunsaulus[2] has been lavish in sudden friendship for me, since my introduction and has expressed his high regard for me very openly. I have persuaded him to renew his famous sermons downtown at Central Music Hall, for the good of the young men of Chicago.[3] He says that whatever good he does the coming winter in that way will be due to me. Since he will speak to 2,500 to 3,000 people every Sunday night, and a good many of them young men who haven't good clothes enough to go to church Sunday mornings I think it will be considerable good.

The next day after I met him and he had been so very kind, I asked him why he troubled himself so much on my behalf. (He is a busy man, President of the Armour Institute of Technology with its 1,100 students and all that.)[4] "Oh," he said, "I don't know. People believe in you, though." A moment or two later he added, "The way you came in moved me. Then you gave me a look and I felt it all through me—as though you really were worth while."

I had a similar experience with Alexander H. Revell.[5] He is a millionaire furniture dealer here. I called to see him and he received me most cordially. In fifteen minutes he wrote me letters of introduction to Armour, Field and Deering,[6] and the next day invited me to lunch at the Athletic Club, where I met a dozen dignitaries from the Chicago postmaster up. The United States Controller of Currency was among the number. The same evening the Athletic Club extended me its courtesies for two weeks, issuing me a card, etc, all on his order. I never met the man before in my life.

Its been the same all around, with Harry G. Selfridge,[7] (Marshall Field's right hand man) Duane Doty, (Mr Lincolns aide)[8] and so on. I really have been well taken care of.

But girlie, I never reach my room but what I drop into a chair and immediately fall into a revery forgetting everything but you and St. Louis. I remember with exquisite pain how you so lovingly looked at me, how you told me that when my fingers touched yours on the car, you thrilled all over. Oh, my baby, it is dear to have your love—such whole, consuming devotion, but I am not worth it. I am but a mere, weak, vacillating man, dearest, and never worthy to make you thrill with delight. And yet, just because of that,—because you have given even me such whole affection, I yearn to make you payment with every proof of devotion. I shall live to love you—to prove that I am at least anxious to have you love me so whether I am worthy or not.

I went to the Post-Office Saturday and Sunday morning but got no letter. I shall be here until Friday or Saturday, so great is the pressure of work, and if you have time for another letter or two, write me dearest. I want to hear from you so much. I think of you at every opourtunity, and go over the delightful hours which we spent together, forgetting nothing. You know what joy was ours. I long for that, and for the day when I can enfold you as my wife, and know that from that time on you will be mine, near me, with me, mine to love and caress and care for.

Oh, my honey-girl you were never more precious to me than you are now, never.

Yours Lovingly
Theo.

1. Philip Danforth Armour (1832–1901) owned the largest meat packing company in the nation.

Marshall Field (1835–1906), the wealthiest man in Chicago at this time, had founded the world's largest department-store chain.

2. Frank W. Gunsaulus (1856–1921), minister, educator, pastor of the Central Congregational Church in Chicago and the first president of the Armour Institute of Technology. See Dreiser's interview of him in "A Leader of Young Mankind: Frank W. Gunsaulus," *Success* 2 (December 1898), 23–32; repub. Hakutani, *Uncollected Magazine Articles*, 60–65.

3. In *Dawn* (1931), Dreiser recalls that in 1892 he himself had responded excitedly to the sermons of Gunsaulus on Sunday evenings at the Central Musical Hall in Chicago. He describes Gunsaulus as "a rather pyrotechnic religious yet semi-liberal orator who rejoiced in presenting by way of illustration historic and biographic material in connection with the growth of the world" (555).

4. Gunsaulus had delivered what came to be known as the "Million Dollar Sermon," in which he asserted that with a million dollars he could build a school where students of all backgrounds could prepare for meaningful roles in a changing industrial society. Philip Armour heard the sermon and agreed to finance the endeavor, with the stipulation that Gunsaulus become the first president of the Armour Institute.

5. Alexander H. Revell (1858–1931) made his fortune manufacturing furniture.

6. Charles Deering (1852–1927), a wealthy Chicago industrialist and art dealer, was the first chairman of the International Harvester Company, founded by his father William Deering.

7. Harry Selfridge (1858–1947), Marshall Field's assistant and later his junior partner.

8. Duane Doty worked for Robert Todd Lincoln (1843–1926), the oldest of Abraham Lincoln's children and president of the Pullman Company.

To Sara O. White [H-LLIU]

CHICAGO ATHLETIC ASSOCIATION

[30 June 1898]

My Dearest Jug:

Two of your letters came together Tuesday morning, and in the nick of time I thought. I was getting so discouraged waiting. Went every morning and evening regularly and when nothing was handed out I could scarcely

believe that the P. M.[1] had looked correctly. At last they came however, and I could scarcely contain myself. I had to pocket them, owing to company, but the delight of knowing they were in reach, waiting to be read, was by far the chiefest pleasure that morning. When I was once more alone you may believe I read and re-read both, so hungry was I for your words of love. I cannot explain my sudden restlessness for want of you, but never have I been more impatient to see and keep you with me always.

I loved you always. I used to pine and grieve, but now it is utter impatience, and I strain at my need of being away with all the strength of my nature. You are nearer and dearer to me than ever and I want no other love. I will not think of another woman if you will only love me as you do.

Those first days impressed me most indelibly with the finer qualities of your nature. Your daintiness came home to my heart with a rush. Your sweetness of temper, tenderness and beauty all proved so much above my hopes or dreams. I found you more than all I had anticipated in every sense and now I think of nothing but the delight I would have, were you only my wife—always with and near me.

You must surely realize my Jug that I want you—and not your physical virtue. I could (or I think I could) have taken advantage of you, for there were times when you would have been practically helpless, and what with tender urging might have succumbed. But I want you, Sweetheart, and the other, without you could only have brought me misery. It is your love I need, and your presence, and now I know it particularly. I could speak of a thousend reasons why, but shall refrain. Only believe, sweetheart, that if I do not come for you this September it is not my fault, but the result of unavoidable conditions. I am going back to New York Friday afternoon, in company with Dr. Gunsaulus, who goes there to speak at the First Presbyterian Church.[2] He is not a Presbyterian however—only a great wholesouled genius, whose mentality and sympathies are as broad as Bryan's.[3] By the way he also is an admirer of our great Silver Colonel and believes he cannot be swept from the field by any combination of circumstances. I consider Bryan and Gunsaulus the greatest living American Orators, and of the two the greater orator is Gunsaulus. I am urging him to take a hand in the political issue next time, but am afraid his duties as President of the Armour Institute will interfere.

When I get to New York I will look up my situation and let you know. Gray[4] is attending to my interests in the Arkell assignment[5] and will let me know where I stand when I get back. I have done good work here, and secured material for quite a number of articles which will duly appear. Visited Lincoln Park and brooded over our first visit to that, together. Also went to Jackson Park and saw what is left of the dear old Worlds Fair, where I learned to love you.[6] Do not like Chicago so well as I once did, but that must be due to the superior attractions of St. Louis and all my interests in New York. Anyhow I shall be glad to get away, and to receive the word from you, which will be waiting.[7]

1. Postmaster.
2. Gunsaulus (see Dreiser to Sara O. White, 2 June 1898, n. 2) was scheduled to lecture in New York, and Dreiser accompanied him on the train.
3. See Dreiser to Sara O. White, 14 August 1896, n. 1.
4. See Dreiser to Sara O. White, 16 February 1898, n. 5.
5. Unidentified.
6. Dreiser is recalling scenes from their first time together, at the World's Fair of 1893. See Dreiser to Sara O. White, 2 May 1896, headnote.
7. The letter ends abruptly, with no signature. It is possible that a page or more may be missing.

To Sara O. White [H-LLIU]

SALMAGUNDI CLUB,
14 West 12th ST.
N.Y.

July 27–98.

My Dearest Baby:—

I am in fairly high feather today. This morning McClure's Syndicate sent a man to me to obtain some data concerning my life. They are going to send out an advance notice of my forthcoming book of poems and wish to present true facts about me.[1] That notice of me will appear in fifty leading journals including the St. Louis Globe-Democrat.

Tonight a clipping came from the Evansville (Ind) Courier concerning me and my poem on Sonntag, "One Who Dreamed."[2] According to the accompanying letter from the writer it seems to have created quite a stir there. I have received assurances from all the journals here that my book will be largely reviewed. That means it will create a stir.

I am hard at work now, for us, and hope the day is not far off when you can join me—you whom I love so much. Your last little note told of yearning you have for me, so beautifully. I wish my arms could reach you as you desire—lips wound you with the kisses you seek. Oh, the beauty of that wish. It thrills me over and over, read it how so often as I will.

The hour will come dearie—the hour in which I can whisper my final burst of passionate love and my intent. Oh, I shall fold you close, close, and reward myself for every hour of painful delay.

Kisses to you Baby. Kisses long, warm, sensuous. My whole soul wakes restless for you.

Theo.

1. See Dreiser to Sara O. White, 15 May 1898. n. 6.

2. Dreiser dedicated his poem "Of One Who Dreamed" to the memory of William Louis Sonntag Jr. (1869–98), an artist who died of malaria while in Cuba on assignment to illustrate naval ships during the Spanish-American War. Dreiser's sketch of him, "W. L. S." in *Twelve Men* (1919), is a tribute to a friend whose work and character he admired.

To Sara O. White [H-LLIU]

SALMAGUNDI CLUB,

[29 July 1898]

Sometimes the imagination becomes all powerful and I grasp with a tremor of passion at—nothing—and bury my face in the pillows in despair.

I wish you could see the view from my window. I expect you would make me move however. I have the sweep of a number of open rear windows, of the houses which face on 15th Street, and in these rear rooms dwell a number of lovely maidens. They are unconscious of my existence and the summer heat seems to make them reckless. Such a display of beauty I have never witnessed since the days of the Midway,[1] at the Worlds Fair, and without expense. You remember I sent you a description of the lovely farmer maiden, retiring in solitude. Well I have that enacted for me conspicuously a dozen times an evening, whenever I choose to occupy my window from 10 to 11:30. I am thinking of inaugurating a telescope and charging admission to my chamber.

Man is ever an iniquitous beast, don't you think. I suppose I am criminal in thus employing my time admiring loveliness at a distance. It shows the failing of the sex, when the opourtunity thus presented, proves irresistable.

I would I had you though, with me. The panorama opposite might go on unheeded. The curtains would be drawn and my own girl would engage me with her beauty as no one else can—ever has before. I would dwell with you in thought, dream—closest embrace, all the hours and rise pure and content to the work I have to do. Now it [word unintelligible] to a new day of longing, ever.

Lovingly, Theo.

1. The Midway Plaisance was a mile-long, six-hundred foot wide avenue that was a major attraction at the 1893 Chicago World's Fair. Dominated at one end by the first Ferris Wheel, it offered many types of entertainment, ranging from staged replicas of world villages to Turkish and Arab dancing girls.

To Sara O. White [H-LLIU]

SALMAGUNDI CLUB,
14 WEST 12Th ST.
N.Y.

Sept. 2nd '98.

My Dearest Baby:

In writing my letters, I nearly always reserve the privilege of writing to you to the last, because then, other worries are disposed of and I may give my heart with ease to you. You must be busy, for I hear little. Since Monday night I have been traveling all the time, and I am very tired. That evening I had such a funny experience. (Monday night). I went up to Ilion as I told you I intended. Missed the New York Central train and went over the West Shore. The train was scheduled to arrive at 3 something, so I did not take a sleeper. It was hot and the West Shore is a bad road, but I met a girl who looked like you, and there was the interest. She did look so modest and quiet looking, but she followed me with her eyes, and every now and then I caught her looking at me. The result was that I finally took advantage of her uncomfortable position to help her arrange her seat, and so began a talk, which lasted from 12:30 midnight until almost 5A.M. when the belated train reached Ilion. For all her white dress tho', her auburn hair and wide eyes she proved a disappointment—wholly untrained and quite of the shy girl order. When I shook hands to leave I really ached at heart for her, because anyone could readily see that better parents and an intellectual home would have made a refined and lovely creature of her altogether. Her instincts were all right, but her language and deportment poor. She drew readily to me, which made me even more sorry. I learned however, that even in the only woman whom I found to look like you, I could not find any of the delightful qualities that I love in you.

Tuesday night I came back via Albany, and from there down the Hudson to New York on the night boat. It was my misfortune to get left on a berth—so crowded was everything. I got a cot tho' and did well enough. What grieved me most was a little incident which occurred about 11P.M. A young man and pretty girl strolled along the gallery and entered such a comfortable state room. I could just feel their delight in doing it for they were in love and on some pleasant outing. Afterward in passing along the lea deck, I came to their window, which was opened, but shielded with fine slats so that nothing could be seen—and then I heard such a joyful little laugh, and then a sigh of satisfaction—and a kiss. The moon was up silvering the water, the air was cool—their state room was wide and comfortable and all the sweet night before them. "Oh" I thought "Jug, Jug, if we were only together there."

I think that after marriage I shall wait. We will come direct to Jersey City and take the night boat for Albany. We will have supper looking out on the water, and then our state room and the long night. We, too, will be blissful and some other may hear our sighs and groan, as did I, in despair.

On Wednesday I went to Larchmont to visit Miss Strumm[1] who helps me with critical advice and got back at 10 P.M., having had a swim during the P.M. in the sea at that point. Thursday I left in the morning for Shrewsbury River, a place 40 mile away in New Jersey where I looked up an historic article. This morning (Friday) I went to Haverstraw 40 mile up the Hudson and looked over the great brick works there, getting back after 3 P.M. Since then I have been cleaning up and writing letters, one of which is this. You may know I am tired—worn out.

Tomorrow night (Saturday) I leave by boat for Portland, Maine, and do not get back until next Wednesday

However I shall put paper in my grip and drop you a line. Blaine lived up there. Tom Reed does yet. Longfellow lived there and so did Harriet Beecher Stowe once.[2] There are other things I am to look up. It does seem I have traveled all the time this summer. I have been east, west, north and south and made twenty trips, so that I can hardly be said to have had any rest. However, I hope this fall to take it more complaisantly than since spring opened.

I enjoyed what you wrote about Gertrude's[3] wedding and your own feelings. Ah, sweetheart, they were mine. I shared all your longings—would have given anything I have to have joined you when you wished it—the time I most wished it, also.

We have exactly the same opinion about publicity of affection. I could not kiss you before a crowd—nor friends, nor relatives. When I fondle you it must be wholly alone—when we can have each other in the silence of a secret chamber. It is so much sweeter—the heart is so much freer. Then I am nervous and perhaps over-refined. Anyhow, people who make public display of affection sicken me. They are dull, beastly, I think. Animals do that, and only people with strong animal natures. It was never a trait of mine.

What I want to write of is not all this but my love. The wind is blowing, there is a moon and the scent of flowers. Over the way, where some lamps burn softly in the shadow some men are singing quite sweetly

"In the evening by the moonlight
You could hear those darkies singing
In the evening, by the moonlight

You could hear those banjoes ringing.
How the old folks would enjoy it
They would sit all night and listen
To the music of the banjoes by the moonlight"[4]

And it brings back the country houses around Danville—the little cabin which we saw coming back from Mineola Springs when the old man sat and sang by his window. The fine evenings we spent on the porch, in the yard, in the hammock under the trees and stars. Oh those were delicious days—days of dream—days of paradise. Ah, if we could love on and on, forever, young, light-hearted and fair. If we could only always be Jug and Theo—boy and girl, sighing in each others arms—how would it be heaven.

But this is not good. It is morose. We have still days and years. Still have I all your splendid affection to look forward to, all your tenderness and care. And I do. It is my one thought, my dear dream. You will be mine, you will love me, we will dream, side by side, in company.

Your own
Theo.

My darling, darling Jug.

1. Unidentified.

2. James Gillespie Blaine (1830–93), senator from Maine and secretary of state in the Garfield and Harrison administrations.

Thomas B. Reed (1839–1902), congressman from Maine who became Speaker of the House. Dreiser interviewed him for *Success* 3 (June 1900), 215–16; repub. Hakutani, *Uncollected Magazine Articles*, 78–85.

Henry Wadsworth Longfellow (1807–82), American poet, translator, professor.

Harriet Beecher Stowe (1811–96), best known for her novel *Uncle Tom's Cabin* (1852). See Dreiser to Sara O. White, 10 July 1896, n. 1.

3. Sara's sister.

4. These are lines from the minstrel show tune "In the Evening by Moonlight," written by James A. Bland (1854–1911). Dreiser misremembered the last line: "when we sang in the evening by moonlight."

Dreiser (ca. 1905).

1907

To Edna Kenton [TS-CU]

Edna Kenton (1876–1954) was born in Springfield, Missouri, and attended the University of Michigan before beginning her career in Chicago as a critic and journalist. She wrote one of the first reviews of Sister Carrie *for the Chicago* Daily News *(30 November 1900; repub. Salzman,* Critical Reception, *2–3), and her praise of the novel resulted in a long-term friendship with Dreiser. Soon after, she arrived in New York and settled in Greenwich Village, where she had a remarkable fifty-year career as a writer and critic. A member of the literary avant-garde, she was an editor for the short-lived but influential* Seven Arts *and wrote for publications such as* Smart Set, The Bookman, *and* The Century. *Her many interests resulted in books on subjects as diverse as the Jesuits in North America, Zen Buddhism, Henry James, the Provincetown Players, and a well-received biography of her frontier ancestor, Simon Kenton. In 1907 Dreiser turned to Kenton for assistance in promoting a new edition of* Sister Carrie *published by B. W. Dodge & Company.*

BROADWAY MAGAZINE
EDITORIAL DEPARTMENT

NEW YORK March 27th, 1907

Dear Miss Kenton:—

When you talk to Mr. Henry B. Fuller[1] of Chicago, I wish you would ask him to write to Mr. B. W. Dodge,[2] 24 East 21st Street, this city, and express his frank opinion of "Sister Carrie." If he does not want to do that, you get him to address a letter to you telling you what he thinks of it, and then you send it here so that I can give it to Mr. Dodge for advertising purposes. Mr. Dodge is getting up a circular which contains the history of the book and some various testimonies and I want this letter from Mr. Fuller.

Yours very truly,
Theodore Dreiser

1. Dreiser considered Henry Blake Fuller (1857–1929) one of the pioneers of American literary realism. Although his diary entries of 23 January and 12 February 1903 (Riggio, *American Diaries*, 86–87; 105) record his first reading of Fuller at a relatively late date, he subsequently pointed to *With the Procession* (1895) as "the first piece of American realism I encountered" (Dreiser to Constance M. Griffin, 10 October 1932, in Elias, *Letters*, 612). In 1913 the two men would meet in Chicago at the Cliff-Dwellers' Club. Dreiser appreciated Fuller's realism and his depiction of Chicago; but his sensitivity to the mixed responses to *Sister Carrie* may have

led him to identify also with the negative critical reaction to Fuller's social views that had shortened his career. Dreiser later wrote that Fuller published his realistic Chicago novel *With the Procession* (1895) "and finding himself facing social as well as literary ostracism, he desisted" (in *American Spectator* [December, 1932], 1).

2. Ben W. Dodge (?–1916) headed B. W. Dodge and Company, which reissued *Sister Carrie* in 1907. Dreiser had a financial interest in Dodge's new firm: as a stockholder he bought fifty shares of stock at $100 a share, putting up $1,000 in cash and agreeing to deduct the remaining $4,000 from his royalties. He was, in effect, financing his own book, but in return he became one of the directors of the firm and would share in any of its future profits. Dodge enthusiastically promoted the novel, producing the brochure that Dreiser describes in this letter. A heavy drinker, Dodge's personal life fell apart over the next decade; letters to Dreiser shortly before his death in 1916 show him working at a New Jersey chicken farm and longing to get back to "the book world." His death by drowning in the East River may have been a suicide or an accident resulting from a drinking spree.

To Edna Kenton [TS-CU]

From 1906 to 1910 Dreiser served as editor-in-chief of the Delineator, *a prestigious women's fashion magazine published by the Butterick Company. He selected authors for projects that interested him and edited their work to suit his needs. The following two letters to Kenton are representative examples of Dreiser's editorial practice, his business dealings with women, and the sorts of topics that occupied him in this period.*

THE DELINEATOR
NEW YORK

July 2, 1907.

My dear Miss Kenton:

I want you to undertake for me at once, an article on Chicago society. I am having a series of articles done, one on Philadelphia society, by Anne Rittenhouse, one on Boston society, by a Mrs. Kennedy, and this one on Chicago society by you, if you will do it.

The only reason that I switched from you to Miss Forsythe on the Jane Addams matter[1] was because Miss Leckey assured me that Miss Forsythe had been close to Miss Addams as a sort of private secretary for some time, and I thought it would be more difficult for you to get at the matter. I told Miss Holly[2] at the time that I would replace that order with another within a few days, and I have intended ever since last Wednesday to write the letter which I am writing now. Please do not feel that I under-value your ability in the least, because you must know that I do not.

I want you to undertake this story, and give me a picture of society as it exists. I want it done in a realistic fashion. I want you to tell me who the big society people are, where they live, how they spend their time, what the sources of exclusive social amusements are, what are the big annual social events, how is a girl introduced into society in Chicago, what do they spend annually in the way of entertainment, are the women as a rule good looking or homely, is the Chicago type differentiated from that of Boston, New York or Philadelphia. You see I want a good realistic informative story, and I want you to write it as though our readers knew absolutely nothing about the situation there, and you were giving them a plain, complete analysis of it.

Now I would like this within a month at the outside, three weeks would be better.

I want you to gather me pictures of the leaders, fifteen or twenty in all, and I want you to write on the back of each just what their standing and significance is, then I want you to give me suggestions for three or four drawings to be done by Mr. Harry Hutt, of our staff.

Please communicate with me at once, relative to your willingness and ability to do this, and as soon as the manuscript is in shape, I will see that you get a check.

With best wishes, I am

Yours,
Theodore Dreiser

Editor

[3]I will pay you $200^{00}

1. "What Jane Addams Has Done for Chicago," which appeared in the October 1907 issue of the *Delineator*. By this time Jane Addams (1860–1935) had attracted worldwide attention for her work at Hull-House, which she had established in 1889 with Ellen Gates Starr (1859–1940). It was named Hull-House to honor their generous benefactor Helen Culver (1832–1925), sole heir to the fortune of Chicago millionaire and real estate developer, Charles Hull (1820–89). By the time Dreiser commissioned the article, Hull-House had had a long history of providing housing and education to the citizens of Chicago's industrial neighborhoods.

2. Flora Mai Holly served as Dreiser's literary agent for the 1907 Dodge edition of *Sister Carrie*. She was also working as a part time advisor to Dreiser at the *Delineator*.

3. Dreiser added this in longhand.

To Edna Kenton [TS-CU]

PARIS NEW YORK LONDON
THE BUTTERICK PUBLISHING COMPANY. LTD.

August 21, 1907

My dear Miss Kenton:

I have gone over this CHICAGO SOCIETY article by you, very carefully, and I am going to have to ask you for a revision. The article has color, but not enough to make it exactly the picture I want, and what is more important, it does not contain the facts that I want.

What you have failed to cover is the people in Chicago society, entirely. Of course, you will say that you mention a number of people. So you do, but you do not give an interesting account of their station, influence and characteristics. Personally, I am interested in the people who make up society. For instance, if some one were going to tell me the state of society in Havana, Cuba, I would want to know what are their characteristics, how they live, who is the Harry Lehr of Havana, who corresponds to Mrs. Stuyvesant Fish,[1] of New York, how do they entertain themselves, where do they dine, where do they go in the Summer, where do they go in the Winter, are they easy going or energetic, is the life easy or strenuous, do they dress differently from what they do, let us say, in New York or Philadelphia?

I want, as you see, a contrast and an estimate story. This you have not given me. Remember that the key-note in an article of this character is information. If I were running a society journal, and my readers knew all about the people who constitute Chicago society, an inside critical estimate would be worth something. Since I am not, only an A, B, C primer of facts can be of value.

Now, won't you take this article, preserve as much of the color as you can, and build me the kind of story that I want? I want to know, of course, about the neighborhood divisions. For instance, that one set of Chicago society lives on the Lake Shore Drive, another out on the South-side, and possibly a third on the Westside. I want to know that the charity ball is the main thing and that the list of hostesses constitutes an array of the elite. But after you have laid down these primary facts, I want to know about the people and what they do, and how they live as per my opening description.

Please let me hear from you at your earliest convenience, and oblige,

Yours sincerely,
Theodore Dreiser
E D I T O R.

1. Harry Lehr (?–1929) and Mrs. Stuyvesant Fish (1855–1915) were members of New York's social set. Mrs. Fish had married into the family descended from Peter Stuyvesant (1592–1672), the last Dutch governor of New Netherland. Harry Lehr had neither great wealth nor a distinguished pedigree, but he insinuated himself into the world of high society by playing the role of court jester. Together they kept their friends amused, hosting eccentric parties and balls. On one occasion they gave a "Doggie Dinner" where the dogs were served a three-course banquet at their own table. Mrs. Fish's pet arrived wearing a diamond collar valued at $15,000.

1910

To Thelma Cudlipp [HP-DPUP]

In 1910 Dreiser had become infatuated with Thelma Cudlipp (1892–1967), the eighteen-year-old daughter of Anne Ericsson Cudlipp, an assistant editor at the Delineator, *the women's fashion magazine of which he was editor-in-chief. Born in Richmond, Virginia, the younger Cudlipp had come to New York with her mother to study art. The scandal of Dreiser's brief and seemingly platonic flirtation with Cudlipp eventually caused him to lose his job. She soon after studied in England and then with Kenneth Hayes Miller, one of Dreiser's closest friends among painters. Later Cudlipp became a well-known illustrator whose work appeared in high profile newspapers and magazines such as* Harper's, McClure's *and* The Saturday Evening Post.

439 W. 123rd St.
N.Y.C.

July 21–1910

Dear Thelma:

I have meant each day to write & tell you how much I like your sketches. I think they're dandy. I will be glad to send my photo on one condition—that you take one of yours & work out some joint scheme so that we can both appear on the cover.[1] Will send you some more rhymes soon & eventually we will throw the poor ones away. By the way I met a girl friend of yours down at Warm Springs, Virginia —Miss Johnston, who studied art with you. I met her through Mary Johnston[2] & she mentioned knowing you & said she thought you were very clever. So there now—

Theodore Dreiser

1. Thelma and Dreiser composed light-hearted nonsense jingles and drawings. Dreiser proposed that they turn them into a children's book: he would write the verse and Thelma would supply the sketches. There survives a booklet called "The Complete Jingler," with poems by Dreiser and sketches by Cudlipp. An example of the doggerel verse is "Lines to Bourgereau":

"Oogle boogle six and eight
Ev'ry artist is a skate,
Ev'ry artist that I know
Rarely seems to have the dough"

2. Unidentified.

Thelma Cudlipp.

To Anne Ericsson Cudlipp [HP-DPUP]

This letter is written to Thelma Cudlipp's mother—who was party to the "fateful discussion" alluded to here, which had resulted in a mutual agreement that Dreiser and Thelma would refrain from direct contact for a limited period of time. Dreiser wrote such a scene into the two versions of his quasi-autobiographical novel The Genius *of 1911 (chapters 95–96) and* The "Genius" *(1915) (chapters 19–20, Book 3).*[1]

Park Avenue Hotel
New York

Oct. 11th 1910

Dear Mrs. Cudlipp:

The question which I meant to ask Thelma the other night & which was lost in the more fateful discussion was this.

Mrs. Dreiser had proposed to me over the phone Monday morning that I return for 10 days as a boarder to the apartment at 439[2] on Friday of this week in order that Ida,[3] who has been told I am away in the country might not learn the truth until she could write her from out of town. The proposition she made was that in all fairness she should be allowed, in appearance at least, to desert me. I agree to this latter. As to the former I wanted Thelma to say what she thought. I still wish an opinion, indirectly of course, but I think she ought eventually to know that I put this up to her. Whatever the outcome I am guiding my life by what she would think.

Very Sincerely
Theodore Dreiser

And I am paying beyond my wildest fancies, believe me.

1. The 1911 version is available only in the Dreiser Edition: *The Genius of 1911*, ed. Clare Virginia Eby (Urbana: University of Illinois Press, 2006).
The "Genius" (New York: John Lane Company, 1915).

2. Dreiser moved out of their apartment at 439 West 123rd Street on October third and took a room at the Park Avenue Hotel, on Fourth Avenue and Thirty-third Street.

3. Ida was Mrs. Dreiser's unmarried sister. She and Sara Dreiser were on staff at the *Delineator*.

To Thelma Cudlipp [HP-DPUP]

To abort Dreiser's relationship with her daughter, Mrs. Cudlipp had taken Thelma to Saluda, North Carolina, to stay with relatives. Although Dreiser wrote daily, his letters were intercepted by the family. Suspecting this, Dreiser had sent Thelma a telegram that required some form of receipt. When he received no notice, he wrote a letter to the general manager of the telegraph company, threatening to sue and demanding an investigation of the Saluda agent's actions.

608 Riverside Drive
Phone—Audubon-1600

Nov. 7th 1910

Dearest Thelma:

In regard to the agent at Saluda—I am not bringing other action of any kind. At the time that I filed a message with you and paid double rates for personal delivery only and a reply, I demanded immediate acknowledgement or a return of the message. When neither came I wrote at once to Mr. Belvedere Brooks the general manager of the company stating the facts. He wrote stating he would investigate the case but having heard nothing more I thought it was all over. I told your mother after the original complaint had been filed I would do nothing.

If there is any real danger of the man losing his job I will write Brooks and ask him to do nothing, though a scare wont hurt an agent who connives at betraying the company. Your mother phoned that I had broken my word to you in this matter. Do you recall any word I ever said to you in regard to this?

Oh, sweet, I am so lonely. In the shadow even this chance to explain is something. I love you, love you, love you, past all words to describe.

Theo

Your mother stated that you felt that I had broken faith with you.

And sometime I would like to show you a letter I have from Krog[1] which will make clear how groundless are the charges I understand he made against me to you.

1. Fritz Krog was an editor and writer who had been hired by Dreiser at the *Delineator*; in 1909 he served as nominal head of *Bohemian*, a magazine that Dreiser briefly and secretly operated. The emotionally unstable Krog also had fallen in love with Thelma Cudlipp and asked his boss for advice without knowing of Dreiser's interest in her. Learning of the scandal, Krog threatened to kill Dreiser and slandered him to Thelma. Dreiser wrote a semi-fictional account of these events in "Emanuela" (*Gallery of Women* [1929]), in which the character of Ernest Schieb is based on Krog.

1911

To Edna Kenton [H-CU]

Dreiser was in England at this time, on the first leg of a tour of Europe, an account of which he gave in A Traveler at Forty *(1913). He was much concerned about the fate of his new novel,* Jennie Gerhardt, *which had been published two months before. As one of his earliest advocates and an influential reviewer, Kenton helped shape early critical opinion of Dreiser's writing.*

Hotel Capitol
1 Regent Street
St. James Square S.W.

Dec 11th 1911

My Dear E. K:

Your note & clipping came to me here. You know I scarcely know what to say to you at times—you've been so uniformly fine.[1] I treated you so badly about your travelling bag that night at the Gilsey[2] but that's my way. I cant help it. I feel far more human and sympathetic toward you always than I act, I think, & I hope & suppose—in fact I know,—that you really understand. The human interest story promised will be good if you do it, just as this in the Chicago Post is good & as all you have said in the past is good.[3] I'm grateful because I rejoice in the thought of having so sane and kindly an interpreter & friend.

I'm going to stay here until January 15th I think—or 20th. Then to Holland, Nice, Monte Carlo, Rome, Sicily, Athens (I hope) Paris, Berlin & possibly here again.[4] You will be interested to know that the book really hasn't started here but I think it's going to.[5] Conditions are promising. Europe is interesting to me—very. You will want to read my privately subscribed impressions when they appear.[6] They will really be interesting.

Th. D

1. Dreiser is referring to Kenton's constant support of his writing, particularly her early advocacy of *Sister Carrie* and her recent efforts to encourage good reviews of *Jennie Gerhardt*.

2. The Gilsey Hotel, located at Broadway and Twenty-ninth Street.

3. Dreiser may be thinking of Kenton's recent article, "Some Incomes in Fiction," *Bookman* 34 (October 1911). Earlier she had written one of the favorable reviews of *Sister Carrie* when it first appeared (*Chicago Daily News*, 30 November 1900; repub. Salzman, *Critical Reception*, 2–3). The *Chicago Post* piece is the "clipping" he mentions, and probably refers to Floyd Dell's praiseful review of *Jennie Gerhardt*,

Edna Kenton (left) with John Reed and Ethel Plummer (ca. 1919).
(Courtesy of the Sheaffer-O'Neill Collection, Connecticut College.)

"A Great Novel" (3 November 1911; repub. Salzman, *Critical Reception*, 64–68), which Kenton had a hand in arranging.

4. Dreiser later visited all the places he mentions here, except Sicily and Athens.

5. Dreiser is referring to *Jennie Gerhardt*, which had not yet been reviewed in England.

6. His "privately subscribed impressions" were in a diary he kept throughout his European tour; they later served as the basis for *A Traveler at Forty* (1913), although more than half his "impressions" were expurgated by the publisher. The uncensored version is available in the Dreiser Edition: *A Traveler at Forty*, ed. Renate von Bardeleben (Urbana: University of Illinois Press, 2004).

1913

To Kirah Markham [H-DPUP]

Dreiser first met Kirah Markham (1891–1967) in January 1913, when she was performing the part of Andromache in Euripides' The Trojan Women *at the Chicago Little Theater, founded in 1912 by the British-born Maurice Browne and his wife Ellen Van Volkenburg. Markham was born Elaine Hyman into a solidly middle-class family that ran a prosperous jewelry company in Chicago. She resisted conventional options, studying art and acting while her sister went to Vassar. Over a long career she worked in many artistic fields—as actress, writer, painter, sculptor, costume and set designer, and founder of a theatrical school in Haiti. She and Dreiser were immediately attracted to each other and became lovers before he left Chicago on 10 February 1913. In June she came to New York, and, bankrolled by her indulgent father, made an attempt to find steady work in theater. Over the following year, she intermittently rented several Manhattan apartments between stints at the Chicago Little Theater or on road tours with the company. Dreiser's earliest letters were written when Markham was either in Chicago or at theatrical venues in other cities. He often addressed them from an apartment at 3609 Broadway (see n. 1). In July 1914, when he moved to 165 West Tenth Street, Markham joined him. For a brief period the couple offered a weekly open house for avant-garde artists and intellectuals who were their neighbors in Greenwich Village. Their invitation card read: "Friends can always find Kirah Markham and Theodore Dreiser at home on Sunday evenings, November-March," along with their address and telephone number. Dreiser's relationship with Markham had no rival for intensity, with the notable exceptions of those with Sara O. White and Helen Richardson. (When Robert H. Elias interviewed Markham for his 1949 biography, he noted that she thought of herself as "the second Mrs. Dreiser" [DPUP].) Markham contributed variously to Dreiser's writing. She helped him to edit the manuscript of* The "Genius," *wrote the songs for his play "The Spring Recital," and did the book designs for* The Plays of the Natural and Supernatural *and* A Hoosier Holiday. *She was the model for the character of Stephanie Platow in* The Titan *(1914), and later she would appear as Sidonie Platow in the character sketch "This Madness: The Book of Sidonie" (1929).*

3609 Broadway

Mch. 1–1913

Elaine Sweet:

I've been in such a quandary ever since I learned on Thursday that you were still in St. Louis & might be for days more as to where to send mail. I didn't know and you didn't say whether you would be in St. Louis for the remainder of the week or longer and even now I don't know and cant know until Monday and not even then unless you tell me or your letter shows whether you are to be in Chicago or St. Louis. I've not wanted to send any more letters to 4830.[1] I've sent enough there for your father to forward & speculate over & so I can only address this care of the Little Theatre at Chicago. I wish sincerely I had known or knew now. It makes me feel restless and disturbed. Please give me your itinerary for at least two weeks or three by return mail when you get this.

I was so glad to get a letter from you today enclosing notices of your work in St. Louis.[2] It seems to me that neither you nor the company have any cause for complaint. Some of the comment is, of course, vapid. It always is. But in the main you have been well treated and as time goes on you can hope for so much more. You are young and enthusiastic and naturally artistic. What more could you want.

I have to smile at your depression over my willingness as you say, to surrender you to the stage. I didn't say that, you know. I said if I couldn't keep you I couldn't. That is all. Neither could I. But there is no need to tell such a philosopher as you how it all works. If love is to endure it will. If it dies, it dies. I love the opera Carmen for the picture it gives of hopeless anguish, rage, revenge but I could not share in any such mood as that.[3] I am too fatalistic. My life has always seemed as though it were something willed to me—things given or taken away—and that in all things where I have put up the best fight—made the most brilliant struggle I have lost. So I, speaking for myself at least—and solely—might well say what will be, will be. You may come of a different order and by struggle create and retain the things that you want.

This sounds a little gloomy perhaps but I am not so pessimistic as to permit myself to cease struggling. I like life—even its losses on occasion—and make a virtue of them. Defeat can easily be turned into a kind of victory though not the victory in the thing that was first sought. We progress quite as much through disaster as through success. So when I say, if I lose you, I do, I merely mean that I should stop all complaint and wish you luck. I would be like your monk in the story of the Monk and the Dancer[4] who returns to his monastic cell. I often think that unless my life shall take on a very definite direction fixing me permanently in this wonder of affection & companionship I shall wind up in a Trappist[5] or some other monastic order. It is almost the only way. I crave affection of a high order so desperately that unless I can have it, only complete resignation & withdrawal from the sight of the universe & the world will help me. It is, with my temperament, all or nothing and I am not so hopeful of life as to be sure that it will be *all*.

But, Elyhon,[6] sweet, you represent so much that is wonderful to me that I wish-I wish-I wish. I crave the tenderness that used to make you—almost unconsciously it seems—take my hand. I remember one day—or several days in fact—you were phoning, and standing in the booth, waiting, your hand sought mine to hold it. I might have been a five year old child then snuggled by its mother, for all the difference I felt between me and it. I fight quite freely and vigorously without affection but when I get it, it does strange things to me. It somehow makes it clear to me what it is I need. A true confession this.

So you looked so nice in your boudoir costume and yellow cap! Would I had been there. Did you ever get my letter asking you to make plans to stay with me a day or two in the East. You never said. Remote Elyhon! I wish you would answer and indicate what you hope for at least: I have never received the 3 first letters, nor yet the one sent via the New York friend. I would give a lot to know what became of the first three anyhow—or should I say three first?

The world goes apace. I work & work & wait for letters from you. Don't let this letter depress you, if it has any such tendency. Tomorrow is another day. I will write and try to be very cheerful. When I stop to think I know I have reason to be for I believe you love me in a rich tender delicious way. Would you were in my arms.

T. L. M[7]

1. The addresses used in this letter suggest the complicated nature of the relationship. Dreiser at first sent letters to Markham's family home address, but became concerned that Markham's parents might take note of the number of letters coming from him and confiscate them. Instead he began to address his letters in care of the various theaters in which she worked. As for his address, 3609 Broadway was an apartment that Dreiser was sharing with his wife Sara. Although they had unofficially separated in 1910, they continued to live on a business-like basis at 3609. Dreiser would often retreat to his room there from Markham's apartment or various Greenwich Village residences to write without interruption. If Sara happened to have family or friends coming, he would leave immediately.

2. Most of the Markham letters, including this one, are not among the Dreiser Papers.

3. Georges Bizet's opera *Carmen* (1874), which tells the story of a spurned lover whose jealousy after being rejected by Carmen leads him to kill her. In his autobiography Dreiser recalls hearing selections from *Carmen* at the Warsaw Opera House in Indiana, and even in his early teens "they smacked of romance" (*Dawn*, 360).

4. Markham's gift of Arthur Cosslett Smith's novel *The Monk and the Dancer* remained in Dreiser's library throughout his lifetime.

5. The Trappists (or the Order of Strict Observance), Roman Catholic monks who in the eleventh century broke from the Benedictines to create a reformed group,

originally known as Cistercians, which emphasized a return to the simplicity and primitive monastic observances outlined in the Rule of Saint Benedict.

6. One of Dreiser's two favorite nicknames for Markham (the other being Cryhon), of uncertain origin.

7. The initials represent one of Dreiser's coded names for himself: The Lonely Man.

To Kirah Markham [H-DPUP]

Markham visited an art exhibit in Chicago that showed many of the avant-garde paintings that had been displayed at the New York Armory Show from 17 February to 15 March 1913. The more experimental of the painters (such as Duchamp, Picabia, Matisse, and Picasso) were lambasted by the National Academy of Design and the Art Institute of Chicago (where Markham had studied) with accusations of immorality, quackery, and anarchism. Dreiser responds here to her enthusiasms and reservations about the new styles of the cubist and futurist movements.

Hamilton Grange[1]

April 2–1913

Elyhon Lamb:

What a wild kid you are! My, my, how this letter describing your career at the Futurist exhibit[2] does indicate your spirited temperament. Don't get too wild, Elyhon. We all have to live at best amid a rather commonplace drift of things and the nearer we remain, conscientious, to the bedrock facts of life the better. I like to think of you, though, whipping yourself into a foam over the significant reaction against a too much formalized art. We need everything that the Futurist exhibit represents and more—much more. I agree with you that the long limbed lady has a poetry of line & spirit which has nothing to do and should have nothing to do with the idea of the so-called perfect human form as we knew it. It is a piece of form beauty in itself like that of a wasp or any other wonderful shape. I felt that way when I saw it. I liked also the Cubistic presentation of nuns walking which some people saw only as strange cubes and squares and cones.[3] It has its place & the idea will no doubt be much used in the future. I wonder how you would like Gertrude Stein's writing ?[4]

Well my lady-lady-oh—enjoy yourself. I'm glad, truly, that Chicago offered you so much wherewith to divert yourself immediate on your return. I don't want you to feel lonely or broody. I am temperamentally much given to that sort of thing and I'm sure there is small profit in it. As a literary mood it sometimes has uses—not always. Joy felt and expressed is probably more wonderful. The curse of some of us is that we cannot always intellectually share it.

I am afraid this letter is going to seem dull to you though. I do not feel dull toward you. My arms—spiritually—are conscious of an emptiness all the while. I cannot have today or tomorrow or the next day or any day soon the things that I most want—looks in your eyes, the smile of your mouth, the sound of your voice—that something about you that always told me you were glad to be with me. I feel like saying "Ah, well a day—so must it be." I can only work now & wait & wish. But don't you let me depress you. We must all take this world as we find it. Have a good time, write me and know that I—what?

The Mourner

I do not know what "seared" means unless it relates to the result of the flame of passion. The position might suggest as much, wouldn't you say?[5]

1. Dreiser probably wrote this letter from the Hamilton Grange Branch Library on West 145th Street, though he may have been visiting Hamilton Grange at 287 Convent Avenue, the last home of American statesman Alexander Hamilton (1755–1804). The house had been relocated in 1889 from the area where the library now stands.

2. Chicago held a "Futurist Exhibit" at the Victory Gardens Theater in 1913, which consisted of the works displayed at the New York Armory Show. Dreiser had seen the paintings he mentions in this letter at the Armory Show.

3. Dreiser had become interested in the cubists on his 1911–12 tour of Europe, when he had seen in London's private salons his first Picasso, as well as postimpressionists such as Cezanne, Matisse, Gauguin, and Van Gogh (see his responses in Bardeleben, *Traveler at Forty*, 133–39; 232–34).

4. Dreiser is correctly associating the experimental writing of Gertrude Stein (1874–1946) with cubist and futurist works. Stein had been a patron of modern art and helped to make American painters aware of various postimpressionist movements. Futurism began in Italy with the theoretical writing of F. T. Marinetti on language, painting, architecture, and music—and influenced writers such as Stein, William Carlos Williams, and Ezra Pound. For literature, Marinetti's writing advocated "words-in-freedom," promoting the breaking of conventional syntax as an aesthetic goal that is in keeping with modern urban and technological realities.

5. Dreiser seems to be responding to a query from Markham, apparently about a figure in one of the paintings.

To Kirah Markham [H-DPUP]

Saturday, April 12–1913

Elyhon Sweet:

I might almost say Elyhon Myhon. Two letters came together last night apparently written the same day and quite long ones. Why this sudden burst of speed I asked myself, even as I rejoiced. The box of fudge "Lyhon's Candy" with the card in it was also there, and finding it better fudge than usual—better than I have ever had made for me, I ate the most of it. It wasn't broken in any way—not one of the ten pieces—not even the nuts were loosened. So your fears are not realized.

But the letters were best—the one quoting Whitman whom I so much admire, being the better of the two. I had a crush on Whitman years ago and have cut out and pasted in my scrapbook "When I Heard the Learned Astronomer," "Ah Poverties, Wincings, Shallow Deceits," "Grass," "Camps of Green," "The Noiseless Patient Spider," and others. But the poem of his I most like I think, is called "Brooklyn Ferry."[1] That to me is really wonderful.

You're a strange maid, Elyhon. I think of you constantly—the peculiarities of your mood. It is so hard to understand anyone in this world—perhaps least of all one of whom you are fond. The angle of your dreams and your logic mystifies me but you are none the less delightful for that, rather more so. I always wonder what new marvel of this to you new world is to take your fancy next. You are just a kid yet, Elyhon, stepping out of the coop and looking around and yet you are strangely wise too, and resourceful. I sincerely think you are a very exceptional person but I only hope you are big enough not to attach too much weight to any seeming manifestation. Life is always compelling our enthusiasms but it needn't do it to our utter despair in many cases subsequently. I rather think though at bottom that you really are very wise—that you are two persons—one who enthuses and one who stands by and looks on. Or is that so in your case.

But I cannot help but rejoice in your love of beauty. It is poignant and it reaches me. I have suffered so much through my admiration and my love of beauty. Perhaps I always shall. I hope so, anyhow. But you with your dreams of me and my letters in your arms—that is a picture worthy of Keats. I have never heard you talk of him but St. Agnes Eve, the Grecian Urn and Ode to Melancholy[2] ought to be delights to you. Are you not familiar with them. Yes, all your letters have come—averaging one a day and I have them all together. Those pictures I sat for turned out badly but I sat again & must now go and see. Mary Elizabeth[3] has never written, Floyd Dell dislikes the mss of a novel[4] I let him read—etc., etc. Amid much hard work and dull days your self-revealing letters are about all I have—all that is really worth while. They are best because they constantly suggest the wonder of your presence—the feel of your living body in my arms.

Mr. Writer

N. B.

The Princess Theatre[5] here is giving one act plays of the strongest kind—quite brutal at times. They have a capable company. It is a very little place.

I wish I could get you in there. I am going to see what I can find out about this. Some of their one act plays are very charming indeed.

1. Dreiser does not always correctly recall the names of the poems by Walt Whitman, but his references are to, respectively: "When I Heard the Learn'd Astronomer"; "Ah Poverties, Wincings, and Sulky Retreats"; "Grass" might be a reference to "The Prairie-Grass Dividing" or perhaps to "Leaves of Grass" collectively; "Camps of Green"; "A Noiseless Patient Spider"; "Crossing Brooklyn Ferry." Markham's letters showed a special fondness for Whitman, especially "Out of the Cradle Endlessly Rocking," a poem that she said brought tears to her eyes (Markham to Dreiser, 24 May 1913 [DPUP]).

2. Poems by John Keats (1795–1821): "The Eve of Saint Agnes," "Ode on a Grecian Urn," "Ode on Melancholy."

3. Likely this is Mary Elizabeth Titzel, secretary at the Chicago Little Theatre. Another possibility is mentioned by Richard Lingeman: Mary Elizabeth Barry, a poet associated with the Little Theatre who had a brief flirtation with Dreiser before he turned his attention to Kirah Markham (see Lingeman, *American Journey*, 77).

4. For Floyd Dell, see Dreiser to Kirah Markham, 15 April 1913, n. 1. The novel Dreiser wrote in 1911, then called *The Genius*, was significantly revised in 1914 and published as *The "Genius"* (1915). For the version Dreiser sent to Dell, see Clare Virginia Eby, ed., *The Genius of 1911*, in the Dreiser Edition (University of Illinois Press, 2007).

5. The Princess Theatre: a theater with only 299 seats, it opened in 1913 on Thirty-ninth Street, off Sixth Avenue. Originally built as a venue for one-act plays, it soon became known for its musicals.

To Kirah Markham [H-DPUP]

Dreiser's ire and suspicions were aroused by Markham's accounts of her conflicted involvement with Floyd Dell,[1] with whom she was having a relationship when she met Dreiser.

Tuesday, April 15–1913—No 1.

Elyhon Sweet:

Baby peaches,

Your letters certainly show your disposition from day to day. They indicate your trials and moods to me—very barometrically to say the least. But why aren't you more explicit at times. You tell me just edges of things. Are you afraid to tell me all? Have you never yet? Or do you think you have. This letter of April 12th (no 2)[2] written at midnight tells of the Dell's Studio and a storm of tears which it caused but not why. The exaggerated Bohemianism and the rapid intimacy—what were these? How did they manifest themselves? How did they come so close to you as to make you cry? Were you compelled to do something you did not want to do? And who made you? I cannot see a cause for a storm of tears unless the provocation was personal & severe. But will you tell me? I feel so often as though I were hearing but the faintest part and that our seeming intimacy was really not intimacy after all but a kind of lovers illusion. You wouldn't want it to be like that would you?

You see I have followed your lead and began numbering my letters. You need not fear that one will not be written unless exceptional conditions arise but I cannot always write at the same hour & so I cannot guarantee regular deliveries (this sounds rather formal doesn't it). But I'll write & you will know they are on the way. I look forward to your daily word more eagerly than I do to anything else—meals, visits, work—anything. I like to see your handwriting (which by the way I am going to have read & interpreted) and to feel that you have written it just two days before. It brings you close to me—close & human.

Are you still wearing glasses? What a shame. I hope your eyes get rested up. I am afraid glasses don't become you—yet. Later on they might look well enough. When you get to the place where you take a very solemn view of life.

You know my mind keeps running on Dell & you & what may be between you these days and I cant somehow shake it off. It seems rather silly to me at times, too. I have an idea sometimes that because it does and because I cannot quite get rid of it, though I want to, that there is something. Are you really keeping faith with me? I wish you would tell me once more for I want to quit thinking about it. I don't care from one point of view. If you like him so much that you want to be intimate with him I will promise to be friends with you but I wont be intimate—not for the present anyhow. I think he is very strong for you. He is no doubt greatly piqued at your tendency to be interested in me. That would make him anxious to win you back. I can stand the knowledge of your continued relation quite well enough—life has made me hardy & stoic—but I cant stand deception—innocent or intended, or being one of two when I don't want to be. I told you that once before and you became angry. I repeat it though now because unlike so many other things I cannot ever forgive it. Something in my nature goes back on anyone who thinks so lightly of my capacity as to think I can or ought to be deceived. I can be—I know that—but if chance unlocks the door on the fact then alas I am no longer the same person. We would get along so much better (so much longer perhaps I had better say) if we were quite frank. I want to be. If you have ever thought of the other way, abandon it for it is no way, if luck should ever turn your seeming awry.

But I would be so desperately solemn. I am very fond of you but only on one basis and I want you to be fond of me in the same way. I can be friends in many ways and you might like me that way best—but I could never be one of two lovers if I knew it. I am too vain I suppose, or too individual. You might be the type that would like more than one, but then you surely would not want me for one if I did not want to be and did not want you to deceive me, would you? That would be most unfair. It would be taking advantage of me after I have protested that I do not want to be taken advantage of. So there—I said my final say on this & I'll stop.

Its raining again today. Last night I went to Patterson to get some color for a one act play I am thinking of doing.[3] I believe I have a good idea. I am also working on my book (chapter 30)[4] and thinking of a short story that I want to write. Tis a mad world Elyhon and my only hope is that out of its madness I can pluck one flower of sincere, uncold affection & faith. Can you guess who's?

The Grumbler.

Honey Sweet if you want to come as much as I want you to come in June & your father wont arrange it & I can I will see that you come on. I wish we could take some sort of place together somewhere.
Here's another.[5]

1. Floyd Dell (1887–1969), journalist, novelist, editor, memoirist, playwright. At this time, he was editor of the *Friday Literary Review* (the literary supplement of the Chicago *Evening Post*) and had already favorably reviewed *Jennie Gerhardt* (1911) as "A Great Novel" (repub. Salzman, *Critical Reception*, 64–68). In December 1912 the two men got together again when Dreiser was in Chicago conducting research on Charles T. Yerkes for *The Titan*. Although Markham was then romantically involved with Dell, she and Dreiser soon became lovers. Dell continued to pursue her after Dreiser returned to New York, arousing the novelist's jealousy and insecurities. Despite having lost Markham's affection, Dell responded well to Dreiser's request for help in editing *The "Genius"* (1915). In general he remained a literary booster for Dreiser's books (though his next two reviews—of *A Traveler at Forty* (1913) and *The "Genius"*—were at best lukewarm and in spots nasty). In *The Titan* Dreiser based the character of Gardner Knowles on Dell and made him the first lover of Stephanie Platow, an actress modeled on Markham. When Dell relocated to Greenwich Village in 1914 to pursue a career as a novelist and playwright (and become managing editor of the *Masses*), he and Dreiser moved in the same circles. Dell discusses Dreiser in his memoirs, *Love in Greenwich Village* (1926) and *Homecoming* (1933). For a fuller discussion of the Dell-Dreiser-Markham relationship, see Thomas P. Riggio, "Dreiser and Kirah Markham: The Play's the Thing," in *Studies in American Naturalism* 1–2 (Summer-Winter 2006), 109–28.

2. Markham was in the habit of numbering her letters.

3. Dreiser is referring to the play he would complete in 1913, *The Girl in the Coffin*. For the background of the play Dreiser used the events of the historic textile worker's strike waged at Paterson, New Jersey, which had begun at the Henry Dougherty Silk Company on 27 January 1913. Within a month twenty-five thousand silk workers had joined the strike, and the abuses suffered by the strikers

led to wide support among Dreiser's associates in Greenwich Village. In June 1913 such support was dramatized in *The Paterson Strike Pageant* written by John Reed and played in Madison Square Garden with a cast that included a large number of the actual strikers.

4. His novel *The Titan* (1914).

5. At the end of letters to Markham Dreiser often placed such comments beside comic bits he had cut from newspapers or magazines.

To Kirah Markham [H-DPUP]

3609

Sunday-April 20–1913—No 6.

Elyhon Sweet:

Just consider that I have recited this well known litany of Elyhon this Sunday morning as my contribution to faith & perhaps that will make up in part for my letter of yesterday. I was "acting up" very badly as I look back on it now. It is blowing like sixty here this morning—white caps on the river—but otherwise it is as clear & radiant as a day can well be. An April blow. Do you remember the blowing figures of March in "Primavera." with their cheeks extended.[1] They are like this day.

Yesterday, after the accident of the night before I saw another accident on Broadway at 113th St. Things always go in twos for me—an old man knocked senseless and broken by a ripping motor cycle. When he fell on the track he looked like a frog that had been hit with a club. The rider who struck him came down in a heap also with his machine & getting up & seeing his victim began to cry—sob in an odd kind of way. A woman coming up offered up a prayer. A fool worked himself into a rage on the assumption that it was a motor cycle policeman who had run the old man down. It was a fine crowd of delivery wagon drivers, Saturday afternoon marketers, butcher boys, grocer clerks and citizens generally, to say nothing of idling authors. Someone brought a policeman: someone else phoned for an ambulance. The cyclist was arrested & so ended that incident. I shall not soon forget the spectacle of the smash. I saw it quite clearly & sharply—like a scene in a play.

Last night I went to George Rector's[2] to see the dancing between the tables. New York is surely crazy over this sort of thing. There was the wildest abandon—a sort of drunken orgy—so rhythmic and sensuous that it put me in a strangely savage mood. But there was only one girl I wanted and alas she was not with me. The young lady opposite complained that I was engrossed with other things. Very true indeed. I kept thinking all the while how you would look dancing & wishing I might dance with you—were graceful enough to match your utmost mood. Failing that I would like to see you dancing with another.

My one act play is growing apace.[3] I'll tell you about it when I see you—if you haven't deserted me by now. I have an idea for a dandy individual book which I will tell you about latter, too. I'm eager to do it—only The Titan is almost draining my heart's blood. I am to be the guest of honor next Friday evening at the Playwrights Club[4]—and I have never written a play. Two playwrights however want to dramatize The Financier.[5] I wish someone who really knew how would. Next Tuesday I meet Madame Kalish.[6] More news than that I cannot think of at present.

But as for you—you may depend on it—my thoughts never change. I go over my hours with you—each little thing—and the crucial hours with violent feeling. I want you so much, Elyhon. I want to get you in my arms & hold you close and tell you all the soft things that only we two can say to each other. Don't you want me *so*?—much?

The Fair Weather Philosopher.

1. The Florentine painter Sandro Botticelli's *Primavera* (ca. 1448) or "Springtime." Among the numerous classical figures of mythology in the painting, there is one "blowing" figure, usually regarded as Zephyrus, the god of the winds depicted as groping at a fleeing nymph.

2. George Rector's restaurant at Forty-fourth Street and Broadway sought to produce a nightclub atmosphere and employed women to dance as part of the entertainment accompanying dinner.

3. *The Girl in the Coffin*. See Dreiser to Kirah Markham, 15 April 1913, n. 3. The play first appeared in *Smart Set* 41 (October 1913): 127–40.

4. The Playwright's Club, which met in the studio of the painter Robert Amick at 63 Washington Square, gave aspiring playwrights an opportunity to discuss their work and to hear talks by established writers. Dreiser was invited to appear on Friday, April 25.

5. There is no record of interest in a dramatic version of the novel in 1913. In later years, Dreiser attempted to dramatize the book, but he eventually felt the material was not amenable to such a treatment. See Dreiser to Rella Abell Armstrong, 26 October 1929, n. 1.

6. Madame Bertha Kalish (1883–1939), actress born in Lemberg, Galicia, achieved her first success in the Yiddish theater in Bucharest. She later came to New York and had a renowned career in both Yiddish- and English-speaking theaters.

To Kirah Markham [H-DPUP]

Dreiser often addressed Markham with various forms of "Asia" or "Egypt"—terms he used to express his responses to her dark hair, eyes, and complexion as well as her sensual nature.

Friday, April 25–1913—No 11

My peaches sweet:
You dark Red Asia Rose:

Your letter last, no 13, caused me to feel so sorry for myself and for you & yet it cheered me, too, for it proved as much as writing can—and sometimes much can be proved that way—that you truly love me. It all springs from love, as you know, that hungry craving that goes with the thought of another. You represent so much that is sweet to me that the mere thought of your sharing your looks and graces with another is maddening. But as I wrote you I am not going to think of that anymore. I am not going to believe you are unfaithful. I really do not. I am just going to think of your loving me whatever you do and that when you get here all will be perfect once more. So there.

Owing to an engagement the dinner with Mme Kalish[1] was put off until next Tuesday and I went instead to dine with Lillian Russell.[2] What a strange type she is—smooth, blond, placid rather cow-like. I question whether she ever suffered a great emotional storm in her life. She is 62 (she says) and she can actually put it all over the average woman of forty. It is almost impossible to believe it is true. At about 9:20 or :30 she left to go to the vaudeville theatre where she was performing and having put on a red and black dress and a chic black hat she looked much younger still —not more than 30. Wouldn't that, as some one used to say, make you bust out and cry? She comes of common stock, however, or her experiences have been coarse for I could see quite plainly that it was an effort for her to maintain that smooth level of polite language which is so easy for others. Every now and & then she would drop back, quite by accident, into the parlance of the vulgar rounder or the bagnio even. However she is charming, good natured, kindly, and courteous which helps a lot —doesn't it. Her husband (no 4) lives in Pittsburgh & comes on every Friday night, returning Sunday night.[3] He owns *The Leader* there, the principal afternoon paper. He is 49 to her 62. He owns a house in Atlantic City which she wont live in, one in Pittsburgh which she will not occupy & an estate somewhere which she will not visit. This apartment is her own, done Chinese style. Two maids, a Japanese servant, her sister & her sister's son make her life comfortable while she is here. She has six automobiles & is earning $6,000 a week at present. How is that for 62.

Wednesday night I went to dine with Laura Jean Libbey.[4] She didn't know me from Adam's off ox and all the while (I went with a newspaper friend) called me Mr. Ceaser, which I refused to correct or allow to be corrected. Short, stout, red headed (brick red) genial, skittish, 53,—that is Laura Jean. She lives in Brooklyn. Her house is a fright—stuffed with all the old, dull stuff for which Brooklyn is noted. There is two billion dollars worth of junk masquerading as furniture and art in Brooklyn. I expected to see a landscape with a mother-of-pearl moon set in the sky (real mother of pearl) but I escaped that. Yet they had Champagne, $7^{50} Victorola records, a library of dictionary sized volumes of history. Police!

Last night I went to see Adachi[5] (the Jap) who is as grouchy as ever. He says when you come east again he will cook us that Japanese diner. He saw you on the subway & you saw him. An interesting but sombre person.

So, Elyhon, thus goes my time but I wish you were here. Life, outside of love (where you are is love) is dull business. I have to smile when I think of Miss Goodrich's[6] solicitude for your age and conduct. At twenty-one you perceive more than she will at fifty or ever. There is no limit to vision or mentality except as our temperaments bind us, but all are so bound—some much, some little. She is bound much. She needs an effusion of temperament. You have so much that life is nebulous to you. But, my sweet, that's why I love you so and when you come to me again I am going to be happy. Now is the time—the spring is so wonderful. But I shall stay in New York all summer with you & if it can be arranged & you will, we live together. Oh, these "them" happy days.

Mr. Lonely.

Here is a lone page but this story isn't bad.[7] If I have missed a letter I have made up in the length of others—haven't I. Write me another poem or send me a sketch. The second picture at Hellinger's[8] was better.

1. Mme Kalish. See Dreiser to Kirah Markham, 20 April 1913, n. 6.

2. Lillian Russell (1860–1922), born Helen Louise Leonard in Clinton, Iowa, actress and noted operetta singer celebrated for her beauty as well as her stage presence. Dreiser may have misheard or misremembered her age, because Russell was a decade younger than he says here. In Chapter 41 of the early version of *Sister Carrie*, Dreiser shows Carrie tiring of her work in choruses and envying the fame of Lillian Russell, whom she thought of as one of "the high and mighties" (see the Dreiser Edition of *Sister Carrie* [Philadelphia, 1981], Chapter 41, p. 391). The reference was edited out of the book published by Doubleday in 1900.

3. Despite her many marriages, Russell was the constant companion for forty years of the famous business tycoon "Diamond Jim" Brady.

4. Laura Jean Libbey (1862–1925), prolific best-selling novelist specializing in heartthrob romances, which reportedly earned her as much as $60,000 a year.

5. Adachi Kinnosuki, prolific writer whose articles on Japanese and other Far East topics appeared in mainstream magazines, including Dreiser's *Delineator*. His books included *Iroka: Tales of Japan* (1900) and *Manchuria: A Survey* (1925). He had written to Dreiser, highly praising *Jennie Gerhardt*.

6. Elizabeth Goodrich, actress who played Helen in the Little Theatre production of *The Trojan Women* that featured Markham as Andromache.

7. As was his habit, Dreiser enclosed a clipping of a comic newspaper sketch and wrote beside it "Do you get tired of these stories?"

8. Markham often sent Dreiser photos of herself, in this case one most likely taken at the Ciminello & Hellinger Theater in Chicago.

To Kirah Markham [H-DPUP]

Sunday, April 27–1913—No 13

Asia Baby:

My Peaches Pet:

Its raining tonight—the queerest little rain—fine and soft with spells of dryness in between. New York streets are almost bare but in the houses here about the windows are all open and the sound of the piano & the Sunday Evening Party is heard in the land. It is most interesting to me how the middle class & almost every other for that matter delights to hold Sunday evening parties and have Uncle John and cousin Mary and her husband in to participate. Life is so gay then. From the outside looking in it tinkles like a cymbal. It seems so eminently worth living and it is.

Honey Sweet, what do you think of true love anyway? Do you think there is any hope of a mating that endures for this life. Have you seen any examples. I have always had such a strange craving for my mate intellectually, emotionally & artistically. I have always dreamed that I would live with her always—if I could find her-year in and year out—never to stray anymore. I have known so many women in one walk and another but so often, almost invariably I have been alienated—as a rule instantly—by one characteristic or another. I have never really found her until now. Are you she? Have you meditated seriously on me and what if anything you would like to do with me. If you married me would you truly expect it to endure—would you try to make it endure or do you think as I so often think there is no binding the artistic temperament. Only hard cold reassuring can help to make an at times troublesome state last & would you feel that you ought to make it or is this just love for an hour—a gay day to be dissolved at will. My feeling is that I would truly like to keep you for my own—that I would love to grow into a sweet companionship with you & quit seeking—that I would like you for my true heart's mate—to consol me & let me love you all that my heart wishes. Years & years do not seem enough in time for me. How is it with you?

This morning I wrote and also until 3 PM when I went down to look at the paintings of an artist by the name of [Dreiser left a blank space here] a most serious and interesting person but quite likable. And the work is beautiful—in the best sense—temperamental, reflective, philosophic, ideal.

It shows sculpture & painting in a strange blend if you can believe it—a charming harmony such as I have never seen before, but successful. The figures are so iron, so material, so gross & heavy & yet so ideal. The landscapes are in some cases enchantments of delight; the skies are rain skies, created in the lively mood of the author. They were delightful pictures all.

Elyhon pet I went the other night with several people into the restaurant which is a part of the Hotel Empire at Broadway & 65th Street where once one Sunday in March you & I were.[1] I had the most poignant sense of lost beauty—beauty that I can only think of now and anticipate for the future. I think of you so often—your lithe body, your black hair, that curve of the throat, the full perfectly formed hips and breasts. What a flower like armful! How like a rose on a tall stem you are. And then to hold you so close—to feel the beat of your heart, to hear your loving voice. If I could just press my face into the round of neck, between chin and shoulder and feel the smoothing caress of your hand.

It's late now & I am going to sleep but I'll wish I may dream of you. My bed & my arms are always empty save of your spirit. I think of you beside me—wish & wish and then sleep. Be my Sweet Elyhon—be only for me, honey. I want you so.

Your Lover

1. Markham had visited New York briefly after her appearance in Boston with the Chicago Little Theater, which had been on tour at the time.

To Kirah Markham [H-DPUP]

New York

Wednesday-April 30 [1913]—No 16

Elyhon Sweet:

My Own Peaches Pet:

I went last night to see Madame Kalish.[1] She is a woman I am told of about thirty-seven years. To me she looks a little older but then she has recently been ill. She lives in a somewhat splendid apartment house at Broadway and 89th Street with her 19 year old daughter. She was married at 15 and as I understand it her husband is dead. She is a Polish Jew.

I was rather interested in Madame because I have seen her act several times and because she made a special effort last night to be nice to me. She has only read Jennie Gerhardt—the one accursed book which all women like—and is particularly mad about it. She could not say enough. She wants it dramatized, set to music —even danced I fancy, if it could be done. She finally got on the subject of me and then—but I am a pretentiously unpretentious person and so I wont say a word. Sunday, however, as I understand, she is to buy and read Sister Carrie and The Financier—neither of which she will care for. Accursed be all women: By the beard of the Prophet!

When you come, however, if you want to, I will take you to see her. She is most friendly now and wants to be neighborly with us. I have her copy of Thais[2] and an invitation to dinner. The daughter who is good looking with reddish hair is intelligent and artistic to a certain extent. Madame Kalish is as tremulous as dramatic and as high blown as the divine Sarah[3] herself. Nevertheless I like my Elyhon best. Your ways in so far as I can see are always your own, which pleases me much.

Is this a dry account? Sorry. It wasn't a dry evening. It was twelve o-clock before I knew it. We had candy, crème de menthe, champagne & black coffee. I was even offered cigarettes. She unconsciously attitudinized and bubbled. Her costume was black and gray. Once more, however, I would trade one Elyhon for nine Madame Kalishs. *If* Elyhon will only love me. But I believe Elyhon does. Yes I do. If I thought she didn't I would feel very bad today.

I get such strange letters. There is coming here today from Chicago a woman who lives in Boston but who is stopping out there. She first wrote me a long mysterious letter asking me to meet her & advise her in a very serious affair which she could not explain except in person. She enclosed fifty cents for a telegraphic reply. I wrote her I was in New York and was fairly sure that I could not be of any service anyhow. Today I got a telegram saying she is to arrive here at 4 PM. & will I please be in. She is, according to her description, 53 and with grey hair. When I hear what it's all about I'll let you know.

My dearest dear, your yesterday's letter was cute but surely you are the wild Elyhon. I wonder what you will do when you find me heavy, phlegmatic, stolid. You seem to be so busy living, but I keep hoping I have seen enough of you to know that there is a touch of the phlegmatic and the meditative in you. I have noticed, with a breath of consolation that you love to dream & the way you have sat beside me for considerable periods in silence makes me think that some of my quiescent moods will suit you. You don't bubble always—certainly not with me. Why? Are you different with others?

Now that you have read Keats Eve of St. Agnes I will get you a copy of Matthew Arnolds poems and let you read Dover Cliff.[4] There are six or seven lines in that I should like to hear you read.

Well (as I used to say in my boyhood letters) I will close. I had word yesterday that an actress by the name of Florence Reed[5] is raving over The Financier and hopes to encounter me soon. Is she a good actress? The best testimony I have had as to that book comes from Cotton & Finance—a financial paper whose subscription rate is $10 per annum. It does not review novels but it reviewed The Financier & praised highly the fine interpretation of finance.[6] This is the last word. I never knew I knew so much about it.

Th. D

You asked why I wasted time on Laura Jean.[7] Curiosity merely. I never saw her. It was just odd enough to take my fancy. I wish I might spend an evening—in time with Jack Johnson—or Mother Jones.[8] It is the high brows that I really dislike.

1. Madame Bertha Kalish. See Dreiser to Kirah Markham, 20 April 1913, n. 6.

2. Anatole France's novel *Thaïs* (1890), the story of an Alexandrian courtesan, which inspired film, play, and opera adaptations.

3. Sarah Bernhardt (1844–1923), famous Paris-born actress who played on the French and English stages and toured the United States nine times between 1880 and 1917. In *Sister Carrie* (Chapter 40 the 1981 Dreiser Edition text; Chapter 37 of the 1900 Doubleday edition) Dreiser shows Carrie interested in one of Bernhardt's American appearances, wondering how such theatrical success is achieved.

4. John Keats's "The Eve of St. Agnes" (1819) is based on a fable that unmarried women can catch sight of their husbands-to-be on the eve of the saint's day.

Dreiser means Matthew Arnold's poem "Dover Beach."

5. Florence Reed (1883–1967), actress noted mainly for her Broadway performances, especially for her parts as oriental women in musicals; she also worked in film and television roles.

6. *Cotton & Finance* (New York) reviewed the novel on 5 April 1913.

7. Laura Jean Libby. See Dreiser to Kirah Markham, 25 April 1913, n. 4.

8. Arthur John (Jack) Johnson (1878–1946), the son of a former slave who became the first black boxing world champion in 1910. Johnson's flamboyant lifestyle heightened racial discrimination against him throughout his career.

Mary Harris "Mother" Jones (1830–1930), charismatic Irish-born labor leader, was an organizer in many fields and one of the founders of the Industrial Workers of America. She became best known for her work among coal miners, and was often referred to as "The Miner's Angel." In 1913 she came to national attention for her work during the Paint Creek-Cabin Creek miner's strike in West Virginia. On 12 February 1913, she led a protest that resulted in her arrest, and, at age eighty-three, she was sentenced to twenty years in jail; but the new governor of the state overturned the conviction just a week after Dreiser wrote this letter.

To Kirah Markham [H-DPUP]

May 1–1913–Thursday. (17)

Honey Sweet

Honey Lamb:

I am longing for you so today I can scarcely tell you how much. It is "heimweh"[1] for Elyhon. Last night I went to the P.O. at midnight, coming home, and got your little school time story which I thought at first must be a long confiding letter—it was so heavy, Dear, but I was happy. I carried it home to read. When I discovered that it was a school day story my face fell, I think, but I read it with pleasure then & there because you wrote it. It made me think what a charming school girl you must have been and what promise you give of real writing. This thing has undeniable charm it its way, morbidly sad as it is.

I wonder sometime why it is—what chemic riddle is back of my craving for affection—or perhaps I had better say the smile & sympathy of beauty, the loveliness of soul in a given woman. Then I ask myself what is beauty and loveliness of soul in woman & I do not know except as I find it expressed by some one—actualized. You, for instance. No individual, not even Jennie Gerhardt, craved affection as much as do I. It seems when I haven't it—when it is dangled before my eyes in the happiness of others—as if I should gladly die to escape the pain—and yet I live and have lived for years quite ruggedly without it. As I said before to you, I can truly say that I never had the woman I wanted—the one woman. I have always been dreaming of her, tender, intellectual, gracious, artistic in heart and body, naïve, faithful but I never found her—until. I wasn't sure at the moment that I had found her in you and yet I kept thinking and feeling so keenly. All the while—every hour you had a strange pull for me and it has grown and grown so that if you are faithful to me you can make my life quite full. Oh Elaine—my Elyhon. I could be so happy with you I am sure—I can be—But you have the capacity also of making me very unhappy even though I should bring my utmost stoicism to bear which I can & will if ever the time comes. To be quickly done with misery is a rule with me. To pluck out the thorn & throw it, though the ache remains. But oh the ache—peaches, pet.

I was so pleased in your letter of yesterday, to find you talking of "we"—really planning. It shall be "*we*" darling if it can be arranged—and it can be. The small apartment I mentioned is charmingly furnished—very conveniently, with linen, dishes & all the elements of service. I know Lee McCann[2] who lives there but she would never know anything about us unless we wanted her to & and she wouldn't care if she did. She designs for stores & cafés, paints and does—oh, I scarcely know what. She & her mother live there. It will be charming. I have already suggested that she wait to hear from me. But there are other apartments, lots of them that can be had in the same way. To think of living with Elyhon: "Would juice[3] get breakfast for me darling?" Or would we go out every morning.

This is May 1 and for me my Elyhon is queen of the May alright. You are so sweet. I wish I were with you so that I might run and play with you—catch you as you suggest. Do you ever think of Revere Beach and those dear

Dreiser (ca. 1912).

Boston days.[4] How sweet those hours were. And how cute you were. I shall never forget your "oh dear, oh dear" voice that first day over the phone. You were "so-o-o nervous."

Honey Sweet I can only think over & over how I long for you. I wish you would spend all your time writing me. I wish I might have six or eight letters instead of one. Every day I look for word from you with such joy. I take the letter out with such satisfaction. Think of *me*—so eager. I can scarcely believe it, and when I think of you sleeping with all my letters in one bundle I can only smile but it makes me happy. It is as it should be for there is real love in them—true longing, passion, hope, everything. Peaches sweet I love you, love you, love you! Do you love me as much.

ThD

Write me a long letter.

1. Homesickness.
2. Unidentified.
3. Dreiser and Markham often used this affectionate play on the word "you."
4. Dreiser is recalling the week in March 1913 that they spent together in the Boston area, where she had an acting engagement.

To Kirah Markham [H-DPUP]

Wednesday, May 7th 1913—23.

Roses Red and Roses Black:

My Asia Lily:

I took your second warning and called up Mrs. Gonled[1] again last night and was promptly invited to dinner for Thursday at 7. So I shall have to listen to Gonled orate on his views. But much more would I do for Peaches Sweet—my Flower Face. I worked in a kind of dream of you all day yesterday—the breath of the art of Elaine—seeing you dimly in the background. You are so much nicer to me than the picture of Florence Reed[2] you sent me—though that serenity of pose is yours; so much nicer than Madame Kalish[3] who may have been but certainly is no longer as charming as you are. I doubt if she was. She called up yesterday but I was out. I expect it is an invitation to come to dinner. You are just art of line, & art of motion and art of feeling & art of thought. You are so beautiful that often I want to get away a little distance so that I can sit and look at you. Then your beauty comes in on me like a soothing song. I get richer & stronger for it—elated & yet composed. You supply just what I want—near me—all the time—the living image of beauty. But will you be good & love me much and very, very long?

I was thinking when I read your letter last night about the Mathison[4] reception that when you come here & get away from Chicago for a while you will get very homesick. All your friends & your home & the Little Theatre and the things with which you are so familiar in Chicago will begin to take on appealing significance and then if I am not just everything you will gather up your belongings and return. The illusion will be ended—the dream over. Did you ever think of that? I fancy you wont thank me for the thought but it might be true. I am such a cantankerous creature intellectually. I insist on turning every angle of the prospect toward me for inspection. I notice that you also have the habit of digging up woes in advance and yelling about them—weeping, as it were, very early and premature tears.

Certainly old Dr. Foster[5] is a strange one but you know I sympathize with him keenly. I know what the lure of beauty is and if it will not die—will not down—it is terrible. I have now reached that state where I can stoically set aside certain charms with an aching eye. But some men never can. The lure is too great. I have a perfectly wonderful novel in my head to be called *The Rake*[6] which ends—but I will not tell you where it ends. It is something really to cry over. But The Rake is the victim of the lure of beauty. I might not be able to commend Dr. Foster. I wish he would learn to keep his hands off for that is futile—the sorrow of unsatisfied longing is always terrible to me.

Do you recall this by Hardy?[7]

THE LOOKING GLASS

—

I look into my glass
And view my wasted skin
And say: "Would God it came to pass
My heart had shrunk as thin!"

—

For then I, undistrest
By hearts grown cold to me
Could lonely wait my endless rest
In Equanimity.

—

But *time*, to make me grieve,
Part steals, lets part abide,
And shakes this fragile frame at eve
With throbbings of noontide.

Thomas Hardy.

I can imagine the lusty & vigorous in life smiling at this perhaps a little contemptuously. They simply do not understand.

But no more. I am on chapter 42 of The Titan. The first 40 have gone to the typewriter. I am struggling with the annoying intricacies of the street car situation in Chicago. I greive over life and then I take a hitch in my belt & stand up & feel quite perfect—equal to anything—Life, God, man or devil. The spring is so wonderful here—it is like a song. Write me dear, thoughtful letters & be my lovely Damozel —my Blessed Damozel.[8]

Th. D

1. Markham had been encouraging Dreiser to visit Mr. and Mrs. Gonled, who had been among her family friends in Chicago.

2. Florence Reed. See Dreiser to Kirah Markham, 30 April 1913, n. 5.

3. Madame Kalish. See Dreiser to Kirah Markham, 20 April 1913, n. 6.

4. Edith Wynne Mathison, actress known for her classical and Shakespearean roles; in the 1930s she joined the faculty at Mount Holyoke College in the Speech department and in the English Playshop Laboratory.

5. Dr. Foster, a personal physician who compromised his professional relationship by becoming romantically attached to Markham.

6. The history of Dreiser's writing of *The Rake* has never been satisfactorily explained, perhaps because he began a novel with this title more than once. (For different views on the subject, see Pizer, *Novels of Theodore Dreiser*, 205–7; 364, n. 10; and Riggio, *American Diaries*, 8, n. 5; 37; 123, n. 15.)

7. Probably working from memory, Dreiser misnames the poem, which is entitled "I Look into My Glass."

He slightly misquotes the following two lines:

> "And view my wasting skin
> With Equanimity"

8. A reference to the work of one of Dreiser's favorite nineteenth-century artists, Dante Gabriel Rossetti: either his early (1846) poem "The Blessed Damozel," with its theme of the heavenly "damozel" yearning for eternal bliss with her earthly lover after his death or Rossetti's later sensual and more secular painting of the same title. The fact that the lady in both works had famously abundant auburn hair did not deter Dreiser from applying the image to the dark-haired Markham. For an earlier reference to Rossetti's poetry, see Dreiser to Sara O. White, 16 February 1898, n. 6.

To Kirah Markham [H-DPUP]

Monday, May 12th 1913

Peaches Pet:

My Own Black Haired Kid:

You must be easy in your thoughts of me these days—these last two or three—for your letters breath a strange content which is sweet to me. You love in such a delicious way Elyhon. You come forward with an eager step—matching my thoughts and my mood with a sweet and delicious abandon. That is the charm of you—the wonder—and it pulls me so exquisitely. I shall never forget the many delicious things you have said—the direct assurances given "before this I throw my body after my spear."[1]

Well, Peaches Pet, be happy. I only wish I could go to sleep & forget everything until your train arrives, the 29th or 28th. I am like a ten year old —expectant—and when you come we will hurry to our secret embraces if we may—to the holding of each other close until—for the moment—this ache be satisfied. Then just sweet pettings and talks until the fever that is

passion returns. I shall never forget you at the Hall of Fame[2] exclaiming so passionately—"oh I want you so"

With the letters today—there were none yesterday—came the copy of Nordfeldt's portrait of you.[3] It is delicious. I like the rhythmic swing of you and the delicious Jewish cast of your face. I wonder how much of a Jewish woman you are going to look as you grow older. That is the race of faithful women and of happy families —perhaps more so than any other. I have always admired the loyalty of most of the Jewish woman I have known. They give, in so many cases, for keeps. But you have New England in you, too,[4] and heaven knows what errantries of romance. But it is delightful this picture & I wish I owned it. With your consent I may secure it someday soon ahead of you—for myself.

Honey Lamb I cant write much more today. It seems to be raining people. I went to see Madame Kalish[5] last night in "The Kreutzer Sonata"[6] on the East Side —she is splendid. Mr. Karl Lewis,[7] of Chicago is at the Astor & phoning hourly. Mrs. Jarmuth[8] an old friend of mine is almost dying of heart trouble & wants my counsel as to her will & effects. I have my work & 20 other things. But I could write you by the week—if I might—just soothing reiterations of thoughts of you—of how much I want you. Write me each day—love me as you do, with that intense feeling which seems to take my very soul in your arms and shield it. And yours are the arms—the only ones in all the world that can.

T. D.

1. This appears to be a line made up by Markham. No specific source has been found for it, though it echoes references to classical heroes in general as, for example, Herman Melville does in the opening lines of *Moby Dick*: "with a philosophical flourish Cato throws himself upon his sword."

2. The Hall of Fame for Great Americans, completed in 1900 on the original site of New York University; today it is on the campus of Bronx Community College at 181 Street and University Avenue.

3. Bror Julius Olson Nordfeldt (1878–1955), Swedish-born painter who had studied at the Art Institute of Chicago and became known for his portraits and landscapes. He painted portraits of the leading figures of the time, including Dreiser and Thorstein Veblen; he also illustrated magazines and painted camouflage for American ships during World War I. He had painted the set for the Chicago Little Theatre's production of *The Trojan Women* in which Dreiser first saw Markham. In a letter to Markham on 29 April 1913 Dreiser recalls his first meeting with Nordfeldt in his Chicago studio: "he had been doing city scenes—bridges, buildings & what not. As I recall them I thought they were very good" (DPUP).

4. Markham's mother, whose maiden name was Belle Bushnell, was raised in Lakeville, Connecticut, and came from a prominent family that went back to the earliest settlers in New England.

Kirah Markham as Andromache in Euripedes' *The Trojan Women* (ca. 1913).

5. Bertha Kalish. See Dreiser to Kirah Markham, 20 April 1913, n. 6.
6. Kalish was playing a role for which she was famous on the Yiddish stage: an adaptation of Leo Tolstoy's novella about marriage, jealousy, and murder, *The Kreutzer Sonata* (1890).
7. Unidentified.
8. Edith De Long Jarmuth had separated from her husband in Colorado, moved to New York City, and become active in avant-garde and radical circles. She divorced her husband in 1918 and married Dreiser's friend, the journalist Edward H. Smith. In June 1919 she died of what was thought to be influenza. Later Dreiser wrote a semi-fictional sketch about her as "Olive Brand" in *A Gallery of Women* (1929).

1914

To Kirah Markham [H-DPUP]

Markham had come to New York on 29 May 1913 to live discreetly with Dreiser in an apartment at 611 West 152nd Street. She returned to Chicago during the Christmas and New Year's holidays and remained there to work in theater during the winter, often on road tours with the company. Dreiser stayed behind to finish his work on The Titan.

Thursday, Jan. 22nd 1914

Peaches Sweet:

I hate somehow to think of your being in a company such as you are in now where the presence or attitude of such a woman as you describe is tolerated. It is one thing to know life thoroughly—another thing to be compelled to live its wretched phases day by day. I know from trying to represent it day by day that art is not concerned with degradation and vulgarity save as the most distant suggestion of a deadly fact. Vulgarity is the soil out of which many things grow. It is a kind of mulch or manure that fattens the earth perhaps but the flowers of art need little of it and you are a flower of art, sweetest kiddie. Life for you should be lived with your equals—or peers—at least on the basis on which they would expect it to be taken. To have to live it with your inferiors adds nothing save a disgust and memories you would rather not have.

People are so dull. Because of the mouthings of an ignorant Christianity they have come to identify all sex joy with vulgarity. I can think of no greater indictment of Christianity and current conventional morality than that. You and I know better. We know the art and spirit in loving physical contact. I wish you could rise by sheer refinement of art so that the vulgar would be sloughed off as a snakes dead skin or a grub's homely shell. You are entitled on the larger stage to some such atmosphere as prevailed at the Little Theatre only eventually you will have to create it for yourself.

It was a short letter you wrote me today. I wonder how long you will be in Chicago? Harpers are nagging me to hurry and I feel the necessity of driving to get this thing[1] done but it takes so much time. I feel as though I ought to stay here long enough to get this thing done which I keep hoping from day to day will only be a matter of a week or so but I cannot be sure. At the end I thought I would take a little vacation and wherever you are (Chicago I presume) run out to see you. It seems sometimes that if I could have a few days every three or four weeks I could get along but I need our deliciousness only to help me live.

Concerning the little sketches[2] why not put them in a perfectly plain envelope without word of any kind save the address on the outside & mail them. Don't draw any signature of any kind or use paper that could be identified. Then it would be well enough. They could not be identified as being either solicited or sent.

I miss you so much. Often I look at the crumpled sketch and wish it were once more real—my delicious, forceful, pagan girl. No tremulous, halfway measures for Lyhon Cryhon. The utmost and with all the force of being. I miss the delight of that more than anything else. When shall we twain meet again.

L—

1. His novel, *The Titan*.
2. Markham had been a student at Chicago's Art Institute and was drawing and painting as well as acting. Markham wrote Dreiser of the sketches of herself she had been doing "sitting here in my dressing room gazing in my mirror" (Kirah Markham to Dreiser, 23 January 1914 [DPUP]).

To Kirah Markham [H-DPUP]

Dreiser had been writing disgruntled, accusatory letters, full of suspicion and jealousy about her relationships with other men.

Wednesday, Feb 4–1914

Honey Sweet:

I had two such lovely letters from you today and in turn sent you a short telegram. Your letters must have been written Monday. I love the love in them & I love the way you make love. I never knew a girl in any way like you—so willful, so sensuous, so loving. I long for you all the time. You are never out of my mind for a single moment. I feel a physical material pull to you that is as strong as anything material could be. It seems to me that I feel it—like a filing being drawn to a magnet. Do you feel that way about me.

I am so sorry about Sundays letter but I couldn't help it. I even wrote a second which I wanted to make slightly different but I couldn't. I had such a wretched feeling of something which irritated, hurt & cut me beyond endurance. It seemed to come direct from you. If I had been near you and there had been anything—what an ugly story. As it was I suffered intensely. From your letters today so loving & coaxing I should judge it was all a fancy of the mind—a temperamental aberration and I hope so. I really trust you completely, ordinarily, except that at times—far weeks apart—there comes the uncontrollable fits of doubt that leave me sick at heart. Then & then only I want to quit for ever & ever and never think of you any more. If you value me at all peaches lamb don't trifle with me until you are satisfied that you will not want me anymore. I suffer so—horribly. You have no idea.

It is beautiful here today. Like spring—one of those days I once spoke to you about. I have been at work—hustling—since 7:30 A.M. Last night I was up here reading proofs until 1 A. M.[1] So you can see how hard I am working in order to reach you quickly. This book could not possibly come out February 26 and I could not leave here for weeks yet without inconveniencing the work greatly unless I were working so. Yesterday I wired Miss Tatum[2] to come to New York & help correct proofs & copy & she is here today hard at work & will be until Saturday when I hope to have things done. Oh dear, sweet heaven I hope so. I do want to start so much. You haven't any idea how I yearn & yearn. My nerves are all on edge—so much so that I can scarcely work at times.

It is a strange book Lyhon. 143 galleys are now in page form—over 450 pages and there will be at least 100 pages more when all is cast—making a book as long as Sister Carrie or a little longer, since the type here is smaller. It has gone through amazing changes, cutting, rearranging, rewriting, filling in. It has gone much farther than where you stopped & has been filled in with many disturbing scenes. To me it is a godless thing,—cold calculating, draining—but it is one angle of life as sure as anything & as true. Whether anyone will read it remains to be seen. Pray to heaven that it sells.

I have solved for myself at last philosophically what *God* is. Hows that?

Since I wrote you I have not seen anyone except Miss Tatum this AM. Hitchcock[3] said no word of his marriage & I saw him again today. He looks no worse for wear. Hayns[4] said today Harpers would try to push the Titan—but who knows. I had a card from the Liberal Club[5] announcing dancing lessons by a Miss Kurger or somebody & a reception at which Edna Kenton, Henrietta Rodman & Miss Potter would receive.[6] Police! Think of it! Great Christ! I haven't seen Courtenay Lemon[7] yet. No time. The Katz[8] dinner was dull—he is so vulgar. And the lady about whom so much curiosity was involved didn't materialize. Doty[9] is sick in bed. Nervous breakdown. & I had a letter from Gertrude Barnum[10] inviting you & I to a reception. I wish you were here but more I wish I were in Chicago. When I think of your nice little room—ours—waiting I could weep. But oh I shall come really soon now & I shall be so glad to get there—to rest a few days & have you love me & let me love you. I long for your sweet body Lyhon. I want to get it close to me, hold it tight, kiss you & feel the warm loving heart of you. Oh dear life is so short & love is so sweet—this love. If only I can rest in it now without any more aches or pains. If only I can. Love me, honey baby. Send me sweet thoughts. Write me & when I come make over me as only you can. I love every inch of you everything about you. I wish I could hold you tight & never let go except to die

L—

1. Proofs of *The Titan*.

2. Anna Tatum (1882–1950). A devotee of Dreiser's work, Tatum met Dreiser in 1912. Her story of her devout Quaker father's career was the inspiration for the story Dreiser worked on for decades and was published as *The Bulwark* (1946). The couple lived together for about eight months in 1912. As Dreiser notes here, Tatum worked closely with him on *The Titan*; she would also type and edit his writing in the 1930s. Dreiser wrote a semi-fictional account of their relationship in "This Madness: The Story of Elizabeth," *Hearst's International-Cosmopolitan* 86 (April 1929): 81–85; 117–20; and 86 (May 1929): 80–83, 146–54.

3. Ripley Hitchcock (1857–1918), journalist, historian, editor. He had edited *Jennie Gerhardt* (1911) while at *Harper's*, and at this time was working with Dreiser's manuscript of *The Titan*.

4. Unidentified.

5. Located at 137 MacDougal Street, the Liberal Club was "The Meeting Place for Those Interested in New Ideas," as its letterhead read. Founded in 1912, it was insistently leftist in its politics and held discussion sessions and lectures with members such as Emma Goldman, W. E. B. Du Bois, Eugene O'Neill, Margaret Sanger, John Reed, Jane Addams, and Walter Lippmann. H. L. Mencken haughtily dismissed it as containing "all the tin pot revolutionaries and sophomoric advanced thinkers in New York."

6. Edna Kenton. See Dreiser to Edna Kenton, 27 March 1907, headnote.

Henrietta Rodman (1878–1923), teacher, advocate of women's rights.

Grace Potter, progressive journalist, author.

7. Courtenay Lemon, writer, editor who was briefly married to Djuna Barnes.

8. In other letters Dreiser identifies Katz as a wealthy art collector.

9. Douglas Z. Doty (1874–1935), editor, publisher. As an editor at the Century Company, Doty had recently handled the publication of *A Traveler at Forty* (1913).

10. Gertrude Barnum (1866–1948). Born into wealth, Barnum became a well-known reformer in the settlement movement and in campaigns for women's rights.

To Kirah Markham [H-DPUP]

Feb. 8th 1914

Darling Kiddie

Darling Baby Girl

Didn't get any letter Saturday at all but went round to P.O. at 1³⁰ P.M. & found your telegram as well as your letter telling me of your father's financial troubles and your row with your mother.[1] She will certainly think you twain are conspiring together to ignore her and I think there is some truth in that. For I think you are much nearer your father and he to you than is he to the others[2] or you to them. You are such a wonderful little Kiddie, Lyhon—so warm and optimistic & courageous in your way. I love the loving heart of you sweet heart. It wouldn't make any difference to me if you never had a cent in the world if only I could make it. My ragged girl would be finer than any Princess to me just because of her swell soul, but you wont be that. It is quite possible that even doing my best financially I shall not make so much—but you will get along in some way & if fate is not tough we both will. All I want now is the delight of living with you—of loving & being loved & not to leave you anymore. I never knew I could suffer so much over the absence of anyone. To be without the sustaining feel of your affection has been plain hell & is to me.

It was so sweet of you to telegraph. Fortunately this morning my throat was better. Last night I worked from 8 to 11 with Miss Tatum[3] revising galley at her boarding house—135 W. 72nd & when I came home I coughed & coughed for fully thirty five minutes at bed time. I fairly ruined three handkerchiefs with phlegm & thought I was getting worse but after that it quit & I slept well. This A.M. I was feeling much better & got up at 8 & worked until 1:30 when I went round to the P.O. Am just back. I had what I call great luck in finally managing to properly organize a chapter on the Illinois (Springfield) situation in my story—one of the big points in the last final climax.[4] It gave me courage to go on the last two or three scenes—four perhaps that are now before me & then!—but I scarcely believe the book can ever really get done. After struggling with it one whole year & more—13 months—I can scarcely believe that it could get done. It seems to me it should go on interminably. If I do the 3rd volume it probably will—but what a story. I wish I might do The Stoic.[5] It would make a splendid book as I see it now. If I had the courage —if it didn't sound too boastful, I would call the whole thing "The Epic of Cowperwood" instead of "A Trilogy of Desire"[6] or perhaps both would do—the one as a sub-title of the other. Then (1) The Financier, (2) The Titan (3) The Stoic. Would that I might.

Sweetest Peaches you make me terribly hungry when you speak of the costume consisting of a pair of jade earrings. You know how I love your body anyhow. As Amick[7] used to say—"Everything goes black before my eyes" I often think of the terribly thrilling moments that have come to me through you. The moments that seemed about to cause a break somewhere. I remember how lovely you were at Holland Beach[8] in the big picture hat & nothing more and how perfect the night you danced for me! What an exquisite girl! How graceful & spirited. Oh Lyhon baby peaches don't you see how really much you mean to me.

It is clear today but windy—awful. The wind just blows & blows here all winter long from November to April one and then some. There are little flows of mildness or stillness but not many. I should love to live in a climate where all was still for awhile. Next summer if you don't get an engagement—but you will though & besides you ought to be in N. Y. Lets see if we cant find some nook on Staten Island or Long Island. If you do catch a stock job I would so love to come & be your stage door Johnnie. I do want you to get along Lyhon not half so much because we need money as because I want to see you attract some real attention. What a horrible ass & fool your mother is—not to see you. It gives me her measure completely. And as for your sister let her cut you. Hell she hasn't a suggestion of the substance or grip or spirit that makes you. You are my girl—the one girl for me—& if I can just come Thursday I shall be willing to make such an effort at anything in order to be able to stay and keep us comfortably together

But woe is me. My financial troubles are many. I read that A Traveler has gone into a second printing but I owe them \$853—\$300 of which I will be able to pay out with an article. I owe Harpers \$3000 against which they have Jennie, Carrie, The Financier & The Titan. If that should sell all would be well for the three thousand would melt away like snow on a stove.[9] If it don't I'm up against it until I can produce something that will. I have The Genius which is being typed & which I will let be published next fall.[10] I think I shall bring An Amateur Laborer[11] along & work at that outside of short stories or articles—if I can think of any. I won't do anything pending my final decision as to the next thing I really want to do—play or book & if book—which one. I have in mind "The Rake" (which is really too much like Cowperwood or The Genius). "The Bulwark"—which is truly different, "Asshur-ba-in-fal"—which is the historical novel,[12] and one more which I have always wanted to do under the title "Howley, Haviland, & Co." or "The Simpletons."[13] Either title fits. Then there is "The Stoic" of course. I forgot to say that on Feb 22 I must pay \$237^{00} on my life insurance policy or lose it. Woe is me! These are parlous times aren't they.

But Honey with your love I can do anything. Honestly if you will back me up and never be unfaithful to me & love me as you do so wonderfully I can try & try & try. Life takes on new lustre with you. The game is worth while. With your dear sweet white body in my arms, your mouth to mine—your loving soul to cuddle to at night—to drive away all the agonies & miseries why I could live & go on & make a real showing. There must be a place for me sometime. If I really try I can write something that will get over. Then—well then I'll just go on living with Lyhon, being loved & loving & not caring about anything else at all but just her and maybe a baby or two. What? Did anyone say baby carriage! And who would heat the milk bottles at night?[14] Police! But you could tame anybody, Lyhon, baby, honey Sweet, even me. If I have any luck, this week sees me in Chicago—

L—

1. For Markham's mother, see Dreiser to Kirah Markham, 12 May 1913, n. 4. Markham's father, Harry Hyman, had inherited the family business but proved to be less than successful running the firm. His financial problems led to marital tensions that ended in divorce. Kirah, often at odds with her mother, took her father's side in the matter. In addition, Mrs. Hyman disapproved of Kirah's involvement with Dreiser. The tone of their relationship is captured in a letter from Mrs. Hyman to "Elaine," in which she talks of the distress caused her by the affair: "It is especially heavy at this Christmas time, when I think of the disrupted home, as the result. I am utterly undone, and know that you can never know the price paid for your illicit love" (Dorothy Hyman to Elaine Hyman, 10 December 1913 [DPUP]). Mrs. Hyman committed suicide in 1922 (Mrs. Hyman's granddaughter Dorothy Ruddick to Riggio, 12 February 2006).

2. The "others" are Kirah's sister Dorothy Hyman, then a student at Vassar, and her brother Robert Bushnell Hyman.

3. Anna Tatum. See Dreiser to Kirah Markham, 4 February 1914, n. 2.

4. The sequence referred to in *The Titan* has Cowperwood negotiating successfully with the Illinois state legislature to pass a law that would allow municipalities to grant long-term franchises. In the end, however, the Chicago City Council is influenced by a number of forces to turn down Cowperwood's bid for a franchise that would give him a monopoly of the streetcar lines in the city.

5. Dreiser would not finish the novel for decades. It was published posthumously in 1947, with the last chapters organized from his notes by Helen Richardson Dreiser.

6. The novels came to be known as "The Trilogy of Desire."

7. Robert Amick (1879–1969), painter. See Dreiser to Kirah Markham, 20 April 1913, n. 4.

8. In Queens, New York.

9. Dreiser's financial trouble was not alleviated by Harper's; the company shortly sent word that it refused to publish *The Titan* (see Dreiser to Kirah Markham, 18 February 1914). It was published by John Lane, on 22 May 1914.

10. *The "Genius"* was not published until 1 October 1915.

11. Dreiser offered the manuscript of *An Amateur Laborer* to the Century Company, but there was no interest in it. The incomplete manuscript was published nearly forty years after Dreiser's death (see *An Amateur Laborer*, ed. Richard W. Dowell; textual editor James L. W. West III; general editor Neda M. Westlake [University of Pennsylvania Press, 1983]).

12. There is no evidence of Dreiser's work on a novel of this name.

13. This is the germ of a satirical novel Dreiser discusses elsewhere. It was to be based on his experiences at Howley, Haviland, which employed Dreiser as editor of *Ev'ry Month* in the 1890s. See Dreiser to Sara O. White, 2 May 1896, headnote; and 14 August 1896, n. 2. This project was never realized.

14. This question of having children was not simply a joking matter between them. They seemed at various times to seriously contemplate having a child: "Well, honey, about this infant question—I feel almost self righteous. I have made such an honest effort. Stop using a douche—at least immediately after—and see what happens. Or go to see that doctor at 253 Broadway to whom the Ouija referred. If it can be done I am willing. At the time I was having my prostate treated 1908–9 —about 6 years ago—I was told my fertility was beyond question. It may have been a wrong diagnosis—or they may not have wanted to tell me. I might undergo another examination and see again" (Dreiser to Kirah Markham, 8 February 1916 [DPUP]).

To Kirah Markham [H-DPUP]

Monday, Feb 9–1914

Darling Kiddie:

Such another dandy letter today. When you write me so lovingly as you have recently I feel so near to you—not far away at all. Your feeling bridges the distances and gives me the firm support I need. Do my letters—my love—sustain you in the same way. They ought to. My feeling ought to, for it is pouring out to you in a steady stream—wireless.[1] I know truly that real feeling does obviate space and strikes where it strikes instantly. I'm sure of it. Your love helps me as you feel it—at the same time. Your indifference would hurt as much.

I'm so sorry Lyhon that you wrote Dell[2] about me. I didn't intend to stir up to any action. As a matter of fact I don't mind at all. To tell you the truth I like the review,[3] because it is a good ad & it confesses some merit even where it assails. I wasnt sending it to indicate I was hurt and to prove it the next day I sent down for fourteen copies to send it to people who would enjoy it. What I wrote on there was in a spirit of gayety and jest. I do not feel that he can do me any harm. I do not feel that critical reviews of that type are dangerous. Anyhow the critics in bookland cannot really break you. They can only help make you. Books—like other things—more or less make themselves. Your writing gives him the chance to feel that he can really hurt you through me or yourself—which is just what he wants. He would like to feel no doubt that he can hurt me. That is ridiculous. He will have to grow awhile & considerably. I don't mind your sending the play back.[4] It would never have served you much, but to roast him never. I wish you hadnt done that. Don't attempt to defend me. I will take care of myself & you too later, I hope.

It is still blowing sixty here—cold & clear. The novel is toiling along. I believe you will think if I don't finish today or tomorrow that I am lying to you—but all last night & this AM I was interrupted by the necessity of stopping to correct first & 2nd revises. A new batch—15 galleys—has just come & it means careful work just now. However it helps me to have the whole book in page form before I leave which I had not hoped to do. Two or three more chapters including the one I am on ought to do it & then there will be nothing much else to do. Wednesday ought to see it done. Miss Tatum[5] who has read the story to date likes it. Hitchcock[6] says it is good as far as he has gone which is farther than you went. Sutphen[7] says it is fine so far. I don't know. The end must tell & it is the end—a real, colorful dramatic one that is causing me all my trouble. I have worked and worked over phases of it. You know how I do.

You spoke in your letter of having no part in this story. Wait till I show you the parts that are you (new) & that you have not seen. Actual scenes. I draw on your character all the time for inspiration.[8] You are my model—my leading figure—from which I borrow much of my working psychology. I study you & love you at the same time & the more I study you the more I love you—warm, sweet, baby kid. How we have fought & how loved but love wins with you. I want my baby girl all the time —want to hold her tight. I mentioned having a baby yesterday & here yours comes today, suggesting the same thing. We will kiddie, first chance. Lyhon's little tummy will look as round as an apple with Lovers baby wont it? Huh. I'll tell you as soon as I can how soon I start—& oh how I want to . . . .

L—

I suppose you got my message. I didn't know where to send it club, house, or theatre. Didn't know whether you were living at 2426 as Mrs. Markham or what. Finally I gave two addresses—club & theatre. Hope it reached you Sunday. Kisses, Kisses, Kisses for your sweety mouth.

1. Dreiser had a strong sense that individuals communicated with each other through mental—and emotional—telepathy. This was not unique to Dreiser; in this period the image of human "wireless" messages (derived from the model of telegram, radio, and telephone systems) was a widespread idea in many psychic, philosophical, and spiritualist movements. Literary figures such as Upton Sinclair (*Mental Radio* [1929]) and Hamlin Garland (*Forty Years of Psychic Research* [1936]) wrote books endorsing the concept. And scientists such as William James and Alfred Russel Wallace (see his *World of Life* [1910]) also sanctioned the idea.

2. Floyd Dell. See Dreiser to Kirah Markham, 15 April 1913, n. 1.

3. A reference to Dell's largely condescending review of *A Traveler at Forty* (1913), "Mr. Dreiser and the Dodo," *Masses* 5 (February 1914); repub. Salzman, *Critical Reception*, 162–64.

4. Dell had sent Markham a play he wrote, asking her opinion of it and about her willingness to play a part in it.

5. Anna Tatum. See Dreiser to Kirah Markham, 4 February 1914, n. 2. Tatum, who also did work for Harper's, played a large role in helping Dreiser find a new publisher after the firm rejected *The Titan* (see Dreiser to Kirah Markham, 18 February 1914).

6. Ripley Hitchcock. See Dreiser to Kirah Markham, 4 February 1914, n. 3.

7. Van Tassel Sutphen (1861–1945), author, editor at Harper's.

8. More specifically, in *The Titan* Dreiser modeled the character of Stephanie Platow on Markham.

To Kirah Markham [H-DPUP]

Wednesday Feb 18–1914

Lyhon Sweetest:

Yesterday at this time I thought that by today at this time I should be en route. I had thought as I rather indicated in a very brief note that I had fixed things up. I talked with Leigh[1] and he said he saw no objection to making an advance and that he would let me know this A. M. by phone. Personally he said he liked the story very much as did others there. This AM. much to my chagrin and anger he phoned to say there was a hitch—no money and he wasn't sure whether Harpers would want to publish it! Would I come down & see him & Duneka.[2] I went. A very brief conference. Duneka had just been reading it.*[3] He said he didn't like it. It wasn't immoral. There was no inartistically vile situation. It was interesting but the critics would say it was merely a catalogue of amours and Harper & Brothers couldn't stand for it: They were playing another game.

I asked just how this book stood. 10,000 copies of the first 336 pages had already been printed. The rest was practically paged He had only read to 336. He wanted me to take this book away & give him the next one or the refusal of it! And also to leave the three books they now have. I laughed. I asked what terms he would make any other publisher. He offered to go on completing this book & printing an edition of 10000 which he would make over to whoever took it plus plates at cost. On that basis I saw Scribner, Century and Doran.[4] Scribner was most cordial—will read the pages (which will come up tomorrow) at once & let me know. He said he had read Sister Carrie, Jennie Gerhardt & The Financier and liked them—The Financier particularly! Doran was quite anxious. Wanted pages at once. Would rush the edition into book form if he could stand the story & make an advance of $500. Doty[5] said the same, though of the Century I have some doubt for I believe Ellsworth[6] is getting cold feet. He wants to run a conservative house. Still they may bid also. There the matter stands. I have no immediate cash—not enough to leave on & clean up other things & so I am compelled to wait now until I hear. Isnt it hell. I cant tell you how bad I feel.

However, honey sweet, if your letter was discouraged and showed that you felt bad it was balm to me in my wretched state for it showed that you care truly. I was beginning to fear from the light letters of several days past, or none at all, just what you were beginning to feel about me (aren't we the silliest?) that you didn't care. This letter with its longing & suggestion of indifference actually made me happy for it showed me that you love me. With your true love & loving I can stand anything. Without it I am down and out. Don't give up your job but wait a few days more. I know I must be able to make some arrangement somewhere & the moment I do I'll bolt.[7] If worst comes to worst I'll take your offer until I can rest a little & do something on the side. Then we'll come back together.

Lyhon sweet never think that I don't love you. I love you *all the time*. My mind is really never off you. There is a physical pull out to you that never stops & that hurts all the time, actually hurts. When you say you feel as if you would go mad you feel no differently from what I do. I am sad, angry, impatient but with your love able to bear it for a few days more only.

Honey Sweet don't give up. Don't get tired of me or let a reaction set in. Something favorable is bound to happen. I had my brother-in-law Brennan[8] handle the insurance for me for the present until I get on my feet. Oh how I truly love you. I love every inch and atom of your sweet body & heart.

L

You never mention Miss Kiper or the wondrous Tobey[9]—Why?
In regard to Red Book. I wrote young Lengel[10] (who by the way is here now) and he (writing for Red Book) told the editor. Hence etc

1. Frederick T. Leigh, the treasurer at Harper's.

2. Frederick A. Duneka, editor, at this time the secretary of Harper's.

3. Dreiser used the asterisk here and wrote at the bottom of the page "* This is all so much like the Sister Carrie incident of 1900." Donald Pizer speculates that Harper's may have been warned by its London branch that the book might open them to charges of libel because the character of Berenice Fleming was based on Emilie Grigsby, a well-known British socialite (see Dreiser to Albert Mordell, 6 March 1914, n. 2, in Pizer, *New Dreiser Letters*).

4. Three publishers. In the end, *The Titan* was published by John Lane from the unbound sheets prepared by Harper's.

5. Douglas Z. Doty. See Dreiser to Kirah Markham, 4 February 1914, n. 9.

6. W. W. Ellsworth, publisher, at the time vice-president of the Century Company.

7. Dreiser did go to Chicago three weeks after this.

8. Austin Brennan. See Dreiser to Sara O. White, 26 December 1896, n. 3.

9. Miriam Kiper, actress with Maurice Browne's Chicago Little Theatre.

Berkeley Greene Tobey (?–1962), journalist, author, at this time general manager of *The Masses*.

10. William C. Lengel (1885–1965), editor and author. Coming to New York in 1910 from Kansas City, he was deeply impressed with Dreiser and became his secretary when the novelist was editor-in-chief of the Butterick publications. A life-long friendship followed, with Lengel acting as Dreiser's editor and agent at various times.

To Kirah Markham [H-DPUP]

Despite the problems with The Titan and his lack of ready money, Dreiser managed to visit Markham in Chicago during March. He then followed her to Philadelphia, where she had a role in a play at the Adelphi Theater. When she returned to New York, he remained at this address to work without the interruptions of New York.

1142 Parkside Ave.
Philadelphia, Pa.

Monday, April 20–1914

And its raining.
Honey Cryhon:

I had your letter bright and early this A.M. but not my breakfast. When I finally kicked they announced that they didn't know whether I was in! No Knife —coffee for two, milk for two, but only two rolls. Then I had four or five letters—one from George Sylvester Viereck offering to publish my "suppressed" novel in The International—for nothing.[1] How unconsciously humorous people become at times. Also a nice letter from young Hecht,[2] wanting me to read somebodys poems and a letter from Clarence Darrow.[3] I wish that by all means if you can, you would get me the copies of the Evening Sun,[4] only make it 25 instead of 10 if you can get so many.

I can sympathize with your feeling walking around N.Y. alone on Sunday. It's a despicable place from that point of view. When your absence began to soak in I grew restless and at 6 oclock struck out to find Mrs McCord.[5] I found her—a typical Jennie Gerhardt living with her old mother & father at 2219 W. Huntingden Street—a meagre little neighborhood—Mulo St.—only worse. The two children are the image of Peter & as smart as mice. Mrs. McCord's mother (I forget the family name—probably Rousgrogge or something like that) had just fallen down stairs and wrenched her shoulder. She was unconscious from administered dope. Old Rousgrogge—aged 70—was flittering about like a moth—quite useless. I didn't stay long—but Jennie Gerhardt is so brilliantly true.

Well Cryhon—be a nice girl and get a good job. If you get too lonesome find a place & I'll move over though its charming here. This A.M. I woke & not finding you got up early. There was no use staying in bed with no one to torture—excuse me—I mean play with. If any bad men look at you make them a snoot—but don't bite them—tis not lady like. And write me every day.

Lovingly
L. D = Lover Darling
L. H. = " Heart

G = Guffo.
S. B. (! ! ! !) = Sweetie Baby
Etc
Etc
Etc
Etc
Etc
Etc
Etc
Etc
(To be continued in our next)

1. George Sylvester Viereck (1884–1962) journalist, editor, poet. When Viereck offered to publish *The Titan* (and in 1917 *"The Genius")* serially in his pro-German journal *The Internationalist*, Dreiser refused.

2. Ben Hecht (1893–1964), journalist, novelist, playwright.

3. Clarence Darrow (1857–1938), labor lawyer, liberal reformer, lecturer, writer.

4. An anonymously written article in the New York *Evening Sun* (April 11), 9, "What Happened to 'The Titan,'" explored the decision by *Harper's* not to publish Dreiser's novel.

5. The widow of Dreiser's friend Peter McCord (1870–1908), an illustrator and painter who worked with Dreiser on the *St. Louis Globe-Democrat*. Dreiser wrote a memorial sketch of him, "Peter," in *Twelve Men* (1919).

To Kirah Markham [H-DPUP]

Between the spring and the late fall of 1914 Dreiser and Markham had been living together in New York at 165 West Tenth Street. She had then returned to Chicago to spend the December holidays at home and to renew her theatrical connections while Dreiser remained behind to write and maintain the apartment.

Dec. 22nd 1914
8:30 A. M.

Honey Sweet:

I had such a nice first letter from you yesterday and it cheered me up greatly. You would be surprised how dumpy I get at odd moments when I realize that you are really not here. So far I have been so busy trying to get these floors painted, my book done, Emma instructed etc that I find the days too short. And I work all the time. Last night I worked from six thirty until 11, if you please painting the back room, varnishing the bathroom for the second time, painting the last half of the bed room for the second time etc. When you think that every room is receiving four coats you can see how it works out. And the rear room floor is so rotten and porous it's a wonder the piano doesn't fall through onto the [word unintelligible].

Say, our new servant Emma is a peach. Emma Heinsberg is her name. She can cook, after a fashion, and she's clean and is industrious and willing and good natured into the bargain, if she is as homely as sin. I got to talking to her about her home life yesterday—she comes from near Munich, Germany—and her experiences here appear to have been very rough. She nearly bowled me over by saying —"Jesus Christ, what a experience I haf had here. Damned talk, I haf had a hell of a time." I could scarcely keep from laughing at the top of my voice.

It appears she has been kicked around a good deal. The people she spoke to you about as working ½ day for have already pitched her out after using her to do a lot of dirty cleaning. She expects her meals wherever she goes and these gave her a cup of coffee! For lunch. I am treating her better. She gets my breakfast and does it fairly well,—only when we get away from chops shes gone. She cant cook anything fancy. Yesterday I stopped at Wannamakers and bought her 3 flat irons (detachable handle), 1 Wash basin, 1 wash board, 1 ironing board, bluing, soap, beeswax etc. & today she is starting in on the wash. She does the marketing & general cleaning & doesn't seem to forget much of anything. I think we'd better pay her for the week we're away, in order to keep her.

By the way I leave Saturday at 11—you know for Malden[1] & will stay as long as it interests me. Mail should reach me here up to Saturday morning. Then Mordell[2] of Philly. He had been to the Wood Street Opera House to hear Powys[3] lecture on me and was evidently much excited thereby. The mere fact that I am getting along by degrees seems to disturb some people greatly. I want to send this letter to Lane[4] for commercial reasons, but if I can work out a copy on the typewriter I will enclose it. He says 1500 people were present and congratulates me "upon the honor thrust upon me." Isn't that funny.

I'm glad your family is getting along so well. It's nice to think that the normal readjustments of life can take place in at least one family without all the customary ensuing rancor and bitterness. You know the more I think of your father[5] the more remarkable I think he is. He is no silly American Moralistic ass apparently but a man who sees through to how things really are. If for one minute the world could be persuaded to drop theory and look at plain everyday life with seeing eyes—thc cats, birds, dogs and common men around us, there would be an end of all this fol-de-rol about immutable social laws and we would see how time and chance shot through with inherent quality and love of balance as well as of sentiment or rather beauty governs everything and makes all the theories and religions that there are.

But Life is better than religion and fact better than theory, and the man who is a kindly opourtunist, saving his soul as best he may, or throwing it away if necessary to his feelings is best of all.

Tons of love. I hope you have a fine time. Do rest and get those blue rings from under your eyes.

L—

You know I think Powys may lecture on me in Chicago since the Philly affair was so successful.

1. Dreiser occasionally went to Bigelow Homestead at Malden on the Hudson, New York—a kind of secular retreat house run by an eccentric journalist, Poultney Bigelow, and his wife. It catered to those who wanted a place to combine exercise (mainly walking tours and splitting wood) with the chance to discuss books and ideas in a pastoral setting.

2. Albert Mordell (1885–1965), lawyer, author, critic. He published *The Shifting of Literary Values* (1912), a book Dreiser had read.

3. John Cowper Powys (1872–1963), British novelist, lecturer, critic from Wales who lived in the United States from 1905 to 1934. Dreiser met and befriended Powys when in Chicago in 1913. The two men considered themselves to be kindred spirits, and their friendship deepened when they became neighbors in Greenwich Village. They shared, among other things, a quasi-mystical belief in supernatural forces at work in the universe and, at the same time, a deep aversion to organized religion.

4. Dreiser's publisher John Lane. After hearing the Powys lecture, Mordell wrote Dreiser to congratulate him on becoming the subject of a lecture, though he disliked Powys's "mannerisms, his epileptic enthusiasm, his unrestrained exaggerations" (Albert Mordell to Dreiser, 20 December 1914 [DPUP]).

5. H. S. Hyman. See Dreiser to Kirah Markham, 8 February 1914, n. 1. He reluctantly had acquiesced in his daughter's affair with Dreiser.

1915

To Kirah Markham [H-DPUP]

In the winter months of 1915 Markham was away from New York, either in Chicago or on tour at various midwestern venues. Occasionally in this period she was able to spend a few days in New York with Dreiser. She had begun to complain in her letters of her suspicions that he might not have been faithful to her, perhaps because his letters lacked the passionate intensity of those of 1913. In response, Dreiser generally dismissed her fears and filled his letters with his daily activities (such as the reading program he had devised for himself), as well as projections of future plans for them as a couple and news of his attempts to obtain a divorce from Sara White Dreiser.

Feb 19–1915

Honey One:

Whats become of my kids letter. The bell rang just now and brought more clippings and a renewal by the Authors League of America[1] of it's request to join —this time signed by four members—but no letter from you And really the only thing I care about in the mail. I've had you with me in spirit all day for I've been up to the old book stores in 59th Street—those about our old studio in 59th near Madison first and later that one near 9th Ave and then one in 42nd near 9th & then that one in West 23rd Street. I was looking for Pere Goriot, Hugh Wynne, Free Quaker (since The Bulwark is a quaker) and Vandover & the Brute.[2] As I rummaged around I thought of our various expeditions & Cryhon's delight in books. I would have given anything to have had you hanging on my arm. (Didn't I tell you the moment you got away I'd begin to appreciate you at your full value. Wont you forgive me all my bad hours when you were here?)

A funny thing. As I was coming down 8th Ave from 59th on the car—thinking where I might find Pere Goriot cheap—wondering if I should have to go down to Cortlandt Street, I passed a moving picture place, just below 42nd (I had ridden a block from 42nd) when I saw a movie sign "Pere Goriot Today." I jumped off and went in and in two minutes a two reel film started which refreshed my memory greatly. It was badly done (in America-Biograph)[3] & the man who played the father overplayed it, but the general idea was well enough. (How is it we cannot do a classic in any form?) I came out, met a cross-eyed kid & soon found Hugh Wynne & Pere Goriot—price 35 cents each. I've been going over them ever since.

Mrs White cleaned today & gave the floor a good polishing so that the rooms look as bright & fresh as we could wish. She asked after you & wanted to know if you weren't coming home soon to which I replied "no, worse luck in so far as I knew." She offered to do some mending but I know of nothing to mend just now.

Its still bright & fair outside. I get a wild desire to go out into the country every few hours with you. I saw a steamship ad today which read "Bermuda & back $25^{00}. 45 hours on the Water each way" & having read & known before that we can get simple accommodations for $12 a week per person I wished immediately that we could go there. A week or so ambling about in that sunny world would be such fun.

Well I'm wondering now how your stage work is turning out. I'll like you to work at the stage but I do wish I could be close all the while. This separation business doesn't please me at all. I'm not uncomfortable at all—physically—nor neglected in so far as people are concerned but just unhappy—like I was in Europe—surrounded by friends all the time but still unhappy.

There is no news. The bell rang twice today & I didn't even answer. Saw the Village Christ at Pa Gallups[4] this A.M. and some girl from the Liberal Club[5] standing inside Cushmans bakery as I passed this P.M. but nothing more. Am invited to an Authors League dinner next week which I think I will attend

Do you love me much? And how are you behaving? If you act up when I am so pathetically faithful I'll sure have grounds for a divorce

So much love
L—

Did you wash your teeth this A.M.?

This is me running in a cap & looking back as I go.

1. The Authors' League of America, founded in 1911 as a civil liberties group devoted to safeguarding the rights of authors. In 1916 it would organize the protest against the suppression of Dreiser's *The "Genius"* (1915).

2. *Père Goriot* (1835) by Honore De Balzac (1799–1850), an important literary influence on Dreiser.

Hugh Wynne, Free Quaker (1897), historical novel in two volumes set in Philadelphia during the American Revolution, written by S. Weir Mitchell (1829–1914).

Vandover and the Brute (published posthumously in 1914), by Frank Norris (1870–1902).

3. Biograph, the oldest movie company in America, producing films since 1895.

4. Dreiser is referring to Gallup's Italian restaurant on Greenwich Avenue. The "Village Christ" has not been identified.

5. The Liberal Club. See Dreiser to Kirah Markham, 4 February 1914, n. 5.

To Kirah Markham [H-DPUP]

Wed. Feb. 24–1915

Hey Bill:[1]

I'm very lonely. Isn't that new? Here I sit at 5:30 P.M.—these rooms sweetly lighted and wish you were here. It seems always as if you must be here for this place is redolent of you and the things that you like. And because you made it so nice & because it looks like you and because we've had such delicious hours here together I write or read or dress or go to bed always feeling as though you were lurking about in spirit and as though I might come upon you unawares at any moment. I'd be startled and then I'd be glad but somehow it wouldn't seem very unnatural.

I've been reading "The Turmoil" by Booth Tarkington[2] today—a light weight work but not unamusing. Also I had hours argument with Mrs. D- who flatly refuses to give me a divorce.[3] Whatever will I do? One thing I am going to do,—stop paying (since I haven't any money to pay with) and see what happens. That may bring about a change of spirit although she can get alimony without my getting a divorce. I know that. Still I'm going to try it out. Supposing she does divorce me—then what. Sometimes, you know, I feel sorry for her. She is so almost futilely cadgey.

It's raining heavily here today—a dark, gloomy rain. I've had to burn the gas most of the time. Between my reading my mind keeps running out to you as the only one I want to be with. I keep thinking how, if you were here, instead of pushing you away I would take you now and hold you close. I was never cut out to be a bachelor nor even a promiscuous liver, strange as it may seem. I'd like to settle down somewhere with you and just live in a simple, homey way. It seems silly, but it's true—silly after all the rolling to and fro I've done.

How did you come out on your question of pay during rehearsal. The telegram distinctly promises payment and unless they match the eastern magnates in their readiness to go back on agreements, a mere showing of that ought to adjust everything. I think you ought to demand it & get it. You are working for so little that this additional $100 wont really make a decent salary all told at that.

The papers here, in spite of my enthusiasm for Elga, have been unfriendly to the Reichers and to John Blair, the leading man.[4] I am sending you the World clipping which is typical. The tenor of the thing causes me to believe there is a conspiracy to protect the old line people—or an instinctive resentment of the criticism which this movement and its fruit involves. John Blair does not mouth, and he gave a splendid interpretation of the leading role. Miss Reicher was adequate and the darkening of the theatre in order that the prayers for the dead might be heard between the scenes was an artistic thought far beyond the Shubert—Klaw—and Erlanger Theatre of stage art. Beside Reichers work, the Washington Square Players & most of the better art work I have seen pale into nothing. The man is a poetic producer with an eye for real actors and he ought to succeed and will. I wrote him my compliments today & I mean them

Sweetie—think of me & work hard & be a fine actress. I want you to succeed so much for I see such a fine future for the two of us together—such dandy things to be done. Do work hard & love me much. If I get any money I'll come out to Chicago. If not I'll pine here.

L—

1. Bill (at times Billup), one of Dreiser's nicknames for Markham.

2. Booth Tarkington (1869–1946), Indiana-born novelist and playwright, among the best-selling writers of his time. Having recently completed *The Financier* and *The Titan*, Dreiser may have been especially interested in reading *The Turmoil* (1915), the first of a trilogy, which would eventually include *The Magnificent Ambersons* (1918), dealing with the rise of industrial tycoons in the years between the Civil War and World War I. Unlike Dreiser, Tarkington lamented the passing of the older order of society replaced by the financiers and industrialists.

3. Mrs. Dreiser, the former Sara O. White. The issue of divorce was complicated by the laws of the day. New York had the strictest requirements, allowing only adultery while living together as a basis for divorce. Even if he wanted to, Dreiser could not accuse his wife of this, and if Mrs. Dreiser refused to grant a divorce, there was of course no way to charge himself.

4. "Elga," a play by the Nobel Prize dramatist Gerhart Hauptman (1862–1946), was brought to the stage by the actor and director Emanuel Reicher (1849–1924), who often appeared with his daughter Hedwiga. Reicher, director of the New York Theater Guild, attempted to introduce a style of German naturalism to the American theater. The political climate during World War I made this difficult, and he returned to Berlin after the war. As Dreiser goes on to say, he feels that both the popular Broadway theater in the Shubert mode and the little theaters such as the Washington Square Players look pale in comparison to Reicher's work.

To Kirah Markham [H-DPUP]

Markham began voicing her suspicions of Dreiser's relationships with other women, and, at the same time, trying to get him more involved in sharing her life by suggesting he come with her on tour for such productions as a vaudevillian adaptation of Owen Taft's one-act play Conscience.

Friday, March 5–1915

My Honey Girl:

Such a moaning letter as I got—today—the one written Wednesday when you were so sure I was so happy that I couldn't even take the trouble to tell you about it. I'm glad it didn't come alone for I would have had to enter on a long and exculpatory explanation which now I scarcely think is necessary. I'm not running around with anyone. The time gets terribly dreary on my hands about 6 P.M. I feel sometimes as though I could not stand another minute of being alone. It doesn't do me very much good to go anywhere to tell you the truth. I can go as a rule somewhere but many an evening I prefer to stay right here and go to bed early rather than to bother with anyone. When you are here it is entirely different. I may fuss and fume about something or nothing—its all about the same, but I'm never lonely and I never have been since I have been with you. You have cured me of those terrible depressions. I feel content if I just have you. Just to sit and hold you or be in bed and pull you close is all the solution I need for spiritual difficulties—those moods which have no relation to money and money troubles—but when you are away I feel as though half of me were gone and I don't know what to do—so I just suffer. Like yesterday. I felt as if I must leave here soon unless I could see you again. Now comes your letter saying you may come back about the 20th and that cheers me a little, only I'm afraid you wont and that I wont get to come out there. If you don't I don't know what I shall do. The idea of using "Conscience"[1] as a vaudeville sketch appeals to me a little but the thing that is worrying me is where do I get off. If you are jumping from town to town a week at a time or less I don't suppose I ever could do it and write—though I might come to some places & besides I don't see where I am to get easy money soon—so the situation looks very dreary to me. But wanting to be with you and not being able to is depressing me and scratching me all the time like a hairy shirt and that's the truth. I wish you wouldn't think I'm forgetting you for others for I'm not. There are some blooming fools whom I meet who wouldn't want to come here knowing that we are not married—and aside from seeing them out of sheer weariness of being alone I should not and do not want to see them at all. There are people no doubt as you say who would not want to see me at all unless they thought I was free—and who for the same reason would resent and not want to see you, but I do not want to see them at all and do not run after them. I give you my solemn word I haven't. Such a person is Mrs. Halton; another is Edna Hume, another is Mrs. Herbermann but I do not seek those people out and have not (Mrs Halton is not here of course) since you left.[2] Over at the Holliday restaurant[3] the other night three ladies descended on me en masse and one made her attention conspicuous seeing that I was alone, but I immediately came away not because I was morally trying to preserve myself but simply because I was not interested. I could have amused myself. She would have hung on to me fast enough but I did not want to. That makes me seem unsocial to some. It gives me some lonely hours which I might otherwise fill in that fashion, but that would not be satisfying the real loneliness that I feel and so there you are. You are the one that I want but on some days owning to some idle comment of mine you don't seem to believe it. But I'm jealous of you & the things that keep you away from me and if you don't believe it, I can only hope that something will show you one of these days. I should think you could almost see if you'd stop & think. Why should I stay hear if it isn't to get you back. I don't need to. Its only because I cant be happy any other way—and that's the truth.

But why don't you write me how the play is doing? I'm so anxious to know. Today I went to hear Jack Powys[4] lecture at the Hudson Theatre & it was really very good. He and this C. E. Chesterton[5] (or something like that) debated & they did it very well indeed. Powys is fiery—like a half-starved library lion and Chesterton is as fat and suave as an English pug—albeit a scholar & lover of letters. The audience laughed & cackled & applauded to the very end. It couldn't help it. Afterwards Powys, M. Powys,[6] a Mrs. _____ and myself went to lunch & talked it over. Powys announced that he is to lecture soon (Mch 28th) at St Marks on Arthur Ficke,[7] whom he seems to have concluded is the leading poet. I think he is making a great mistake when he does not pick on Masters.[8]

However, it is evening again & I have been all afternoon. I told you the Grist-Herrick bunch had reneged on the new bath tub & today to cap the climax they refused to connect the gas stove which I bought & paid for—with the water tank—a matter of 5^{00} more in costs. I asked Grist very pointedly what he proposed to do and he said "nothing more." I would give anything to tell him to take his floor & go to but where can we do better. Isn't it the limit.

But enough of that: do tell me about the play. If it doesn't succeed what are your immediate plans? I am wondering gloomily when we will see each other again.

Much, much love-

L-

1. Markham currently had a part in Taft's *Conscience*.
2. Perhaps Mary Halton, noted advocate of birth control.
Edna Hume, actress.
Mrs. Herberman, the niece of Dreiser's brother-in-law, Austin Brennan.
3. Polly Holliday's, on Fourth Street between MacDougal Street and Sixth Avenue, was a famous meeting place for the artistic and political avant-garde of Greenwich Village.
4. John Cowper Powys. See Dreiser to Markham, 22 December 1914, n. 3.
5. Dreiser means G. K. Chesterton (1874–1936), English lecturer and prolific author known as the leading apologist for Christianity in his day.
6. Marian Powys, the sister of John Cowper Powys.
7. Arthur Ficke (1883–1945), Iowa-born lawyer and well-known but now forgotten poet of his day. He and Powys met in 1914 and established a life-long friendship.
8. Edgar Lee Masters (1868–1950), lawyer, poet, novelist, and biographer whom Dreiser had befriended in Chicago in 1913. Dreiser was instrumental in getting Masters's *Spoon River Anthology* (1916) published.

To Kirah Markham [H-DPUP]

At this time Dreiser was on an automobile trip to Indiana with his friend, the illustrator Franklin Booth (1874–1958), who also had spent his formative years in the state and maintained a home there at Carmel. Dreiser's tour of the towns and landscape of his childhood became a central subject of his travel book, A Hoosier Holiday *(1916), which was illustrated by Booth.*

Carmel, Ind

Sat: Aug 21–1915

My Glossy Kid:

Letters pour in here so regularly that in spite of all my cards I feel rather behind and in your debt. But as I said on the road I had so little time and Monday I'll be on the road again, hurrying to get done. This A.M. a registered package of proofs from Jones[1] arrived—galleys 1 to 34 inclusive & I had to sit down & read them at once—which took from 9:30 AM to 4 P.M.—so you see how my time is used up. Then in spite of a pouring rain Franklin wanted me to go out & see a fine beach woods near here, which we did, returning in time for dinner. After that a neighbor who likes my books—a Miss Somebody, school teacher—came in and I had to be pleasant for an hour. Now I'm getting my first chance to write you, but it wont do much good as I understand that in this Christian country no mails are carried on the trains on Sunday! And the last bags are sent out of here before 7 Saturday—so if this reaches you way late you will understand.

It's very charming here as the country always is. This town is nothing—a few Churches & Stores. Booths house is nice—a conventional frame house with a nice veranda on two sides & green and white awnings. He has a fine studio at the back of the long lot which runs through from one street to another. His studio faces the other street.

I wish we could have a hut or studio on the lake at Warsaw.[2] The two nearest lakes—the most convenient to this town are untouched. What little summer life once existed on them has gone to Winona 5 miles away in another direction, so one could get a most wonderful place cheap. And a row boat would put you at the door of the shopping center in 10 minutes. Isn't that wonderful, when you think of it?—a beautiful little lake between you & the heart of town. We ought to go out there some time.

So the dog arrived at last![3] It never rains but it pours, does it. Your work for Grace Potter interests me.[4] I know you'll take fine pictures. I wish you could rig yourself up now and have the Greek pictures[5] taken. You'd take such wonderful pictures that I'm sure they'd sell and you'd make some money that way.

Well, I cant think of a word more to say save that I love you & I wish you were out here or I were down there—only every time I get in the country I wish we could live in the country always. I guess I'm a regular country jake anyway. The town don't interest me so much anymore. Here the bed is so good and the air so fresh the food so tasty that I could stay here weeks if you were here. Booth's people are simply farmers moved to town. They farmed east of here for years until finally they sold the place & moved here. His father is nearly 80 and very feeble. His mother is quite old too—and an old maid sister looks after the place with the aid of the mother.

Well, honey, Monday, we move again. My route for letters will be
Monday— Terre Haute—Gen Delivery
Tuesday— Sullivan & Vincennes— Gen. Del
Wednesday—Evansville & Bloomington— " "
Thursday—Carmel—and then home.
I am getting interesting notes and can certainly make an interesting book out of it.
Well, so long Kiddie. I think of you at various hours and wish I could turn you over and handle you to suit. Be a nicey girl. You'll see me next week again.

Love
L—

The "Genius" reads fine in type.

1. J. Jefferson Jones, the American director of the British publisher John Lane. Dreiser was reading galleys of *The "Genius."*

2. The Lake District town in northern Indiana where Dreiser lived from 1884 to 1887. He later wrote of it as "a town to which I owe some of my most hopeful as well as most pleasing hours—hours of schooling, of play, of romance, of dreams under the shade of great trees or in swimming holes, lakes, the Tippecanoe River, on ice ponds and snow-covered farms and woodlands that made this region a kind of paradise" (*Dawn*, 180–81).

3. Markham had agreed to care temporarily for a neighbor's dog.

4. Dreiser may be referring to Grace Potter, progressive journalist, author. It is unclear what, if any, working relationship Markham might have had with her.

5. With Dreiser's encouragement, Markham had been planning to have marketable photos taken of herself in various Greek costumes such as those she used as Andromache, the role she had been playing in Euripides' *The Trojan Women* when they first met. Her work in Maurice Browne's Little Theatre productions also might have encouraged Markham in this activity, because Browne as a director "drew his inspiration from the Greek chorus and pantomime" (Newlin and Rusch, *Collected Plays*, xi).

1916

To Kirah Markham [H-DPUP]

Exhausted, sick, entangled with a number of women, and feeling unable to work on A Hoosier Holiday *in the cold winter climate, Dreiser had left New York and arrived in Savannah, Georgia, on January 29. Because Markham had a role in the Garden Theater's production of Gerhardt Hauptmann's* The Weavers, *she remained behind. After the play closed in mid-March, she would join Dreiser for a brief period. During his stay in Savannah, Dreiser finished* A Hoosier Holiday *and again began work on* The Bulwark.

103 W. Taylor St
Also, P.O. Box 28 Z

Feb. 2nd 1916

Honey Kid:

Your telegram certainly ended though it did not solve a mystery which is puzzling me yet. Telegram in hand I went down to the Chief Clerk and asked how long mail took in coming from N. Y. One day, as a rule, he replied. And here it was a week. He said he would make a search and finally produced one letter—that of Jan 31—and a form card from the Superintendent of Station O. saying that a package of clippings was being held for want of postage—that no package of clippings, once delivered would be forwarded unless a new stamp was put on it. So I have to wait now another week I suppose for that to come back. In the meantime I'm wondering where all the letters since Friday are. I am due three more from you, plus any written since the 31st.

Cryhon, dearest, I wish you would bear with the meanest man in the world. I don't know what gets into me. Actually I think I'm a little crazy at times or possessed by a devil. I dont mean what I say. I'm intensely in love with you. I should think really you could feel it—at times anyhow—the atmosphere of union which holds between us. Why at night as a rule, I never feel that I can get close enough. I want to hold you close so that life wont seem as hard as it does, and though I rant and storm and crave freedom of action and a certain amount of loveliness, only knowledge of your true affection for me sustains me these days. I feel always as though life were a thin and pointless game—for me—but so long as you believe in it or in me, it is alright. I absolutely sink to suicidal depths when I think how pointless the whole game is without love. And truly I need you. I should think you could see that. I must have you as a staff to lean on and yet it seems as though I must have moments of separation too. I cant understand myself—honestly and truly I cant. I must be insane—or life itself is lunatic. Here when I thought that you had decided not to write me anymore and to use this as a good time in which to break I have been so upset that I thought of returning to New York. I know at bottom that when all was over and I knew what the worst was I could weather any storm—and live—but I would not be particularly interested in doing so. When I think of you and your work and your possibilities I would like to live to help you. I would like to share in the things that I know you can and will do. As for myself I would like to write a little more if I can do it and not be miserable but otherwise I shall not long hold out. The game isn't worth the candle. I think of you and your art and your naturalness and you bring lovely emotions all the while. I know you have faults—not nearly as many as I have. But they are unimportant beside your real worth. Only if you can—and you really love me—give me a certain amount of latitude. You do already as a matter of fact —much more than any other woman that I know anything about would—but try not to turn on me. Time will certainly make some changes in my composition and we will probably be happier as we go along. Last night I lay and thought of you for hours and wished you could percieve my thoughts and feelings. You would never really doubt my need of you or what a place you have made for yourself in my life and do write me every day for awhile, anyhow. I need your letters.

As for this place, if I weren't so much alone, it would be delightful and it is anyhow. The older portion of the town is beautifully planned according to the sketch I have made on this page.

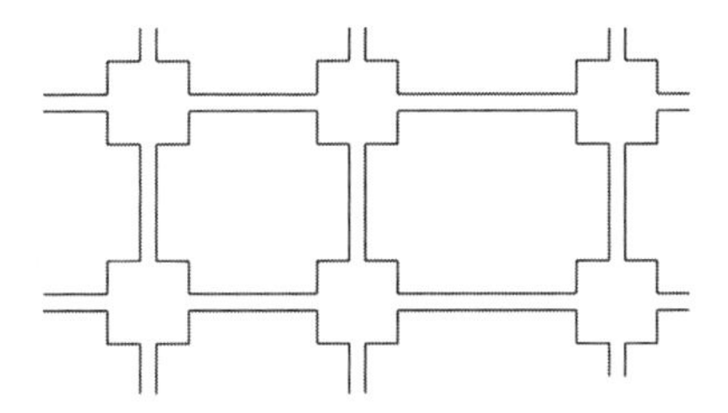

These are all large squares at each intersection, set with palms, flowers, evergreens, and sometimes—not always—decorated with monuments, stone benches and the like. It's somewhat like living in a park. To my horror and disgust I find that in the newer sections this plan has been abandoned and the houses are built in long rows like everywhere else. This old portion was laid out nearly 200 years ago by an Englishman[1] and it looks like the work of someone who loved art and life. Since then—but America will have to be reborn to be anything. All that fine old understanding and taste seems to have gone out of us.

It is gray today—almost the first gray day. Yesterday I wrote all day in the cemetery park just back of me, under a palm if you please. Negro maids & children were here and old men and pedestrians. By dint of not thinking of your silence I managed to work after a fashion. It blew up slightly cool toward six and then I went to dinner. But I do wish you were here—if only for a short time. You would like it so and we would have such a good time.

I have lost all faith in Ouija boards.[2] God knows what it is but it lies all the time. If one's subconscious Self betrays one like that then indeed we are damned for good. If it is a low order of spirits one ought never give them any encouragement. I hereby swear off. Sunday night when it was saying to you that I had a new sweet heart I was lying here wishing you were here so that I might take you in my arms and caress you. What can you think of a thing like that—after that. And the German emperor being dead. Rot.

However forget all that. If you'll just stand by me things will come out alright. Only love me and don't grieve and in a little while I'll come back or you'll come down here, or if you go west I'll join you. I don't know whether I can stick it out as it is. I need rest and I feel rather down and out physically, to tell you the truth, but I'm lonely too—and perhaps that's the hardest and worst thing on me—even worse than sickness in N. Y.

Much love. I wish I could see you coming in the door & could take you in my arms.

Now can you make me out

L—

Don't mind my letter of yesterday I was very much wrought up.

1. James Edward Oglethorpe (1696–1785) received the Charter for the colony of Georgia from King George II in 1732 and founded the city of Savannah in 1733. It was Oglethorpe's design for the city, to include twenty-four squares placed at regular intervals, which so impressed Dreiser.

2. Markham and Dreiser at times entertained themselves with friends at the Ouija board, often playing with H. L. Mencken and George Jean Nathan. Here he mocks her latest reading and reminds her of the absurdity of past predictions, such as the one that revealed the Kaiser would be poisoned by a cook.

To Kirah Markham

By this point Markham and Dreiser were at odds, largely as a result of Dreiser's unwillingness to enter into what he was coming to see as a conventional "marital" relationship. He argued that they might live apart with freedom on both sides and still maintain a relationship, but he could not live with her unless she was devoted to him alone. He also maintained that he was to be allowed freedom to be with other women. On 16 May 1916, Markham wrote him, rejecting that proposition and claiming at least equal freedom for herself while they lived together: "The self-abnegation act isn't in my line. You can decide now what our course shall be, and don't forget in your desire to fix things easy for yourself that I love you and will do as much to keep you happy as I can" (DPUP). Despite the apparent finality of their letters to each other, including this one below from Dreiser, the couple reunited, and in certain moods even spoke of having a child together (see Dreiser to Kirah Markham, 8 February 1914, n. 14).

165 W. 10th St.

Thurs. May 18–1916

Cryhon:

If I could for any living woman I would for you, but I can't. You are a ranging, vigorous intelligence, each day growing more individual. Our paths are slowly, but surely, diverging. I see that. You will not believe perhaps that my deepest affection follows you whatever you do, but it does. On the long roads that we go alone my thoughts—loving thoughts—will always be with you. Goodbye and good luck. If I can serve you in any way let me know. And whatever disposition you want made of things here, say.

Bubs[1]

1. Markham playfully called Dreiser "Bub," and he often signed off his letters as "Bubs."

To Kirah Markham [H-DPUP]

168 W. 10th St
N.Y.C

May 30–1916

Cryhon Dearest:

Two letters came yesterday morning which I tried to answer yesterday but couldn't. I was really too much put out by the last one to discuss the subject further. I had the misfortune to meet Alice Frank coming back from dinner and to submit to being interviewed by her for some paper. Result—a very bad time. In the course of the discussion she made the statement that because Isadora Duncan[1] had never told her a lie in three years that she never told a lie to anyone—was in other words absolutely truthful. I laughed at this which seemed to put her out. One thing led to another and I left confirmed in my original impression of her that she is merely a satellite—a creature willing to spend its life in seeming something that it is not. Her opinion of me (that being without truth myself I could not see truth in anyone else), sounded so familiar that I began to wonder whether it had become a theme for general discussion in the dear village.

Your this mornings letter puts a somewhat different aspect on things. You know that you are welcome here—that there is no one I would rather live with if it could be done peaceably. Actually I have concluded that never anymore must I put myself in the position of having my movements controlled by a domestic arrangement, however wonderful that may be, for the simple reason that it does not accord with the way my mind works. I see that now clearly and once and for all. I love you. You command not only my physical but my spiritual respect but if I must lose you in preference to this other then you must go. Not that I am a libertine. I deny it. But there is something in connection with me which seems to smother and decay unless I feel absolutely free to come and go as I choose. You know I do not ask you to accept this situation. If it pains you greatly to do it I would prefer that you wouldn't. Living alone would be much better and if you desire your own freedom you must live alone for I would not want you to live with me, presenting the face of a singular affectional relationship and not maintaining it. I don't care to give anyone the opourtunity of supposing they are undermining a situation which I may seemingly be believing is intact. Alone you can do as you please. I should not mind nor feel that I had any right to. If I found things unsatisfactory to me later I could go my way. Or you could go yours. There is no reason to suppose that we might not (would not) go on indefinitely. I feel always as though I do not want to lose you,—as though we should go on.

I am so sorry that your home conditions are not what they ought to be. With me, coming to Chicago would depend on getting more money before or on the 15th. At present, after paying the rent Thursday I will have seventy dollars out of which will have to come before the 15th 25^{00} for typewriting, my living expenses and the telephone bill which would leave me about $17—if there were no incidentals of any kind, on which to come to Chicago. If only I didnt have to pay for this typewriting I would save about $65, but most of it is given out now.

Under the circumstances, unless you feel interested in Chicago I would advise you to come back. If you do I wish you would look for some cheap place in the country where we might go, just shutting this up. I have nothing on hand now save the writing of The Bulwark and the correcting of the typewritten and galley forms of "A Hoosier Holiday" and that can go on anywhere. Please don't think because I write this way that I don't care for you or that if your mood were different mine would not be. Love is a question of mood—not of rules or conditions. If the mood is with one all else can go. In my case, in so far as you are concerned, there is nothing to recapture—merely to clear away the obstacles. We can have lots of happy days and it would mean so much to have you in my arms again providing you are single to me. I liked your little poem. It has less of the lyric in it than some of the others but it is lyrical. I wish you would write me a whole book of them.

L. B.

Cecile Greil[2] (according to Alice Frank) was arrested two weeks ago and locked up in Jefferson Market and the Tombs for alleged malpractice. A girl, sent her by that little pigeon[3] who runs this Twilight Club[4] was operated on and is dying. According to what I hear it may mean 10 years.

1. Isadora Duncan (1878–1927), internationally acclaimed dancer noted for her innovations in modern dance and for her flamboyant lifestyle.
2. Cecile Greil was a physician who performed abortions. For the story behind Dreiser's allusion here, see Dreiser to Kirah Markham, 31 May 1916.
3. The "little pigeon" is identified as a Mr. Tucker in Dreiser to Kirah Markham, 31 May 1916.
4. The original Twilight Club was established in the late nineteenth century by the British philosopher Herbert Spencer. The group sought to foster social reforms and public ethics. The loosely knit "club" was taken up by various intellectuals and artists in the United States, and at this time in New York it met in various private homes, most frequently at the residence of Richard Watson Gilder. Speeches would be given and members (among others, Andrew Carnegie, Hamlin Garland, and John Dewey) would discuss possible changes in social conditions, such as the elimination of sweatshops and the establishment of child labor laws.

To Kirah Markham [H-DPUP]

Dreiser's circle included such figures as Margaret Sanger, Emma Goldman, and other advocates for women's rights to birth control and abortion. The interaction with Dr. Greil described in this letter is indicative of Dreiser's position on such issues. Also see Dreiser to Margaret Sanger, 20 April 1929 (in Pizer, New Dreiser Letters).

165 W. 10th St
N.Y.C—

May 31–1916

Cryhon:

The two letters which came this morning are such a revelation of you. I like your eccentricities and your characteristics so much that they hold me to you almost in spite of myself. Imagine bursting out of doors because father and sister are indulging in a dull past time and bursting into Byronic verse. Your delightful. The poem isn't as good as some of your others but it can be made into one. And that other different thing about the four leafed clover. Your almost too good to be true.

I'm not going to quarrel anymore. I've said my say. But I want you to be a lot happier than you are if it is humanly possible. You don't belong in that family—your too different, but then you really don't belong in any limited realm. It's your privilege and your duty to rise on wings and do splendid things and you will. Your such a fine, big, sixty horse power girl. Your sudden shifts and turns fairly make me want to burst out and applaud. I hope before you start that you let me know when you arrive and let me meet you and bring you here. We're surely not far enough apart for anything less are we?

Last night I went over to see Dr. Greil.[1] She was in the dumps—all gone to peices really—in a dreadful nervous and melancholy state. I took her in hand and left her quite defiant. Evidently she is living with some Jew physician who seems fairly interesting—a typical Jew medic. She told me that Mr. Tucker of the Twilight Club[2] sent a girl to her not more than 18 years of age. She was three or four days overdue and frightened. She operated on her and sent her away. A few days later she comes back feeling badly and with temperature of 103. Evidently Greil lost her head for without any instructions as to how to act or what to say she sent her to the Lying In Hospital in 2nd Ave. There the medics seized on the girl, scared and pumped her and took an ante-mortem statement. She was so badly frightened that she told who and where Greil was. Then the officers came and arrested her and took her before the girl. When she saw Greil she tried to pretend she didn't know her—then said the doctor had made her say that she had been operated on and paid for it but that what she had said was not true. This was to help Greil. The girl then got well, but having signed an ante mortem statement the District Attorney decided to use it against Greil. Hence the trial.

This A.M. I sat in Jefferson Market from 9:30 to 12—waiting for her case to be called, but when I left she was still waiting. Charles Le Barbier and Justus Sheffield are her lawyers. Tucker's wife was there with a lawyer, trying to get evidence on which to base a divorce. So far Tucker's name has not been divulged officially and it may not be. The girl was not present and had said that she proposed not to testify. Greil was hoping that she would beat it to another state. But Greil's mother was present—or had been—and was trying to expose Greil—or make trouble for her! How is that? And what has Greil done to her mother in times past. It's a great mess. The German papers, because of her [word unintelligible] testimony, are down on her and young Viereck[3] shouts to heaven that she is a scoundrel. What a little rat he is, anyhow. I am trying to find out now before I finish this letter what disposition of the case was made in this court. I phoned just now and can tell you. It was postponed until next Tuesday

How are you, Cryhon, physically? Worse, or better? I think we both need a rest in some out of the way place for awhile. Aside from tending to the typewriting of the Hoosier as it comes in I am working on "The Bulwark" and waiting for further word from Franklin.[4] Sorry you dislike his schema so much. Haven't you one to propose?

In spite of all this raving I think of you right along and never feel as though you are very far away or ever would be. Perhaps you don't agree with me. But I cant help that, it's the way I feel. Yesterday being May Day—or rather Decoration Day[5]—I joined a Rosenthal[6] May party which went in autos to Sands Point (Long Island). It turned out grey and sprinkly and we all came back stopping at some road house —the Oceanside—for something to eat. I was back by eight—and over at Greils. Since the thing didn't begin until 1:30 I worked here until 1.

Do you love me anymore? I am almost afraid to ask. But you must know how I really feel toward you.

L. B.

Greil asked after you. She has that Italian shawl waiting. I'll get it for you today or tomorrow.
I started a letter to you on the 29th recalling 3 years ago but got in such a state over it that I decided not to write at all.

1. Dr. Cecile Greil. See Dreiser to Kirah Markham, 30 May 1916, n. 2.
2. Twilight Club. See Dreiser to Kirah Markham, 30 May 1916, n. 4.
3. George Sylvester Viereck. See Dreiser to Kirah Markham, 20 April 1914, n. 1.
4. Franklin Booth: See Dreiser to Kirah Markham, 21 August 1915, headnote.
5. Decoration Day is the old name for Memorial Day, so called because people would "decorate" military gravesites with flowers.
6. Elias Rosenthal, a prominent lawyer, in whose home Dreiser lived briefly after the breakup of his marriage to Sara White Dreiser in 1910.

To Kirah Markham [H-DPUP]

Markham had left for Los Angeles to perform in a Provincetown Players production.

Wed. Sept 22nd 1916

Honey Kid:

Although you've only been gone a few hours various things have happened which will interest you for a moment anyhow. In the first place Mrs. Jarmuth[1] phoned to ask if I wouldn't lecture before various organizations on the modern stage here and in Europe. I told her of course that I can't lecture, as much as I would like to.[2] Then she wanted to know if you wouldn't—whether you couldn't get up a lecture and deliver it. Thinking that might be a good thing for you I told her that I would try and induce you to so to do. If you are interested write her as to what you think you want to say in that letter.

Next Jones[3] called up and said he had arranged with Brentano's to put my portrait in their window for two weeks and wanted me to deliver it to here next Tuesday or Wednesday.[4] I thought the frame needed doctoring up with gilt or that we ought to borrow a good frame from some dealer for two weeks. What do you think and how shall I go about it? Do you suppose Nordfeldt[5] would object to having the frame retouched? Lastly I had word from Hale[6] that he had dropped a note to Scribners and found them interested in my travel book[7] and that he may be able sell it there though he isn't sure yet.

When you left I came straight home and did some work on my travel book but something I have eaten has upset me very much and I've been working all P.M. against a feeling of nausea. I'm not hungry but I thought I would try potatoes and milk and see how I came out. I hope to feel better tomorrow. For another thing I'm going around to Mame's[8] about 8^{pm}, take her her dog litter and swing awhile. Maybe that will fix me up. Haven't heard a word from Powys[9] though somehow I expected to.

Well, by now you know how your trip is coming out and whether you are going to enjoy it. I hope you are for I think you need a change of some kind. I wish you'd practice dancing and some exercising to loosen yourself up. It just occurs to me that skipping the rope—an old pugilistic stunt, would be great for you and you could do it here in the front room when at home while I do my dumb bell work. I must get them today or tomorrow.

It's lovely here now, warm and pleasant. I found your cards awhile ago and am sending you some. Whenever you really get away & I think how nice you are and how much I really care for you & how much you care for me, I feel ashamed. I must have a lot of Peer Gynt in me but I don't believe in old button moulders.[10]

So much love. Write and tell me how you are.

L—

Here's a nice kiss to you

1. Edith DeLong Jarmuth. See Dreiser to Kirah Markham, 12 May 1913, n. 8.

2. At this time in his life, Dreiser had difficulty speaking before large groups.

3. J. Jefferson Jones. See Dreiser to Kirah Markham, 21 August 1915, n. 1.

4. Jones had arranged to have a display of Dreiser's books, including his portrait, at Brentano's bookstore.

5. Bror Nordfeldt had painted the portrait Dreiser planned to have in the display. For Nordfeldt see Dreiser to Kirah Markham, 12 May 1913, n. 8.

6. Ralph T. Hale, editor at Small, Maynard & Company.
7. *A Hoosier Holiday*.
8. Dreiser's sister.
9. John Cowper Powys. See Dreiser to Kirah Markham, 22 December 1914, n. 3.
10. Dreiser is referring to the central character in Henrik Ibsen's play *Peer Gynt* (1867). Gynt is a roisterer, a braggart, and a liar who lives a dissolute if colorful life. The Button-Moulder is a mysterious creature that appears to Gynt in his old age and tells him he must be punished by being melted down in the Casting-Ladle.

To Kirah Markham [H-DPUP]

Markham had written Dreiser about her distress over what she considered her lack of success in the performance she had given in Los Angeles.

165 W. 10

Oct 25–1916

Honey Cry!

Goodness, goodness, such ructions over a career—and you so talented. If I had one half your ability along twenty lines I wouldn't worry over anything. I always think of you as supremely gifted in so many ways—but cursed with such a fineness in all of them that you will have to have special conditions created for you in order to show you off at your best. It may be that I'll have to create them for you—that I'll be fortunate enough so to do. In any tragedy that I do—if there is a part for you that you really want and that will do you any good you shall have it.

I'm terribly sorry to hear of your troubles there but why cry so much. Your young & your sure to get along. Various things are coming your way sure. I think there'll be a return to tragedy and Greek—or poetic things—pretty soon in various fields. So your opourtunity is certain to come. Just now things are in a preliminary or fumbling seeking state. Better come East if things don't turn out right & try your hand here again. For heaven's sake don't cry or give way to nerves. Your too gifted for that. Think how really talented you are and how truly attractive in your field. Its pathetic to think of you crying—but not justified in you and you know it—really.

My tragedy[1] goes on apace. Just finished Act II and had it typewritten and now am on Act III. It's all worked out in my mind before hand so I cant fail in this, anymore than I could on a novel. Have a plan for a second tragedy and expect to do my farce comedy too, soon.[2] Then comes the struggle of getting it produced

Jones[3] & I are about ready to break. He refuses to stand by me on The "Genius"—even to the extent of selling a few copies so Sumner will have a case against him.[4] John B. Stanchfield one of the most powerful & costly lawyers in the city has come to my rescue and offered to take the case for nothing—freeing Jones of any expense. I am getting endless publicity here & in England & mostly in my favor. I can win the suit I think but my publisher at least ought to stick by me long enough to make people think he approves of me—and he wont. But I'll win anyhow, I believe.

Masters[5] was here recently & looked me up—as loving as a cat. Wilkinson[6] is back & is calling on me this evening. I saw Jack Powys[7] a few weeks ago—he and his new girl—a queer half-fed looking Flemish girl. Mencken[8] was here Sunday night and Wright & Clair[9] the Friday before—He bores me stiff. Mordell[10] called once!! Also Waldo Frank[11] There is in town now Mr & Mrs Gerard Grant Allen. He is the cousin of Grant Richards who played Santa Claus at Richards house in England.[12] He's over here raising money for some war fund & incidentally trying to connect with the theatrical business as a producer. He and his wife are coming down here Friday evening for a few hours. I met her once on Fifth Ave. She's a dreadful type really—a cockney English Musical Hall actress I think, but he's always amusing & interesting.

What else? Nothing much. My fight goes unevenly on. The publicity end of it has been enormous but since the book cant be sold its of no value to me—yet—and may never be. Next week I'll send you a copy of "A Hoosier Holiday." When this play comes out, if your not back here—I'll send you that. Will send you a typewritten copy as soon as I get it done for judgement. It's been a wonderful fall here cool & clear & yet not cold. Ed has made quite a hit here in "Under Sentence."[13] His picture, is all over the front of the Theatre. Gertie is still with Warfield.[14] Emma is moving to 120 W. 96th. Mame is finally getting settled at 130 W. 13th & expects to do well. She's going to call her restaurant "Mrs. Brennan's Cozy Corner"!![15] Jack Powys is in Chicago. Marian[16] has opened a lace store or studio at 60 Washington Sq. She phoned today wanting me to come over to see it & asked after you.

Outside of tears & disappointments how are you? What a tempestuous Kid you are. I was looking over your drawings the other day & thinking what a really splendid human being you are—and here you are having your eye lids lanced because of tears. Kind heaven! I'd like to lay you over my knee and give you something to cry for—something really worth while.

Aren't you going to behave? So much love to you

L—

I'm sending the stencil design & a copy of The Born Thief.[17] Cut it yourself & say I did it, if you wish.

1. *The Hand of the Potter*, published in 1918, was Dreiser's four-act "tragedy" about a deviant sex crime that afflicts a family in an immigrant Jewish community in New York. For a more detailed discussion of the play, see Introduction, Newlin and Rusch, *Collected Plays*, xx–xxxiii.

2. Nothing came of these projects.

3. J. Jefferson Jones, the American director of John Lane, the British publisher of *The "Genius"* that refused to release copies of the novel for sale.

4. John S. Sumner (1876–1971) led the New York Society for the Suppression of Vice, an organization that conducted campaigns against what it considered obscenity in art. Sumner's group succeeded in suppressing the sale of *The "Genius"* by threatening in July 1916 to bring charges against the publisher John Lane. As Dreiser notes, Jones and publisher John Lane gave into the demand and refused to distribute the novel. Aided by, among others, H. L. Mencken and the League of American Writers, Dreiser took the case to court.

5. Edgar Lee Masters. See Dreiser to Kirah Markham, 5 March 1915, n. 8.

6. Louis Umfreville Wilkinson (1881–1966), English author.

7. John Cowper Powys. See Dreiser to Kirah Markham, 22 December 1914, n. 3.

8. H. L. Mencken (1880–1956), writer, editor, critic, and Dreiser's longtime friend.

9. Willard Huntington Wright (1888–1939), author, journalist, editor. A close associate of Mencken, Wright was an editor at *Smart Set* and, at this time, the literary critic of the *New York Evening Mail*. Later, as S. S. Van Dine, he wrote the popular Philo Vance detective novels.

"Clair" is the actress Claire Burke, with whom Wright was living.

10. Albert Mordell: see Dreiser to Kirah Markham, 22 December 1914, n 2.

11. Waldo Frank (1889–1967), radical journalist and editor, cultural historian, novelist.

12. Grant Richards (1872–1948), English publisher who encouraged Dreiser to return to writing novels after the misfortunes of *Sister Carrie* (1900). In 1911 Richards organized Dreiser's first trip to Europe, about which Dreiser wrote in *A Traveler at Forty* (1913). For the Christmas celebrations with Gerald (Dreiser means Jerrard) Grant Allen that Dreiser describes here, see Bardeleben, *Traveler at Forty*, 235–50.

13. His brother Edward Minerod Dreiser (1873–1958), an actor until an accident left him blind for over two years. He was performing in *Under Sentence*, an adaptation of a story by John Ford that was made into a film in 1920.

14. ["Gertie"] Nelson, the daughter of Dreiser's sister Emma, had a part in a revival of "The Music Master" at the Knickerbocker Theatre, starring David Warfield.

15. Dreiser's sister Mame was attempting to open a restaurant, which eventually became known as "The Green Witch."

16. Marian Powys Grey (1882–1972), the sister of John Cowper Powys, was a leading authority on handmade lace.

17. "The Born Thief," a story based on a Greek fable that Dreiser had hoped to sell either to a magazine or to a film studio as a scenario (Swanberg, *Dreiser*, 178).

To Kirah Markham [H-DPUP]

Markham had recently been married.

Dec 14–1916

Honey Kid:

Your letter causes me to wonder whether you are seriously unhappy and whether you feel that you have made a mistake. In so far as I am concerned you couldn't make any real mistakes—any which your art and temperament couldn't and wouldn't excuse and make of no real moment—any more than could a humming bird—or a bird of paradise. Like Jennie[1] you are seeking affection and you are entitled to find it—only I often wonder whether I was the one to attempt to provide it for you. I always felt that I could not always give you all you deserved in that way and that in a fashion I seemed to interfere with the natural free swing of your temperament and your development (I sometimes sit and wonder whether we are really separated at all—or ever will be.) You were inclined to subordinate yourself to me and my minor & negligible whims—and what a brute I was really.

I don't know whether I may talk to you freely or no—now that you are married[2] but you must know that you are always the same to me—just Lyhon Cryhon—and that unless your new ties make a vast difference you will remain so. You will always be Lyhon Cryhon here—wonderful and desired wherever you are. I want you to be famous & happy—famous if you can be so—being happy—otherwise not, unless you want it anyhow.

Life with me here is just the same as it's been. I've just finished "The Hand of the Potter"[3] and like it in a way—though I'm by no means sure it's as good as it should be. Am trying to begin on another—"The Reformer"[4] but without success, so far. The Bulwark waits, but I'll do it soon. Saw Dixie Hines[5] one day recently & he advised me to keep my plays out of Little Theatre.

Laughing Gas[6] was tried out successfully I hear in Indianapolis Dec 2nd. The trial of The Genius[7] comes up either next week or, if postponed after Jan 1. I paid Adolph Wolff[8] for that statue yesterday.

If you can come back here and want to see me—or feel that you want to come back to me out of some storm wire me—or come on. I'll do the best I can. I would want to comfort you & make you happy as best I could, only I would want you to be tolerant of me too. I wonder—sometimes—whether with your temperament you should have married or should want to (it can become very inconvenient at times as I can testify) but you must judge of this—end of me & my opinions.

But enough of this. Always think of me, if you can, as you used to, that is, as very close to you spiritually & every other way. I think of you a hundred times a day it seems and always as I did—as Lyhon Cryhon, the wild, gay, weeping, dreaming girl.

Luck—and Ill always be
Bubs—my-bubs to you
and L

1. Jennie, the main character in Dreiser's novel *Jennie Gerhardt* (1911).

2. Markham was at this time married to Frank Lloyd Wright Jr., known as Lloyd Wright (1890–1978). The marriage was conflicted from the outset and did not last long. Markham later told her niece Dorothy Ruddick that she married Wright mainly out of attraction to the work of his famous architect father, but soon found that the son had none of the strength of character or genius of the elder Wright (Dorothy Ruddick to Riggio, 22 March 2006).

3. See Dreiser to Kirah Markham, 25 October 1916, n. 1.

4. No play by this name has survived.

5. Dixie Hines (1872–1928), producer and influential theatrical press agent who wrote a widely read newsletter on plays and productions of the day.

6. *Laughing Gas*: Dreiser's symbolic and expressionistic play was first produced by Carl Bernhardt for the Little Theater Society of Indiana. Opening on 7 December 1916, it received mixed reviews, some very good. For a more extensive discussion of this production, see Newlin and Rusch, *Collected Plays*, 333–36.

7. Dreiser would attempt fruitlessly for years to obtain a legal ruling to force the publisher John Lane to distribute the novel that had been pronounced obscene by the New York Society for the Suppression of Vice (see Dreiser to Kirah Markham, 25 October 1916, n. 4). There never was a ruling on the charges, and in 1918 the case was dismissed by the courts.

8. Adolph Wolff (1882–1944), Belgian-born anarchist, sculptor, and poet associated with the Dada movement in New York.

1917

To May Calvert Baker [H-DPUP]

In the fall of 1884 Dreiser's family moved to Warsaw, Indiana, where for the first time, at age thirteen, he attended a public rather than a Catholic parochial school. It was then that he encountered May Calvert, his teacher at the B Ward School who taught a combined sixth and seventh grade class. She was a delightful change from the nuns of his earlier classroom experience. Because she was young, only twenty-two, enthusiastic, kind, and gave him special attention and encouragement, Dreiser developed a schoolboy's crush on her and enjoyed being a student for the first time. "This girl who was to be my teacher and who did really teach me in the best sense of the word, spelled opportunity instead of repression" (Dawn, *174). Dreiser first mentioned her in his travel memoir,* A Hoosier Holiday *(1916), which recorded his impressions of his youth during a 1915 automobile tour of his home state. He had written that Calvert was "dead now, so someone told me later"* (Hoosier Holiday, *317), but a letter from her on 6 February 1916 assured him that she was "not dead but very much alive and still teaching the young to aspire" (DPUP). By this point she had been divorced for over twenty years and had an adult daughter.*

Feb 15–1917

Dear Mrs. Baker—

Or perhaps better—Dear Miss Calvert—Nothing could be nicer than to have you write me as you did. It pleased me so much that I was happy all day long. You see you are and have always been an integral part of my most pleasing memories and to have you return so—isn't it charming?!! I haven't been as happy as I should have been, all things considered perhaps and all due to a bad disposition I suppose. I am not as happy yet as I might be—who is—but I am much more philosophic.[1] And I'm so glad your not dead and still able to write me. That day I went into the school room and found my little desk—or one just like it—it was you I was thinking of and of that new blood time—and it made me quite sick.[2] Indeed it did—very.

Yes I wish you would write me and tell me about yourself. Nearly all I can tell is in Hoosier Holiday and my other books. I have been working, working, working and still am. The teacher who came to me in Chicago was Miss Fielding[3]—may the deep fates keep her whole. (What does not America owe to its teachers! I want to write something about them someday—collectively and singly—and that last means you and others.)[4] I have thought of you for years, always with pink cheeks and a warm girlish smile

185 WEST 10 STREET
NEW YORK CITY

Feb 15 – 1917

Dear Mrs. Baker –

Or perhaps better – Dear Miss Calvert – Nothing could be nicer than to have you write me as you did. It pleased me so much that I was happy all day long. You see you are and have always been an integral part of my most pleasing memories and to have you return so – well it

Miss Fielding – may the deep fates keep her whole. (What does not America owe to its teachers! I want to write something about them someday collectively and singly – and that last means you and others) I have thought of you for years, always with pink cheeks and a warm girlish smile and kind eyes – haloed by the affection and the fancy of youth

Dreiser to May Calvert Baker, 15 February 1917.

charming? !! I haven't been as happy as I should have been, all things considered ^perhaps and all due to a bad disposition I suffer. I am not as happy yet as I might be—who is—but I am much more philosophic. And I'm so glad you're not dead and still able to write me. That day I went into the school room and found my little desk—or one just like it—it was you I was thinking of and of that nose bleed time—and it made me quite sick. Indeed it did—very.

Yes I wish you would write me and tell me about yourself. Nearly all I can tell is in A Hoosier Holiday and my other books. I have been working walking, walking and still am. The teacher who came to me in Chicago was

There must be many other boys
and girls who have carried you
onward in the same way.

All my best wishes and thoughts
to you. If I had known where
you were we would have motored
over that summer. Would
that I had.

Yours
Theodore Dreiser

Do you recall that I couldn't learn
grammar? I don't know a single thing
about it yet

and kind eyes—haloed by the affection and the fancy of youth. There must be many other boys and girls who have carried you onward the same way.

All my best wishes and thoughts to you. If I had known where you were we would have motored over that summer. Would that I had.

Your
Theodore Dreiser

Do you recall that I couldn't learn grammar? I don't know a single thing about it yet.

1. In her letter Baker had said that in reading his book "it does not appear that you have won happiness with fame."

2. Dreiser is referring to his emotions during his 1915 visit to the classroom in which May Calvert taught him.

3. Mildred Fielding was Dreiser's high school freshman algebra teacher in Warsaw. In 1889 Fielding, by then a principal at a Chicago high school, rescued Dreiser from a dead-end job in a hardware store by helping him to be admitted to Indiana University (Bloomington) and reportedly paying his tuition for the 1889–90 academic year.

4. Dreiser never wrote an extended study of teachers, but in response to this letter, Calvert wrote about the rewarding nature of the work but also its difficulties: "When you write your book about teachers I hope you will make this great, rich country ashamed forevermore, of the salaries paid its teachers" (30 March 1917 [DPUP]).

To Kirah Markham [H-DPUP]

April-19–1917

Honey Cryhon:

Don't you think your foolish really, to suggest that I don't want to hear from you. I'm always delighted when I get a letter from you and for weeks and weeks your pictures have been standing in a row on my mantle and four of your little drawings on the rear mantle and Nord's[1] portrait of you in the rear row and your sketch of yourself in the red frame—and that youngish photo of you in the back room—and four letter files full of your letters. What more do you want. You seem to run this place even at a distance. However you really know I want you to write me, only you want to hear me say it. Isn't that it?

Yes, I saw Nju[2] and I thought that Miss Andrews,[3] if that is her name, was very bad in the part—a flapper attempting to make a serious artistic role. She imitated a Russian accent which half the time she forgot. For the best scene—that with the letters—she was entirely inadequate (or was it his picture?—the restaurant scene I mean.) Absolutely no emotional power. If this is a sample of Ordynski's[4] casting ability—with you at hand

& ready to do the part I give up. He needs to recover his artistic sense—cut it loose form the domination of pink underwear. If he assigned you to the part of the nurse he is a fool. That you should assay it is a testimony to your own generosity & highness. To me the whole play was miscast—the actors inadequate. The lover, to me—was a scream—the stage pictures not very satisfactory—entirely unsatisfactory—the restaurant scene in particular. However it proved an absolute failure here, when with fine actors it might have made a great stir. So much for so much.

As for my own play Arthur Hopkins[5] has accepted it and will produce it next fall. We are about to enter into a definite arrangement concerning it—the usual useless contract. He appears to be quite moved by it and has engaged Jack Barrymore[6] to play the boy. I have another play—The Bad Girl[7]—that I am trying to do but I am not getting along as fast as I might. If I ever get it done and it is accepted and I can control the casting of it and you like the part—but so many ifs are scarcely worth discussing are they. I hope some day to [word unintelligible] of just [word unintelligible] for you—to write a part around you. When I do it is yours wherever you are or whatever you think of me. I want to do it for you—and for myself.

Now as to other things. Only a few people have read The Hand of the Potter so far—Ed, Arthur Hopkins, Jack Barrymore, Hutchins Hapgood, Mencken, Frank Shay, Jones (of the Lane Co—who refused to publish it), Yewdale and my lawyer—Joseph S. Auerbach and Messers Stanchfield & Levy. [8] All but Mencken like it very much. Mencken froths at the mouth—in opposition. Frank Shay weeps tears of enthusiasm. So there you are. I offered to send you a copy but you never mentioned it—so—

I have practically broken with the Lane Co and am seeking a new publisher. I never make any money through them and Jones came to look on me as a beggar or dependant—finally writing me a superior letter which I never answered. I have The Bulwark also a book of short stories and a book of poems which I will issue one of these hours. A new edition of Sister Carrie which is being called for is being brought out by Frank Shay.[9] I thought I'd let him see what he can do. Also, if he succeeds—I'll let him produce The Hand of the Potter—about the time the play goes on. It's so grim & terrible I don't expect to make a dollar—not one.

Wright & Claire Burke[10] split up but are slowly getting together again. Claire Burke went off and lived with an actor. Wilkinson[11] was in here yesterday & asked after you. Said his wife had just given birth to a girl and would write you soon. Jack Powys is on the coast. Floyd Dell & Marjorie Jones[12] seem to be hobnobbing together once more. Met them this A. M. in the little French restaurant at 11th St. Mencken & Miss Bloom still hang together. She has an apartment in 19th Street near Eighth Ave with her sister.[13] I see all sorts of people you know from time to time but on the street only. I never go visiting or so rarely it's not worth mentioning. I've been writing articles & short stories and selling them to the Cosmopolitan & Hearsts—hence my ability just at the present to tell Jones to go to:

Im so sorry about your married troubles[14]—since it seems so ideal—but if you cant stand it you cant and your wise to cut it all. You're a free soul and deserve to be free. Please rise very high on your wings. Whatever I can do to help I will. And now don't say I don't ever write you or that I don't want to hear from you. When you come East I want to hear much.

Bubs—

Are you as slender as ever? Or are you getting stout (Horrors!)

Do you read many plays?

Hopkins says he thinks he will follow The Hand of the Potter with an evening of four or three of the 1 act plays. [15] I'll get all your books together when you come.

Jig Cooke & Ida Rau,[16] running the Provincetown Players threw out the Nordfeldts[17] upon whom they were sore. There is feeling over that of course.[18]

1. Dreiser's shorthand for Bror Nordfeldt. See Dreiser to Kirah Markham, 12 May 1913, n. 3.

2. *Nju*, a play by the Russian playwright, actor, and screenwriter Ossip Dymow (1878–1959) was translated from the Russian by Rosalind Ivan and produced at the Bandbox Theater, one of the many little theaters in New York City. Dymow had emigrated from Russia, claiming that the new regime stifled artistic individuality and discriminated against Jewish authors. Many of his plays and later films were written for American Yiddish theaters.

3. Ann Andrews (1890–1986), actress in her first professional performance who played the lead role of Nju.

4. The Polish stage and film director Richard Ordynski. The reviews of the play tended to agree with Dreiser's negative assessment of the production, and the show closed after one month.

5. Arthur Hopkins (1878–1950), the producer-director who paid Dreiser $1000 for the rights to *The Hand of the Potter* but never staged it. Dreiser believed that H. L. Mencken's negative opinion of the play influenced Hopkins's decision not to produce the play.

6. The actor John Barrymore (1882–1942).

7. Dreiser never completed a play with this title.

8. Ed, Dreiser's brother who, like brother Paul, used the stage name Dresser as an actor until an accident ended his stage career.

Hutchens Hapgood (1869–1944), journalist, social commentator, novelist. His autobiography *A Victorian in the Modern World* (1939) contains a portrait of Dreiser in these years.

Frank Shay (1889–1954), Washington Square bookseller and publisher.

J. Jefferson Jones. See Dreiser to Kirah Markham, 25 October 1916, n. 3.

Merton S. Yewdale, at the time an editor with Dreiser's publisher John Lane.

Joseph S. Auerbach (1855–1944), the attorney who argued Dreiser's case against the suppression of *The "Genius."* He published an account of the argument he made before the Appellate Division of the New York Supreme Court in *Essays and Miscellanies*, 3 vols. (New York, 1922), 3:130–65.

John B. Stanchfield and Louis Levy were the heads of the firm that represented Dreiser in the legal case connected with *The "Genius."* Given his experience with the novel, Dreiser sought advice from them and Joseph Auerbach on the legal ramifications of producing *The Hand of the Potter.* On Levy's response, see Dreiser to H. L. Mencken, 21 December 1916 (Riggio, *Dreiser-Mencken Letters*, I, 285–88).

9. Frank Shay printed the novel but was drafted into the army before he was able to bind and publish it. In 1917 Boni and Liveright published the novel using the gatherings from Shay's printing.

10. Wright and Claire Burke. See Dreiser to Kirah Markham, 25 October 1916, n. 9.

11. Wilkinson. See Dreiser to Kirah Markham, 25 October 1916, n. 6.

12. Floyd Dell. See Dreiser to Kirah Markham, 15 April 1913, n. 1.

Marjorie Jones began her career as a Chicago photographer, then moved to New York where she acted in little theater productions and wrote screenplays.

13. Marion Bloom and H. L. Mencken had a long-standing affair that had begun in 1914; her sister, Estelle Bloom Kubitz, and Dreiser had become lovers. For more detailed accounts, see Dreiser's diary entries for 1917–18 (in Riggio, *American Diaries*, 149–256) and Martin, *In Defense of Marion*, passim.

14. Markham's 1916 marriage to Frank Lloyd Wright Jr. had begun to sour. See Dreiser to Kirah Markham, 14 December 1916, n. 2.

15. Dreiser's one-act plays were published as *Plays of the Natural and the Supernatural* (1916).

16. George Cram Cooke (1873–1924), novelist, playwright, and founder of the Provincetown Players at Cape Cod. The company moved to MacDougal Street in Greenwich Village in 1916.

Ida Rauh (1877–1970), actress, poet, sculptor, social activist who was married to the writer Max Eastman (1883–1969) at this time.

17. Bror Nordfeldt. See Dreiser to Kirah Markham, 12 May 1913, n. 3.

18. Dreiser added these two lines in the left-hand margin of the page.

To Kirah Markham [H-DPUP]

Dreiser had left the distractions of New York and was writing at a farm in Maryland owned by a relative of his companion Estelle Bloom Kubitz.

July 3rd 1917

R. F. D. 10
Westminster, Maryland

Dearest Cryhon:

It was fine to get your letter, which just now came here—along with one from Maurice Browne.[1] I'm up here working in the woods and had

not intended to return to N. Y. before Aug. 1, but I may get there earlier. Of course I'll see you. Did you get my letter about my conversation with Browne—a month or so ago. He wanted you to come back to him. Said he could pay as much as the Washington Square Players & would feature you. If you haven't seen him, do.

What a picture you give of father-in-law.[2] I should like to meet him sometime. What're you doing—writing any—you should. I think of you everyday—wonder how you are and if you are doing all that you should. Write me here.

Lover as ever,
Bubs

1. Maurice Browne (1881–1955) and his wife Ellen Van Volkenburg (1882–1978) (aka Nelly Van) founded the Chicago Little Theater in 1912. Although it existed for only five years, it was among the most influential experimental theaters in the country. Dreiser first met Markham in 1913 when she was acting with the group.

2. Markham was married to the son of the architect Frank Lloyd Wright. See Dreiser to Kirah Markham, 14 December 1916, n. 2.

To May Calvert Baker [H-DPUP]

Dreiser spent parts of June and July with Estelle Bloom Kubitz in Westminster, Maryland, at a farm owned by Harry Baile Smith, a relative of the Bloom family. The rail table he worked at was in a cabin designated for his private use. There he tried to finish The Bulwark, *a novel about Quakers in contemporary society begun in 1914 but interrupted to complete other writing. His former publisher John Lane had earlier announced the book's publication date as spring 1917; but despite the work on it at this time, he did not complete the novel for another quarter century. He was also now working on* Newspaper Days, *which would be published as* A Book About Myself *(1922).*

R.F.D. 10
Westminster, Maryland
c/o H. B. Smith

July 23rd 1917

Dear Mae Calvert:

Thats the way I always think of you,—just May Calvert: No I haven't forgotten you and I do want to write. On my desk in New York is a letter begun to you—but thats all. Other things intervened and I was pushed off. Up here in Western Maryland in the woods at a rail table I am trying to do two books at once—one a novel called "The Bulwark," the other a reminiscence book ala "A Hoosier Holiday" entitled "Newspaper Days." I spent

The young May Calvert at the time she taught Dreiser (ca. 1881). (Courtesy of Robert Craig.)

a little over three years—nearly four as a newspaper reporter, critic & what not and I'm thinking it'll make a good story. So far I've done 28 chapters of the novel and 12 of the Newspaper book so I'm not loafing exactly.

Your letters are charming. The news of the row in Warsaw is amusing.[1] Those things never trouble me anymore. I've been clubbed so long. Judson C. Morris, son of the bookstore man—a hunchback—I wonder if you remember him?[2]—is coming to N.Y. Aug 5 and wants to see me. I expect to be back there for awhile by then. In his letter which came only 2 days ago he enclosed a notice of Mary Gibson's death in Chicago. It said she was a Sunday School teacher!—healthy, animal, daring Mary![3] Well, so life runs.

No I don't remember Eschbaugh at all. Nor do I recall your sister Anna. For the sake of Mae Calvert though I'm coming to Huntington[4] one of these days and you'll have to put me up for the night & give me a meal or two. Do you agree to do that.

This evening—it's 6 now—is wonderful in the woods. I have a lovely hill and valley prospect—as delicately colored as an Inness or a Vermeer[5] and the evening sun is streaming over this letter. I feel as cheerful & youthful as ever I did—just now anyhow. Mentally I think we never grow old or change much—some of us anyhow. But physically we don't do so well, do we? I cant complain though—standing 6 ft 1 1/2 inches & weighing 190 lbs. Am returning to N. Y. this week so write me there. And dont think I am forgetting you. If I have thought of you once I have done so 100 times.

Theodore Dreiser

1. Baker had written him that "The Warsaw 'elite' are having horrors that you dared to tell the truth [in *A Hoosier Holiday*] about some of their friends" (16 July 1917 [DPUP]).

2. For Dreiser's memories of Morris, see *Dawn*, 244–45, 269, 285, 287–88. Also see Dreiser's letter to Morris, (Pizer, *New Letters*, 1–2).

3. He recalled Mary Gibson (disguised as "Dora Yaisley") in *Hoosier Holiday* as the great love of his adolescence: "I used to dream about her all the time . . . from my fourteenth to my sixteenth year . . . she was the one girl whose perfection I was sure of" (289).

4. Huntington, in northeastern Indiana, was Calvert's residence at this time. Dreiser did visit her at Huntington in June 1919. Among other things, they drove to Warsaw together, where they visited with old friends such as Jud Morris and John Shoup, and even spent time rowing on a lake together in Culver (see Riggio, *American Diaries*, 259–63).

5. George Inness (1825–94), American landscape painter; Jan Vermeer (1632–75), Dutch painter.

1918

To May Calvert Baker [H-DPUP]

Nov. 23–1918

My Dear May C

You say write often. I wish I could. I think of you often—several times everyday. I fancy and wish I might spend a few days with you, but here I am & here I stick, largely because of the convenience of doing things & the number of things for me to do here. And New York doesn't make me sadder or more cynical than any other place in America or elsewhere. Life makes me sad—not cynical—because I realize what poor flies we are. And the hopes of most people come to so very little. You seem to have discovered as much from the things you told me.[1]

Anyhow I am glad you are not as dull as we all were in our youth. Most of us are as blind as kittens and the majority remain so. It is a privilege and a reward to grow mentally and I think it repays for most other ills if we really grow.

Some day I shall surely walk in on you & stay a few days—possibly in the spring—maybe before.[2] I have many things in hand and as usual the critics discuss me most savagely, but I can stand it. Im used to it. And besides they become more ridiculous every year. I'm glad I'm one of your blessings. An elusive blessing—What?

Theodore Dreiser

1. She confided in Dreiser about her marital problems.

2. Dreiser kept his word and visited her home in June 1919. See Dreiser to May Calvert Baker, 23 July 1917, n. 4.

1919

To May Calvert Baker [H-DPUP]

Baker had suggested her willingness to go on a promotional book tour for Dreiser in order to help him realize his dream of having a publisher issue a complete set of his books, a near-impossible task because he had published with so many different firms that it would have been very costly for any publisher to purchase the rights for such a set.

165 WEST 10 STREET
NEW YORK CITY

Aug 16–1919

Dear May C-B:

My reputation must be rather down by you but still—here I am. No need to say that I'm always being hurried by someone—the crag to crag stuff, you know. I'm due for a long rest somewhere but whether I'll get it on the other side of life is a question also. My sins may prevent. Have arranged with Boni and Liveright to put a portion of your plan in regard to my books into force this winter.[1] That is, they'll assemble a number of sets from different publishers & get up a poster such as you suggested. I'd like to get an estimate from you of the cost of two or three months canvassing trip such as you might make next summer. I can get Boni and Liveright to finance it I believe. Work it out. The idea is to visit various bookstores & start local booms. The enclosed leaflet—particularly the last few lines—shows that they are interested in your program.

How are you, my good angel. Please dont think I've forgotten or am ungrateful. I'm not, just busy. Will send you more of my books as soon as you notify me that you are reading any of them. If you should undertake a canvass you would need to have read them all.

And I haven't forgotten the small or the large Craigs. I want to send Virginia a fan. What would the boy like.[2]

Love & best wishes.
T. D.

If the state of Indiana will make me a present of a small house & garden on the Wabash, I'll come back there & live.

1. Boni and Liveright had become Dreiser's publisher in 1917 after he left John Lane for its refusal to distribute *The "Genius."* Horace Liveright (1886–1933), the firm's founder, was willing to entertain Dreiser's promotional idea, but Baker never did undertake this task.

2. Dreiser is referring to Virginia and Calvert Craig, the children of Baker's daughter, Mrs. Jessie Craig.

1920

To Margaret Johnson [H-DPUP]

Margaret Johnson was a young actress associated with the Provincetown Players. Dreiser had met her in the spring of 1919, in the company of her mother. Afterwards she began a sporadic correspondence with him, but they did not see each other again until she visited California in the summer of 1922. In 1920 Dreiser was living in Los Angeles with Helen Richardson (see Dreiser to Helen Richardson, 1 December 1923, headnote).

P.O. Box 181
Los Angeles
Calif

July 29–1920

Dear Margaret:

Call me anything you want to—anything you are emotionally moved to call me—and no more. You know I am drawn to you and you know why. When you describe the upbringing and the logic and the reality of life battling in you—and I think of you as you really are—a kind of Pink Hebe[1] hung with silver Methodist chains I feel a little sad. For I have lived and I see others living and to no least hurt—for life is not a reflection of a divine order, sad as that may seem to one taught to expect and demand a divine order, but a loose and unstable chemic movement which at one end is emotional and magnetic and at the other economic—nothing more. Here—and everywhere—I look about me & see people acting according to their internal impulses and restrained only by external & economic (which is another phase of social) conditions. Where they have the force & the beauty they do as they will and nothing comes of it—not a thing—save a measure of happiness & success. For some life is literally all success & all pleasure—crossed by the inevitable stresses of industry or action. For others—with the same stresses of industry & action it is all pain—or dullness—or indifference. Beauty, strength, brain, taste are gifts—and most partial and unfair ones. Weakness, homeliness, smallness of mind are curses & dealt to all & sundry almost accidentally it seems. If I could I would blow out of your mind every trace of religious & moralic cant & faith. Whether you ever exchanged another word with me or no, I would take from your mind faith in any ultimate justice or reward and leave you only generous where the balance of your affairs permitted you so to be. I would have you give yourself to happiness in your youth—so that in the latter days you could not complain. Those who have been happy do not. Look up sometime the true meaning of the old biblical quotation, "Remember thy creator in the days of thy youth."[2] That word *creator* does not refer to God. That is a horrible, slavish Christian perversion. It refers to the male organ—once worshipped as a symbol of the Creator. And it is, certainly is as good as any other symbol. If you ever came to me it would have to be because you very much wanted to—and if you did—and we lived together—all these trashy lies—save as economics & policy—exterior policy—guide one, would be blown away. I could neither love nor live with anyone who was not a happy pagan. The day of social lies for me is dead. I face life willing to earn & pay my way economically, anxious for a square deal & willing to give it & stripped clean of religious & moral theory & bunk. When love is dead it is dead. No chains other than those relating to a fair economic division of things which are purely economic should hold one. When it is aflame it should be gratified if conditions permit. Each one must save himself whole as best he can, or live his life passionately & will it as he chooses & without complaint. When I watch these men & beauties in this seething movie world where success & pleasure hold their proper place as goals I see what a fine brilliant interesting thing a pagan world is. Moralic cant & religious theory kill life. They are cancers, horrible growths that should be cut out before they kill life itself. Note the results of Mohamedan theory, Budhist Theory, Christian theory—Christian morality. We are not so. Nature is not so & I like only those born so strong & so courageous & so mentally well equipped that they can see & do as wisdom & strength indicate.

You are beautiful & full of fine physical & mental strength & lust. Don't waste the next ten years. If ever we meet & you are very much drawn to me don't temporize. The years slip by so quickly. But whether we ever chance along the path of happiness together don't you let musty Christian morality hold you to commonplace meditative failure. It will be too bad.

Theodore Dreiser

The John Lane Co. has 500 copies of The "Genius"—1st edition & won't even sell one to me. I paid $10^{oo} last May for a worn copy. They sell for as high as $5^{oo} just as does Sister Carrie. But I may win my suit yet.[3] *The Bulwark* is a novel & a good one, if I ever finish it.[4] *A Novel About Myself* is really a part of my life which I may issue as *Newspaper Days*. It has a sort of *novel* quality—hence the idea of the title. But I think I'll call it plain old *Newspaper Days*.[5] Does that sound interesting.

I wish you'd send me a dandy picture of yourself sometime. Movie schemes—& the need of the ready cash blowing about here—hold me here. If I come East I'll come up to Provincetown but it would be to move you—and you alone.

1. The Greek goddess of Youth.

2. Ecclesiastes, 12:1. The term "Creator" has puzzled commentators as an unlikely source for the counsel expressed within the context of this passage. Though not impossible, the idea that it stands for the male sexual organ is highly unlikely. Recent commentary suggests that "a very similar Hebrew word meaning 'your grave' suits the context" (May and Metzger, *Oxford Annotated Bible*, 814, n. 12.1).

3. When in 1916 John Sumner and the society for the Suppression of Vice threatened to bring obscenity charges against *The "Genius"* (1915), the publisher, the John Lane Company, gave in to the pressure and refused to sell the novel despite there never having been a ruling on Sumner's charges. Dreiser attempted for years to force the firm by legal means to release the copies held in storage, and in another suit in 1922 he sued Lane for damages resulting from the loss of sales. See Dreiser to Kirah Markham, 25 October 1916, n. 4.

4. Dreiser completed the novel in 1945, just before his death.

5. Horace Liveright published the memoir as *A Book About Myself* in 1922, and it was reissued under the title *Newspaper Days* in 1931.

To Margaret Johnson [H-DPUP]

P.O. Box 181
Los Angeles
Calif

Aug. 27–1920

Dear Margaret:

Yes, I judged my letter had acted like a bucket of cold water suddenly dashed over you. I felt as I wrote it that it might and that you might drop out entirely. Not that I wanted you to but I thought you might as well have a taste of my mind. Really I'm not as bad as I write, I think. We always attribute to writers—or I do anyhow—more than they say, when less would be truer. In short I lead a very simple life & have—working-working-a very great deal—stopping never more than an evening to browse about. I never go on wild trips, haven't been to an all night party or an orgy of any kind in years. Haven't been more than tipsy in fully seven years I think. I get all sorts of bids. I could go nightly & daily but plainly I love work more than pleasure. Judge for yourself. I have written fourteen books in the last 10 years & have two on the stocks now. One must be in fairly forceful condition to write and a waster cannot write. The nervous system will not permit it. I play at times of course. When I do I want only brilliant men—or women—or both & they are not so terribly numerous. Mere cuties & flappers never interested me. I like to talk too much—and that intelligently—so I seek circles wherein people are emancipated and they are to be found. In fact as I say I could go & go, but I don't. If we were very much drawn to each other we might settle down for a long period—indefinitely. It depends on the flare. I look on you as very dynamic and engaging person—beautiful & magnetic. You might grow on me—we might grow on each other. A mental understanding is the finest cement as you know. Between a man and a woman it makes for wonderful hours & years even. When I talk of the pagan spirit I mean that I want that to be the character of all those who interest me. They have to think wisely & tolerantly. I cannot bear people with hard & fast rules or secret moral reservations—who cannot play without thinking how terrible it is! They torture themselves & everyone else. I like only those who take life as it is. That does not mean that work or pain or gloom is eliminated. It simply means that they stand all things better—more sweetly, courteously, beautifully. The Christian, the moralist & religionist are always awry. They make life look like a terrible joke. The pagan makes it look what it is—grim, dangerous, subtle, pathetic—but always attractive, often beautiful—a fit thing for ones best years. I only like such people. I like people who think what is best for themselves and do it—because it is best for themselves,—who are not taken in by clap trap rules made by other people—for them. So I really hate people who stop & moralize over everything and then do what is best for themselves while pretending they are serving some great moral law or God—or something. Heavens, how I despise them.

But I am just talking. You know all this. If you really were intensely drawn to me, theories wouldn't trouble you at all. Since your not you speculate & worry. Perhaps the best thing to do is to wait, without words until we meet sometime. I may be back in N.Y. Oct 1st or 7th. If so & you were really drawn to me we could soon decide. If we separated instanter there would be no harm done. If not—well—

So don't worry over me anyway. Just dismiss me for the time being and if you feel inclined to write at any time do so. I know you are a fine dynamic thing and if you ever did like me intensely it would be some like—

Th. D.

1921

To Louise Campbell [TS-DPUP]

Louise Heym Campbell wrote to Dreiser in February 1917 to praise his writing but also to criticize him for judgmental remarks about Pennsylvanians in A Hoosier Holiday *(1916). At his invitation she came to New York to meet him, and he immediately put her to work on the autobiographical material that later was published in two volumes as* A Book About Myself *(1922) and* Dawn *(1931). Campbell's friendship with Dreiser lasted until his death in 1945, and over the years she acted variously as his editor, lover, literary advisor, typist, researcher, translator (she was fluent in German), and confidant. He relied heavily on her critical and editorial skills, notably in her work on* An American Tragedy *(1925), a major revision of* The Financier *in 1927, and his last completed novel* The Bulwark *(1946). Her account of her marital problems became the basis for his story "Chains." Dreiser helped edit the stories she sold to the magazines, and encouraged her career as an editor, notably for* Ladies Home Journal. *She published a bowdlerized selection of Dreiser's letters to her, together with a brief but valuable biographical narrative, in* Letters to Louise: Theodore Dreiser's Letters to Louise Campbell *(1959).*

P.O. Box 101.
Los Angeles.

Feb. 16, 1921.

Dear Louise:

A word of advice, please. You recall that volume about myself—"Youth" I think I called it. It is as I probably told you volume one in a four volume work—*The History of Myself*. Last spring I finished volume two, which I called "Newspaper Days." It is now typed and in the hands of Liveright.[1] Being about grown ups and principally newspaper life, it has little in it to shock the puritans. But what I need to know is this. Harpers, who have also seen this second vol. are most keen to undertake the entire set—a volume a year. They want to make a great fuss about it. Now comes the question. What about volume one. Can I show it as it is? Ought it not be edited before I let anyone see it.[2] Please give me your advice. You read it and I recall your saying that you thought much of the stuff would have to come out. Do you still think so. If I gave you a key to a trunk in my studio would you go there and get the volume out and look it over and give me your opinion. There is no immediate rush about it but I would like to know what you think. I would like to know just how much of that stuff I would dare to use in my life. Would you advise my letting Mencken see it as it is?[3] Please give this your serious consideration and let me know. No one has ever seen the thing but you,

Thanks for the word about Powys.[4] Why am I so much in your mind these days, Loose.

Dreiser

1. Horace Liveright published "Newspaper Days" under the title *A Book About Myself* in 1922.
2. Volume one, which Dreiser here refers to as "Youth," was published by Liveright as *Dawn* in 1931, along with a reissue of *Newspaper Days*. Dreiser's concern is that "Youth" is not principally "about grown-ups" but about childhood and adolescence, which included the sexual misadventures and social transgressions of his siblings and himself.
3. H. L. Mencken: see Dreiser to Kirah Markham, 25 October 1916, nn. 1 and 8. Dreiser's concern about having Mencken see the manuscript is rooted in what he considered Mencken's conservative responses to *The "Genius"* (1915) and to his play *The Hand of the Potter* (1918). Although Mencken was willing to defend Dreiser against artistic suppression by the "puritans," he felt these works violated the boundaries of literary propriety.
4. John Cowper Powys. See Dreiser to Kirah Markham, 22 December 1914, n. 3.

To Margaret Johnson [TS-DPUP]

P.O. BOX 181
Los Angeles
Cal.

April 18, 1921.

Dear Margaret:

Now wouldn't I be a fine specimen, indeed, not to be willing to write you or to meet you in the spirit in which we first met, especially after such a simple and human request. And all because, for a little time, I might be talked about in the meretricious and evanescent prints of the day. Believe me I value human affection and honest fellow interest above all the conventional palaver that goes on in the prints anent literature. I am not a vain, posing ass and you, of all people ought to sense that, because you do me the honor to like me and our intellectual tastes are much the same. Though I haven't had a word from you in how long now?—eight or nine months?[1]—still you have never been really out of my mind. There is a nicely furnished chamber there that concerns all the charming things that relate to Margaret Johnson and I step into it ever so often and close the door. You are too fine, not to be visited in memory from time to time, though I notice that you can and do, walk briskly off and forget, or try to with the greatest ease. You did that the very first time, if you will recall.

But I am not just that stripe of bird exactly. When I like, I like, and it is not possible for me to begin to dislike or forget quickly. I hang around, thinking, long after the other fellow has stopped thinking of me, I fear. I think I have pictured you doing just about the things you tell me you were doing and wondered how you were making out and whether I ever stepped into your thoughts. For, after all, you are my type of girl, aren't you,—spirited, vigorous, seeking, dynamic, hopeful and sensual and that is just what I like and why I have always liked you and always will. I will only be too glad to trade letters with you and when I come east, if I do soon, which is not unlikely I will be only too happy to step about and see where you are or at least to call you up and see what you have to say for yourself. As I say, I have thought of you regularly for lo, these many days and will continue to so do, you may be sure.

Yes, Atlantic City is one of my favorite sea places or, better yet, really the only sea place in America that I truly like and much more interesting than any I saw in Europe. There is something spacious and quite noble about Atlantic City, a baronial sort of resort. The Traymore, The St. Charles, The Chalfant, the Chelsea and those several exclusive little ones between the Marlborough and the Traymore, I know them all.[2] I always liked to live in one and then amble out to dinner in one of the other ones. And winter, January, has always been my favorite time, with snow on the great walk and an angry sea. I like it in summer almost as well, though not quite. The throng is almost too much. But, just the same, crowd or no crowd, on a hot night to feel the breath of the sea there and listen to the surf is exhilarating. There is nothing on the west coast that compares to it. The only other place that even approaches it in my estimation is the Jersey coast about Asbury Park. The boardwalk there is a thing of almost exquisite beauty. I saw nothing abroad to compare with it.

As requested, I am enclosing a clipping but with an ulterior purpose. After you have read it, do this. Write a personal note to Frank Harris,[3] care, Pearson's Magazine, 40 Seventh Avenue, New York, and say, in your own way, as follows:

"I notice with some interest your comment, in the current Pearson's, on Edward H. Smiths article on Theodore Dreiser.[4] It interested me the more because of your sketch of him in your book, Contemporary Portraits, Second Series.[5] I also recall your quoting his opinion of your study of Oscar Wilde.[6] Not that I am by any means an enthusiastic follower of Dreiser but merely that I have been interested by the manner in which he appears to invite and provoke discussion. How do you explain that. The clatter in regard to him never ceases. From a recent issue of The Nation, for instance, I take the enclosed study of him by Prof. Carl Van Doren of Columbia University, eulogistic in the main.[7] And, as you know, Mr. Mencken, in the Smart Set and elsewhere, never ceases to plead his cause. It would interest me no little to have your opinion as to this, all the more, because, as I say, you yourself have made several kindly references to him in the past."

This note will certainly rub the noisy Frank in just the wrong way. At the same time it may provoke him to further silly assertions which is just what I want. I like to tease him and this will carry on the work for a moment anyhow. I bear Harris no real ill will, as everyone who knows will tell you. I have done him many favors, contributing material free which would have cost another hundreds. His present rage against me springs from my refusal to praise his second volume of portraits. Do something like the above and favor yours.

Are you as ruddy and Hebe[8] like as ever? I always think of you as I saw you in New York. Your just a strong man's girl, that's all.

T. D.

Jim, the Penman.

It now appears likely that I shall be in N.Y. in May—to stay.[9]

1. See Dreiser to Margaret Johnson, 29 July 1920, headnote.
2. Hotels in Atlantic City, New Jersey.
3. Frank Harris (1856–1931), Irish-born author and editor.
4. A sympathetic essay: Edward H. Smith, "Dreiser—after Twenty Years," *Bookman* 53 (March 1921): 27–39.
5. The portrait of Dreiser in *Contemporary Portraits: Second Series* (1919) led him to write a damning letter to Harris, accusing him of "vaulting egotism" in his treatment of authors (see 3 November 1920, in Elias, *Letters*, I, 294–95). Harris printed the entire letter with a mocking rebuttal in "Dreiser vs. Harris," *Pearson's Magazine*, January 1921, 234–35.
6. *Oscar Wilde* (1916). For Dreiser's high praise of the book see Dreiser to Frank Harris, 14 January 1917 (in Elias, *Letters*, I, 247–48).
7. Carl Van Doren, "Contemporary American Novelists: Theodore Dreiser," *Nation* 112 (16 March 1921): 400–401.
8. See Dreiser to Margaret Johnson, 29 July 1920, n. 1.
9. It would be eighteen months before Dreiser returned to New York, in October 1922. Dreiser wrote this postscript in longhand.

1922

To Margaret Johnson [T-DPUP]

Johnson had recently sent Dreiser a letter with a photo of herself and a report on the 1921 production (and mixed reviews) of his The Hand of the Potter *at the Provincetown Theatre in New York.*

P.O. BOX 181
Los Angeles,
Cal.

Feb. 6, 1922

My Dear:

Feb. 6. And you wrote me, when? I have an idea that it has been all of a month. I am writing a play,[1] or, trying to write one for a certain celebrity and it is just about flooring me. Unless you have tried play writing at some time you can never guess how absolutely entangling and brain racking it can become. The profoundest puzzle you ever essayed isn't a patch. It seems at times as though neither the psychology nor the arrangement would ever come right. And yet, as in the case of the puzzle one is lured back at times to have another go at the damn thing. All the plays *so far* (get that) that I ever tackled I finished. *So far.* And I hereby tap on wood and cross my fingers and spit to the right for luck. Even then I don't like that *so far.* Its kinda sorta like defying the lightning.

That is a cute picture of you and the dog on the sand by the old boat. You look so calm and speculative and rather unbelieving, though friendly. Certainly that beach as the picture shows it, has charm. One of these days I must go to Provincetown. But, as I once wrote you, my favorite sea place is Atlantic City in January and February when the great crowds are not there. Then I love the immense hotels and the sea and the board walk with snow on it. Nothing better in this world, I do believe.

What is behind the barrage of publicity? Not a blessed thing worth mentioning. A dreamer who walks and looks at the sky and the kids playing and housewives stirring around in kitchens or feeding the chickens and wonders what it is all about and why, and why we can't get a line on it. Who started it? What did he do it for? Was he tired of being disembodied energy or energy in some other form. Where is mind when it isn't,—that is when it is asleep. Why the passions except to keep this going. Or, is it just for the fun of them, and the race has to be in order to keep up the fun of sex.

Why should we just live seventy years,—or so little more. Who figured out the chemical combination that makes the machine run just that long and incidentally reproduce itself? (Some inventor) And he looks to me like a great thinker.

But why does he want to waste his time being a clog dancer, for instance, or a hop-head? Or a loutish, bull necked, grafting politician. Or, a thick-necked, narrow minded profiteering butcher or grocer? Or, a fuzzy wuzzy housewife who believes that God insists on her having one a year? Why the long upward (?) pull from swamp protoplasm to John D. and Wilson with his fourteen fool points.[2] Why, if it isn't just for fun, is every blessed thing forgotten after a time,—wiped out,—the slate washed clean so that the mind of man runneth not to the contrary. And if its for fun, why so much devilish cruelty here and there. Can't it be worked any other way?

But it doesn't make me sad any more. Not a bit. It used to but now it doesn't. Loss of sensibility I presume, and illusion. But that don't insult me either, now. And it doesn't give me any qualms or pains. I didn't invent it. I can't help it. I see no profound reason the other side of charity for so doing.

Well, that's all there is behind the barrage. Not another thing. And all old stuff,—every bit of it. It's been recited litany fashion since the Greeks began to think. So you see, I'm a waster and a dub. I fiddle my time away thinking aimlessly when I might be making shoes wholesale or manufacturing pants or selling oil or real estate,—something useful,—and laying aside a wad for my old age. I might have married at twenty-one, brought forth several children and sent all the boys over the top for the good of the flag. But I didn't. Wrong, unpatriotic wasteful instincts. God,—the fellow who does the clog dancing in part, will punish me. Or, so I hear, here and there. Well, even that doesn't disturb me. I've seen him or his system do worse than that. And then betimes, it occurs to me that he can't help himself, any more than I can,—that he is fiddling at something trying to make eternity and nothingness a little better than eternity and nothingness. Pretty rough on him, isn't it? He has my profound sympathy at such moments and I wish I could help out in some way. I really do.

But enough. Farrago and bombast. Hot air. Old stuff. But that is all there is behind. "An lesson arf a that before."[3] You've gone over it a thousand times yourself. If I couldn't put an occasional book together I'd never be heard of because I'm not constructive. And everybody ought to be constructive. And, if they eat, in nine cases out of ten they have to be.

But I wish I could see you once more. I'd like to have a talk even though it only consists in removing ideas from one shelf to another. Don't be angry because I didn't answer sooner. This play may be the death of me, at that. If it isn't it may bring me to N.Y. Then, if your not dead, as you say, you may do me the kindness to let me come round and look you up. I certainly hope so.

Ivan the Fiddler.

Per TD.

1. Dreiser was attempting to write a play based on his novel *The "Genius"* (see Dreiser to Kirah Markham, 13 July 1922, n. 1).

2. John D. Rockefeller (1839–1937), oil magnate.

[Thomas] Woodrow Wilson (1856–1924), the twenty-seventh president, introduced his "fourteen points" to Congress on 8 January 1918, a program that attempted to enunciate the basic premises of a just and lasting peace in the face of European territorial ambitions at the end of World War I.

3. Unidentified.

To Kirah Markham [H-DPUP]

Dreiser was still living with Helen Richardson in California when old friends such as H. L. Mencken and Kirah Markham began pressuring him to return to New York. They felt he was not getting any good work done in Los Angeles and that he was losing his connections in the East. Markham wrote saying that she had "heard from various sources that my name is anathema to you," but still felt compelled to write him about the present dangers to his career: "People are saying you are done, finished, but I know that you are only finished at fifty if you choose to be. I have a deep rooted conviction that senility and softening of the brain will come to any one over twelve years of age who stays in that decadent state and I want to know when you are going to get out of it" (Kirah Markham to Dreiser, 6 July 1922 [DPUP]). Dreiser did return to New York in October 1922.

P.O. BOX 181
Los Angeles,
Cal.

July 13, 1922.

Dear Cryhon:

No one better than you knows that there are no such things as bitter moods in my mind in connection with you. And you know that no one would dare to speak of you to me except in terms of friendly understanding. You know that all too well. The dreadful moods you are thinking of would be more likely to follow any such attempt. Any one who tells you anything else lies.

As for California, what you say is true, but not so true for me as some. You know how I crave sunshine. And it does not seem to enervate me. I think I have felt better here than in most places,—certainly than I felt in New York. And when I left there in 1919 I was rather run down. Out here I picked up not a little. As for being through at fifty,—well, words won't help to counteract that save words in book form. Since coming here I have done several things. 1. Dramatized the "Genius" as you will see, presently, I hope. And a fine play it makes.[1] But it was hard work. Took me nearly five months. 2. Completed volume two of a History of Myself, which same volume,—entitled *A Book About Myself*, is even now being set up by Boni and Liveright and will be published this fall.[2] It has, for me at least, the quality of a novel and I believe you will like it. Wait and see. 3. Have completed, lying here, awaiting its day a second book of short stories which I hold to be my best in that line. I judge by their effect on others,—not on myself. And I am not trying them on California moving picture people. 4. (This is between you and me. You must not give my title away.) *A Gallery of Women*. It contains some fifteen intimate studies of interesting women, grave and gay. They are selected from a large number of studies made. Some grave, some gay. Will you object if *Lyhon Cryhon*[3] makes one of the most colorful of them all. The Bulwark I never finished. It is half done. But I can do it now and have just contracted with Dodd Mead to finish it.[4] Another book, *Mirage*[5] is much farther along. That comes next unless I finish the *Bulwark* forthwith. 5. I have *completed*, a book of pictures of American Life. It contains some eighteen studies. One, on New York, I sold to Hearsts. Another, "Hollywood, Now," I sold to McCalls. I had a lot of letters about it. Fall River was sold to the Atlantic long ago and so on.[6]

No, Cryhon, I am not sour on life. Why should I be? In some ways I have not had a square deal. In others ways few men have had more. Or, so I feel. I am in good health. I work about five hours a day. I read some and I enjoy all that this summerland can give one, nearly. At various times, for one reason and another, I have thought of returning to N.Y. Because of The Genius,—the play, I would like to return this fall. I want to try to stage it. And I may. (Do I hear you saying "bluff"? Not at all.) Tell me about rents in your region and what chance one has of obtaining a floor or one very big room. I would like to see you again. Indeed I would. Jack[7] came alone and told me just little bits about you,—all complimentary you may be sure. And Mencken wrote me that he had dinner with you and that you treated him royally. Will you cook me a nice dinner and promise not to lecture me, much, if I come back.

I like your letter, Cryhon. I respect the spirit that prompted and that informs it. You are a big, wise, sane girl, with a wonderful grip on the facts of life and you know that I know that that is so and that I respect you as much as I like you. Only *like* isn't the word really and you know that too. You will always be Lyhon Cryhon to me.

Theo

1. Dreiser had recently completed a draft of a dramatic adaptation of his novel *The "Genius,"* but the project never went beyond this initial stage.

2. *A Book About Myself* (1922), later called *Newspaper Days*, was published in December.

3. Dreiser did not use "Lyhon Cryhon" (changed by 1928 to "Sidonie"), a semi-fictional sketch of Markham, in *A Gallery of Women* (1929), but he drew from this material a shorter sketch that eventually was published as "This Madness: The Book of Sidonie" in the June and July (1929) numbers of *Hearst's International-Cosmopolitan*.

4. See Dreiser to May Calvert, 23 July 1917, headnote. Dreiser did not finish the novel until 1945.

5. "Mirage" was Dreiser's working title for what became *An American Tragedy*. He had completed about twenty chapters at this point.

6. Dreiser never gathered these articles into book form.

7. Jack Powys. See Dreiser to Kirah Markham, 22 December 1914, n. 3.

To Kirah Markham [H-DPUP]

Dreiser responded to Markham's concerns about the portrait of her he was thinking of including in A Gallery of Women.

P.O. BOX 181
Los Angeles,
Cal.

Aug. 7, 1922

Dear Cryhon:

No, the study of you won't be anything like the other thing.[1] These are broad-gauge and intensive, things out of which I would prefer to make novels if I only had the time. You can guess how I am working when I have done nine and have not even begun on the really important ones. Of all done thus far I see only three that I would like to use. Practicing on the piano, as it were.

Whenever you talk of Howard's studies and inventions I feel that writing is a silly business.[2] Artificial anthracite. And a new petroleum series. That makes a book seem rather thin. And yet all one can do is to do what he can do, like a potato bug or a fiddler crab. It may be poor stuff but if you haven't anything else in you what are you going to do.

Do you remember how I use to encourage you with your drawings. And how I always longed to see you get a decent shot at the stage. This is the day of hard little snipes who are called upon to do little more than pose about. And the swill that is published in the magazines,—without a spark of real mood.

Yes, I saw the Gold Shod[3] and liked it. I might have known by my interest in it that there was a person back of it.

And, yes, I'll come accross with a novel, soon, now. I have done about all of the other things that I want to do.

And then the hammers.

T. D

1. The "other thing" is likely the fictional rendition of her in *The Titan*, in which the character of Stephanie Platow was loosely (and not altogether flatteringly) based on Markham. For his new work see Dreiser to Kirah Markham, 13 July 1922, n. 3.

2. Howard Scott, to whom Markham was now married, was an engineer and an advocate of a new economic theory called Technocracy, which called for an overhaul of the economic system with engineers in charge. In the 1930s this idea influenced Dreiser's social thinking by impressing him with the significance of technology in promoting a more equitable society.

3. *Gold Shod* (New York: Boni and Liveright, 1921) by Newton A. Fuessle (1883–1924), a novel about three men who miss their chances for a creative life and, to their regret, pursue careers in business and lives of economic security. Dreiser had a copy of it in his library. His syntax here suggests he is referring to a film or play, but no record of such a production has been located.

1923

To Sallie Kusell [H-UV]

Sallie Kusell (1892–1982) was born in Aurora, Illinois, and had been working for her brother Daniel Kusell, a theatrical writer and producer. Dreiser met her in the spring of 1923, when she applied to him for a secretarial cum editorial position. An aspiring writer, she began to help Dreiser to edit his writing, working principally on the first two books of An American Tragedy *and on a number of sketches that would later be included in* A Gallery of Women *(1929). At the time of this letter Dreiser had retreated to a cabin in upstate New York to work on* An American Tragedy.

Monticello, N.Y.
R.F.D. 1

Aug 4–1923

My Little Yankee Zulu:[1]

A nice sporting letter charming and full of an unchanging affection. And not being worth it I get it—forth with. But I like you much, just the same—because well—because you make yourself liked. There's something so innately decent & kindly about you that you would naturally appeal to me anyhow. I have this feeling that you couldn't be made to do a really small thing—which is wonderful, as people go. Yes, I have someone cooking for me and Gertie is here today & for this week, a little sick & run down.[2] She needs this woods even more than I do. But if I had my druthers now or anytime while I'm here I'd have you here. There's a lot that could be done between us and it would be fine to talk to you. The trouble with you is that you have a gripping sex appeal for me. I doubt—apart from that if much would be done because I'd fag myself daily & then lie about, I know. As it is I really work a lot—as you'll see, soon. But with you here we might bring about that classic tragedy discussed the night I was last with you. I've fixed up all the newspaper headlines[3] in advance. Just the same the mere thought makes me want to lay aside composition & fancy & get down to the real business of life. And your the boy that can tend to business.

Thanks for Rona[4] which you say you are sending. What about the others, now? I had a long oily letter from Liveright yesterday promising much for the future but not explaining the discrepancy. As a sop I presume he announces that the poems[5] are great. But he's such a damn liar I would not know whether he meant it or not. I'll send you his letter to read, next mail. I want to answer it first.

Sorry your lonely but cheer up. I'll fix things soon & then we'll work together for a while anyhow. And I'll try to balance play with some work anyhow. It's bright & yet cool here today—rained all night. I'm writing at an improvised table under a tree—in a small thicket really. Flies, worms, spiders & mosquitoes visit or buzz about but not enough to disturb my work. And I'm breathing pure air—lots of it. When I think of N.Y.—I only think that I don't want to think of it. But when I think of you—well thats something else again—a nice girl, a good sport—a good fellow—and a genuine spiritual help. The other part you know. Love & whatever else you would like.

John—The Piper's Son

Or

TD

1. A term of affection, not unlike Othello's "my fair warrior" for Desdemona.

2. Gertrude Nelson was Dreiser's niece (the daughter of his sister Emma) who stayed two weeks longer than Dreiser notes here. She and Helen Richardson (the "someone cooking for me") were at a woodland cabin that Dreiser had rented for the summer at Monticello, New York. He had discovered the site on an earlier research trip with Richardson to the site of the 1906 Chester Gillette-Grace Brown murder trial, upon which he was basing *An American Tragedy*. See Dreiser to Helen Richardson, 1 December 1923, n. 5.

3. Dreiser is referring to headlines and newspaper clippings concerning the Gillette-Brown case, which he collected and used as a biographical source for the "classic tragedy" that he was writing.

4. "Rona Murtha," one of the portraits included in *A Gallery of Women*; it is loosely based on events in the life of Anna Mallon, the second wife of Dreiser's friend Arthur Henry (see Dreiser to Helen Richardson, 21 April 1924, n. 2).

5. Dreiser was generally annoyed at his publisher, Horace Liveright, for delaying a new issue of *The "Genius"* (1915) in an attempt to accommodate *Metropolitan* magazine, which at the time was running a condensed serialization of the novel. Liveright published the poems Dreiser is referring to as *Moods, Cadenced and Declaimed* (1926).

To Sallie Kusell [H-UV]

Monticello, N.Y.

Tuesday, I guess

Aug 7–1923

Dear Sallie:

(Did you know that Mrs. D's first name was Sallie!)[1]

Received Rona and have already revised it—its final revision. Shall I send it back for two copies for my files? Have had three letters so far—one

Sallie Kusell.

today and they read charmingly. But I wish you wouldn't worry & would be a little patient. I'm not going to leave you. And I'm not going to stay here beyond September! Don't want to. At the same time I expect to be in before then—a day or two anyhow—to see you. My one interest now is this novel[2] and I want you to help me with it. I feel that I need your encouragement & honest critical help. So I expect to arrange things so that we can work together on it. And there's no one here but Gertie and a farmer & his wife about a block up the road who provide meals.[3] I have a card today from Mencken indicating that he would like to drift up here.[4] And there are some others who would like to come but wont be allowed. I am sleeping pretty well at nights & not doing a thing the most puritan person in the world would object to. I really need to build up a little energy in the fresh air & hope to. The first week I was here I felt as limp as a cat—no energy at all and no strength. Just now I am feeling better.

I'm sorry its so hot in New York & that you are so depressed. I wish you were more interested in just life and could communicate some of it to me. I need more zest for just the humdrum face of things. And if you have none at all either!

Wish you could find it in your heart to clean up those other studies[5] so that they will be out of the way. But if you can't—and I don't think you ought to try if this job palls on you, I think they ought to be returned to me—gotten out of your sight & mine—for the time being. Its best always. Then as soon as I get six chapters of the new book I'll send them in—or bring them & you can tell me what you think.

Enclosed is Liveright's letter.[6] Send it back. And don't think that I don't think of you. There are almost too many times when I stop & think of what we do & where & how. The woods around here are delightful. And this cabin itself would be an ideal place for two—for a while. Have a little patience with me & see.

T. D

1. Dreiser's reference is to his first wife, Sara Osborne White, who was known as "Sallie" to her friends.

2. *An American Tragedy*.

3. Helen Richardson had returned to New York City. It was the beginning of what turned out to be a long estrangement in which she moved to the West Coast to visit her family in Oregon and to try to revive her film career in Hollywood. For Richardson, see Dreiser to Helen Richardson, 1 December 1923, headnote.

4. At this time Mencken was hard at work preparing the first issue of his journal *American Mercury* and expressed no interest in visiting Dreiser, whom he jokingly suggested should return to the city for the sake of his health (see H. L. Mencken to Dreiser, 2 August 1923, in Riggio, *Dreiser-Mencken Letters*, II, 498.)

5. Dreiser is referring to a number of sketches for *A Gallery of Women*, which Kusell was editing and typing.

6. Unidentified.

To Sallie Kusell [H-UV]

Monticello, N.Y.

Aug 16–1923

Dearie:

No letter from me? Seems to me I've been doing exceptionally well—writing almost every day—every other day anyhow. And that in the face of the damndest qualms & struggles in connection with this book. I have written & written & at last I hope—and if I dont get cold feet on it & change it again, gotten a fair start. The trouble with me when I set out to write a novel is that I worry so over the sure even progress of it. I start & start & change & change. Have done so with nearly every one. What I really ought to have is someone who could decide for me—once & for all when I have gotten the right start—when I am really going ahead—or one who would take all the phrases I pen down & piece them together into the true story as I see it. That is what I eventually do for myself—but oh, the struggles & the flounderings. Am working right along, however, have about six or seven chapters done—maybe more & will bring them in.

By the by, expect to be down Saturday & Sunday. Have various things to do & will have to do them in order—see Liveright, see Towne,[1] straighten out a mistake at my bank, get my sister to give up my apartment for a few days,[2] see my doctor (Rosenthal) about a constant nausea & headache that is troubling me—and so on. But I'll see you not long after I get in—will ring you—if your in town—and of course.

I liked the letter I got today very much—the one about your inability to take an interest in ordinary things. It's very plain your not an ordinary person—and I like that, too, only it makes life hard to endure at times—dreadful. The ordinary individual can so easily lose himself in little things—"petty larceny" you call them—and you cant! I often wish that I could. And I liked the poem. It's good & it's very like you—so like your despondent moods. And yet at times you can get such an immense kick out of things—seeing me for one. It makes me laugh at times. And yet I can relish the zest of that apart from me. I like to see you light up over anything—even over such a bag of wood as myself.

Sorry I cant be with you to see some of these shows you are seeing. Are there any good ones—I wouldn't mind seeing a real live one. By the way I finished Will Shakespeare the other day & liked it ever so much. Theres something quite noble about it—Shakespearean, almost although it does run a little thin in spots. Shake—in this play—is almost as poor a lover as I am. He puts no verbal kick into his love—or no fire into his few protestations. The most moving person is Ann Hathaway.[3]

But I cant ramble on like this. The mailman is due down the road here in about 10 minutes and I want to hand him this. But I'll see you Sunday I hope. And I'll bring down what I have written. And we'll talk things over. And maybe do a few things just to show how we feel. What? Yes or no. Much love & I wish you were here now.

T.

1. Charles Hanson Towne (1877–1949), editor, actor, poet, literary agent. In 1907 Towne left *Smart Set* to join Dreiser's staff at *The Delineator*, where he was a fiction editor; he later served as Dreiser's agent for a short period.

Horace Liveright: see Dreiser to May Calvert Baker, 16 August 1919, n.1.

2. The sister Dreiser is referring to here is either Gertie's mother Emma or her aunt Sylvia.

3. The play Dreiser mentions having read, *Will Shakespeare*, was written by Winifred Aston (1888–1965) under the pseudonym Clemence Dane. She was a novelist, screenwriter, playwright, actress, and director. A number of her plays were produced on Broadway, including *Will Shakespeare*, which opened at the National Theater on 1 January 1923 and ran for eighty performances. Apparently Dreiser had not seen it.

To Marion Bloom [Maritzer] [H-DPUP]

Marion Bloom was the sister of Estelle Bloom Kubitz, who from 1916 to 1919 had a sustained if problematic affair with Dreiser (for the details from Dreiser's perspective, see Riggio, American Diaries, *147–256). Marion Bloom was at the time the companion of H. L. Mencken, and the sisters often lived together and socialized with the two men as a foursome (see Martin,* In Defense of Marion*).*

118 W. 11th St.
N. Y. C.

Nov. 7, 1923

Dear Marion:

Certainly I'll be glad to blow down sometime & camp on your roof or in the vicinity. Maybe a standard hotel would help out on the sleeping problem. And I'll be pleased to meet Maritzer[1] too. I have no prejudices against individuals anywhere. It's masses that give me the large ache—masses that you have to conciliate and can't do anything but dodge. I'm glad you're happily married & hope it works out OK—and for good if it will give you any peace of mind.

I didn't know that Little Bo[2] was in the U.S. I thought she went abroad. Deep down in my central works somewhere I always miss Bosie. She has a spirit that belongs in a dream somewhere. This shabby world is not good enough for it. But don't show this to the 100 percent. It might end my novel[3] where it now stands—1/2 done.

That by the way is keeping my short, unattractive nose close to the grindstone. While it may improve the nose it comforts me not at all. Writing is hard work for me. And if you see Bosie, whisper that she's as close to me spiritually as any mortal will ever be.

T. D

1. Bloom had recently been married to L. S. Maritzer and lived in Washington, D.C.

2. Little Bo and Bosie were among the nicknames Dreiser used for Estelle Bloom Kubitz.

3. *An American Tragedy*.

To Helen Richardson [H-DPUP]

Dreiser's relationship with Helen Patges Richardson (1894–1955) began on 13 September 1919, when they started a long, tempestuous relationship that culminated in their marriage nearly twenty-five years later. Dreiser describes that encounter in his diary: "This day I met Helen. Don't remember much about the morning. Was reading at 11 A.M. when door bell rang." She introduced herself as a cousin, "a 2nd cousin rather distantly removed," and told Dreiser that she was looking for the address of Ed Dresser, the stage name of his brother. Helen was an aspiring actress who had already appeared in vaudeville. "So fascinated I invited her in . . . I learn that she is married and 20 years of age." She was twenty-five, not twenty, but she was indeed a relative: Helen's grandmother (Esther Schänäb Parks) and Dreiser's mother (Sarah Schänäb Dreiser) were sisters. A month after their meeting Dreiser abandoned the familiar New York associations of twenty-five years and accompanied Helen to Los Angeles, where he worked unsuccessfully on The Bulwark *and began what was to become* An American Tragedy, *while she worked in minor roles at the film studios. In October 1922 they returned to New York and there began the pattern of long periods of companionship alternating with interludes of separation that lasted until Dreiser's death. The fullest record of their life together is her memoir,* My Life with Dreiser *(1951).*

At the time of Dreiser's 1923–24 letters to "Babu," his pet name for her, he and Helen were estranged. She had decided to try to revive her acting career in California, where she would also be closer to her mother and sister who lived in Oregon. She did not leave New York, however, until March 1924. Dreiser was in the process of writing An American Tragedy *and was feeling the strain of separation even while she was still living near him. His letters to her both before and after her departure are filled with jealousy, wistful memories of their first years together in Los Angeles and New York, pleas for her to return to him, accounts of his daily activities, and reflections on his novel in progress.*

[1 December 1923]

A Letter for Babu

Babu:

There is something different, something at once mystical & magical about this union between you & me. The way you came to my door,[1] the perfection of beauty that you represented, the perfection of intelligence. I

Helen Richardson.

had known so many. Could one more mean anything—anything more, I mean. And lo & behold not one more—but you—you could & did. The something of youth that came with you—real youth,—springtime. The perfection of romance that carried me entirely beyond the confines of the commonplace and watered my soul as a spring waters a dry and over parched plain. Will I ever forget the voyage south[2]—Key West—like a fairy city accross the waters; the gulf & the flying fish, the Mississippi in the dark of the mornings with its huts & plantations—New Orleans—so hot, so romantic, so Negroid!

The little restaurants, the boats & the clouds of Lake Ponchatrain;[3] the clouds to the west of our verandah where I was sick & Babu made me celery soup. And the gay whites and yellows & blues of your hats & dresses. The classic freedom of your body, your heart, your mind.

Dream with me of New Orleans, Babu—*always*. Dream with me.

And then the long trek to Los Angles. The plains, Denver, Salt Lake and at last L.A. And then the Stillwell, the hours in Alvardo, the house in Highland Park! And the hills. And the little cat. And Babu in summer things always dreaming sweet dreams and viewing sweet scenes. And I with her—happy-happy—for once in my life & at last.

Those evening strolls at sunset—the shadows of the green hills about. Our little bedroom. Our car & motor trips to strange places—San Diego, Santa Barbara, Tia Juana. When I think of the road by the sea to San Diego, to Santa Barbara, little Babu in the car beside, the clouds, the winds, the sunlight the romance of the west and of Babu I know that I seek in vain elsewhere for what I already have. Every hour in Larchmont, in "*Vanbun Vay*,"[4] in Vine and Detroit Streets was too perfect. I think of the great studios, the car, the walks & drives to the shore, the Virginia Hotel, the houses in Beverly Hills one of which we dreamed to own—and somehow my heart sings & cries at once not for beauty missed but for beauty garnered, garnered, garnered—sheaf on sheaf & row on row.

And the song cycle of Glendale above the little house—the little flowers, the flower boxes we made, the little garden I kept. And Babu. And beauty. And the car. No wonder rainbows double & treble arched the skies at times. They were telling of what was—not of what might be.

And here in dreary New York, for all its sorrows. Still I think of the ride toward the sun & Montauk Point—our days in woods on Long Island. Our long ride to Big Moose[5] & all the happy nights—to Atlantic City—to[6] in the Spring.

Ah, Babu love is not dead in my heart—nor romance. I am crying as I write & I am not ashamed. I have cried. I cry not for sorrow but for beauty achieved—the golden bowl placed in my hands and held still, unbroken. Its beauty—the beauty of all of this—all . . . all—is deathless. For me it can never die.

T. D.
New York, Dec. 1–1923

1. Dreiser is referring to their initial meeting. Sometime in 1924, when Helen was in Hollywood, he wrote the following reminiscence of that day:

> HELEN
>
> With what words may one pen one's deepest emotions. With what colors paint that which appears to be the essence and hence the evasion of all sharp shades. I can begin in no better way I think than by referring to a certain gray windy day in September of a certain year when seated at my desk in 10th Street New York, writing, my door bell rang and I sat there for a few moments wondering whether I should answer. The drag and almost despair of a dreary interlude was upon me. At best one feeds so much on husks. Af-

fairs begin & affairs end. But before they end, whatever they are, there is a period of wretched retrospect and dark foreboding than which there would be nothing darker or more dreary. I have described various personages & identified myself with them. Among them, if one looked sharp might be several of those—the romance with whom had paled to greys & sombre days. My soul was really sick of this malaise that concerns the black lees of once sparkling cups. Must romance ever end in disillusion. Must my dreamful searchings for delight end where black night was settling upon a bleak & pathless moor. I was thinking so as I wrote.

And then this ring.

It was repeated.

I got up & slipping on a blue Chinese working coat that lay near me—in order, always, to make myself somewhat more presentable if needs must, I strode to the door. In doing so I noticed I had slipped on the coat wrong side out—a most drastic and inescapable and invariable sign of change. I had never known it to fail. Yet since it looked as well either way—the inside as well stiched as the outside, I left it. The bell rang again & peeping through a dark brown silk curtain which protected the panes of the outer door I observed a girl of not more than nineteen or twenty—I would have said at the most. She was dressed in a long slate blue afternoon frock with a large floppy slate blue hat, in which was fastened a single, immense, and very faintly tinted but delightfully harmonious old rose tinted rose. I opened the door. At once visiting me with such a youthful gladsome, innocent-seeming smile such as I had not (I would have said at the moment) seen in years, she inquired if I knew where I lived, reciting my full name "Here. And I am the person." "Well, then, I am your cousin V's neice" she promptly trilled "and she made me promise—" "If you're my cousin V's neice or any relationship to me near or far come right in," I interrupted welcoming her as I would a beam of light in a dungeon. And her smile & her eyes were all light. I would scarcely have imagined up to that moment that any so glorious a maid could have been kin to me. A painted flower in a meadow, say, as contrasted with a coarse weed in a city lot. A little mincing gazelle and a tusked boar—wild & evil. Pierrette decked for a May party and old Boreas scowling darkly by her side. And yet I was trying to smile—and be young of heart—and was achieving something—I would scarcely venture what. Who is it that has written "Making a gay sun to shine in the dim hearts of those who find beauty a need."

2. Dreiser is here describing their first trip to Los Angeles. On 8 October 1919 they left by boat and leisurely made their way to New Orleans, where they vacationed; from there they traveled by train, first to St. Louis and then west to Los Angeles, arriving in early November.

3. The correct spelling is Pontchartrain.

4. Apparently a private joke between them, a street name they pronounced with a German accent. They stayed in various places in Los Angeles, finally settling in a small house in Glendale.

5. As part of his research for *An American Tragedy*, Dreiser and Richardson visited Big Moose Lake in upstate New York, the site of the murder of Grace Brown by Chester Gillette. For her version of the event, see Dreiser, *My Life with Dreiser*, 83–85.

6. Dreiser left a blank space at this point in the letter.

1924

To Helen Richardson [H-DPUP]

118 W. 11th St

Wednesday

April 2–1924
Babu:

Well this makes the 10th letter to you without one to me in return. And before this I was to have heard about the car.[1] I think it must be that your mood in regard to me is very variable. Or you are working out—or trying to—some policy in connection with me. I needn't trouble to wonder, I presume, since the coming days will presently show. But yesterday when I got no word & today none I was much reduced—very. I was so disappointed yesterday that I said well if she doesn't want to write me I certainly am not going to write her. But this morning, after getting no word, I am writing again. There is a heavy snow on the ground here today. It snowed all day yesterday most heavily. And the trees in these yards here & in Washington Square looked as though they had been outlined in cotton—regular Christmas Card Christmas trees. And Sunday was exactly like May or June. Last night after working all day here until 8^{30} p.m. I called up Jack[2] but he wasn't in. Then I went round to Llewelyn[3] & found him wrapped up in a red shawl basting his toes before a fire & writing. He looked just like an old English farmer. I wanted to go again because he was writing but he wouldn't let me. His sister Katie who looks very much like Jack only—if anything more wild—was getting him a little supper on the top floor. Nothing would do but I must stay to that, too. Alyse Gregory[4] wasn't there (working). We went up at 9 & talked of Whitman, Poe, Africa, Virginia, Greenwich Village. Jack had taken Kate over to see Walt Whitman's house in Camden.[5] Also his grave was there. (What a shrine lover he is.) The caretaker was not present. The house closed. But Jack hoisted Kate through a window which they found loose & she sat in Whitman's chair. So delight reigns.

Llewelyn asked after you. At 11 Alyse Gregory arrived & she asked after you. And I wished you were there. It was all so amusing & pleasant. Then I came back here.

How do you feel, Babu?

How are you?

What are you doing in Portland.[6]

Shall I cease writing you so regularly

I think I must:
I think maybe you want me to—for your own ease.
Is that so.

TD

1. A Maxwell that he and Helen had bought in 1922 while living in Hollywood. Before she left for the West Coast, they had agreed that he would sell the car and send the proceeds of the sale to her. He had recently found a buyer and was waiting for her approval on the matter.
2. John Cowper Powys. See Dreiser to Kirah Markham, 22 December 1914, n. 3.
3. Llewelyn Powys (1884–1939), author and brother of John Cowper Powys.
4. Alyse Gregory was married to Llewelyn Powys.
5. The poet Walt Whitman (1819–92) spent his last years at his home in Camden, New Jersey.
6. Richardson had been visiting her family in Portland, Oregon.

To Helen Richardson [H-DPUP]

118 W. 11th

Wed. April 16–1924

Dearest:

Well at last I got word as to where you were going. I thought, at first, since you kept talking of going but said nothing as to where, that you & Myrtle[1] might be heading for San Francisco temporarily. And maybe you were. But anyhow you changed your mind. On hearing, yesterday, that Tuesday—the 15th was your last day in Portland I wired there about selling the car.[2] Now I'm hesitating as to whether to send the check to General Delivery or wait until I get an address. But I think I'll send it on. Only I wont have it until Monday. I have $100 on account & the balance Monday, when I will turn over the car. He is in the advertising business but is going to take the car out to his mother who lives in New Jersey somewhere—Rutherford, I believe. Farewell to the little boat.

You ask who I'm going with, meaning, what lady have I picked on to devote myself too. *None.* My socializing so far has been slight & very general. Last night—Tuesday for instance, I worked here until 11:30 without any dinner. At 4 p.m. I went over to that little hot dog place at 14th & 7th and ate one dog & two crullers. Then I came back & worked on. Monday night I went with Ernest Boyd[3] & his wife to see a new show at the Provincetown Players—a dramatization of The Ancient Mariner by Eugene O'Neill.[4] They've decided not to do All God's Chillun[5] for the present anyhow. But it wasn't very good as I saw it—an attempt at the fantastic that wasn't successful. One day last week I went to Zoe Akins because Mencken & Nathan & Van Vechten[6] were going to be there. I met a half dozen men & women—one of the latter a smart dressmaker on Fifth Avenue who claimed to be an enthusiastic admirer of mine but I've since forgotten her name. She pretends to be French but I think is Jewish and her first name is Louise. I was interested in her because Miss Akins insisted that she had as many really smart people as any dressmaker in New York—among them some duchess now living here and Mrs. E. R. Thomas, wife of the Domas Flyer (that was).[7] For this coming Saturday & Sunday, if I choose to go—which I doubt very much if I will—I am invited to Laurette Taylor's[8] place above Ardsley. This comes through Tom Smith[9] who knows her very well. I suppose he has been talking to her about me. But as I say, I am not very much interested & may not go at all.

All along, as I have been indicating, I think I have been giving nearly all of my time to this book. Two to three evenings a week will cover the times I have been out—sometimes to no more than a moving picture. Since you went away I have not wanted to go anywhere very much—been in the doldrums. I have suffered a great deal, thinking about you & us & that has not made me feel very social toward anyone. I have not wanted to see any particular person and do not wish to now. Apart from my work my mood has been diffuse & I have not wished to see anyone in particular. I have gone here & there—exactly as my letters have indicated. If I were in the mood for it, it would be no trouble to build up a whole chain of affairs & people—but I am in no such mood. This book & your going away seem to make a combination which holds me steadily here—by myself. I like to think of you & what you are doing. And I like to work on this book.

I may as well confess that I will never be able to write this book fast: It is too intricate in its thought & somehow my method if not my style has changed. I work with more care and hence more difficulty. My style isn't as fluid. Whether its worse I cant say—yet. Two to three chapters a week is the best I can do. But I am not discouraged & I am making progress. In fact I am surer now than I have been in a long time that I will bring it to a successful conclusion. And that explains why I said I was getting along & doing better—also why I said that I was looking to do two chapters in three days. I should have said three in a week.

However I must stop here now. I have a lot of things to do. But your back in L. A.—think of that. And I'll hear now, soon what you think of things down there. Love & the very best of luck Babu.

T. D

1. Myrtle Patges, Helen's sister.
2. See Dreiser to Helen Richardson, 2 April 1924, n. 1.
3. Ernest Boyd (1887–1946), Irish born critic, editor, and diplomat who had served in the British consular service in Baltimore until 1920.
4. A dramatization of Samuel Taylor Coleridge's "The Ancient Mariner" by Eugene O'Neill (1888–1953) opened on 6 April 1924 at the Provincetown Playhouse and ran for thirty-three performances.
5. *All God's Chillun Got Wings* (1924), a play by O'Neill.
6. Zöe Akins (1886–1958), playwright, poet, writer, critic.
George Jean Nathan (1882–1958), drama critic, editor.
Carl Van Vechten (1880–1964) music critic, author, photographer.
7. Dreiser's playful spelling of the "Thomas Flyer," a four-cylinder automobile produced by Erwing R. Thomas, which entered international racing competition in 1907 and became famous for its design and speed. The company stopped manufacturing the car in 1912.
8. Laurette Taylor (1884–1946), actress.
9. Tom Smith, editor at Boni and Liveright who was working with Dreiser on *An American Tragedy*.

To Helen Richardson [H-DPUP]

118 W. 11th St
N.Y.

April 21–1924

Dearest:

Here is the check & please acknowledge receipt by wire collect.[1] I want to know that you receive it promptly. Saturday was a lovely day here—beautiful & at seven after eating here with Mame went for a walk & walked from here through the East Side and accross Williamsburg Bridge—a wonderful walk into Brooklyn. From there I walked south to Brooklyn Bridge & back accross that to Park Place Subway. And all alone. There was a full moon—brilliant. On both bridges all the way accross were fellows and girls walking together or trying to make a mark. Spring sure enough. I got back at midnight quite tired & went straight to bed.

Yesterday Easter—in spite of the wonderful Saturday it rained all day so as to spoil Easter for everybody. So thoughtful that. I think it absolutely malicious & intentional. Today it is bright again—when all have to work. Divine mind, as it were, at its best yesterday. I wrote here from 1 to 6. Then went up to Henry's.[2] He had one dramatic critic—Alexander Woolcott[3] & two actors besides his son-in-law—or rather Clare's[4] & her daughters. She is sick in bed with grippe & didn't come out at all. I got into a knock down & drag out fight over Shakespeare & New York critics. A fine evening. But the dinner was good. And there was plenty to drink and I didn't get drunk. But

I felt pretty good even after the fight. I wished you were there. You would have enjoyed it. Decided not to go to the Peg-o-my-Heart lady.[5] Too far & I didn't want to come down on a late train.

You ask so many questions. And I know you think I have a girl hanging on my arm every night. I'm like a poor man who gets credit for being enormously wealthy. (Now don't throw anything.) Just the same I'm presenting an honest picture. I have four invitations for this week—now. One to Oppenheims[6]—for tonight—if I wish. One to Van Vechtens[7] for Tuesday one to Claire Burkes[8] for Thursday—because Mencken etc are going to be there. One to Mrs. Hackville Johnsons in Madison Square. She is the daughter of H. M. Breen who used to edit the Metropolitan[9]—have to interview me for a movie paper. Her father is coming here on Friday. I haven't seen him since 1907. Hence the invite to dinner. But whether I'll go or not remains to be seen. I suppose other things will crop up. They usually do. But I dodge a lot and I like to work here by myself more these days than at any other time. Somehow when I'm away from other people & just here I feel nearer to you. It's like a wireless station in touch with another. Your thoughts come here to me.[10] I think. I hope so.

Didn't sleep good at all last night. But I'll be well enough to work. I'm sure. No one ever replaces you in my regard Babu. Not for an hour. I wish so much for you out there—for us. Don't let that fierce disease get hold of you.[11]

T. D.

1. Dreiser sent money owed her on the sale of their car. See Dreiser to Helen Richardson, 2 April 1924, n. 1.

2. Arthur Henry (1867–1934), journalist and author who helped Dreiser edit *Sister Carrie* and to whom the novel was dedicated. (See Dreiser to Emma Rector, 4 April 1894, n. 1.) A rift in their friendship had occurred over Henry's unflattering portrait of Dreiser (thinly disguised under the name "Tom") in *An Island Cabin* (1904), in which Henry described Dreiser's brief stay with him on an island off the Connecticut shore in the summer of 1901. Despite the initial hard feelings, the men socialized much afterwards, though their friendship never recovered its former intimacy.

3. Alexander Woolcott (1887–1943), playwright, drama critic, founder of the Algonquin Round Table, and humorist known for his biting wit.

4. Clare Kummer (1873–1958), playwright who was married to Arthur Henry.

5. Laurette Taylor (1884–1986), called the "Peg-o-My-Heart Lady" after she had starred in a popular stage play named *Peg O' My Heart*. The song of the same name was the winning entry in a contest to promote the play, and Taylor's picture on the cover of the sheet music secured her identification with it.

6. James Oppenheim (1882–1932), editor, poet, novelist, author of self-help books on topics such as marriage, sexuality, and writing.

7. See Dreiser to Helen Richardson, 16 April 1924, n. 6.

8. Claire Burke. See Dreiser to Kirah Markham, 25 October 1916, n. 9.

9. Dreiser had often contributed to the *Metropolitan Magazine* during his days as a freelance writer when Breen was its editor.

10. For Dreiser's belief in mental telepathy, see Dreiser to Kirah Markham, 9 February 1914, n. 1.

11. Dreiser is referring to the "infectious" nature of the allure of Hollywood.

To Helen Richardson [H-DPUP]

118 W. 11th St

Saturday, April 27–1924

Babuchka:

This is Sunday again—bright & warm for once, after a week of mostly grey, windy weather and because it's so fine I'm wishing you were here & that we had the car, and that you were in just the mood for an outing. I'd like to ride out along the canal—or near it & maybe stay all night in some little country hotel. Remember the one over near Port Jervis where we first heard "*Bear to the Left*."[1] That was the day we rode along the Delaware clear to Phila & back. And now I am wondering if ever such delightful rides & days will come again to me.

Gertie[2] is coming down this morning. She's up & around taking injections of something direct into the veins—and I think I'll take her out to Long Beach. The trains go so close to the beach. But I wish it was you instead. However, your so down on me that there's no use thinking of any such things any how and I might as well be trying not to think so much as to give myself over to thoughts of you so constantly. But I'm thinking of the time we went out & bathed in the sea there & then ate the hotdogs at the little stand on the corner. Happiness—that intangible distillation of the mind—made that trip & others like it perfect for me.

Went last night with Henry to see Fashion.[3] It's picturesque & funny because it is old fashioned & out of date. Quaint is a better word. I like it. A note on the program said that Kirah[4] selected & arranged all the costumes—a rather fine piece of work I thought.

You dont rave over Los Angeles very much—or Hollywood either. I'm thinking your finding something wrong with it—or what is it? Just a first days impression. Maybe by now you like it better. I wish you'd write me more about it. But your letters to me are very brief & non-committal. I'm beginning to think that apart from business you dont want much of anything to do with me—which wont do at all. I wouldn't want you as just a business partner. I wouldn't get much kick out of that.

Here comes Gertie now,—very spruce looking for person who was almost dying a fortnight ago. I'll wind up for the present hoping for a nice letter in the morning. But I wish it were you I was taking instead of her.

T. D.

B&L dont like "An American Tragedy" as a title. What do you think of *Orion* or *Icarus* or *Xion*.[5] These are all Greek heroes or fabled characters who were misled by & suffered through love. I have still another, *The Love Cast*.

1. "Bear to the Left," a popular song they heard while on a trip to Pennsylvania. Port Jervis, where they stayed briefly, is an upstate New York town situated near the border between New Jersey and Pennsylvania.

2. Gertrude Nelson. See Dreiser to Sallie Kusell, 4 August 1923, n. 2.

3. *Fashion*, by Anna Cora Mowatt, opened at the Provincetown Playhouse on 2 February 1924 and ran for 152 performances. For Arthur Henry, see Dreiser to Helen Richardson, 21 April 1924, n. 2.

4. Kirah Markham was still involved in many aspects of theater production.

5. Dreiser is referring to the opinion of his publisher, Boni and Liveright. *An American Tragedy* tells the story of a poor young man who falls in love with a rich girl, whose main charm for him is her social position. The characters from Greek mythology that Dreiser lists here are doomed over-reachers who commit analogous mistakes, though romantic love is not always the motive. Among these, Dreiser probably does not mean Xion but Ixion, who developed a passion for Hera, the wife of Zeus, for which he was punished.

To Helen Richardson [H-DPUP]

118 W. 11th St

May 3–1924

Dearest Deario:

Two really fine letters from you yesterday. I liked them, ever so much. They cheered me up. But I got a laugh when you referred to my nice new stationary! I only got 1 box of 25 sheets & envelopes & it cost me exactly 39 cents. But they only had this one box left—in a cheap kyke[1] place in Broadway. And its nearly all gone—about 8 sheets left. The stationary I want to get cost me 52^{oo} for 2000 sheets and envelopes (wholesale) or about 70 or 75 cents a box of 25 sheets & envelopes. Which—wholesale—I consider much too much, so I'm looking for a cheaper deal.

This morning I had to go up to the library early to see if I could find—painting or drawing of Icarus falling into the sea. I want it to put on the cover of the book—stamped in green gold. And she showed me a whole book of prints of classic characters drawn by various artists—8–10–15 sketches or reproductions of paintings of each one. Ariadne, Psyche, Hebe, Venus, Minerva, the Bachants, the Menaedae, Helen, Pandora—a long company. And I staid two hours examining them & thinking of the temperaments & skills—or lack of it, of the various sculptors & painters who had done these things—from Greek days on. But among all of them, do you know, I did not find one as beautiful as you or that I thought could have posed as well as you. I was thinking for instance of us up in the little cottage near Port Jarvis[2] & how wonderful you looked when I poured the cold water on you outside the door—or as I have so often seen you fixing your hair & passing around in front of the mirror. You always look so brisk & vital & perfect really. Sometimes I look at the pictures I have of you here & I can scarcely believe that anyone could be so beautiful & not be a sexsation. No one ever sees the pictures I have here of you without commenting on them—not a person that I know. I often regret that you couldn't have gotten into the movies on your own terms just so that your beauty & imagination could not have gotten over to the public. They would have loved them so—& you, of course, because they are you. But as I looked at all of those studies, made in various centuries & lands I wished sincerely that you might have posed for some of the best—beginning with Praxiteles.[3]

Is Los Angeles really so marvelous to you. You speak of that lot in Beverley 75 x 145 going for $5,000. When we were there it could have been had for half that. I'm positive myself that there is to be a very large city there and perhaps one of the wealthiest in the world. And I do wish that we might pick up a building lot in some ideal spot there—Beverley is as good as any—& pay for it on time & so hold it. It could be sold if anything better came up. But at least we would have a site reserved.

You say I don't write you any intimate loving things anymore. No? Well, I think them. Also I thought I had. So often I can just see you coming into the rooms so eager for affection—"hold me"—and so often I feel you beside me & wish you were. Most certainly I'd gather my Babu close & pet her nice beautiful, smooth body. No one in the world that I have ever seen has had a body as really classic in its lines as yours. I once told you that you had a body so beautiful that it rather quieted passion because of its perfection & I meant that. It has that effect at times. At other times your own imagination transforms the beauty or rather infuses it with a lust that is terrible & beautiful, too. Don't think I don't think back or forward because I do.

And today is Saturday—& lovely & I'm wishing you were here to go out in the country with me. Instead being alone I'm sticking right here & working & will be here till evening. You ask how I'm getting along on the book. Pretty good. It's slow work but I'm moving ahead. When I finish part two even I'm going to celebrate for then I'll know that the top of the range is crossed & I'm descending the other side & quickly. For the approach of this story is longer than the conclusion.

I'm so glad you like L.A. & are getting a kick out of it. When I finish this book—& as soon as I do, I'll come out & we'll go to China if you wish. I'll take along my other things & work over there awhile. Love & kisses. I'd like to hold you in my lap now & tell you how much I have missed you.

T. D

If you see Ettinge[4] say hello. And how is your German movie man?[5]

I mailed—registered—the $1,000 check to you yesterday.[6]

1. The word "kyke" (or "kike") is a slang term for a Jew, especially of Eastern European origin, usually taken to be offensive—at the time the equivalent of "wop" for an Italian or "chink" for a Chinese person.

2. Dreiser misspelled Port Jervis. See Dreiser to Helen Richardson, 27 April 1924, n. 1.

3. Praxiteles was an Athenian sculptor of the fourth century BC.

4. James A. Ettinge was a dedicated friend and devotee. He served as a general factotum to Dreiser for years, both in New York and Los Angeles.

5. In her letters Helen often wrote about her various admirers in Los Angeles, deliberately fueling Dreiser's jealousy. An unidentified bit actor, this "German movie man" had become a running tease between them.

6. Dreiser wrote this note on a diagonal in the top left-hand corner of the first page. He is referring to the money he received from the sale of their car.

To Helen Richardson [H-DPUP]

118 W. 11th St

Friday, May 9–1924

Dearest:

Did you get the $1,000. It should have reached you Tuesday or Wednesday. I'm hoping to hear by Monday anyhow, that it came safely to hand.

There isn't a single thing doing with me except for pen pushing. Last night I went to dinner with that Burleigh Rodick[1] & heard all the news in connection with him. He's trying for a job in connection with the International Peace Court at The Hague[2] as an expert on International Law and thinks he will make the job, start himself off as an international lawyer & diplomat and maybe he will. He has a plodding determination which interests me. Among things—a book of short stories finished, etc. he's just about to be granted a Ph.D. (Columbia) for a paper on International law. Not so dumb, apparently. And Liveright is going to bring out his book on me.[3] The other night as I told you I saw The Emperor Jones.[4] It's an interesting play—very good in its way but like most of O'Neill's things based on a false assumption—in this case that a negro who had murdered several people, stolen money & escaped to Africa[5] would be driven mad with fear of his African subjects who had turned on him. I rather doubt it. Desperate criminals don't often go to pieces so long as there is a fighting chance. However, apart from this notion that rather haunted me as I saw the play, I liked it. It is different & has color. Helen Freeman[6] who had seen it before seemed to think it was without flaw. So there you are. Afterwards she & I & James Light, the present stage manager of the Provincetown Players, went down into a Chinese Restaurant which is next door in a basement—(run by Chinese Columbia College Students by the way) and had some chop suey. Afterwards I left her at her apartment in East 9th Street—off Fifth where she is living with her mother & father, she says. After the show we had a long discussion as to the value or true purpose of scenery in connection with a play. My contention is that the more suggestive & less real—the more symbolic really—that scenery is the better as long as it really contributes to the art or mood of the play, whatever it is. This man Light & for that matter Helen Freeman agreed with me mostly—& toward the end I didn't think the scenery for The Emperor Jones in this instance was as suggestive of Africa & the jungle as it might have been.

Today, for some reason, I have been feeling nearer to you than yesterday or the day before. Some days for no reason known to me, I feel as though you were miles away—not interested in me in the least—the psychic chain completely broken. Again it seems to be renewed. And my mind, even while I'm working, keeps running on where you are & what your doing & what thinking, or it takes up some thing we've done together like going down to Atlantic City last time & stopping at Tom's River for lunch and passing through all those lonely little Jersey towns along the coast. But I was never lonely sitting beside you anywhere. Are you getting used to being away from me. And is that why I feel so far off some days? I would be surprised. When I read a hard dogmatic letter such as you wrote me the other day I feel for a time as though I would never want to be with you if you are going to become like that. Then when the anger goes I feel too sad to think of anything contentious in connection with you. I just think of all the times that were perfect—and the times that might be again.

Mame's tea room opens tomorrow night.[7] I saw it for a moment yesterday morning. It looks fine—really very pretty. And she's been around to Wanamakers & bamboozled some twenty or thirty department heads over there into believing in her. I fancy she'll get along. If she does most certainly I will clear out of here, once & for all.

Dreamed of you last night. But dreamed that you were quarreling with me because of some place I had been without you. I was trying to hold you but you pushed me away. I woke up thinking you were beside me for the moment but had gotten clear over on your side of the bed. Then I realized that you weren't here at all & felt very bad. I can't tell you. It was long over an hour I am sure before I went to sleep again. It's all too sad to talk about now, so I won't say anymore.

But write me a nice letter.

It's been raining here hard now, for two days—began night before last. It's very damp & dark outside. And last night it thundered & lightninged heavily. I had to get up & shut the windows.

Here's to all your dreams, Babu. And all my true love.

T. D.

If you want to hear a nice record, stop in somewhere & have them play "The Bard of Armagh" Victor 983–A. John McCormack sings it. I like it very much.[8]

1. Burleigh Rodick (1889–1983), writer, historian.
2. Dreiser probably means the Permanent Court of International Justice, the judicial affiliate of the League of Nations, housed in the Peace Palace at The Hague.
3. Both Dreiser and H. L. Mencken saw the unpublished manuscript of Rodick's book in 1921 (see 8 October and 15 October, Riggio, *Dreiser-Mencken Letters*, II, 451–52). His dissertation was published as *The Doctrine of Necessity in International Law* (1928) and his fiction as *My Own New England* (1929).
4. The Provincetown Players revived the O'Neill play at the Playwrights' Theatre on 5 May 1924, featuring Paul Robeson (in his first stage role) as Brutus Jones and Kirah Markham as the "Old Native Woman."
5. *The Emperor Jones* is set in the West Indies, not Africa.
6. Helen Freeman (1886–1960), actress, writer, and director connected with the little theater movement of the period.
7. Dreiser's sister Mame owned a half share of a Greenwich Village "tea room" called The Green Witch with her friend Ross Freeman, a partnership that dissolved within a few months.
8. Dreiser wrote this note on a diagonal in the top, left-hand margin of the letter beside his address. He is referring to John McCormack (1884–1945), an Irish lyric tenor of international renown for both his operatic roles and his renditions of popular ballads and songs. "The Bard of Armagh" is a traditional Irish ballad.

To Helen Richardson [H-DPUP]

118 W. 11th St.

Monday, May 26–1924

Dearest Babu:

Yesterday, because it was clear, I decided to go up to W. C. Fields'[1] place after all. He has just leased a place for the summer in the Sound beyond Larchmont—a $150,000 show property. He has had a very successful year in Poppy[2] & plainly wants to splurge. No wife but apparently many friends. And he said if I would come as far as Mt. Vernon on the train he would meet me—which he did. In one of two cars that belong to him. And with him were three of the chorus girls of his company and an actor by the name Lionel Brahman, now with The Miracle.[3] In true country-house actor & actress style they were mostly in blues & white, with very trim hats, shoes & the like. The conversation consisted of nothing but bright remarks or attempts to make them. Nothing serious. You know the stuff well enough. You used to call it "wise-cracking." There was also of course much ritzing. And being anxious to hold up my end I did my share.

But that place right in the Sound. I wish you might have seen it. It was built by some rich sugar man for some woman he was living with at the time. And afterwards it was sold to F. E. Albee—or E. F. Albee[4] who leased it to Fields this summer. A long sweeping drive in from the main road, a porte cochere at one side, two lamp standards along the road, a great veranda at the back overlooking the sea—and to one side a large smooth tennis court. The lawn was perfect & went right down to the water. There are trees, flowers, a pagoda—or lounging room near the water & so on. Inside were four big rooms on the ground floor [word unintelligible] down to the verandah at the back & of course all the luxuries—wines, fruits, cigars & a butler & two men servants to look after you. Out on the lawn were swings & benches with parasols over them & tables before them. And all day after I arrived actors or friends, coming up or going down the road, were coming to and going from the place. They arrived in parties of two, four & six, stayed for a little while—some for all day & departed again. That Eddie Jessel[5] that we once saw telephoning his mother from the stage was there nearly all day. He was accompanied by his wife and sister-in-law—the Coleman sisters—whoever they are. Then Halliwell Hobbes[6] (never heard of him before yesterday) arrived with two ritzi girls—actresses—arrived in a car big enough to hold twelve. After them two Jews, a Mr. Lewis & a Mr. Key in a Buick roadster showed up—brokers I judged. And after them that Mr. Benchley[7] who did the polite monologue in The Music Box[8] (the financial secy. making his report) and the leading beauty of his show—a Miss Saunderson. And after them two Jews connected with the Famous Players Lasky[9] who brought out a new movie by Pola Negri[10] which was to be shown in the evening on a screen in the library. Finally, the veranda, the rooms & the lawn were dotted with people. Four played tennis. Others walked over the ground in pairs. I sat with about 10 around a central outdoor table on which they put cigars, cigarettes, whiskey, candy & magazines.

You would have been amused. Of all the dumb-bells & bone heads give me the average actor and actress. Nothing got the least applause or interest unless it was smutty or smart-aleck. Not a thing. There was a copy of the

Theatre Arts Magazine with some really beautiful reproductions of stage sets from the Ancient Mariner, The Emperor Jones & so on. But someone having picked the book up & looked at it casually it went the rounds with such remarks as "do they call that interesting" "Can you beat that stuff" "I can't see a thing in it." But the price of cars, who had bought a new one, who owed who what, whether such & such a show was going to close—who was taking a house where—all this got close attention. And, of course some one asked me if I was related to Dreiser the jeweler.

Then dinner at two. A long automobile ride to a hotel at Greenwich just to promenade & have a few drinks & look at the sea there. Then back for a supper at six-thirty (cold everything). And all the while one actor or another was playing the piano & another was singing. And two or three more monkeying with the radio try to get Pittsburg—or Chicago. And at least five chorus girls got silly drunk & talked about who was a this or a that & what they would do to so & so if they were in such another one's place. I sat for the most part & made mental notes.

But to see the Sound & the little yachts out on the water & the sunlight on the grass from the verandah was beautiful. And there was a library of books but no one picked up one.

Then came the moving picture—a fierce, silly thing about Paris & a girl being ruined & then becoming a great star. And someone said to me thats kinda like your book—Sister Carrie—ain't it? At about 10 dancing began. And since I dont dance I called on Mr. Fields to get me a car to the depot. And he took me down—without any farewells on my part & I was back here at 11^{30}. But when I looked back on it I liked it—as a spectacle. I've really seen the same thing all my life—some actor or financier or manufacturer getting rich & taking a house for the summer & splurging during his little hour around the candle. But it's still interesting because it emphasizes—for me—how the world goes on doing the same thing over & over & over in precisely the same way. Some of the girls & women there were very pretty & well dressed—but quite without exception in this case brassy & unintelligent. I looked at them & talked with a dozen. Unless you talked sex & flirted they wouldn't talk at all. But automatically I contrasted each & everyone with you—how you thought and how they thought. You wouldn't get very far with that group with any thoughts as to the beauty of the skies or the sea or life. "Oh—yes, it is pretty, isn't it?" You never get "I don't want to see anything beautiful any more"[11] out of them.

Well, Babu—this is what I wanted to write earlier in the day but couldn't. It's 10^{30} now. I'm tired and about ready to turn in. But I'm going out to mail this first. You're way out west under the pepper trees & I'm here in 11th Street looking up at the lighted clock of the Jefferson Market Police

Court.[12] And cats always yowl back here at night. It's only 7 *PM* with you. And when you get this you'll have forgotten what you did Monday evening at 7—Maybe. But if you didn't get a loving long distance thought from me then (a wish I were out there just now & could walk in on her) there's nothing much to telepathy between us.

Good night.

It'll probably be good morning when you read it.

Lovingly
T. D.

"When its moonlight with you in Italy it's Thursday morning here."[13]

Syl[14] just telephoned that todays Christian Science Monitor has a long article about me! What do you know. Do you suppose that Mrs.?[15]
112 So. Ardmore will recognize me in it?

1. W. C. Fields, born Claude William Dukerfield (1880–1946), actor and comedian.

2. *Poppy*, a musical comedy by Dorothy Donnelly, opened on 3 September 1923 at the Apollo Theatre and ran for 346 performances.

3. Lionel Brahman (1879–1947) appeared in *The Miracle*, written by Max Reinhardt and Karl Vollmoeller. The play opened at the Century Theatre on 16 January 1924 and ran for 175 performances.

4. Edward Franklin Albee (1858–1930) formed the Keith/Albee vaudeville circuit, which promoted "polite" vaudeville productions that dominated the industry into the 1930s. He was the grandfather of the American playwright Edward Albee.

5. Unidentified.

6. Halliwell Hobbes (1877–1962), English-born stage and film actor.

7. Robert Benchley (1889–1945), author, humorist, theater critic, appeared in *The Music Box Revue* in 1923.

8. The Music Box Theatre was originally built to showcase the songs of Irving Berlin.

9. Famous Players Lasky was a Hollywood production studio owned by Jesse L. Lasky (1880–1958), director and producer.

10. Pola Negri (1894–1987), born Barbara Apollonia Chalupec in Lipno, Poland, began her career in the Polish film industry and went on to achieve international fame in Germany, before coming to the United States.

11. Dreiser is quoting what he felt was Helen's sensitive response to beauty.

12. The Jefferson Market Police Court, a New York landmark built between 1875 and 1877 on Sixth Avenue and Tenth Street, is now the Jefferson Market Library.

13. Unidentified.

14. Syl or Sylvia was Dreiser's sister, who had become a member of the Christian Science church. The article has not been identified.

15. Dreiser left the space blank, with a question mark in place of a name. The reference is likely to a Christian Scientist they knew when they lived together in Los Angeles.

To Helen Richardson [H-DPUP]

118 West 11th

Thursday, June 5–1924

Where are you, Babu:

I miss you so much today. Its bright here. Not warm. Rained a little last night. I've been trying to write since 10^{30} & have accomplished something. Brennan[1] is down in the yard alone here—mowing the 10 x 30 patch of grass, reading the paper & sitting in the sun all alone. He's been all alone since Mame took the restaurant and manages to content himself as most old people do I suppose with himself. As much as I dislike him at times I think it's a little sad—although, of course, he's had his day. And I admire his courage—the dogged way in which he accepts what is. I sometimes think that in the same position I wouldn't do as well.

Are you leaving me for good Babu? That last letter dismissing a divorce as unimportant—save for me—sounds ominous. Heretofore you've never stopped talking about it. And now all of a sudden, you explain it all away. It isn't so essential. You only talked of it because of other things? Who is the other man? Is he rich? Will he guarantee you a career? Take you abroad? I only hope, if your really going, that you are finding someone with whom you can be happy. Since you went away I haven't spent one really happy day. That's the truth. I've worked. And like Brennan below stairs I content myself with what is. But there's something wrong with my spirit, I guess. It doesn't help me to go here & there with people. Maybe it is that I'm essentially contrary & that I will never know peace of mind anywhere—anymore. But when I was with you from Sept. 1919 on I did know a measure of content I never had before & have not had since you went away. Sunshine & bright days & company even—at times—only make me restless. I go here & there. Last night I went with a Mrs. Guitteau[2] whom you do not know to the Briarcliff above Yonkers for dinner. But only thought of you & the little house up at Mt. Kisco (Robins)[3] & our rides up there. I walked about the gardens up there & listened to a lot of palaver about how she would like to devote her life to me. I can have many lives devoted to me. I'd be happier, I know, if I could really devote my life to you.

There's not much outside of my seeing a few people here to write about: Jack & his girl—Phyllis Plater[4]—were in here yesterday afternoon for about an hour. He's not going to England this year. Is going to lecture & write here. I'm going to their place for dinner next Tuesday. Mr. & Mrs. Orrick Johns[5] who live here in 9th Street (43) have invited me to their place to dinner tonight. He's a poet & playwright: His father & I used to work on the Globe together in St. Louis.[6] I have all sorts of places to go really, but I'm not happy just the same & sometimes I wish I could fall asleep & stay asleep. In a way my life seems to have fallen to pieces.

Well—there's no use burdening you with this plaint—but so it is. Write me when you feel in the mood. I think of scores & scores of sweet things in connection with you each day.

T. D.

That Chicago case[7] interests me enormously. If you were here I would like to talk to you about that. It's one of those fantastic things that seems to hold so much more than is on the surface. Just a desire to kill doesn't seem to explain it. There must be something more it seems to me. A great novel there somewhere.

1. Austin Brennan was the companion of Dreiser's sister Mame. Dreiser used their early relationship in *Jennie Gerhardt* (1911) as the basis for his depiction of the liaison between Jennie and Lester Kane. At this time Brennan and Mame served as the rental agents and caretakers for the building in which Dreiser was living.

2. Maude Guitteau and Dreiser had a casual affair. She had been through two marriages and a brief stage career. On 14 May 1924, Dreiser notes in his diary: "She . . . appears to be completely overawed and subdued by the power of a name. . . . Without the fame of my books I personally could not achieve this relationship at all" (Riggio, *American Diaries*, 409–10).

3. "The little house up at Mt. Kisco," owned by Joseph G. Robin (1876–1929), a businessman-turned-author, editor, playwright. A Russian immigrant originally named Rabinovitch, he came to the United States in 1887. He first wrote Dreiser on 22 October 1908 to praise *Sister Carrie*. According to Dreiser, Robin was the model for the central character in "'Vanity, Vanity,' Saith the Preacher" (in *Twelve Men* [1919]). Under the name "Odin Gregory," Robin published *Caius Gracchus* (1920), a verse tragedy for which Dreiser wrote the introduction.

4. John Cowper Powys and Phyllis Playter (1893–1982) met in 1922 when she was a proofreader for Powys's publisher Haldeman-Julius. Twenty-two years his junior, she lived with him from 1923 until his death in 1963. For Powys, see Dreiser to Kirah Markham, 22 December 1914, n. 3.

5. Orrick Johns (1887–1946), poet, playwright, novelist.

6. Dreiser worked for the *Globe-Democrat* in St. Louis from November 1892 to April 1893.

7. Dreiser is referring to Nathan Leopold and Richard Loeb, who kidnapped and murdered fourteen-year-old Bobby Franks in Chicago on 21 May 1924. The two men were convicted in a famous trial in which Clarence Darrow represented them. Citing early-life social and psychological pressures, Darrow argued that the young defendants were not totally responsible for the murder they had committed, an argument that has its parallels in the novel Dreiser was then writing, *An American Tragedy*.

To Helen Richardson [H-DPUP]

118 West 11th St
N.Y.

Wed. June 18–1924

Honey Girl:

So now it is Temaine Street in the West Adams district. (Fatty Arbuckle).[1] He lived over there. And who are you really mooing around with. I'd like to know. I think I'll send a detectatuff to peep through the curtains & shrubbery & report. What news would come back. I think I might get news of the blonde German that way—to say nothing of Dwan, Noah or Wallace Berry & a few others.[2] Your mind runs to gross Rhinasocerii these days and no doubt they are about like pachyderms from the zoo. The streets will be resounding with them. No doubt one of them has a yellow car & sits up beside you like a wall while you scuttle him here & there. And he doesn't deserve it, of course. All he is, is in luck. You happen to need him & so he shines on the front seat whereas I take my lone hat & stick & walk. And all the time you write me of bathing girls only—you who like women about as much as I like sawdust. Well, the classy yellow car has arrived but I'm not in it. All I draw is paper & pencil and a thousand chapter job. Aren't you ashamed to be such a hypocrite. And one of these days I'll be hearing reports. And I'll be expected to love you as much as ever.

Summer has come at last here. It's hot & sultry with some mosquitoes. Mame is out of the Green Witch entirely.[3] She & the lady fought but she must have been valuable for the creature came over here & wept after using her very badly as I know. The downstairs room is rented to two girls who are working in the movies here. I haven't seen them but she says they say that they work all the time. It was rented to someone else but there's been a change. And on Sept 1 they plan to take this floor. So I go out—I know not where.

All my time is being devoted to this book. I do nothing else. You imagine, no doubt, that it ought to be through by now—but if you knew how hard I find it to work (get ahead I mean) even when I lock that door & hold to silence in here all day long, you'd never censure me for not accomplishing all in a day or a year. I am getting on slowly but sure. I'm to where the factory girl & the rich girl in Clydes life are enlarging & by degrees destroying him. Hard! No name. It seems simple. I know the story. The right procession & selection of incidents should be as nothing but it just chances to be everything. And so I write & rewrite. Sometimes I write enough to make two chapters or three—in a day—& get 1/3 of one chapter that is eventually ok. But just the same & failure or no failure I feel it an honor to be permitted to even attempt to tell such a tale & on that basis I am working on. If I fail at least I have tried.

And what am I doing. Last night I went with a Miss Davis—Magdalen Davis—connected with the Greenwich Village Theatre & the Standard Oil Company—to see "The Goose Hangs High."[4] A trashy worthless, comedy-drama much lauded here. How did I meet her? Through Ridgely Torrence,[5] a poet who has moved in to Patchin Place & is having groups drop in every so often. Tonight I am not going anywhere. Expect to eat at Cavanaughs in 23rd Street, take a walk & then come back here & read in Fort's Book of the Damned[6]—which I like to read in. Do you remember that you were going to give me notes once for a study of that amusing girl who used to hang about [word unintelligible]. But you never did. Wont let me have it, will you? I told you I took lunch with Robin[7] the other day. He wants me to share a house in the country with him, but I can't. I expect to spend every blessed summer week day here in this room. He asked after you and wanted to know whether you weren't soon to appear in a movie. I think he thinks of you as some remote genius really who should only be seen on the screen. He cant forget you. But according to your program the movies are out. Three years of study and then what? Europe or America?

Do you think I dont miss you? There's many a night I go over one after another of heavy sensuous hours we've spent together. I can lie & think by the hour until I find that it's a little too much,—that first night in New Orleans—those days on the boat going South—the Sunday morning I came in from Robin's place at Mt Kisco & you were at the Prince George. We went down to St. Luke's place & played until nearly three in the afternoon. Dont tell me. Sunday night or—morning I got up at 1 AM & took a cold bath.

Well, so long for today honey. I'm glad you rented the house. I wish I were free—no load on my mind . . . that I were out there & could push the German out into the snow.

T. D.

Speaking of seeing beautiful skies—Sunday evening (June 15th) I went up to Central Park for a walk—walked all the way to 59th Street up 7th Ave. & then into the Park, far away—along that path that leads to the west of *The Mall.* And up in the sky above the Century Theatre & Columbus Circle were various clouds that looked in some instances like processions of people in a frieze—Greek or Assyrian figures blended in rows. Now & then there were single figures of women with great wings folded to their sides. But high above them all—so that I had to look more directly up overhead was a splendid white & gold cloud that looked for all the world like a heroic figure of a dancing Bacchante or the posed figure of Victory[8]—most gracefully & beautifully draped. Her legs & neck & arms were bare. Her head thrown back. Only the torso was gauzily draped in pink & gold. You could see her face & the hair blowing wildly about it. I was transfixed & I stood by the edge of the walk & looked up until by degrees—during the course of an entire half hour, the light faded & the beautiful cloud faded to a thin dull gray. But to the very last the figure endured without change. There was no wind & just hung there undisturbed. I thought of you—of the skies above Hollywood & of how we used to see winged seraphs floating above in the light air of the dreamy world.

You are like that. Your spirit is like that of such a Victory or Bacchante dreaming in the clear skies above a sordid world. I wish that my soul might find such a still rosy world in which to dream.

Do you realize that I write
no letters to anyone else at all.
—just 20 word notes—if so much

1. Helen was living in the same neighborhood in which the comedian Roscoe "Fatty" Arbuckle (1887–1933) had lived. Dreiser may be associating her actions with those of the scandals attached to Arbuckle's recent trial for murder and rape.

2. For the "blond German" see Dreiser to Helen Richardson, 3 May 1924, n. 5.

Allan Dwan (1885–1983), film director, producer, and actor.

The actors Noah Beery (1882–1946) and Wallace Beery (1885–1949) were brothers.

3. See Dreiser to Helen Richardson, 9 May 1924, n. 7.

4. *The Goose Hangs High,* written by Lewis Beach and produced by the Dramatists Theatre, Inc., opened on 29 January 1924 at the Bijou Theatre and ran for 159 performances.

5. Ridgely Torrence (1875–1950), journalist, poet, playwright. Dreiser had known Torrence since his freelance days in the 1890s.

6. Charles Fort (1874–1932), journalist, iconoclastic author, who did battle against what he considered the limited empirical viewpoint of modern science. The two men had known each other since 1905, when as editor of *Smith's* Dreiser published his work. Dreiser insisted that Horace Liveright publish Fort's *The Book of the Damned* (1919), which was a gathering of strange and often inexplicable happenings that science had "damned" as unworthy of serious notice. Fort went on to finish three more books before he died, *New Lands* (1923), *Lo!* (1931), and *Wild Talents* (1932). With all his eccentricities, he became something of a cult figure, and in 1913 a number of his admirers such as Dreiser, Booth Tarkington, and Alexander Woolcott supported the founding of a Fortean Society to promote and preserve his ideas.

7. Joseph G. Robin. See Dreiser to Helen Richardson, 5 June 1924, n. 3.

8. Dreiser is probably referring to the Greek statue called "The Winged Victory of Samothrace," which dates from the second or third century BC. Unlike the figure in the cloud formation he is describing, however, the sculpture is headless.

To Helen Richardson [H-DPUP]

118 West 11th St
N.Y.

Friday, June 20–1924

I'm just up. Its 8:45 and before I dress or bath I feel like writing you a note, just to be talking to you. Your in my mind, just as you were last night. I keep wondering about you & wishing I were out there so I could peep in on you & find if you really wanted to see me again. Last night, I went to one of those crazy musical shows all by my lone—*Vogues*.[1] Its just like all the others. Greenwich Village follies & so on & I knew that but the comedians—Fred Allen & Jimmy Savo[2] I have seen in vaudeville before—years ago I had a good laugh at them or rather at Fred Allen who reminds me of some old time quirky character I have seen somewhere. He talks in a high piping voice & very slowly & correctly & learnedly. I really laughed 40 times I guess. They're kinda like Savoy & Brennan[3]—in method I mean. The curtains part & there's a door labeled *Insane Asylum*. The door opens & a keeper in uniform lets these two out. Then they agree to write the show. Some of their jokes just killed me. For instance they were figuring on how to count the receipts in the box office.

"Well, Mr. Savoo let's see if you can count now. How many is 4 & 6" | "Eleven" | "Oh, no 4 & 6 aren't 11. Count again. How many now." | "Nine." | "entirely wrong. Cant you count? 4 and 6 dont make nine! Think again now. Four plus six." | "Seven." | "Oh, what ignorance. Dont you know that four and six make ten?" | "Huh—uh. It aint so." | "Why isn't so?" | "Because five & five make ten." |

Another time an actor comes out with a piece of paper—the script for an act presumably & asks "Did you two write this?" and Allen says "Yes, but we'll go quietly." Still later Allen comes out with a small banjo & sits down & says that the management has asked him to make a test. The fire commissioner says that with every seat full & with every one walking leisurely the house can be emptied in 3 minutes. "So I will now play just three minutes." And so on. This is the show in which Otto Kahn's son[4] plays a banjo in a jazz orchestra. There was much talk of it here in the papers at the time.

There isn't anything else I have to tell you except that I wish you were here with me today. I wished you were with me last night. You would have laughed I knew. The show itself was nothing. The leading woman Odette Myrtil[5]—French & with an accent—didn't interest me & the chorus wasn't much. But two such Sillies always make a good show. I know Allen would make you laugh. And I love to hear you laugh when anything really hits you. It seems to come clear up from your heels.

Is my Babu studying hard? And is she going to be a real singer & sing for me some day. I wish I might hear you. It's all cloudy now & going to rain. I think. But I don't care. I'm going to be at my writing board all day & I work better when it's gray. If you were here I'd hold you on my lap & rock & pet you—man handle you afterwards. How would you like that? I see there's a movie called *Manhandled*.[6] Isn't that a scream.

T. D.

1. *Vogues* (book by Fred Thompson and Clifford Grey, music by Herbert P. Stothart) opened 27 March 1924 at the Shubert Theatre and ran for ninety-two performances.

2. Fred Allen (1894–1956), writer, performer, composer.

Jimmy Savo (1890–1960), producer, performer.

3. Savoy and Brennan: The vaudeville act of Bert Savoy, born Everett McKenzie (1888–1926), and Jay Brennan (1882–1961). Savoy was a female impersonator and Brennan was the straight man.

4. Otto Kahn (1867–1934), banker and financier. His son Roger Wolfe Kahn (1907–62) was a musician who in 1925 started his own band, Roger Wolfe Kahn and His Orchestra.

5. Odette Myrtil (1898–1978), actress.

6. *Manhandled* (1924), directed by Alan Dwan.

To Helen Richardson [H-DPUP]

118 West 11th St

Thursday July 3rd 1924

Dearest:

You have asked in several letters about the convention[1] excitement here. If I had thought you were so much interested I would have written before. It has been intense,—I cannot tell you how intense—the one topic in every restaurant, beanery, stationary store,—on every corner. The newspapers from the first have just been convention, convention, convention. One reason for the excitement—& with some intense interest—has been the determination here on the part of the Catholics & Tammany Hall to put over Al Smith[2] who is a Catholic. Also he is for free beer & wines. Priests and rooters from Tammany Hall, the Cook County Democracy of Chicago—which is Catholic, and others from Philadelphia & Baltimore & Boston also have packed the hall & every time Smith's name has been mentioned have yelled & stormed. Also, they have—so all who have attended the convention report, booed down everyone else—hissing Bryan,[3] the name of McAdoo[4] & anyone else who spells any danger to Al Smith. Also the newspapers with the exception of the Hearst papers have been for Al Smith & not only that but violently anti McAdoo because neither Wall

Street nor Tammany nor the Catholics want McAdoo. They feel that they cannot run him. So all pro Catholics & the dubs boo McAdoo & yell for Smith. Smith's name (in poster form) is in many windows. Wagons have it plastered on the side. In all the parks & most theatres I hear—and hotels—a radio has been set up & between acts, or all the time in the parks the voice of the vote counters in the hall can be heard—even as you walk along the street. There is a radio in the drugstore around the corner. The last vote, 53rd ballot—only an hour ago was McAdoo 446—Smith 361, others scattering. Necessary to a choice—732. Total number of delegates 1098.

Madison Sq. Garden is hung with flags. A set of search lights placed in Madison Sq. Park plays on it all the time. Fifth Ave. is hung with red, white & blue lights & banners. All night is as bright as day almost. Thousands of strangers are here. You see them everywhere. The buses carry great crowds. In honor of the delegates Mayor Hylan[5] caused Washington Square to be fenced in and two great dancing floors holding several thousand each built. A Paul Whiteman[6] and a[7] orchestra attend every night. Also a policeman's chorus of 500 voices assembles nightly & sings. The convention convenes each day at 10^{30} am & runs until midnight. One night it ran until 2^{30} am. No decision has been reached today. I expect one tomorrow or late tonight. Personally I prefer McAdoo but would not mind Underwood or Glass.[8] No Catholic for me. Yet for few days now I have not gone. Gave my tickets to Gertie & Mr. Armstrong.[9] But tonight, late, since a decision may now be reached, I think I'll go. I wish you were here. I would have been so glad to have taken you every day.

Is this enough convention?

I should add Bryan dominates it. He killed the chances of John W. Davis[10]

—a Wall Street candidate—by one speech. Up to that time Davis had 161 votes. Three ballots afterward he had fallen to 67 & is now *out*! So much for Bryan who has no power, *they say*.

You know I mentioned Sterling.[11] Speak of the devil. Today comes an ms from San Francisco—an essay which he is publishing in pamphlet form & which[12]

Last night I was reading in John Davidson's poems "A Ballad of a Nun" and "A New Ballad of Tannhauser."[13] They are both about love—exquisitely done as ballads and I thought of you all the while for they are like you—probably as you are to others now—as you certainly were to me for so long. I loved them both—but not so very much else in the book—but I read them over twice & thought—somewhy—of Highland Park & our quaint little trips to Los Angles & elsewhere thereabouts on the street car. And of the first time you went out to see about the movies because you were troubled over me—then gave over bothering with them for awhile because we were so happy out in *Herman* (that name).[14]

Tonight I am having dinner with that Bowers[15] man & his wife. But tomorrow & Sunday I plan to stay right here & work. I have so much ahead of me yet to do & see no certainty of finishing it all on time.

It is very bright & green where you are, isn't it? I suppose Sycamore is as pleasant as Detroit Street. You can sit & look out on that wonderful sunshine & read. Here one fine day seems like seven anywhere else because it comes so infrequently. I wish so much this morning that I were out of all this—that we had our little car & were going somewhere—anywhere—just to ride & see & dream.

T. D.

1. The 1924 New York Democratic Convention, the longest in history, lasted seventeen days from 24 June through 9 July.

2. Alfred Emanuel Smith (1873–1944), governor of New York from 1919 to 1921 and from 1923 to 1929. He went on to win the Democratic nomination for president in 1928, but he lost the election to Herbert Hoover. Dreiser's emphasis on the Roman Catholic aspect of Smith's campaign comes from his own strong anti-Catholic biases.

3. William Jennings Bryan. See Dreiser to Sara O. White, 14 August 1896, n. 1. Bryan was the Democratic presidential nominee three times: in 1896, 1900, and 1908.

4. William Gibbs McAdoo (1863–1941), a candidate for the presidential nomination in both 1920 and 1924. He was Secretary of the Treasury in Woodrow Wilson's administration, and he would later be the Democratic senator from California (1933–38).

5. John F. Hylan (1868–1936), mayor of New York from 1918 to 1925.

6. Paul Whiteman (1890–1967), bandleader called "The King of Jazz" who pioneered "sweet style" jazz rather than its traditional form. He increased the size of the band to nearly symphonic proportions, which allowed him to attract a wider, mainstream audience.

7. Dreiser left a blank space at this point in the letter.

8. Oscar W. Underwood (1862–1929), senator from Alabama (1915–27) and a candidate for the presidential nomination in 1912.

Carter Glass (1858–1946), senator from Virginia (1920–46).

9. Gertrude (Gertie) Nelson. See Dreiser to Sallie Kusell, 4 August 1923, n. 2.

Mr. Armstrong is unidentified, possibly the writer Paul Armstrong.

10. John W. Davis (1873–1955) eventually won the nomination on the 103rd ballot. He had been a Congressman from West Virginia and the Ambassador to Great Britain. He lost the 1924 election to Calvin Coolidge.

11. During his time in California, Dreiser met George Sterling (1869–1926), a flamboyant and talented poet, dramatist, & critic; Dreiser helped publish and wrote the foreword to Sterling's tragedy *Lillith*.

12. Unidentified. There is at least one page missing at this point in the letter.

13. John Davidson (1857–1909), poet, playwright, novelist, essayist. The poems

Dreiser mentions are, as he says, about love—in both cases about illicit love (or love branded as such)—which is vindicated at the end. Both poems represent institutional Catholicism as sexually repressive.

14. Dreiser was baptized Herman Theodore Dreiser, so the street name had personal significance for him.

15. Claude Bowers (1878–1958), writer for the *New York Evening World*, who often editorialized against censorship. Like Dreiser he was born in Terre Haute, Indiana. He later became a historian, published *The Tragic Era* (1929), and served as the Ambassador to Spain (1933–39).

To Esther McCoy [H-DPUP]

Esther McCoy (1904–89) was an author of novels, stories, screenplays, and political journalism. In the second half of her career she became a renowned architectural historian; of her many books, Five California Architects *(1960) is a classic in the field. Born in Kansas, she spent her childhood in Arkansas and was attending the University of Michigan when she and Dreiser first met. She initiated a correspondence with Dreiser on 7 May 1924, writing from Fayetteville, Arkansas, to describe her enthusiastic reactions to his books.*

118 W. 11th St.
N.Y.

July 9–1924

Your a quaint & elusive and maybe a just slightly affected person. I can't say. But I like your letters. And I think I can tell you what you are going to be—eventually if not now,—or right soon. A *writer*. Your mental compass seems to point thusly. You have such a flare for the visible scene & present it with so much simplicity & force. You might as well begin scribbling forthwith. Only, of course, one does need variety of contact & experience. By no other method are worthwhile tales to be come by. You know that, too. I know you do.

How old are you, anyhow? You have the brain of a person of thirty-five or—if you are by any chance still a kid—a most precocious brain. You say so directly so many things & so neatly & clearly—and by implication more. And you calmly ignore questions. Well, two can play at that game. Letters for instance. And how many I get. And what I do about them.

So you are coming to see me & stand in my door. And I am to say "run away." Precisely. Well, where is Radcliffe?[1] And does next winter mean October or there about. If so I'll most certainly be looking over proofs. That I'll be in this suite of rooms I doubt. I'm supposed to surrender them Sept 1. And, yea, how I dread it. And where I shall go forth with I know not. (Where is Radcliffe? A quiet place for a harassed author?)

Just the same you wrote speedily,—a most salutary result from a few comments. Or was it? Anyhow its another quaint & interesting letter. But—whisper—I'd more enjoy a tabloid or thumbnail of one E. McC, done deftly & truly, than many pictures of Life on the Mississippi. "Ah's been on the Mississip."

It's stunning bright here today. This room is big & cool & bare—very, very few things in it. A glass bowl filled with water makes a delightful rainbow on the ceiling. And I'm trying—(on either side of a letter to one E. McC) to think out a certain phase of this book[2] and not doing well at it either.

It's odd—by damn—that your letters can invariably extract replies from me. I don't get it. There's a stack in the corner three inches high & I haven't the zest to answer one. Now just why, pray?

An honest tabloid might elucidate here.

A most solemn
and harried
Author

1. McCoy was contemplating a transfer from Washington University in St. Louis to Radcliffe College to continue her studies. Although Dreiser may be writing tongue in cheek here, his lack of knowledge would not be unusual for the time: the Harvard Annex for Women's Instruction was chartered as Radcliffe College in 1894; it didn't merge with Harvard College until 1 October 1999.

2. *An American Tragedy*.

To Helen Richardson [H-DPUP]

118 West 11th St

Friday July 18–1924

How' s the Babu this night. Comfortable. I hope so. I've been sending helpful messages your way all day because I've been thinking that maybe you needed them.[1] I hope not but I was glad to send them just the same. Is Wilshire[2] as attractive as the other street.

It's been very fine here today—clear & cool. I've been working steadily from 11 a.m. to 10 p.m. As I write I can look out through my window & see the Jefferson Market Court Clock. Hows that for a days work? (Jack a good boy?) I'm tired now, but I'm going out to eat a little—in a dinky place called *The Coffee Pot* recently opened around the corner. A western sandwich and a *cowp-a-cowpy*[3] as a little kid I used to know used to say about my speed. "Low living and high thinking." That was once the Boston Transcendentalist Movement watch-word. You know me Al.[4] If I'm not transcendental what the h- - - am I anyhow. Then I'll come back in & read in Llewellyn's latest book "Black Laughter."[5] Its about Africa—his life there & very interesting. Fine, I think. Then—

To bed, to bed, said Sleepy head.
Lets wait awhile said Slough.[6]

I'm getting silly—due to hunger & satisfaction with an honest days toil.

Do juice still think nice things of me. I hope so. And I wish I was in L.A. this day—or night rather.

Love—and lots of nice squeezes & maulings for you.

T. D

1. Dreiser is referring to telepathic "messages." See Dreiser to Kirah Markham, 9 February 1914, n. 1.
2. Wilshire Boulevard, where Helen had taken an apartment.
3. "Cup of coffee."
4. Dreiser is alluding to Ring Lardner's baseball classic *You Know Me Al: A Busher's Letters* (1914), which had as its main character a brash and conceited bush-league pitcher.
5. *Black Laughter* (1924) by Llewellyn Powys.
6. A variant of the opening lines of an old nursery rhyme:

> "To bed, to bed!" said Sleepyhead
> "Tarry awhile" said Slow.

To Helen Richardson [H-DPUP]

118 West 11th St

Friday July 25–1924

Dearest:

There are times when I grow profoundly sad & I do not know why. Always though when you are so far away I attribute some unhappiness of spirit to you & that you are reaching out to me. All day yesterday & quite all today I have been depressed. My book is hard—very. I see so much to do. I regret sometimes that I have not the right person to help me,—more, that you are not the one person who could & would. It is a trick of fate which causes the one person I desire most to be one person who other than by the wells of her spirit can do little for it. Spiritually you seem like a spring to which I can go in thirst—an absolute anti-dote for soul misery—the only anti-dote I have ever known. Mentally you betray my work to happiness—lead me dancing along paths of ease—lead me into a garden where nothing other than happiness matters. And I have suffered so—trying to work without & with you—in either case feeling myself lacking some necessity—in the first case you & your support & your content & your love—in the second instance the fillip to energy—the hard compulsion that compels one to put all but work aside. What a struggle! What a life! Today I have been wishing to know if anything were wrong with you and where you are—and that I might see you. Those wishes have made me restless. I find it hard to concentrate.

Once in awhile you write me a beautiful letter. One that you wrote on Saturday (July 20) was such a one. You enclosed a little picture of Hubbard[1] & talked of the oneness of our temperaments. I loved it. It was fine & helped me a little,—a great deal. I wished when I got it that I might see & be with you—that you were the one who could & would supply my every working need. Yet I feel that maybe that is not as it should be,—that I should work perhaps exclusively within myself,—to myself—in work needing no or little advice. If it were possible at the moment I would go with you anywhere & settle down—leaving you for such time as you needed to your dreams & taking such time as I needed for mine. I am hoping that in some way that will soon be solved. It must be if ever I am to be happy any more. I think.

You must write me something about the trip.[2] How long will it take to ride to Portland. How many days or weeks to Boston. What is the fare. What is the latest date you propose to start. I want to come & in the face of the necessity to stick close to what I am doing will break away I think & make the trip. I want to. It would be delightful. And I would get to see my Babu again.

T. D.

Don't worry about "little snakes" writing me. They might charge you with many things—all the crimes in the Decalogue.[3] I might believe nearly all of them to be true—some of them anyhow, but it wouldn't alter my attitude.

I like your friend Hubbard's face only fairly well. He may be a great teacher. He looks not at all astute or temperamental. Interesting however—some.

1. Arthur J. Hubbard was Helen's voice teacher. While she studied with him, Helen and her sister Myrtle lived in his home (see Richardson Dreiser, *My Life*, 95, 101–2).

2. Preoccupied with his novel, Dreiser did not make the trip West to see Helen. Instead, she spoke of coming back East, with the idea of attending Arthur Hubbard's voice class in Boston. She did not return to New York, however, until late October. At that point the couple took an apartment in Brooklyn, and Helen saw him through the last stages of writing *An American Tragedy*.

3. The Ten Commandments.

To Esther McCoy [H-DPUP]

McCoy had sent Dreiser a photograph of herself. She had decided to continue her studies at the University of Michigan, and she continued her exchange with Dreiser from the Ann Arbor campus.

118 W. 11th St.
N.Y.

Sept. 2–1924

I didn't want to say any smart things about the picture because there's more to it than just flaws. The arm isn't well posed. The mouth looks dejected a little—or hurt. And I judge from the picture that you can be hurt. People who are without emotion or do not understand it—do not understand me and do not trouble to write me. A primary letter is a primary confession. The costume is conventional to a degree & might well be worn at a church lawn social. But what of it? You are not conventional. And your mind besides being daring is also endowed with beauty and tenderness. You may have the mind of a man—(you have a darned sight better one than most men)—but you are a woman and it is colored, as your letters show—with sufficient feminine traits to keep it classified as sufficiently feminine to make it attractive to a man. Anyhow its attractive to me—and your not writing to me like a man would write to a man but as a woman would. And if you don't want to be admired as an attractive girl—why this photo—costumed & posed to win the admiration of men.

Well, anyhow—let that be as it will. The combination of a party dress, a band of ribbon about the forehead, graceful arms & a mind such as yours is pretty strong bait for one of my temperament. The combination seems, as I said before—the candy—and I guess it won't irritate you terribly to know it. And I like the idea of you coming from dreary old corn-tassel Kansas—the home of Sockless Jerry Simpson and the Grass Hopper.[1] I went to school with a kid who lived in Medicine Lodge. I liked him, too. He died of a fever in Mexico, prowling crazily here & there as an engineer. I would like to talk to you some day—for an entire evening in a good restaurant. Why didn't you come to Adelphi College—Brooklyn? That's famous. When you get to Ann Arbor—if you have time & would like to come on here over a holiday or so—well—I could scrape the price of a round trip ticket with berth & you could give New York the once over. And no questions asked,—by me, at least.

I love your interest in fairy stories—I know them all—or did—the Brothers Grimm and Hans Christian Anderson[2] were companions of my youth. Also a lot of lovely Japanese fairy stories that I have never forgotten.

T. D.

My last letter wasn't a dirge. Your preceding letter was skimpy and almost too high handed for me. Hence the comment.[3]

92 in the shade here today.

1. "Sockless Jerry" refers to Jeremiah Simpson (1842–1905), Populist Congressman from Kansas who accused his opponent of being a tool of big business, as evidenced by the silk hosiery he wore. When his rival answered that it was better to wear silk stockings than no stockings at all, the name "Sockless Jerry" took hold and helped Simpson to win his first election.

Kansas is known as the Grasshopper State because of the grasshopper plagues of 1873 and 1874.

2. Hans Christian Anderson (1805–75), Danish novelist, poet, and short story writer, was most famous for his fairytales.

The brothers Grimm, Jakob Ludwig Karl (1785–1863) and Wilhelm Karl (1786–1859), two German philologists famous for their collections of fairy tales.

3. Dreiser had been hinting that perhaps she was simply playing with him with no intention for them to meet.

To Esther McCoy [H-DPUP]

118 W. 11th St.
N.Y.

Sept. 24–1924

Well, it's nice to get your new address but 'tis a sad tale you relate. I swear I can scarcely grasp the stupidity of men, at times, as much as I have witnessed & even been the victim of it. So called *mind* seems to me for the most part an illusion. The actions of men have little to do with it or it's primary principle logic. In fact men act & read by some system of responses—chemic or psychic which has nothing to do with what we have been dreaming of as mind. So when you tell me of your Dean & his comments on Dostoievsky, Turgenev[1]—& others I see him as a chemic or psychic sign of his time—little more. And the average run of professors is but symbolic of some mass mood. They thumb over books & harvest unrelated notions. Your explanation of your un-academic mind was wonderful. But he didn't get it, of course.

But you know. I can't tie up your letters with your picture or your reported age. Is this a hoax? Are you one? And are you just kidding me? If so, I'll laugh—I'll have to. And the joke will be on me. If you aren't, your the oddest combination of girlhood & wisdom that has come down the track in my experience. What's the *real* answer? Are you a myth?

I got the little green cloth *Alice*[2] & liked it for the inscription. I got your nice letter saying sure you would come down here. But now because of the Dean—you seem to regret being so nice. Why didn't you try Columbia or N.Y.U? There's opera here. And you must tell me when your interested to come and I'll send you your trip.

Haven't been feeling so well, recently. And can't get what it is. Weary nerves, maybe. I'm very tired—too much so—& prefer to sleep—or lie about to anything else. Am thinking of going to the country for a few days—to a work-farm like Muldoon's[3] used to be to see if I can be pulled into shape.

Meanwhile you must write me more about yourself. I've had five different annual invites from student groups in Ann Arbor to lecture before them, but I never have—or will I guess—since I can't bring myself to feel that I can lecture. Writing is my game—and thats about all—books & an occasional play.

I hope when this reaches you you'll be feeling better—liking the University better. If not—come down here & see what you can find to study here. I'd like to talk to you. All my best wishes for you.

T. D.

1. Feodor Mikhailovich Dostoievsky (1821–81) and Ivan Sergeevich Turgenev (1818–83), Russian novelists much admired by Dreiser.

2. McCoy sent him an edition of Lewis Carroll's *Alice In Wonderland*. At the bottom of the title page, she wrote: "bound by E. McCoy," which is a reference to the green cloth she placed over the original binding. On the inside front pastedown, she wrote: "To my beloved Theodore Dreiser."

3. William Muldoon (1845–1933), best known as a professional wrestler, he ran a health clinic called the Olympia in Westchester, New York, where Dreiser spent six weeks in the spring of 1903. Muldoon is the original for Dreiser's character sketch "Culhane, The Solid Man" in *Twelve Men* (1919).

To Esther McCoy [H-DPUP]

Dreiser's schedule forced him to cancel a trip to Ann Arbor for what was to be his first meeting with McCoy.

Theodore Dreiser

Oct. 29–1924

You don't quite grasp the situation with me here. Saturday night I had a fixed engagement with Dr. Brill returning from a visit with Freud in Vienna.[1] Since I am to see Freud through him, later, it was fairly necessary to keep it.[2] Sunday was more difficult to handle if not so important, Clarence Darrow.[3] I had an engagement with him—he to call for me at 7. But he was travelling & I hadn't his itinerary. No chance to wire. Since I have a bit of business that includes him later it was not wise—scarcely possible to walk away. Hence my not coming. The notice was too short.

Really expect—this week—to leave Friday on the Wolverine—5 pm. Arrive Ann Arbor Saturday a.m. 8:12. Will confirm this or any change by wire. The uncle idea is of course best.[4]

What a rambling, sociable person. You have the spirit of Chaucer's Canterburians.[5] *Hail-fellow & give us the news*. And plainly you gather much news. A gypsy soul, maybe. But I am less casual & social. Experience has taught me the value of a certain amount of shyness. And the room in Seneca road is quite satisfactory.

If any plans of yours conflict with this, wire—collect.

Th D

1. Abraham A. Brill (1874–1948), Austrian-born psychiatrist, author, and translator of Sigmund Freud (1856–1939). Brill's translations made Freud's work available for the first time to many Americans, including Dreiser. He and Dreiser met in 1918 and collaborated on an informal "conversation" on psychoanalysis and Freud that was recorded by a stenographer but never published.

2. Dreiser asked Brill for a letter of introduction to Freud, which he received, though the meeting never took place.

3. Clarence Darrow. See Dreiser to Kirah Markham, 20 April 1914, n. 3.

4. The plan was to pretend that he was McCoy's uncle during his visit with her in Ann Arbor.

5. Dreiser is referring to the ribald characters in *The Canterbury Tales* by Geoffrey Chaucer (ca. 1340–1400).

1926

To Sallie Kusell [H-UV]

An American Tragedy *had been published on 17 December 1925. Dreiser had left New York and driven to Florida with Helen Richardson, hoping to escape the northern winter and the fatigue he felt after completing the novel. He had not yet had any word about the critical and popular success the book was beginning to enjoy.*

Ft. Lauderdale, Fla.

Jan 5, 1925[1]

Dearie:

Well here I bees in this burg—and rather glad to get here after Georgia. There was much talk up there of the "coldest spell in 16 years" but that did not cheer me any. The roads were beastly and full of old water and mud. And the air—despite southern Ga was biting and so much so that I had to wear an overcoat. Down here in such roads as there are—and they're pretty good—we can walk anywhere, mostly without a coat and the vegetation is different—tropical. You can see sugarcane and pineapple groves. And cocoa nuts hanging by forties & fifties on the coconut palms. Out here on a road not ten miles from this inn one fell within five feet of me. And if coco had met coco there would be at least one less indigent author in this world.

Had your telegram about Mr. Sherman & his review yesterday which was the second day after I got here.[2] Interesting very—such a "switch"—and it was nice of you to send it. Apart from your letter concerning the boat & this message I have had but one other word concerning it—and that from a woman in St. Louis who writes that she thinks the first 2/3rds trivial. So you see how you critics agree.

I'm sorry about letters. I cant write much because I feel too relaxed mentally. But I think of you a great deal & I guess you know that. If you have written me more than three letters all told I have never received them. As I said in my telegram all mails in Florida are horribly congested & delayed. This place contains maybe 5000 people. Possibly eight but there are so many strangers—some 800,000 on wheels in the state, they say that they pack every general delivery window to suffocation. The queue at St. Augustine was about 70 people long all day long from 8 until six. Here it is over 150 long all day long & the two windows with four clerks stay open from 7 A.M. to 9 P.M. At 9 P.M. they close the doors but serve all who can crowd inside.

Great state. Great climate—in this southern part. The skys are blue. Porpoises cruise along the coast in schools. You can see pelicans and cranes (white & blue) and blue herons by the dozens in every pool. Fish really leap out of the waters by the dozen. Twenty miles west of here in the Everglades are real alligators. You can see an occasional one on the bank. And the new architecture of the new towns is beautiful beyond belief. The Riviera, Mentone, Biarritz—the old Mission of Mexico & Spain all are here in profusion. It's a wonder world & growing like mad. In this one town I think easily $200,000,000 in construction work is now under way—houses ten strong, business buildings, canals, sea walls, bridges, parks. In the little artificial canals & inlets here only 100 handsome small yachts costing not less than 40,000 each are riding at anchor. From the banks you can see people under awnings drinking and hear them talking or singing. There is no danger in my humble estimation that Florida will not go over. And prices are not much different to what they are anywhere apart from rooms. A room single is from 3 to five or six almost anywhere—in any decent place I mean. The indecent ones are probably much higher.

How are you? And how is N.Y. I ask but the way the mails are I don't suppose I'll ever hear. I had one telegram from Liveright[3] yesterday—dated New Years night saying the book was starting off pretty good and he hoped for a good sale. Scripticly I certainly shut myself off when I blew in here. Did you get a letter in which I asked you to look in the papers for a studio or something about 59th between Brdwy & the Hudson and not farther north than 72nd. I asked that in the letter.

All my nicest thoughts. I'm not much on love as you know. But I'd like another afternoon like that last one. Write me here—c/o Las Olas Inn-Box 1215. I've found a clean pleasant place & much territory around here that I want to look into. I may write an article on what I've seen.[4] If so I'll send it to you to be copied. You never heard more from Masters[5] did you? Did you get a check for 15^{00} from Winston-Salem.

Its 6 P.M. I'm going out bathing—then to eat & then to bed. If you are otherwise engaged for the night—

Well—
T. D.

1. Dreiser meant to write "1926."

2. Stuart Pratt Sherman (1881–1926), professor of English at the University of Illinois (1907–24), literary critic for the *Nation* and later for the *New York Herald Tribune Books*, author of numerous books of literary criticism and editor of the *Cambridge History of American Literature*. After the publication of *The "Genius"* (1915), he dismissed Dreiser's naturalism as embodying merely a theory of animal behavior.

However, Sherman's critical opinion of Dreiser changed with the publication of *An American Tragedy*, which he considered "massively impressive" ("Mr. Dreiser in Tragic Realism," New York *Herald Tribune Book*, 3 January 1926, 3; repub. in *Salzman, Critical Reception*, 445).

3. Horace Liveright: see Dreiser to May Calvert Baker, 16 August 1919, n. 1.

4. Dreiser did write an article, "This Florida Scene," which was published in two installments in *Vanity Fair* 26 (June 1926): 43, 98, 100; and 26 (July 1926): 63, 94, 96.

5. Edgar Lee Masters. See Dreiser to Kirah Markham, 5 March 1915, n. 8.

To Sallie Kusell [H-UV]

Kusell had asked Dreiser to inscribe a copy of An American Tragedy *to her. His response was the sort of reaction he had whenever he felt his celebrity was being exploited.*

61 W. 48th St.
N.Y.

Feb. 13–1926

Dearie:

The trouble between us springs in my mind at least from the firm conviction that your interest in me is somehow based more on a desire for mental & artistic recognition through me than it is on any innate, personal and ineffective as well as effective qualities which may characterize me. In other words as a searching, blundering faulty male—however constructive my unrecognized aspirations might be—you would not see me. As a writer who has achieved this or that yes—and in spite of weaknesses & lacks as a male—perhaps. A hard thing to say—but on the other hand—a hard distinction to make. The matter of inscribing the book was one of those chance flashes which reveal so much. There must be some form of written recognition consoling to an ego that sees—or did see in me as a writer,—not as a man,—some form of personal achievement & stimulation for you. And excellent—and fair enough perhaps as it may be, still scarcely the basis for a temperamental affiliation. Meaningful & moving affections are like that. One likes or loves—not because—but after all I need not explain that to you. I have missed the note I have described & for want of which I have always been dubious & resentful. Does that fully explain my silence. And would it not always explain it?

T. D.

To Sara White Dreiser [H-DPUP]

Sara Dreiser had written Dreiser a letter congratulating him on the success of An American Tragedy *and the sale of the motion picture rights to the novel. She also wrote "wondering if you wouldn't be willing to give me something, now that you are able to do so, & let me go back home & and have little Rosemary"*[1] *(7 April 1926 [DPUP]).*

My dear Jug:

Your congratulations on the *financial* outcome of my labor in connection with An American Tragedy are appreciated. What interests me about this prompt notice of your pleasure in connection with the sale of the moving picture rights of the book is that in the last twelve years or so I have written eight or nine books, all of which seemed to me at least to be worthy of some form of congratulation,[2] however little the financial return. They represented the best I could do. It remains for you, however, to congratulate me only on the financial outcome of the only book that has achieved a financial outcome worthy of the name. To me there is something rueful in the thought of your very special & purely financial interest in my career.

T. D

1. Sara Dreiser's sister Rose had died at a young age and left a daughter whom Sara wanted to adopt.

2. Sara Dreiser responded by saying she did not know that he had "written 8 or 9 books. I read nothing. I have no time for reading. I know of only three books you have written during that time. Your trip to Indiana with Booth, which I have never seen, Twelve Men which I stood in the book Dept. in Wannamakers to run hurriedly thro' the stories of Peter & Mr. Paul to see if you were able to write of them as strongly as you felt & and as you did of my father, & the 3rd was Hey Rub a dub dub which one story you sent me out West & I wrote then of your great power—power to make people believe almost what they do not believe" (Sara White Dreiser to Dreiser, 19 April 1926 [DPUP]). She is referring respectively to A *Hoosier Holiday* (1916), illustrated by Franklin Booth; to the sketches "Peter," "My Brother Paul," and "A True Patriarch," in *Twelve Men* (1919); and apparently to some "story" published in *Hey-Rub-A-Dub-Dub* (1920).

1927

To Sallie Kusell [H-UVL]

Feeling low physically and mentally, Dreiser went on a walking tour in an attempt to improve his health. Starting in late March from Elizabeth, New Jersey, he walked for three weeks through Pennsylvania, Maryland, West Virginia, and finally into Virginia and the Shenandoah Valley.

Hotel Brunswick

Lancaster, Pa.

April 2nd-[1927]
Dear S:

I just realized from your letter today that you were thinking something must be amiss with me. There is nothing wrong. In one way—physical strain, the trip has been very trying. Toward evening especially I am always worn out; on the other hand I see & feel a real improvement. Have lost eight pounds & feel stronger. Today—just now—purchased a new kind of shoe (arch supporter) which I hope will relieve this foot strain. Find it hard to write at all—en route. Mornings too restless & eager to be off—at night all in. Yet I am not overdoing it. Got covers[1] just now (Sent on from Reading.) Like gold well enough—but want script (like hand-writing) used for text on cover—*without box* and same reduced to lower right hand corner. Raining & cold here today. Disagreeable. When it clears up next will wire you where to come.

T. D.

Sent cover direct to Gross[2] with an explanation—but you follow it up. Beautiful country between Allentown & here. Have found the wellspring of the Mencken physical & mental compost. Can produce one hundred photos of men of or near his age—bankers, bartenders, farmers, clerks, tradesmen—all Menonite Dutch—and all his living image.[3] It is amazing. They live between Allentown & here.

1. Dreiser is referring to the sample book cover of a revised and shortened version of *The Financier,* which was published later in the month.

2. Carl Gross, a design editor at Boni and Liveright.

3. Dreiser's banter is aimed at H. L. Mencken's German lineage; unlike Dreiser, however, Mencken had no Mennonite ancestors.

To Helen Richardson [H-DPUP]

Along with a group of world-class intellectuals and artists, Dreiser was invited to Moscow for a weeklong celebration of the tenth anniversary of the Russian Revolution. He asked for (and was granted) permission to make an extended tour of the country, which lasted for three months. He boarded ship at New York harbor on 19 October 1927.

ON BOARD THE
CUNARD
RMS "MAURETANIA."

Thursday-Oct 20–1927

Dear Babe:

I was wrong about the introductions as I wired. They turned up ok at the bottom of the bag.[1] The long trip is on. And I am somewhat oppressed. The passengers trucking to & fro around the deck do not interest me. And at breakfast each morning now the food has been wretched. That Danish boat was the best of all. Worse—just now I feel a little seasick. But I enjoyed the start off—our going down to the boat first & getting off afterward. Also the dinner[2]—though not so much. Things like that are a strain. Am editing Robin's script[3] which I will send to you. Wish you would read it over & think about it before turning it back. You may have things to suggest. I have made quite a few changes which I feel are most important. I wish now you were along. Things wouldn't be so dull.

Friday-Oct. 21–

Think I may as well add things as the days go on. Had your wireless last night saying no letters were there. But by then I had wired you. Have met Ben Huebsch[4] the publisher who is on C deck & sometime today—by the aid of an interpreter if we can find one—I am going to look up that Spanish-Mexican painter.[5] He is travelling 3rd class. If we don't find an interpreter I am going down anyhow & maybe he will find some one. I shall always think of him as he talked at that dinner. Yesterday it was gray & with quite a sea. Last night there was a thunder-storm with rolling thunder & great flashes of lightening that lit the waste of waters in such a grim, mysterious way. Today it is partly clear & part showery with lovely rainbows here & there and your flowers are as good as new whereas the others—the roses—are beginning to flutter down. Between editing the Genius, writing an article for Elser,[6] keeping a diary & writing letters I have scarcely a moment to myself. But I lie in bed & write & that's something

Saturday. Oct. 22

It's grey today & cooler. And I'm still working. Theres to be a prize fight this P.M. on the sun deck. That may help a little. You will not believe it but I miss you and I wish your wire to me had contained a personal word—something over and above the mere statement that there were no letters there. Are we so completely apart that a word was not worth while?

Saturday midnight

Diego Rivera has just left my cabin. He has been here all evening showing me and Ben Huebsch and Joseph Anthony[7] a writer, his paintings. Before dinner I took a bottle of whiskey and went down & looked him up. He talks almost no English but I got Mr. & Mrs. Ernst[8]—a lawyer & his wife whom Heywood Broun[9] introduced by telegraph to translate for me & I learned a great deal about Mexico. He is very friendly & promises on his next visit to N.Y. to come & see me. So you'll see him sometime. Also Huebsch—and this Joseph Anthony who represents Hearst in London. The Ernsts remind me of the [word unintelligible]. There is no more news tonight. But I wish now that you were along. Travelling (for me) together is hard enough, but alone—well. Think a few nice thoughts and maybe the relationship will not remain as bruised as it seems right now. If anything important comes up cable.

T.

1. Among other things, Dreiser was writing an introduction to the Constable edition of Albert Londres's book *The Road to Buenos Ayres* (1928), a study of the white slave trade between France and Argentina.

2. Before returning to the ship, Dreiser attended a farewell party at Schwartz's, a popular restaurant on MacDougal Street. The group included, among many other leftist-leaning celebrities, Floyd Dell, Joseph Wood Krutch, Konrad Bercovici, Ernestine Evans, and Diego Rivera.

3. The Russian-born Joseph G. Robin (see Dreiser to Helen Richardson, 5 June 1924, n. 3). At this time Robin was attempting a dramatization of *The "Genius"*—a project that was never realized. Dreiser was unhappy with Robin's text and wrote Helen on 22 October to "persuade Robin to make all of these changes. In his text in the instances of Angela, Suzanne, and Christine, the emotional beauty and visibility of the book is wanting. This has sprung from his attempt to create an allegory apart from the book. But apart from the allegorical frame he has nothing but the force of the book itself to offer and I am trying to inject that force into his frame. If he will not accept these changes here & work to make the play a presentation of the spirit of the book, then I will have to do it when I return or reject his frame entirely" (DPUP).

4. Benjamin W. Huebsch (1876–1964) founded the prestigious B. W. Huebsch Co. and was known for publishing many European writers such as Joyce, D. H. Lawrence, Strindberg, and Chekhov. In 1925 he merged his list with the Viking Press, for which he was at this time serving as vice president and chief editor.

5. Dreiser is referring to Diego Rivera (1886–1957), the Mexican painter whose off-again, on-again relationship with the Communist Party led to his official visit to Russia at this time. Habitually contentious, he was eventually expelled from Russia at the request of the Soviet government.

6. Max Elser, an editor at the Metropolitan Syndicate in New York, which distributed articles to various newspapers and magazines throughout the country. Dreiser had accepted $1,000 on account from Elser for a series of articles on Russia.

7. Joseph Anthony, a journalist for the Hearst newspapers.

8. Morris L. Ernst (1888–1976), a lawyer with leftist political sympathies.

9. Heywood Broun (1888–1939), a columnist and a member of the Round Table at the Algonquin Hotel.

To Helen Richardson [H-DPUP]

Arriving in Moscow on 4 November, Dreiser began to record his first impressions of daily life, the people, and the new regime.

[9 November 1927]

Dear Babe:—

At the same time that this goes I am sending you a letter. But letters can never make the impressions on you that coming here will. It is all so different to our world. They are like some other kind of a tree or animal—large, stolid, easy-going and not bad natured—more inclined to be genial & smiling but indifferent to many things. And the country is so backward. There are 2,000,000 people here but just a few automobiles—maybe 500 or a thousand or two. And a few busses. And some street cars (put in only 15 years ago!) The rest are little draschkas or troikas—holding scarcely more than 1 fat Russian each—maybe two Americans. And then small crater-shaped wagons—with one horse. And the only difference between the Russian government & ours that I can see is that it is poorer—as yet. And that no one is allowed to pile up large fortunes—or not to work at something. Otherwise it goes on fine as it does everywhere. People with taste have tasteful little places and people without have places that are not so tasteful. The city is artificially attractive because of large squares everywhere and buildings which suggest the East—not the west. There are 484 churches here—all with gilded or green or blue or red or brown pineapple shaped domes & when the sun shines they look like oriental mosques or glittering palaces out of the Arabian tales. And then the bearded men—with tall or broad fur caps—and wide heavy skirted coats & boots. And the stout women—with shawls over their heads & boots on their feet. Only once in a while do you see a woman or girl who is trim—in our sense. And the shops are poor as yet because the government is trying to raise all of Russia at once—1/6th of the earth—to build railroads, power plants, machines & equipment of all kinds. And it takes money—or taxes. But the radio is everywhere, and the electric light and gas, and the telegraph & telephone & cable. The Soviets vote just as we do and I think in 10 or 20 years Russia may be as gay & wonderful & happy a place as any on earth. I hope so. There is no lack of liberty. You can go & do as you please. I think really there is much less liberty in America than there is here. For one thing there is no Negro or Catholic question:—the church is down here. A child cannot receive religious instruction & education is the watchword everywhere.

Personally I like it so far and am sure if given time, it will teach the world something new. We must come here in a year or so.

My plans are rather clear—though not exact—as yet: I am going from here to Leningrad (St. Petersburg). From there to Omsk or Tomsk in Siberia.[1] From there to some big city in the Volga—from there to the Caucasus—and Tiflis in the Caspian sea. From there, I will either return to Moscow & go south to Kiev, Kharkoff & Odessa and take the transcontinental at Constantinople for Paris—or I will go to Odessa direct & come north through Kiev, Kharkov to Moscow. In that case I will return as I came—via Berlin, Paris. But I prefer if possible—the other route. In any case we can meet in Paris or London or any other point as you will.

I hope you are well. In spite of lordly treatment everywhere travelling is hard work for me. I am getting old or lazy. And wonderful scenes are enticing—new lands but so often I wish I were up at Mt. Kisco[2] with you sitting on the porch or going to the spring for water. I hope all is well. Aside from one cable here & a letter which I got the day I arrived I have had no other word since I left. (Yes—the cable at Berlin.)

Love
T

1. Dreiser never did get to Siberia; he struggled with bronchitis for much of the trip, and because Russian officials thought the trip would adversely affect his health, they persuaded him not to go.
2. His country house at Mt. Kisco, New York.

To Esther McCoy [H-DPUP]

Grand Hôtel
Moscow

Nov. 24–1927

Dear Esther:

Recieved your one letter so far just three days ago. You've probably forgotten all about it but it contained news of the fire in your basement, ptomaine poisoning & the "Graphics" handling of Harding's child.[1] It was nice to get it. For my part I have been leading a full and busy life and I report for your benefit, that traveling is hard work—especially traveling in Russia. It is very cold here. The hotels are—alas—not American hotels. But the sights and the people perhaps make up for the hardships. A strong and interesting people—but again I am sure one would need to have been born here to enjoy them thoroughly. I scent a hyperborean strain. They are a little like their bears, friendly—but bears. And the living equipment is—as yet—not so far from what bears might enjoy. The country is changing; everything is just ahead, but since it is not quite here—it is all mixed up with old stuff and old clothes & customs. And then because of the cold one has to wear too many clothes. Some days I think of Florida or Los Angeles and sigh.

But how is the wilding of the heath? Leading a satyric and critical life I fear. A good girl? (You say) But do you know what a good girl is? Just the same I think of you with not only affection but admiration. Your so genuine. And so kindly, and so girlish with it all. I can listen to you talk by the hour. I get a genuine response. You should I think watch your physical health. Don't injure your charm (physical). It could all go so quickly with illness and you have everything before you. As for me—(us) we shall have a happy companionship I know if you do not decide (for reasons of another maybe—who can say) to move out of my life. . . . . . I am (in 3 hours) leaving for Leningrad (St. Petersburg). It is a twelve hour ride. Distances in Russia are enormous. I am to be there four or five days. Then I come back here to interview Stalin, Bukharin and Tchicherin[2]—three chiefs of the Communist Party. Then to Kharkoff—30 hours ride south of here—a large manufacturing city. Then to Novgorod,[3] on the Volga—Omsk and Novosibirsk in Siberia[4] (Also Kusbaz). Then back to Saratov on the Volga. Then to Stalingrad, the Caucasus Mountains, Tbilisi, in the Caucasus (Georgia), Baku on the Caspian Sea; Batumi on the Black Sea, The Crimea, Odessa & Kiev. From there I shall go through Odessa to Constantinople & so direct to Paris & London. I have been so delayed here that I am worried about my time—but I hope to have a week or so in London. Will let you know. Meantime love. I think of you in your wonderful little room. And I wish I could sit there with you now.

Love,
T. D.

1. The reference is to an article on former President Warren G. Harding that focused on the child he had fathered with his mistress, Nan Britton. She gave birth to his only child, and went public with the story after Harding died, when his family refused to continue the child support he had been paying. She told her story in *The President's Daughter* (1927).

2. Dreiser had been promised an interview with Joseph Stalin (1879–1953), but the opportunity never presented itself. He interviewed the Bolshevik leader and coeditor of *Pravda*, Nikolai Bukharin (1888–1939), on 5 December 1927, and he also spoke with Soviet Foreign Minister Georgi Tchicherin (1872–1936).

3. The city east of Moscow on the Volga is Nizhniy-Novgorod.

4. Bronchitis attacks led Dreiser to cancel the trip to Siberia.

1928

To Ruth Kennell [H-DPUP]

Dreiser met Ruth Epperson Kennell (1893–1977) in November 1927 during a tour of the Soviet Union, which had begun with a weeklong observation of the tenth anniversary of the October Revolution. An author, translator, and political activist, Kennell became his secretary and companion during his three-month trip through Russia. She was an American expatriate who had been living in Russia for five years, initially with her husband as part of a group of Americans that sought to bring manufacturing skills to Siberia. By 1927 her ailing husband had left Russia with their son, and she was supporting herself by editing and translating so-called anniversary editions of American writers, including Dreiser, for the state publishing house. Throughout their travels in Russia, Kennell kept a diary for Dreiser of his experiences, which she submitted to him daily for expansion and emendation. She also kept a private journal of her own, which in later years she used as the basis for Theodore Dreiser and the Soviet Union *(1969). She returned to America in 1928, and though they rarely met, she edited Dreiser's book on Russia and maintained a spirited correspondence with him in which she influenced his ideas on foreign affairs and American politics. She published novels and stories, including children's books set in Russia, such as* That Boy Nikolka and Other Tales of Soviet Children *(1945) and* Adventures in Russia and Other Stories about Soviet Children *(1947). Dreiser's semi-fictional portrait of Kennell appears as "Ernita" in* A Gallery of Women *(1929).*

THEODORE DREISER

Feb. 24–1928

Dear Ruth:

It was fine to hear from you here today. I didn't expect so interesting a letter so soon. Yes I'm back—and in the ring, as these clippings show.[1] There were a lot of others in the afternoon papers. Being back among, to me, more agreeable conditions even than in Europe, led me to much quiet thought. I felt that I should not confuse my personal discomforts and temperamental reactions to a changed world with the actual Russian approach. Most of all I decided that however little I might I should not seriously try to injure an idealistic effort. Besides, learning that there were bread lines here—the first since 1910 I became furious because there is too much wealth wasted to endure it. Hence, while I am going to stick to what I saw favorable and unfavorable I am going to contrast it with the waste and extravagance and social indifference here. I may find myself in another storm. If so—well & good.

I'm glad your working for Wood. I like him. He's a fine fellow. And so is Reswick.[2] Tell them both that they are bright spots in my Russian days.

And now several personal things. If you come to America stop here in New York and see me. If you need a little extra money to get out with, cable me. And as for data over there—send me rough mental sketches of these things—from your own point of view: 1. The New Bolshevik Art. 2. Theatrical conditions—old and new. 3. The Woman Question—(that is morals, marriage-divorce). 4. The condition of the Peasant as you see him. And lastly that contrast that you suggested of the difference between the Siberian and Russian peasant. Think these things out in extended letter form. If I can weave them into sketches here I'll make it up to you in ready cash.

You know I always think the very finest things of you. In fact if it hadnt been for you where would I have been. I hold you very close to me and will do what I can for you at any time. You know that. Do you still like me a little?

By the way, honey, Otto Kyllmann[3]—the president of Constable & Company of London (address 10 & 12 Orange Street, Leicester Sq. W.C. 2–) is very anxious to get hold of good books out of Russia. He's really a wonderful man, the most wise & kindly & engaging fellow imaginable. I told him I would get him in touch (if you were still there) with you, Dynamov,[4] and [word unintelligible]. I want you or Dynamov to write him & help him. He is a power in London—close to the London Times—controls the 19th Century and the Hibbard Journal & can do wonders in the way of furnishing European information—books—authors—magazines anything you will. If you are going to stay awhile write him—mention me & put him right. If Sergey should stop in London, Kyllmann can & will—at my request, make his stay wonderful. Therefore—

So long honey. Be a bad girl.

T. D.

Why not send Kyllmann that book about the new kind of love in Russia you were telling me about.

1. Dreiser had returned to New York from his Russian excursion on 21 February 1928. The newspaper clippings to which he refers are those in which his comparative views on America and the Soviet experiment were widely reported. She read eleven articles by Dreiser, five of which were sent by Junius Wood (see n. 2) from the *Buffalo News*, the rest by Kennell's in-laws from the *Morning Oregonian*.

2. Junius Wood was the Moscow correspondent for the Chicago *Daily News*. William Reswick was a Moscow Correspondent for the Associated Press who encouraged Dreiser to become involved in an effort to bring the Russian Ballet to America.

3. Dreiser met Otto Kyllmann, of Constable & Co., Ltd., in London in 1926. Kyllmann was one of the few publishing executives or editors Dreiser counted among his good friends.

4. Sergei Dinamov (1901–39), Russian author, translator, and editor who had served in the Red Army during the Revolution and was the director of the Institute of Red Professors. He admired Dreiser's writing and edited the first Soviet edition of his collected works.

To Ruth Kennell [H-DPUP]

Dreiser had received Kennell's justifiably severe criticism of the manuscript of Dreiser Looks at Russia *(1928) and here responds to a number of her editorial suggestions.*

200 West 57th St.
N.Y.C.

Sept 5–1928

Dear Ruth:[1]

Thanks for that very severe Dutch-Unclish letter which came last Friday. I went through it with the greatest care and reverence and made almost all of the changes which you suggested. For instance I reversed chapters 17 & 18. Then I took Captain Lenin[2] & put him last. I meditated on all your side corrections & where they were sound (as nearly all were) I incorporated them. In one or two places you failed to get my meaning. For instance philosophically & practically there is a vast difference between *religion* and *dogmatic religion*. There is for instance the religion which is a response to as well as an awe or reverence before the beauty and the wisdom of creative energy. Many people, free of any dogma, enjoy it. Then there are the dogmatized religions of the world. I think many are likely to approve of the differentiation. In regard to your objection to the description of the Russian huts with cows & pigs as a part of the family ménage, where do you suppose it came from? No less a person than Tolstoy's daughter Olga who wished me to stay over one more day in order that she might show me not four but a dozen or two. And all adjoining Yasnaya Polyana. I questioned her closely as to the arrangement, food, sanitation, clothing, etc. It was during the afternoon & evening before the Tolstoy reading.[3]

But if you are so doubtful ask your friend Wood who told me of things he had seen. And there is Reswick who testified of village conditions he knew. And Sergey[4] who told me, in your presence, if I am not mistaken, of plenty such in the Caucasus. And there is Albert Rhys Williams' book[5] which he recently sent me as well as the personal testimony of Leon Levinson,[6] the Jewish Critic with whom I visited the Jewish Art theatre in Moscow. He saw them twenty miles east of Rastov and what he told me tallied exactly with Olga Tolstoy's pictures. These things are a part of 1928 Russia and no fair picture is complete without them.

And next the secretaries. All your "*interpreters*" are incorporated. But next, what about the little dub with whom I quarreled from Moscow to Baku?—or your devoted Trevis,[7] who accompanied us to Leningrad, or the youth who before you came guided me through the Moscow penitentiary & afterwards accompanied us to Novgorod? Or the various soviet representatives who took up the noble work in different cities. Anyhow—and apart from that—what about the possible situation here in America—(a personal one I mean) which might (sympathetically let us say) dictate silence in regard to any particular female secretary.[8] So often we see our own plans & state so clearly,—those of the other fellow not at all.

As for the "bad construction of sentences," "inexcusable superfluity of words & parenthetical clauses." Guilty. I have been so offending all my life. All my books are full of them. You should have begun with Sister Carrie. But there is at least one chapter that is satisfactorily done I am sure—the state of the ladies in Russia. I am supposed to be at my best in that field, am I not?

In this connection I am amused. You speak of Chapter III as "a rambling & dull philosophic discussion." As a matter of fact it is the same chapter which as an article in Vanity Fair[9] you enthused over, saying that it was succinct and illuminating and that the Soviet government ought to be grateful for so clear & fair statement of its case. And because of those particular remarks I decided to incorporate the chapter. I have only one consolation. If you were wrong in your first impression of it you may not be absolutely right in your second. Is not that possible?

What I really fear though is that my writing the book has crossed you in some way. If so I'm sorry. But I could scarcely escape doing it. The International Newspaper Syndicate that first bought the series wished to issue the newspaper stuff in paper form at a clip. Liveright who has contracts with me objected and claimed the stuff as a book. Covici & Friede, publishers, and Simon & Schuster, publishers, both urged me to print and Constable wanted it for England. Finally, therefore, I took out my book of notes & went to work. The sad mess which now troubles you so is the result. But I'm doing my best to improve it. And regardless of these few counter squeaks I am honestly grateful to you for pointing out the bad as well as the good. I know you wish me only good. And if I can be of service to you, you have only to call on me to see whether I make good or not.

Affectionately—very
T. D

1. Dreiser wrote the following in the upper left hand corner of the first page: "I would like to do Haywood but I fear my picture would be irritatingly gloomy to some. And just at the moment I have no heart for it. T. D." Dreiser's reference is to William D. "Big Bill" Haywood (1869–1928), who had died on 18 May. Haywood was a union organizer for the International Workers of the World (IWW); Dreiser had used the 1913 Paterson Silk Strike, in which Haywood was active, as the background for his one-act play *The Girl in the Coffin* (1917). Sentenced to prison for his labor activities, Haywood had jumped bail in 1920 and escaped to the Soviet Union. Dreiser had visited with him in Moscow, but Haywood was then a sick man who had become a pensioner of the government.

2. Dreiser's jocular reference to Vladimir Lenin.

3. On 21 November 1927, Dreiser took the train from Moscow to Yasnaya Polyana and then a sled to the home of Leo Tolstoy. By chance the visit coincided with the seventeenth anniversary of Tolstoy's death. His youngest daughter Olga welcomed Dreiser to the celebration, which included recordings of Tolstoy's voice, musical performances, reminiscences from local residents, recitations, and a reading of an unpublished Tolstoy story. Dreiser was particularly interested in the peasantry and villagers of Yasnaya Polyana. In his diary, Dreiser records only that he "had a wonderful conversation with the daughter, who told me all about her work" (Riggio and West, *Russian Diary*, 120).

4. For Wood, Reswick, and Sergey, see Dreiser to Ruth Kennell, 24 February 1928, n. 2 and n. 4.

5. Albert Rhys Williams, a Congregational minister from Boston and a member of the American Socialist Party. He visited Russia after the 1917 March Revolution along with John Reed and Louise Bryant, and he later recorded his experiences in *Through the Russian Revolution* (1923).

6. Leon Levinson was the first president of the International Christian Hebrew Alliance formed in 1925, the umbrella group for various organizations that advocated contemporary Messianic Judaism.

7. Trevis was Dreiser's official guide and interpreter who traveled through Russia with Dreiser and Kennell. Dreiser reports in his *Russian Diary* that relations among the three were strained because Trevis made personal overtures to Kennell.

8. Dreiser is arguing that he cannot include many of the people Kennell wanted mentioned, including minor functionaries such as "secretaries." Dreiser also suggests there are many reasons for public silence about individuals, an example of which is his discretion in not mentioning his personal relationship to her (his "secretary").

9. Dreiser is referring to his article "Russia: The Great Experiment" (*Vanity Fair*, 30 June, 1928: 47–48), which was incorporated into Chapter III of *Dreiser Looks at Russia*.

To Beatrice Booth [H-DPUP]

Beatrice Wittmack Booth was married to Dreiser's friend, Jay Franklin Booth (1874–1958), the Indiana-born book and magazine illustrator who contributed thirty-two charcoal illustrations to A Hoosier Holiday *(1916). See Dreiser to*

Kirah Markham, 21 August 1915. Dreiser sent Booth a draft for a dramatization of Sister Carrie.

Sister Carrie[1]

Oct 4–1928

Dear Beatrice:

Wish you two would read this & see if you can make any suggestions for improvement. The key note of the play is Hurstwood's decline. The psychology of Hurstwood's decline was his own social conviction that he had sinned—(morally, socially anyway you please). The chief problem *is* how best to suggest that destructive psychology in the play.[2] Are you enjoying Indiana.

T. D.

1. Dreiser had authorized Hy S. Kraft, a theatrical writer-producer, to develop a stage adaptation of *Sister Carrie*. Kraft hired the playwright and screenwriter John Howard Lawson (later to become one of the "Hollywood Ten" indicted by the House Un-American Activities Committee) to produce the script that Dreiser here sends to Booth. In the end, Dreiser disapproved of Lawson's adaptation and abandoned the project.

2. For Dreiser's detailed ideas about how to present Hurstwood in the script, see Dreiser to John Howard Lawson, 10 August 1928 and 10 October 1928 (in Pizer, *New Letters*).

To Louise Campbell [H-DPUP]

Louise Campbell remained one of Dreiser's most trusted editors and confidantes, managing a good deal of work for him during the brief period of greatest prosperity in his career—the years between the publication of An American Tragedy *(1925) and the outset of the Great Depression.*

THEODORE DREISER

Oct 18–1928

Dear Louise:

I'll send a check Nov. 1. It seems crazy not to do it before but a combination of demands makes it necessary to adjust dates. On second thought I'll get Pell of B&L[1] to send $100 & I'll send the balance & arrange with him Nov. 1.

But why not come over this next Saturday or Sunday & spend the day. I mean come straight through to Mt. Kisco. You can taxi to the Grand Central & get a train within a half hour. They run about 9^{15} 10^{20} 10^{45} 11^{20} or so & get to Kisco in 1 hr 15 min. If you come Saturday to the house here you could go up with us. The Hoffensteins, Roberts, Horace Kallen, Bercovici's daughter Rada, and maybe Bercovici,[2] & so on are coming. But you and I could wander off & talk. At Mt. Kisco there is a taxi man. His name is Davis & he runs about 12 taxis. He knows my place. If I'm not at the station say Mr. Dreisers place & he'll know.

I never expected poor old Yvonne to evoke such a burst. And I still feel that I haven't portrayed McKail.[3] He had had a hard, grim youth. I think for a time he was an apprentice to an iron moulder & ran away. He had been hungry too. I think Yvonne was crazy about his iron courage—his calm ability to wait—and on so little. By the way he's a success now—a real one. John Ferguson is his name. But she has walked off & entirely discarded 250 canvasses. She is one of the really amazing incidents of my life.

Are you coming?

T.

The Russian book will be out Tuesday.[4] At least I'll get 6 copies then & will send you one. I am reading Insull[5] direct. If you can come Saturday you can have a nice room all to yourself. Also you can stay over Sunday night to Monday.

By the way do you know of any old antique shop in Phila which might have an old Revolutionary flint lock gun. I want it for my cabin. I can get one for $30 [00] but in Phila I might do better.

1. At this time, Arthur Pell was the treasurer at Boni and Liveright. Dreiser owed Campbell money for her work on *Dreiser Looks at Russia* (1928).

2. Samuel Hoffenstein (1899–1947), author and scriptwriter who would later write the screenplay for the 1931 film version of *An American Tragedy*.

The Canadian author Charles George Douglas Roberts (1860–1943), whom Dreiser had known since their Greenwich Village days.

Horace Kallen (1882–1974), social activist, author, educator, philosopher, and one of the founders of the New School for Social Research.

Konrad Bercovici (1882–1961), Rumanian-born novelist, playwright, and journalist.

3. Dreiser is referring to Keir McKail, a character in "Ellen Adams Wrynn," one of the sketches in *A Gallery of Women* (1929), which was based loosely on Dreiser's acquaintance with the modernist painter Anne Estelle Rice (1877–1959). "Yvonne" was a working title for the sketch. The model for McKail was John Duncan Ferguson (1874–1961), a Scottish painter whom Dreiser had met in Paris in 1912.

4. *Dreiser Looks At Russia* was published on 11 November 1928.

5. An article Campbell had sent on Samuel Insull (1859–1938), a public utilities and railroad magnate in Chicago, whose career in some ways paralleled that of Charles Tyson Yerkes, the model for the character of Frank Cowperwood in *The Financier* and *The Titan*.

To Lina Goldschmidt [TC-DPUP]

Dreiser first met the German art critic and antifascist activist Lina Goldschmidt (1889–1935) in Moscow during the 1927 celebration of the tenth anniversary of the Russian Revolution. An ardent admirer of Dreiser's writing, which she championed in Germany, Goldschmidt eventually collaborated with Erwin Piscator on a dramatization of An American Tragedy. *In 1933, she and her husband fled the anti-Semitic campaigns of the Nazis and soon after settled in the United States.*

October 31st, 1928.

Dear Lina Goldschmidt:

I haven't written you because I said to myself, "What's the use?" You were constantly moving from New York to Honduras, and from Honduras to Brazil, from Brazil to the Argentine, and I could not hope to follow you.[1] But your letters have been a genuine delight and the services you have rendered me in South America are already evidenced by letters from individuals in Brazil, the Argentine and Chile.

Apparently, one of the most enthusiastic of your admirers is Louis Quintanilla[2] of the Mexican Embassy in Brazil. Because of you he has set out to make me famous in Brazil. I think that is a very startling if not exactly bad effect on one young man.

Because of what you wrote me I sent to your German address some material which I thought might be of interest to you, and now I am wishing that you would forsake Germany and come over here and live in New York where I would be able to see you once in a while. You are so very far away, and as I see it, there's no particular reason for it. You move about so much that you might just as well live in New York as in Berlin.

By the way, now that you are there, won't you go and see the German production of "The Hand of the Potter"[3] and tell me what you think of it?—whether it is really as good as some people say?

Incidentally, if it is not too much trouble, and you could do it conveniently, I wish you would get in touch with Dr. Paul Eter, Friederich, Wilhelmstrasse 8, Berlin. He is the man who translated "The Hand of the Potter" into German, and for my future guidance I would like an intelligent comment on him from you—his intelligence, character, connections, etc.[4] The reason I say this is because he is writing me for another play in case I happen to have one. I would like to know from you how good a translator you really think he is.

Do, please, write me whenever you are moved so to do, because I am charmed when I read your letters. I would be even more delighted, though, if you were here and we could easily talk over all of the things that are so ready at hand to talk about.

Affectionately,
Theodore Dreiser

1. Although Goldschmidt was now in Berlin, she had spent time in Latin America, where her husband Alfons Goldschmidt was attempting to establish guidelines for the immigration of anti-fascist refugees from Europe. Based in Mexico, the couple traveled throughout the southern hemisphere for months at a time.

2. Louis Quintanilla (1893–1978) was a prominent Spanish artist renowned for his murals. He took an active role as a Loyalist in the Spanish Civil War, and after the war he lived in exile in New York and Paris.

3. In September 1928 the play was staged in Berlin by Drei Masken and produced by Gustave Hartung. The reviews were favorable and the play had an extended run.

4. On 3 December 1928, Goldschmidt reported that Eter was "a fine person" with experience as a director in a theater in Hamburg; but she recommended Dr. Max Epstein, a theater critic and producer in Berlin, as better suited to getting Dreiser's plays staged successfully in Germany (DPUP).

To Kirah Markham [H-DPUP]

Dreiser sent Markham a draft of a character sketch about her that he thought of including in A Gallery of Women *(1929).*

200 West 57th St.
N Y

Nov 6–1928

Dear Kirah:

Here is Sidonie—or yourself & myself in one study. I meant to call it Stephanie but decided, because of the other, not to.[1] As it reads now it is laid in Chicago and New York. Maurice Brown and The Chicago Little Theatre[2] are mentioned. In short the thing has the undisguised natural flow of our contact. But these things—especially names & places might be changed unless you feel differently. Personally I should prefer it as it is. If you feel that it should be more disguised I will see what I can do. Am open to suggestion, criticism—even abuse. But I question once when you read this whether you will feel like abusing me.

Personally I always feel that no one ever really knows anyone else. We observe—exteriorly certain deeds & expressions. But what else? You & I lived together nearly three years. During that time we each imagined we sensed certain things in regard to each other. But did we? And if we did not, how are we to do more than paint a seeming portrait from a purely personal view painting—not accurate but as we saw it—or thought I did.

And so with this comment I leave it to you. The critical part if there is any may be due to mis-apprehension. The truthfulness, if there is any, may be indiscreet. But the affection & admiration are not to be concealed. And they are there.

T. D.

I would have sent the sketch had I been here yesterday—(Monday). Have only now returned from Greenwich. And would come to Reading[3] but again visits & trips have to be shuffled like cards here. Some come up unwanted and sometimes are forced on us. Others wanted are delayed. But I'll see about Reading after you read this. Not before.

1. See Dreiser to Kirah Markham, 13 July 1922, n. 3. Dreiser changed the name to Sidonie because he had already used Stephanie Platow as the name of a character based on Markham in *The Titan* (1914).
2. Maurice Browne. See Dreiser to Kirah Markham, 3 July 1917, n. 1.
3. Markham was living in Reading, Pennsylvania.

To Kirah Markham [H-DPUP]

Markham was upset about a number of interpretations in "Sidonie," a sketch based on her years with Dreiser.

Theodore Dreiser

Nov. 10–1928

Cryhon Dear—

Don't cry—Once you pleaded to be buried in the same ground with me. Isn't it a little warmer to live in the same book—as long as such books last?[1]

I didn't mean to be cruel to your father. You know what writing is. You get in the swing of what seems reality—and painter wise you brush as close as you can. Soften it for me. Your realistic soul will keep it true enough I know.

Sure I'll come to Reading one of these days.[2] I walked through there in the spring of 1927—walked all the way from Elizabeth N.J. to Roanoke, Va. And alone. You'll believe that when I say I averaged 25 to 32 miles per day—550 miles

Give my regards to your husband.[3] Tell him to be kind to drunk brutes. That'll fix things for me when I get there.

T.

Can you revise it soon for me.

1. See Dreiser to Kirah Markham, 13 July 1922, n. 3 and 6 November 1928, n. 1.
2. Dreiser did visit her in Reading, Pennsylvania, later that month.
3. Markham was at this time married to David S. Gaither, a stage designer and teacher.

To Kirah Markham [H-DPUP]

Theodore Dreiser

Dec 30–1928

Dear Kirah:

Thanks so very much for the Venus of the Sun & Moon.[1] I am delighted to have it. I was away when it came & they stored it in the office here. But it was brought up yesterday and now I am thinking of taking it up in the country to be hung over a fireplace one of these days when I am a little less rushed. I shall try to think of something for you. This must be my Painting week—or Xmas, for I received one from Jerome Blum[2]—an exquisite south sea thing and another from Katherine Dudley[3]—a negro harmony. Besides—at last, I have a portrait that is one—by Weyman Adams[4]—and I am to get that presently. It's going to [word unintelligible] first.

I think of you too so much & wish you the best of everything. Esherick[5] was in here one day and said you two had been down to his place. Also that you had been offered something with that Crossroads Theatre over near Media.[6] Did you decide to take it?

Things are very well with me. I have a slight touch of flu and an embarrassment of labor—but since work is what I want I am certainly best off when embarrassed that way. All of the [word missing] dreams of the two of you for 1929.

T. D.

Maurice Browne[7] & some allies now have a play on here—*Wings Over Europe*.[8] The general opinion is that it is fine. I haven't seen it.

1. Unidentified. Seemingly a painting by Markham.
2. Jerome Blum (1884–1956), Chicago-born painter who was influenced by oriental art and known for his townscapes, landscapes, seascapes, still-lifes, and figure studies. Dreiser had visited his Chicago studio in 1913. There appeared a month after this letter Dreiser's foreword to the "Catalogue of an Exhibition of Paintings by Jerome Blum at the Anderson Galleries in New York, January 28th-February 9th." Dreiser later made a point of visiting Blum when the painter went through occasional periods of deep depression that hospitalized him.
3. Katherine Dudley, portrait painter and poet, sister to Dorothy Dudley (see Dreiser to Dorothy Dudley, 7 April 1932, headnote).

4. Wayman Adams (1883–1959). In addition to his painting of Dreiser, Adams was known for his portraits of national figures such as Otis Skinner, Alice Roosevelt Longworth, and presidents Harding, Coolidge, and Hoover.

5. Wharton Esherick (1887–1970), a major figure in the Arts and Crafts movement; he created furniture, sculpture, wood block prints, and architectural interiors. He had a studio in Paoli, Pennsylvania, near the Rose Valley Arts and Crafts Community. He did wood and metal work for Dreiser at his country home at Mt. Kisco, New York, including a set of wrought-iron andirons, and he supervised the construction of two thatched-roofed cabins on the property—in effect, putting his personal stamp on the architecture of Dreiser's estate. Dreiser first met Esherick in August 1924 at the Hedgerow Theater outside Philadelphia, where Markham was performing. She introduced the two men, and she and Dreiser stayed overnight at Esherick's home.

6. The Crossroads Theatre, a little theater in Media, Pennsylvania, just west of Philadelphia.

7. Dreiser wrote this note in the upper left-hand corner of the first page.

8. *Wings Over Europe*, written by Robert Nichols and Maurice Browne, directed by Rouben Mamoulian, was produced by the Theatre Guild and opened in New York on 10 December 1928 at the Martin Beck Theatre. For Maurice Browne, see Dreiser to Kirah Markham, 3 July 1917, n. 1.

1929

To Emma Goldman [H—SCHR]

Dreiser had known the Lithuanian-born Emma Goldman (1869–1940) since the 1910s when he lived in Greenwich Village and associated with political radicals in such venues as Polly's Restaurant and the Liberal Club. After her activities against military conscription and America's entry into World War I, Goldman was imprisoned in 1917; she lost her citizenship and was deported to Russia in 1919. Soon disillusioned with the Soviet regime, she went into exile in Germany and then France. In 1926 Dreiser visited Goldman in Paris, and pledged his support for her repatriation efforts and for her attempt to find a publisher for the autobiography he had encouraged her to write. She wrote him of her "joy to find you so eager and so intensely interested in my struggle and the things I want to do. Really it was a revelation, a bright ray from a dark horizon. It warmed me all over and made me feel that I am not so terribly cut off from everything as I thought I was" (29 September 1926 [DPUP]). For the next few years, he continued to help Goldman find a publisher and contributed funds to support her while she wrote Living My Life *(1931). In 1928 Dreiser considered writing a sketch of her for* A Gallery of Women *(1929) and inquired about biographical sources for her.[1] He sent her newspaper clippings he had collected on her public activities, which she returned with a detailed list of inaccuracies contained in them (20 January 1929 [DPUP]). For more reliable data, she suggested that he look through the files of the radical journal* Mother Earth, *and read Hyppolyte Havel's biographical sketch of her, Frank Harris's essay in* Contemporary Portraits: Fourth Series *(1923), and William Marion Reedy's article "The Daughter of the Dream" (1911).*

200 East 57th Street,
New York City,

January 31, 1929.

Dear Emma,

Your letter of January 20, in regard to in the inaccuracies in the newspaper clippings I furnished you, proves very interesting.

I have not as yet gotten hold of Mother Earth[2] nor the William Marion Reedy article,[3] but the book by Hippolyte Havel[4] has been delivered to me and when I get sufficient data together I will see what I can do. I only want to make a sketch of some 9,000 or 10,000 words, but unless the material in my hand is sufficiently intimate and dramatic, I will not attempt it.[5]

I am glad you are getting along so well with your book[6] and am absolutely satisfied that some publisher will be glad to take it and that it will prove a

Emma Goldman. (Reprinted by permission of the Collection of the International Institute of Social History, Amsterdam.)

success—unless you make it so threatening that the American Government will disbar it. I hope not, because I would like to see you with a tidy sum at your command from now on.

1. In 1909, Dreiser "had commissioned a profile of her for *The Delineator,* instructing the writer to pretend to denounce her while smuggling across her ideas. Dreiser

considered her the most important American woman of her time" (Lingeman, *American Journey*, 34).

2. *Mother Earth*, an anarchist journal published and edited (1906–17) by Emma Goldman and Alexander Berkman.

3. William Marion Reedy's celebratory article "The Daughter of the Dream" appeared in the *St. Louis Mirror* in 1911.

4. Hippolyte Havel (1871?–1950), anarchist author and editor who had been one of Goldman's lovers. He wrote for *Mother Earth*, as well as for other radical publications. He collected Goldman's essays in *Anarchism and Other Essays* (1910), which contains his portrait of her.

5. The sketch did not appear in *A Gallery of Women*; it is possible that Dreiser did not find the material sufficient for his purposes.

6. *Living My Life*.

To Ruth Kennell [H-DPUP]

After the publication of Dreiser Looks at Russia *(1928), Dorothy Thompson accused Dreiser of plagiarizing from her book on the same subject,* The New Russia *(1928), and threatened to sue him. Kennell had helped Dreiser with the editing of his book and she was concerned about the implications of a legal suit for her.*

Feb 11–1929

Dear Ruth:

As you see by the legal exchange of letters of which I enclose copies, Dorothy decided not to come into court.[1] It took nearly 1 month to get a bill of particulars to which a legal reply could be made. Meantime my attorneys Hume & Cameron examined Dorothy's *The New Russia* and Anne OHare McCormicks *The Hammer & the Scythe*.[2] I have a copy of their 14 page comparison of parts of the two books. Sometime when you are east you may see that. Both the Times & the World referred to this similarity but no word from either lady. The McCormick book was published 6 months before Dorothys. Please send the World column back to me for my files. There will be no suit here or anywhere for the simple reason that the first question Mr. Hume would ask Dorothy would be "is this work of yours wholly original with you?" If she said yes the McCormick book marked, with hers also marked for comparison, would be given her for explanation. Apparently there is some other work which both read and profited by. Despite or because of all this the Russian book is now being printed without change in England, Germany & Scandinavia. Draw your own conclusions.

And now in regard to your literary future. Let me give you a last straight word. It is what you do in writing—*your thought contribution* & nothing less that makes or breaks you. What people charge you with is always completely overcome by what they can get from you intellectually. Incidentally if Miss

Thompson will come into court I can prove that you had nothing to do with what you call the plagiarized chapter.[3] That is all you need to know, isn't it.

Now as for your book, *sure I'll get it published for you.*[4] Send it to me.

And as for your opinion of my Cosmopolitan material[5]—allow me to most cordially blow you a kiss from the ends of my fingers. You are one & do not get it. I happen to have written the thing as a whole, see it as a whole—and await, as usual, for the significance of the wholeness of it to get to such temperaments as will get it.

Regards, Love, etc.

But send back the clipping. The legal copies are yours for such use as you see fit.

T. D.

1. Dorothy Thompson (1894–1961), at this time foreign correspondent and head of the Berlin bureau of the *New York Evening Post*. Together with her husband, the novelist Sinclair Lewis, she arrived in Moscow in 1927 and socialized with Dreiser for a brief time. Thompson's experience resulted in a series of articles; she collected these in *The New Russia*, a book that appeared two months before the publication of *Dreiser Looks at Russia*. As Dreiser notes, she had just dropped the plagiarism case against him.

2. *The Hammer and the Scythe* (1928) by Anne O'Hare McCormick (1880–1954) described the renowned *New York Times* journalist's experiences during her two trips to the Soviet Union.

3. Kennell was concerned that her editing of Dreiser's book would open her to charges of plagiarism.

4. Kennell's novel *Vanya of the Streets* (1931).

5. Kennell disliked three autobiographical stories (collectively called "This Madness") that he was writing for *Hearst's International-Cosmopolitan*. Kennell felt that the sketches, which centered on the lives of women Dreiser had known, were self-indulgent and badly conceived. See Dreiser to Ruth Kennell, 20 March 1929, n. 4.

To Ruth Kennell [H-DPUP]

As was his habit in connection with the writing of many friends (both men and women), Dreiser offered editorial advice and publication connections to Kennell.

200 West 57th St

Mch 20–1929

Dear Ruth:

I have not only read Vanya of the Streets but it has been read by readers for *Liveright*, *Covici-Friede* and *Simon & Schuster*.[1] My personal reaction is that most of your material is fine but that the story form is weak—almost harmful because not convincingly done. As a study of Vanya, there is plenty of fine material here. But it should be condensed considerably. The conversations especially could be cut—some eliminated, but all the material presenting pictures of Russian life—Xmas, Easter, the anniversary procession—used as atmosphere—bits say in the history and development of how & why this one boy came to be what he was. It would be much more moving I think than it is now. On the other hand the reader for Simon & Schuster thought the story form should be abandoned entirely & the book be made a direct study of these children. He added that the bare facts are stark enough. Smith[2] of Liveright thinks the story form as is is possible but not strong enough in its present form. Naturally I prefer my way. With permission to edit I can get the book done—but do you want that? Say what you wish.

Glad you have had such a fine winter but sorry you are leaving for Russia. Evidently your friend[3] desires to stay as she is extending her passport.

As for This Madness[4] I am sorry that I cannot alter my experiences & reactions to suit you. This situation appears to be my literary fate.

T. D

1. Harper and Brothers published *Vanya of the Streets* (1931).
2. Tom Smith. See Dreiser to Helen Richardson, 16 April 1924, n. 9.
3. Unidentified.
4. Another installment in the on-going debate between Kennell and Dreiser about the three stories published under the title "This Madness" in *Hearst's International-Cosmopolitan* (see Dreiser to Ruth Kennell, 11 February 1929, n. 5). Kennell wrote him that the pieces had "the unreality and romanticism of a schoolboy" and displayed the "false conception engendered by capitalism . . . that woman is a commodity for the use of men" (10 March 1929 [DPUP]).

To Kirah Markham [H-DPUP]

Markham had turned more seriously to writing at this time. Dreiser encouraged her, though he also had a sense that her many talents were something of a curse that led her to dissipate her creative energies, a critique stated here somewhat obliquely as a wish that he could give her "the gift of concentration."

Theodore Dreiser

April 18, 1929

Dear Kirah:

Why the inquiry—almost ironic. We all have so much to do—you know that. I have thought frequently since I read that story of yours that if you were to do a series of such fabulous commentaries on *now*, how interesting it would be. I suppose I should have said that before this. The magazine I was thinking of was The Dial. But there is also *Rejections* published by

Doubleday Page at Garden City and Caravan—or The Caravan.[1] Address unknown. My personal answer to the absence or want of anything was work—It still is—my only solvent. I can suffer or wish, but not when I am creatively tasking or seeking to create. If I could only give you the gift of concentration. The resulting condensation would be so much. But as for writing—I can only occasionally do that.[2]

T. D.

Sidonie—in cut form soon begins in the Cosmo.[3]
The check[4] is what I meant to send you Xmas.

1. *The Dial*, *Rejections*, and *The Caravan*: arts and literary magazines of the day. The most famous, *The Dial*, was being edited by Marianne Moore at this time, but it ceased publication three months later in July of 1929.

2. Dreiser means he has limited time to edit other people's writing.

3. See Dreiser to Kirah Markham, 13 July 1922, n. 3 and 6 November 1928, n. 1. "Sidonie" ran in the June and July 1929 issues of *Hearst's International-Cosmopolitan*.

4. Payment for reading and making editorial comments on "Sidonie."

To Lina Goldschmidt [TC-DPUP]

Goldschmidt was acting in a dual capacity as Dreiser's unofficial agent in Germany and a contributor to the production of a dramatic version of An American Tragedy.

200 West 57th Street,
New York City,

April 27, 1929

My dear Mrs. Goldschmidt,

I have your letter of April 15 and agreeable to your suggestion, I hasten to write Piscator,[1] urging him to begin work on AN AMERICAN TRAGEDY at once, but under no circumstances do I wish the play to be a hash or hodge-podge of four or five people. Piscator should either be able to dramatize it himself or he should get some one whose repute would not interfere with the fame of the book to do the dialogue, but this must be the work of one person and I will sign no contract that does not specify that. In the presentation of the play there should be mentioned only the name of the author of the book and that of the person who has dramatized it from the original version.

I certainly will be grateful to you if you will supervise the dramatization to this extent—i.e. see that it is a satisfactory and forceful presentation of the book in play form. I do not wish any incidents or philosophy that are not part and parcel of the original work. They are not necessary and I do not wish to have any dramatizer placed in the position where he could say that he was doing more than dramatizing the original work or that the finished product as it appears in German is not my personal creation. I want this understood and written in the contract—otherwise I will not accept it.

I think you are exactly right in what you say about having this done by a famous writer such as Heinrich Mann[2]—and I would prefer to have it done as originally planned—that is re-arranged under your supervision or at least with your knowledge—but I would not care to have it entirely claimed by any prominent dramatist or writer with radically different ideas of his own. I know you understand the situation thoroughly and I consider myself fortunate in the extreme to have your able assistance, and I continue in the exceedingly comfortable thought that with you in on this transaction my interests are even better guarded than were I there myself.

I am attaching copy of letter just written to Piscator,[3] so that you may know everything that passed between us.

I am anticipating your "extended" letter, of which you hold out a promise to me, with keen interest, and in the meantime, believe me to be,

As ever,
Theodore Dreiser

1. Erwin Piscator (1893–1966), actor, playwright, director, and theatrical producer, a radical figure in German theater, who had formed his own production company. (A Marxist and a member of the German Communist Party, he went into exile after the Nazis came to power, and in 1937 he moved to the United States, where he remained until after World War II.) Dreiser was arranging to have Piscator adapt *An American Tragedy* for a production in Germany, using a scenario prepared by Goldschmidt. Goldschmidt suggested that Dreiser himself write Piscator "to hurry a bit with your play" since he was dragging his feet with the work (Goldschmidt to Dreiser, 15 April 1929 [DPUP]). Goldschmidt had written Dreiser that she was returning the script Dreiser had sent of the earlier dramatization of the novel by Patrick Kearney, and she recommended that Piscator and she do a completely new adaptation. Probably because Piscator was known for both his doctrinaire interpretations and for his experimental and expressionistic staging techniques, Dreiser here shows concern for the treatment of his novel as well as for his sole rights to authorship. He had reason to be concerned. Unlike Kearney's 1926 stage adaptation, which followed Dreiser's plot and was structurally conventional, the Piscator play emphasized the class struggle in the book by staging the action on two levels, representing labor and capital. An interlocutor asked questions of the two groups, provoking debate on social and philosophical issues.

2. Heinrich Mann (1871–1950), German novelist (and the elder brother of Thomas Mann) famous for his satires on social conditions in Germany—writing that led to his exile from Nazi Germany in 1933. Dreiser had recommended Mann to Goldschmidt for this project, but she objected to Mann's participation in the writing.

3. This letter is not among Dreiser's papers.

To Rella Abell Armstrong [TC-DPUP]

Dreiser met Rella Abell Armstrong in Rome during his European excursion in 1912. She was then married to the American writer Paul Armstrong and she had ambitions to write for the stage, which she later realized. In his diary of the time, Dreiser reveals his admiration for Mrs. Armstrong's knowledge of Italian history and her intellectual and personal independence. In a letter of 21 December 1916 Dreiser suggested to H. L. Mencken that Mrs. Armstrong was among the friends whom he trusted to criticize his work in progress (Riggio, Dreiser-Mencken Letters, I, 286–87). Dreiser's diary of 1917–18 shows that their friendship had evolved beyond the platonic stage of their initial encounter, though by the time of this letter that aspect of their relationship had ended. In 1928 they began collaboration on "The Financier," a dramatization of his novels The Financier *and* The Titan. *He soon became disenchanted with the idea, however, writing that "the financial material is much too congested . . . you would have to rid your mind of at least some of that load, or use symbols rather than directly expressing it in the first act. . . . If you think an outline could be prepared which would more readily convey the natural drama I am talking about, I wish you would let me have it" (Dreiser to Rella Abell Armstrong, 19 December 1928 [DPUP]). By the fall of 1929 he was suggesting she collaborate with someone else, though he clearly preferred her to put aside the project. The opinions of the anonymous "someone" alluded to here are almost certainly Dreiser's own.*

200 West 67th Street,
New York City,

October 26, 1929.

Dear Rella,

I took up the matter of collaboration on The Financier[1] with someone you know by reputation, I think, but whom I do not wish to name right now. He has collaborated on various things here in New York, but he does not want to collaborate on this. He himself, having read both The Financier and The Titan, is of the opinion that they cannot be dramatized, except in a very general way, i.e. by some plot or theory which holds only its general outlines to either one or both of the books.

One of the things he said about this Chicago version was just what I said: that it should not be laid in one city, but preferably three—Philadelphia, Chicago and New York. He insists that there is no possibility of crowding in all of the characters that are in your outline or that are indicated in the book. He said that even to vaguely suggest, let alone stamp any of the complications and the individuals on the mind of the audience would take—using your outline as a basis—about 80 minutes per act, and that would make a show something like Strange Interlude.[2]

I am willing to hand it to some one else if you think fit. I know, for instance, Mr. and Mrs. Spewak,[3] who have successfully accomplished several things, but I don't believe they would collaborate and just another opinion on this text would scarcely help.

I don't see what remains to be done—unless you can work it out for yourself or find some one to collaborate with you.

Let me know what you think.

1. In response to Dreiser's suggestion in this letter that she work with another playwright on the project, Armstrong wrote "I should prefer to make the dramatization of The Financier alone" (Rella Abell Armstrong to Dreiser, 6 November 1929 [DPUP]). "The Financier" was never produced, probably for the reasons Dreiser outlines here. It remains in manuscript among the Dreiser papers at the University of Pennsylvania.

2. *Strange Interlude* (1928), a play in two parts and nine acts by Eugene O'Neill. Relying on the modernist technique of stream of consciousness to reveal the characters' thoughts and emotions, as well as asides that are often in ironic contrast to their speeches, it was thought by many, including Dreiser, to be too lengthy and tedious.

3. Samuel (1899–1971) and Bella Cohen Spewak (1899–1987), a husband and wife comedy writing team who are best remembered for the long-running *Kiss Me, Kate* (1948)—with music by Cole Porter.

1930

To Mrs. Heym [H-DPUP]

Dreiser occasionally wrote to Louise Campbell's mother, whom he visited when in Philadelphia. Because of her marital problems, Campbell preferred to live with her mother and sister.

200 W. 57th St
N.Y.C.

Feb. 27–1930

Dear Mrs. Heym:

The lovely ties made by you and forwarded by Louise have just come. I am so pleased. And so grateful. I know you are sick much of the time and probably sick of sewing, but you dress Louise so well that I thought (enviously, I will admit) that you might help me out: I dress so wretchedly. Besides they've quit making bow ties and I love bow ties. So, mother dear—I mean my dear Mrs. Heym—I want to register here my gratitude. I know you get enough adoration for eight mothers from Louise—but I'll add some more—say enough to—all told—make it nine. Besides I'll remember you in my Prayers—such as they are. They're not so much but in your case I'll do a little better than usual—or try to.

Affectionately and
Gratefully
Theodore Dreiser

To Louise Campbell [H-DPUP]

At this time Campbell was helping Dreiser edit the manuscript of Dawn, *a memoir of his first twenty years.*

200 W. 57th St
N.Y.

Feb. 27–1930

Dear Louise:

The ties are really beautiful.[1] I am moved to incorporate mother as a tie factory—say over in Wilmington, or Chester Pa. or Trenton—Heym Sweet Heym—or Hyman Heym, Inc. Anyhow I am thinking heavily—as per the above . . . . . Next I hear Esherick[2] is to return in a few days. Cheer up.

. . . . Next—Fabri[3]—you know—the porch builder has written a novel or novelette—a sort of comedy of character and temperament. I like it. But he doesn't understand English well enough not to write—"They will own the entire household" when he means "they would own." In short throughout the 261 typewritten pages many, many tenses are wrong. Also many transpositions of parts of sentences would help greatly. But Fabri is sure that his language, apart from this sort of thing is perfect. And if anyone restated his thoughts in fewer or different words I believe he would bleed to death. Still the book ought to be corrected & retyped. I have convinced him that it must be done. What would you charge him to do that? Or do you want to bother?

Chapters 1 to 12 have arrived.[4] I haven't gone over them yet. Revising this thing is very difficult. It seems as yet much too diffuse and not well arranged. Perhaps when it is all worked over an effective thing can be selected from it. But the thing now is to shape it up as orderly as possible and then reconsider it as a whole. Yeah! Just to show good faith I am sending you—on the 1st—a check for 100^{00} . . . . Are we down-hearted. Yep—we are down hearted. Brownskitus[5] seems to have me lashed to the mast or nailed—far side in—to the cabin. I cough & cough. And take electric treatments and heroin (perhaps heros would be better) and gin rickeys—and Browns Mixture.[6] And still I cough. How about a novena—or a few prayers to St. Joseph.[7] Pray for your dear kind old—well you know.

Love
T

1. See Dreiser to Mrs. Heym, 27 February 1930.
2. Wharton Esherick. See Dreiser to Kirah Markham, 30 December 1928, n. 5.
3. Ralph Fabri (1894–1975), Hungarian born artist, educator, and writer. He is referred to here as "the porch builder" because he built a natural stone porch for Dreiser's New York country house at Mt. Kisco, as well as contributing to the design and construction of the various buildings on the property. Campbell did type and edit the prose of the Fabri novel.
4. Dreiser is referring to chapters of *Dawn* (1931) that Campbell had typed.
5. Brownskitus is Dreiser's wordplay for "bronchitis," a condition that plagued him from childhood.
6. Brown's Mixture was a popular over-the-counter, opium-laced medication commonly used as a treatment for coughs and colds.
7. In the Catholic tradition, St. Joseph is known as the patron saint of various occupations, but mentioning him in the context of chronic bronchitis suggests that Dreiser is thinking of him in his role as the protector of those who are dying and hoping for a blessed death.

To Yvette Szekely [H-DPUP]

Yvette Szekely [Eastman] (1912–) was born in Budapest, Hungary, and arrived in the United States in 1919 with her stepmother, a foreign correspondent and designer who hosted a salon in Manhattan for writers, intellectuals, and artists. It was in this company that she and Dreiser met. The fullest account of her long relationship with Dreiser is Dearest Wilding: A Memoir *(1995). Later she married the writer Max Eastman, who had known Dreiser since their days together in Greenwich Village during the 1910s. At the time of this letter, Dreiser was traveling to escape the stress of chronic bronchitis and the mental strain that was making it difficult for him to concentrate on completing his autobiography* Dawn *(1931). In hopes of improving his health and making some headway on the book, he decided to go to Tucson, Arizona. His traveling companion was Kathryn Zayre, a Columbia graduate student in philosophy who drove his car and helped to edit the memoir.*

Santa Rita Hotel

Tucson, Ariz.

April 3rd [1930]
Dearest:

Yesterday afternoon I walked miles out in the mesa here. All beyond the city is mesa—hundreds of thousands of acres perhaps, surrounded by mountains, peopled with cacti, mesquite, chapparal—and except for the cacti, low bushes all. But with such smooth, dry, firm, warm brown earth in between so that you may walk as among the very young trees of a young orchard. And the sky overhead with now & then a single white sailing cloud! And the changing colors of the mountains! And the cool pure wind! No taint of any city—which you smell as you return, as though it were a hot odorous animal. And the lone birds seeking lone prey,—here an owl, there a sand shrike. Perhaps in places cattle browsing, the rough shaggy herds of the mesas, that must make their own way as best they can—find food & water or die. And here & there in a hummock of brown earth in the sun I lay & thought and thought and baked. What is life? What man? Life is so unmindful of him. He is built with a few powers & then pitted, as in an arena, against so many others. But here the drama is so simple. Search for food. Guard yourself or be food for something else. A few ants. A few flies. I lie where there is no single fly but presently, should I throw a crumb of food of any kind on the ground here is one and there two and there ten and twenty. And from where? Over what distance? By what marvelous sense of smell? Or what? Among many things I thought of you, meditating on life—dreaming of what to do about it, how to proceed? What the end—for you?—and loved you for what you are. I wished you were lying with me. That we could look & dream over all these things together. At dusk—under a new moon I walked back—miles. In one lone cabin a half mile distant a radio was singing "Sighing for the Carolines."[1] It was as clear at half a mile as in a room. Our great land! Our far flung people! And all seeing & hearing if not knowing the same things at once.

T.

1. Although Dreiser writes "Sighing for the Carolines," he is almost certainly referring to the line from the chorus of the popular song "Cryin' for the Carolines," which was recorded by Ruth Etting in 1929.

To Yvette Szekely [H-DPUP]

Santa Rita Hotel
Tucson, Ariz.

April 3rd 1930

Dearest:

Just now I received such a doleful and yet really vital and interesting letter from you. Your so unhappy. You see no future or—you are falling all unprepared into one from a great height—youth. And no parachute. Excellent. Excellent. At seventeen and a half you are thinking more than most men and women at sixty. You have weltschmerz[1]—that most upbuilding disease that can attack youth. You really feel so bad that your going to do something about it, by George! Excellent, baby. I can think of nothing more healthful and encouraging. It even inspires me at three and a half times your age . . . . . But what is going to please you most is that you are going to get somewhere. You have youth, brains, health, and looks. Kids at your age are—where they have real brains—always despairing as to their future. But you are going to live in a period of enormous social changes here in the U.S.A. People are going to read. A heavy percentage are going to weary of numbskullery and fol-de-rol and sigh for worlds to conquer. There are going to be vital changes in government. If you want to be in on things—read first chemistry, physics, bio-chemistry and all phases of science. And then sociology. It would pay you to read law—and pay well. A law course would be invaluable in your case. Also a course in philosophy. But read now—and at once. Will Durants Story of Philosophy.[2] And if you've never read it H. G. Wells—Outline of History[3] (which reminds me that I owe him a letter). Get Schopenhauer's The World as Will and Idea[4] and read that. If you want to go to college perhaps that can be arranged. If you were to study science enough you could become a technical assistant at good wages & learn besides. Don't forget too, that the movies are going to provide an enormous field for educational ideas. People are going into Hollywood pretty soon who are going to construct social and scientific documents in film form—things that are going to teach & change the world enormously. Bother the communists over here. Turn your face to gay, thrilling instruction—the conquest of more & more amazing natural facts. Just now I have a bid to go to Hollywood (Warner Brothers) for some such work. If so I may give you a lift. But I am not going to leave New York. Not permanently. And should I go for awhile I'll send for you because I feel you can be of help to me—and to yourself. And even should I go—I'll be back before I go—and arrange some things with you. Will you come? Will Margaret[5] have sense enough to let you. You see how interested I get on the mental side. But there'll be *moments*—too, when you'll want me to "*Hold me*." Well, I will.

Its still marvelous here. No rain. No clouds yet. All sunshine. They say it rains but I havent seen any. And I'm feeling better. No coughing at night at all. And none in the day to speak of. I still wish you were here. It would be fun strolling around with you here. And how.

Write me. Cheer up. Eat an apple every day. Get to bed by noon. And blow me a few kisses and a few hot thoughts. No hot thoughts—no great ideas. I gotta have moments.

T

1. Melancholia, of a youthfully romantic sort.
2. William James Durant (1885–1981), American teacher, historian, and philosopher. *The Story of Philosophy* (1926) summarizes the lives and influence of the great philosophers.
3. Herbert Gregory Wells (1866–1946), British journalist and novelist; his *Outline of History* (1920) is a two-volume general history of the world. Dreiser had praised Wells as a writer in his introduction to *Tono-Bungay* in the Sandgate Edition (1927) of the novel.
4. Arthur Schopenhauer (1788–1860), German philosopher for whom Dreiser had a special fondness. Schopenhauer argued in *The World as Will and Idea* (1819) that the desires and drives of human beings are not the products of individual will but are manifestations of a single cosmic will to live; and since this will creates a continuous striving without satisfaction, life consists of suffering.
5. Yvette's stepmother, Margaret Monahan.

To Lina Goldschmidt [TC-DPUP]

200 West 57th Street,
New York City,

August 25, 1930

Dear Lina:

I have had the Piscator-Goldschmidt version of *An American Tragedy* with Patrick Kearney's American version as well as the book itself and find that it does not in any way overlap Mr. Kearney's text and anyhow, since Kearney's text was more or less bodily extracted from the book itself, I have never given much thought to the matter since I myself worked with him on his particular dramatic version. There is no chance of a quarrel on that ground, but in looking over the Piscator-Goldschmidt version I have the feeling that, while decidedly original and arresting as a stage presentation, it certainly does run counter to some of my Economic and Sociologic principles.[1] I am by no means as final in my conclusions in regard to the ills of society and the government and the way out as the text of this dramatization would indicate. For instance, by no means do I believe that the rich man is a scoundrel or the poor man an angel. Nor do I believe that the rich capitalist is always conscious of the injustices of a system of which he is an heir any more than I believe that the poor man is always conscious of the fact that society has benefited in the past, certainly by at least some of the methods of capitalism.

What I actually believe is that capitalism has shown the way toward Communism or perhaps I had better say that without the organization and direction in mass production indicated and achieved by capitalism and capitalistic minded geniuses, such a thing as the Soviet State would not now exist. It could not exist. No Lenin nor Marx nor Trotsky nor any other of the organic group at the head of the State would have known how to organize the various functions so necessary to the conduct of so enormous a body of people. I even really believe that without the antagonistic state as it came about in 1917 some form of Communism was inevitable. It appears to be arriving here but disguised, at the present, as conflicting trusts and money organizations of amazing reach.

A little group of financiers is already directing the United States through its Congress, its President and its various governments and state legislatures. Just now it is sub rosa—or at least conventionally sub rosa.

Under the circumstances I wish that some of the paragraphs could be modified and others a little, so as to remove what I consider the irrationalities of the principal draft or scenario. To bring about that I am going to forward a corrected copy of your German version only translated into English[2] and I hope that you will be willing to incorporate those corrections in your production in October. Will you be good enough to let me know whether you and Piscator will agree to this.

Incidentally I wish to add that there has been published here in deluxe form a very beautiful set of drawings by Hubert Davis[3] which epitomize and symbolize in drawing form the chief tragic moments of The Tragedy. They might help and be valuable to you in staging the play. Under separate cover I am sending you a copy of this particular book which is limited to five hundred copies and sells for $20.00. It is a personal gift to you from me and inscribed by me.

Very truly yours,
Theodore Dreiser

1. For a brief summary of Piscator's Marxist interpretation and the structure of his adaptation of Dreiser's novel, see Dreiser to Goldschmidt, 27 April 1929, n. 1.

2. Dreiser is referring to Louise Campbell's English translation of the Piscator-Goldschmidt stage version of the novel, *The Case of Clyde Griffiths*.

3. Hubert Davis (1902–77), artist known for his lithographs, published a hauntingly surreal set of prints, *The Symbolic Drawings of Hubert Davies for "An American Tragedy"* (1930) in a signed limited edition of 525 copies.

To Marion Bloom [H-DPUP]

On 5 September 1930 Bloom had sent Dreiser an undated newspaper clipping about Aleister Crowley, reporting him to be "the High Priest of Black Magic" in Paris. It describes meetings of satanic cults in the Fontainebleau forests. He led a group that proclaimed that the "Mephistophelian one is asked to bestow worldly riches upon his followers or to fulfill their sinful desires" (DPUP).

Sep-6–1930

Dear Marion,

Yes, the clipping refers to the Aleister.[1] I'm please to know he's still functioning—making pacts with the devil. According to this clipping, in return for one's soul he'll fulfill all one's sinful desires *here*. The only trouble in my case is they've all been fulfilled, so we can't do any business.

What is the house of Art?[2] Do you own it? I rarely get as far as Washington. Somehow it's easier to get to California or Europe. Don't you get over here? I'm at the same old desk I had in 1915.[3]

In reading of Menck's marriage—well, you know.[4] Also, as you know Gloom[5] has deserted me forever—darn her.

T. D

1. Born Edward Alexander Crowley, Aliester Crowley (1893–1947), British author known for his writing on the occult and for his practice of what he preached.

2. Bloom wrote on the stationery of "Maison D'Art," otherwise unidentified.

3. Dreiser had converted his brother Paul Dresser's piano into a writing desk.

4. H. L. Mencken had recently married Sara Haardt. At one time, a marriage between Mencken and Marion Bloom had been contemplated.

5. Another nickname for Estelle Bloom Kubitz. See Dreiser to Marion Bloom, 7 November 1923, headnote. The relationship between Kubitz and Dreiser had ended in 1919, after Helen Richardson had entered his life. Dreiser may be alluding here to Kubitz's second marriage.

To Marguerite Tjader [Harris] [H-HRHUT]

Marguerite Tjader (1901–86) was the daughter of a socially prominent American mother and a Swedish-born father who had been a preacher in Stockholm. Tjader studied at Bryn Mawr College and Columbia University before beginning a career as a social and religious activist, novelist, biographer, and editor. Dreiser met her in 1928 (she was Mrs. Harris until her divorce in 1933), and their relationship continued until his death. In his final years, she traveled to Los Angeles to assist him with The Bulwark *(1946). She wrote* Theodore Dreiser: A New Dimension *(1965); another memoir was published posthumously,* Love That Will Not Let Me Go: My Time with Theodore Dreiser *(1998). She published a novel,* Borealis *(1930), and later wrote two books on religious topics:* Mother Elizabeth *(1972) and* Birgitta of Sweden *(1980).*

Iroki[1]

Sunday-Dec 14–1930

Dear Marguerite:

I read your letter and in many ways was impressed by it. It is a quality of my mind that it favors every effort toward self-expression and freedom. I have suffered bitterly by that same in others since in many instances it has torn me from them or them from me—and I have bled. But still I favor it! And yet I know also that a condition of such freedom is *self-torture*. One cannot exercise it at the expense of the other fellow alone and unscathed. Mentally and emotionally one pays. There are tearing nostalgias in oneself—in me at least—unconquerable, irrepressible vomits of agony. And out of it comes what? Wisdom? Peace. Durable and delightful memories. I wish I could be sure. In myself I see isolated strength—yet more than that? Peace? Sweetness? Wholeness of heart? A level look into that far amiable land of the heart & all dreams, the future? I wish I could say so. I truly wish.

As to your book—it is good in a concentric personal way.[2] I do not feel that it is sufficiently dramatic or in places—especially at the last—compelling. And yet I also feel that many should like it! It is good.

Marguerite Tjader.

As for another one—if you would devise one out of your knowledge of life in general, paint people as you know them—choose your own drama or comedy and illuminate it with your own thoughts & conclusions—truly I cannot see how it could fail of an audience.

Love from me—who wishes so much for you—so much real good.

T. D.

1. The name of Dreiser's country home at Mt. Kisco, New York. The word is commonly referred to as being Japanese for "the spirit of beauty," though Lawrence E. Hussman makes a case for it meaning "the spirit of color," pointing out that "color in Japanese connotes sex" (Tjader, *Love*, 87).

2. Dreiser is referring to her novel, *Borealis* (1930). He contributed a blurb for the jacket cover.

1931

To Emma Goldman [TS-SCHR]

Emma Goldman's most famous relationship was with her fellow anarchist Alexander Berkman (1870–1936), who had become notorious for his attempted assassination of Henry Clay Frick, the chairman of the Carnegie Steel Company, in the wake of the 1892 Homestead strike in Pittsburgh. Goldman and Berkman were deported to Russia in 1919, after spending two years in prison for their activities in opposition to military conscription and America's entry into World War I. Both became disillusioned with the Bolshevik leadership and spent many years in exile in western Europe. In France, the increasingly unstable Berkman was constantly threatened with exile and harassed for his political views. Goldman had requested that Dreiser add his name to a protest prepared by "well known Frenchmen of Letters" (Emma Goldman to Dreiser, 4 October 1931 [DPUP]), but (somewhat to Goldman's dismay) Dreiser chose instead to use his influence directly with the French authorities to help Berkman.

200 East 57th Street,
New York City

September 22, 1931.

Dear Emma,

I send you this copy of a letter which is going out in the same mail to the Minister of the Interior.[1] I have mentioned the persecution of Berkman to Arthur Garfield Hayes,[2] who informs me that Roger Baldwin[3] is now in France and that when he returns he will probably be in the possession of all the facts. At that time, I think it would be good idea for the American Civil Liberties Union to try to get some effective action on this through the French League for the Rights of Man.

I'm sorry this response to your letter is a little late, but my work as well as moving from this place keep me busy all the time, it seems. But you know that I want to do what I can to assist Berkman, and I hope this letter to Pierre Laval will help. Let me know if there is any action beyond that of the American Civil Liberties Union which I can institute to this end. My address will be Hotel Ansonia, New York City.

I'm glad that your book[4] is coming out so soon; I know it will be intensely interesting and, I hope, highly successful.

Best wishes always.
TD

1. Pierre Laval (1883–1945), four times prime minister of France—the fourth time under the Vichy government in World War II, which led to his trial and execution for high treason after the war.

2. Arthur Garfield Hayes (1881–1954), American lawyer who specialized in civil liberties cases.

3. Roger Baldwin (1884–1981), a founder of the American Civil Liberties Union.

4. *Living My Life* (1931).

To Louise Campbell [H-DPUP]

[17 October 1931]

Dear Louise:

Those ties are very attractive to me.[1] I think some of them might be 1/2 inch longer. Others seem to be ok.

So sorry about mother's ills but you can tell her I'm nearly keeping her company. Brownskitus[2] again—infuriating. I may have to get out of here. I'm in room 1665 Ansonia. You should see it. This room is charming. Helen & the family have another 16–159.[3] They're back & forth. Now the book[4] is done. Just combined two chapters into one. It reads swell. 21 Chapters. Do you know I have been doing those damned things over for exactly 2 years now. You weren't in on the early outline stuff at all. Liveright (the house) likes it very much. The communists have examined it with care & while disagreeing as to points think its the goods & timely.[5] I'll send you a set of the first revise proofs.

Its colder today. Im going up to Kisco. Wish you were going to be there just to cheer up the place. If you'll come over here Ill put you up for the night in one of these 16th floor rooms. Or you can sleep in mine. According to Pell[6] no Savings Bank today is now safe—so if your hoarding wealth get a tin can & put it in the back yard.

Love
T. D.

About the ties again. The thin ones should have a filler. The heavier ones not: I hope mother gets a 70-30 break—70 in favor of good health.

1. Dreiser is referring to bow ties Campbell's mother made for him.

2. Dreiser's familiar wordplay on "bronchitis."

3. Helen's Oregon family was visiting and staying at the hotel.

4. A critique of the political and economic systems of the United States, *Tragic America* (1931), published by Horace Liveright.

5. In fact, Communist Party officials were generally displeased with what they considered the lack of orthodox doctrine in Dreiser's analysis.

6. Arthur Pell, the treasurer at Boni and Liveright.

To Clara Clark [H-RIG]

Clara Clark (1909–2006) was born in the Germantown section of Philadelphia of a prosperous Pennsylvania Quaker family whose American origins dated back to the seventeenth century. In 1931, after reading the newly published Dawn *and* An American Tragedy, *she wrote Dreiser about her identification with his quest to find beauty in life and with the pain and shame he had felt at her age. There was an exchange of letters that preceded their first meeting in November 1931, which began a four-year intimate relationship in which Miss Clark acted as secretary, editor, and sounding board for what Dreiser thought to be his next novel,* The Stoic. *In addition, she edited his articles and a book of poems. After Dreiser's death she published (under her married name, Clara Jaeger) a memoir entitled* Philadelphia Rebel: The Education of a Bourgeoisie *(1988) that includes a detailed account of her time with Dreiser.*

[October] 1931[1]

Dear Miss Clark,

I asked you to be frank and you are, and frankness calls for frankness in reply. In some respects I like your estimate of yourself. It's at least definite and courageous.

Take this confession of yours: "I guess I am in love with myself." Well, then, you have never been in love. I have found beings whom I have loved more than myself and suffered for it. I cannot say that I regret the experience.

Again you say: "I have always been loved and always expect to be." There speaks the egocentric, self-centered to the danger point. Do you always expect to be loved? Such faith. For my part, I have by no means always been loved, and do not expect to be. Yet I have been loved too much, perhaps, or rather, more than I deserve. But loved too much or too little—how sad. Both involve something that is of the very tragedy of life. Of that—if I were to believe you entirely, you could know little. Your always expecting to be loved smacks of one who does not need or care to return love. To me—deadly dull.

You say: "I do not lower myself for another but rather try to lift another to my heights." Have you such immense heights to offer? As for myself, as of heights and depths I am dubious. There are only people for whom I would sacrifice much or nothing. They are heights to me or they are not. If they are—I seek, how eagerly, to find it.

Lastly you say: "I fight to be alone. There are so many people always seeking, clinging."

Fortunate soul. The security and very likely egotism of youth and beauty. But you may not always have to fight to be alone. The thought to me is humbling, for I have been alone much. Yet now the table is turned and I am not alone. Sometimes I must shield myself and garner my time, but for those to whom I must deny myself I am unutterably sad.

Lastly, so much of what you say indicates one who must be pursued and served. Alas, I am not one who vainly pursues or serves anyone. With love or a strong pulling, strengthening attachment, as you will, I will go hand in hand. As one of a rout attendant upon a beauty fighting to be alone I would not endure—would not even set out upon the dusky pilgrimage. For it is not condescension that I am seeking, but a kindred, helpful, meaningful spirit. Your first letter seemed to indicate that you were such—or desired to be. These others, well—yet perhaps at no time had you the intention to convey that. More than likely it is an ideal of my own that has betrayed me. But not too far. You must tell me more about yourself.

Theodore Dreiser

1. This letter is undated, except for "1931" at its head. The late Clara Clark Jaeger had forgotten its exact date but was certain of the month of its composition (Clara Jaeger to Riggio, 24 May 2005).

1932

To Dorothy Dudley [TC-DPUP]

Dorothy Dudley (1884–1962) began her literary career in Chicago after graduating from Bryn Mawr in 1905. As part of the so-called Chicago Renaissance, she began to contribute poetry and articles to leading magazines of the period, including Harriet Monroe's Poetry. *She began a long friendship with Dreiser after being introduced to him by Edger Lee Masters in 1916. Dudley was then married to Henry Blodgett Harvey; in 1925 the couple moved to France, where Dudley continued writing and translating French authors. Her valuable study of Dreiser, the first critical biography, appeared in 1932 as* Forgotten Frontiers: Dreiser and the Land of the Free *(in 1946 it was reissued as* Dreiser and the Land of the Free*).*

Hotel Ansonia,
New York City

April 7, 1932.

Dear Dorothy:

Very recently, Jonathan Cape,[1] who is over here, brought me galley proofs of your study of me, of which both he and his now partner, he said, thought very highly, but he was anxious to get my opinion and that of some of my critical friends because, he said, both he and his partner feared some of the material might be offensive not only to myself but to Mencken and Masters.[2]

Apart from my own reading of most of the book, I had it read by three estimable critics whose judgment I think you would value along with mine. All three agreed with Cape and his partner that the book is brilliantly written and full of interesting material and that it is likely to attract attention and sell. All three objected to this and that and, so that you may know exactly what they objected to, I am sending you a duplicate of my letter to Mr. Cape.

In that letter, you will read what I have to say about the letters from Masters, Mencken and so on, and your excerpts from the same. What I say there in regard to no direct quotations without their consent is my memory of my agreement with you, but, apart from that, I cannot feel that it is fair to any of those who have written me privately, nor that it is good policy to set them forth in a book published other than by myself. I have not the slightest objection to your saying that I allowed you to read them, and that from reading them you gathered certain impressions, but without Mencken's or Masters' consent, you cannot possibly have them say things which will create quarrels for them and unkind remarks as regards my good taste in such matters. I feel that you will be willing to cut them out, and I am writing you now to ask if you will not do this, and inform Cape and his partner, by return mail.

In regard to what you say about my lack of interest, it sprang from enormous pressure on me just then in connection with many things—DAWN, TRAGIC AMERICA, the Russian Ballet[3] and such—all of which were more or less in hand at one and the same time. I don't think you can accuse me of any lack of real interest, though, when the material with which I provided you shows up so extensively and so well.

Further than this, I find no glaring errors of fact or supposition, and insofar as supposition is concerned, I would not want to interfere with that anyway. If you feel certain things to be true about me, it is certainly your privilege to feel that way and to say so. My answer to most that has been said about me is likely to appear in the history of myself which I hope to continue.[4]

By the way, AN AMERICAN TRAGEDY, presented by Piscator,[5] the dramatist and producer, and with a very fine cast including Joseph Schildkraut, and actors and actresses selected from the Reinhardt[6] group, is to open on April 16th, both in Berlin and Vienna. If, by any chance, you could go to either place and see the performance, I would be delighted to hear what you have to say about it. I have been asked to go over, but I cannot possibly make it, as my present intention is to move much nearer the Mexican border than I am now.[7]

In regard to my interest in economics, I have this to say. I have always been interested in economics and the social set—up in this country and all countries—humanity in general. I think that the text of my books shows that from the first to the last. My reason for troubling with the economic phase here is because conditions as they are now are certain to be addled and to make ridiculous literary achievements of almost all kinds other than economic. There is a social unbalance here which would not permit of any sane picture that did not clearly reflect social unbalance. However, at the same time that I am interesting myself in our social conditions, I am concluding the last volume of the Trilogy which, I am sure, most of my critics will pounce on as decidedly unsocial and even ridiculous as coming from a man who wants social equity.[8] Nevertheless, I am writing it just that way.

Thank Katherine[9] for her interest, and tell her I treasure the negro painting she gave me past almost any other that I have. It is so colorful and so richly human.

1. Herbert Jonathan Cape (1879–1960), prominent British publisher whose authors included Ernest Hemingway, H. G. Wells, and T. E. Lawrence. In 1929, Cape developed a partnership in an American company with Harrison Smith, and in 1932 they published Dudley's biography of Dreiser.

2. Dreiser had opened his papers to Dudley, and she had quoted from the personal letters of Edgar Lee Masters and H. L. Mencken to him.

3. To Dudley's complaint that he did not carefully critique her manuscript, or even see her in the last stages of composition, Dreiser responds that he was busy with his autobiography *Dawn* (1931) and his social polemic *Tragic America* (1931), as well as with his campaign to bring to America the Russian ballet company he had seen at the Bolshoi Opera House in Moscow.

4. Although he made sketchy outlines of his literary experiences, Dreiser never did write about this period in his memoirs.

5. Erwin Piscator. See Dreiser to Lina Goldschmidt, 27 April 1929, n. 1.

6. Joseph Schildkraut (1896–1964), Austrian-born actor who had a successful career as a stage, television, and motion-picture performer in the United States. He made his professional debut in Berlin in 1913 under Max Reinhardt (1873–1943), an Austrian American theatrical director.

7. Dreiser was thinking of moving to New Mexico.

8. The last volume of the trilogy was *The Stoic* (1947). Dreiser anticipated such criticism because his protagonist Cowperwood was a type of robber-baron financier; Dreiser did not fully complete the novel in its published form during his lifetime.

9. Katherine Dudley, Dorothy's sister, was a portrait painter and a poet.

To Esther McCoy [H-DPUP]

San Antonio, Texas

June 9–1932

Dear Esther:

So glad to hear from you: to receive one more of your sensitive poetic letters. And I am glad that you are in Los Angles, if you like it so much. I found it refreshing & stimulating for three years.[1] After that I had to get out in order to work—back to New York . . . . . But now, as you see I am out of New York—here in San Antonio,[2] where I have been for a month. *And working*. Had to get out of N.Y. on account of expenses & people. Actually I was being run ragged. Here I see no one & work all day & every day on *The Stoic*[3] which I hope to finish in another month or so. Besides my expenses are very light & they need to be these days. But your letter finds me moving on *this Saturday, June 11*th to *El Paso, Texas* which is the same as the center of New Mexico. I am going there because for 6 cents I can cross over into Juarez, Mexico & buy all I want to drink. And somehow I need to drink to work—but not to work to drink. If you will you can write me there care of General Delivery. If I move I'll let you know.

Honey, I haven't a job for you & I don't know where to send you. If I needed an amanuensis I would take you. But, you would have to take dictation, typewrite, edit, sweep out the house, run to the store & do whatever else there was to do including telling me what the papers say. But I'm not using such a person now.

As for the Le Gros Aged Spaniard[4] I scarcely know what I would do with it. Is it small? I have only two bags—the largest about 18 X 30 & when I move all I have goes in those two. I might hang it on my wall but maybe you'd better save it for a better man . . . . . . Incidentally I may come to Hollywood. I move as I grow restless. After El Paso I may go to Tucson or Phoenix—or Prescott. And after Prescott I might run on over to Hollywood.[5] If so I'll see you. Meanwhile don't tire of your Paradise. And believe me I think of you and wish you every sort of ease this world provides—material & spiritual & aesthetic.

Love from
T. D

Until further notice
—El Paso, General
Delivery, Texas
My permanent N.Y. address is
c/o Evelyn Light,[6] Room 709
1860 Broadway
N.Y.C.

1. Dreiser moved to Los Angeles with Helen Richardson soon after they met in 1919, and they lived there together until his return to New York in October 1922.

2. Upset by the death of his friend Charles Fort (1874–1932), suffering from bronchitis, and tired of New York, Dreiser sailed for Galveston, Texas, early in May with his companion Clara Clark and his Chrysler on board. From Galveston, they drove to San Antonio, where Dreiser wrote this letter.

3. Dreiser was working on *The Stoic* (1947), the third book of the Cowperwood trilogy following *The Financier* and *The Titan*, and at this time he made some good progress on it, though he would soon be distracted by political activity from completing it.

4. McCoy offered him the *Aged Spaniard*, a painting by Alphonse Legros (1836–1911).

5. Dreiser never did get to Tucson, Phoenix, Prescott, or Hollywood. He returned to New York early in July.

6. Evelyn Light (1904–58), Dreiser' s secretary from February 1931 to June 1934.

To Kirah Markham [H-DPUP]

Like many others during the Great Depression, Markham found it increasingly difficult to make living wages.

San Antonio, Texas

June 10–1932

Kyra Dear: The description of the place you want to buy & your reasons for wanting to buy it—your entire aesthetic & poetic approach to life makes my inability to help you now painful. Like everyone else I have gone through drastic things—the total elimination of five sixths of all I thought I was putting safely aside. Just now to save expenses & be able to concentrate (eliminate a perfect swarm of people using up my time) I am out here in the West writing. Have been here in San Antonio—a half Mexican & Negro place—over a month, but am leaving tomorrow—Saturday for El Paso Texas, where I hope to concentrate for another month. It is The Stoic I am working on & it should be done by August first.[1] I've let other things put it aside for a long time—(you were with me when I wrote The Titan) but now I have to complete it. I'm sorry your having a close time. But since 1929 I have had to adopt all of my relations & only now am finding it impossible to go with their allowances at the same rate because of the reduction in my own means.[2] I keep wondering if things are going to get better. Here as elsewhere conditions are bad—schools on part time, stores closing—the most amazing types of people begging—people who never would have begged before anywhere. 11 of the largest movie houses in this state have closed for want of patrons. But enough of that. There are things to do—remedies as I see them, but the American people will never apply them. This year taxes are going to drive us crazy. But if I get another break & you are still broke I will see if I can't find a little spot for you.

Love from
T. D.

If you write me, address me care E. Light,[3] Room 709–1860 Broadway, N.Y.C

All mail is forwarded

1. See Dreiser to Esther McCoy, 9 June 1932, n. 3

2. Dreiser had been helping to support his siblings (particularly his sisters Mame and Sylvia and his brother Rome) with monthly allowances. For years Rome (1860–1940) had not been seen, and the family thought he was dead until Dreiser discovered him in a Chicago flophouse in 1926 and began to support him. Rome moved to New York and joined his siblings there.

3. Evelyn Light. See Dreiser to Esther McCoy, 9 June 1932, n. 6.

To Yvette Szekely [H-DPUP]

Szekely was at this time in Hungary to visit her father and meet her biological mother for the first time.

Friday-After Thanksgiving [25 November 1932]

Yvette Sweet:

You'll think I'm long on silence. I've been to the west coast—San Francisco & Los Angeles. Went to speak for Mooney[1] & to cross-examine a new witness—Paul Callicotte[2] who went to the Oregonian in Portland, saying that he carried the bag that carried the bomb that killed 12 people at the preparedness parade in San Francisco in 1916. Also that the two men he carried it for was neither Mooney nor Billings. I cross examined him privately in the Mark Hopkins Hotel in San Francisco before eight friends in order to satisfy myself that he was telling the truth. I decided that he was. Then I cross-examined him before 18,000 people in the Civic Auditorium in S.F. for 2 hours. He came through in fine form. Very convincing. Then I saw the District Attorney, as well as the judge who may retry him & then departed for Los Angeles to help raise some money for the communists there.[3] We raised $1600. The labor of doing so consisted of sitting around in two very gay parties looking very pontifical while a lot of young enthusiasts told each other that it was their duty to contribute. Sam Ornitz[4] bagged the money for the local cause. I put away about eleven high balls and felt as though I had done nobly by my country. High balls have a way of doing that.

By the way Miss Light[5] mailed you copies of the 1st & 2nd issue of The American Spectator.[6] It sold 60,000 copies the 1st issue. And this second looks to go 80,000 or 90,000.

Next I enjoyed that factory picture[7]—all those ambitious Hungarians anxious to come over here & lead loose immoral lives. A fine comment on what America stands for . . . . . As for me as a monument? I like the picture. My ample lap full of girls and you paying me visits. My future looks better than I had hoped.

What news of your mother? Any. I meant to show those two pictures of your mother to her, but I forgot. Now she wants to see them. So if possible, I wish you'd send them back. For all her sharp words I think Helen[8] likes you. You ought to write her a little letter.

Are you really all set for a year? It seems a long time. And I hope you don't work yourself into any routine frame of mind. Your too brisk & gay for that. Rather I wish you'd write an article entitled The Hungarian Yen for America—or the European Yen For America. You could use that letter almost as you wrote it—or I could incorporate it in a slightly longer article. Want to try?[9]

It's Friday night & I may go out to Mt. Kisco. Helen & I came down Wednesday for Thanksgiving. The weather here just now is perfect—like early October—warm & bright. I'm going without an overcoat. I wish you were here. We'd go over to the Hungarian place or maybe instead I'd take you to 146 East 61. It's almost as charming at the old Stork. Not quite. . . .

Do you miss me. Remember when you were working for the Charity Relief?[10] And afterwards that cloth hand-printing concern? The poor working girl? And her lack of diversions! I can see your playful ironic grin—even now? I'll write again in a few days.

Love from T. D.

On a German movie introduction the other night I saw "dialogue by Hans Szekely."[11] Any relation?

1. Thomas J. Mooney (1882–1942), socialist, newspaper publisher, and union organizer, was in prison serving a life sentence. He had been convicted of planting a bomb that killed ten people during a Preparedness March on 22 July 1916 in San Francisco. Tried and convicted, he was sentenced to death, but later his sentence was commuted to life. The Preparedness March was a demonstration in favor of expanding national defense measures. Despite evidence presented at Mooney's trial that he was over a mile away from the bombing site—and later discoveries that key witnesses lied and that the jury foreman was in collusion with the prosecution—Mooney spent twenty-two years in prison (1917–39) before receiving a pardon from California governor Culbert Olson. In poor health after years of imprisonment, Mooney died three years after his release. Dreiser first visited Mooney in San Quentin in 1930 and for years actively worked for his release. In 1928 Mooney, after having read *An American Tragedy*, had contacted Dreiser by using Ruth Kennell as an intermediary.

2. Paul Callicotte, an Oregon mountain guide who confessed in 1932 to having planted the bomb at the 1916 San Francisco Preparedness Parade without any aid from Mooney.

3. When on 6 November 1932 Callicotte publicly confessed at the San Francisco Exposition Auditorium, Dreiser questioned him. After this Dreiser met with San Francisco district attorney Mathew I. Brady and with Judge Louis H. Ward on behalf of Mooney.

4. Samuel Ornitz (1890–1957), playwright, screenwriter, novelist, and social activist. A founding member of the Screen Actors Guild, Ornitz spent most of his professional life as a successful Hollywood screenwriter until he was blacklisted in the 1950s. In 1931 he had joined Dreiser as a member of the National Committee for the Defense of Political Prisoners in calling attention to such cases as the plight of coal miners in Harlan County, Kentucky, and the death sentence imposed upon the Scottsboro Boys, eight young African Americans accused of rape in Alabama.

5. Evelyn Light. See Dreiser to Esther McCoy, 9 June 1932, n. 6.

6. *The American Spectator*, edited by Dreiser, Eugene O'Neill, James Branch Cabell, Sherwood Anderson, George Jean Nathan, and Ernest Boyd. This periodical

was started in 1932 as a "literary newspaper," but Dreiser eventually left it because he felt not enough attention was being given to broad social and political commentary. James T. Farrell edited a three-volume reprint of the entire run of the paper (New York: Greenwood Reprint, 1968).

7. Szekely had sent Dreiser photographs—one of factory hands at work—with her letters.

8. Helen Richardson, who was not fond of Szekely because of her relationship with Dreiser.

9. Dreiser thought her account would make a good article for *The American Spectator*.

10. For years Szekely was intermittently employed as a social worker.

11. Yvette Szekely Eastman confirmed (to Riggio, on 10 January 2005) that there was no family connection.

1933

To Esther McCoy [TS-DPUP]

Theodore Dreiser
The American Spectator,
12 East 41st Street,
New York City.

February 17, 1933.

Dear Esther:

I have been out of town for the last three weeks, and so have had no opportunity to answer your letter, but I assure you that it has peculiar and valuable interest for me. It illustrates what has so often been proved to me in connection with Communist organizations and efforts, that is, that there is very little organization and very little effort. In other words, just what you say—theorizing and sometimes money-wasting, but with no results worth speaking of.

When I introduced you to Ornitz,[1] it was, as I explained to you at the time, because he had told me what he wished to do, and how much the particular movement he had in mind needed some one person or several who would help to put it over, but even at that, I had no idea that the situation was as higgledy-piggledy as you present it.

I wish I had your permission, though, to make copies of your comments on the situation there. I could send them to some of the leaders of the party here. I think it would be of value. As a matter of fact, in all my browsing around among Communists, trying to do things with and for them, the only effective organization I ever encountered was in San Francisco, where, due to one or two genuinely in-earnest and capable young men, really wonders were accomplished not only in connection with the Mooney[2] case, but in connection with other things that really were important out there. If they had such people in Chicago, Los Angeles and some other American cities, I believe the essential values of Communism would grow in public favor. As it is, they are getting nowhere.

Let me hear from you further in regard to developments there. Of course, I am not going to Los Angeles unless some very significant arrangements are made.

Do I understand clearly that Hynes[3] is now publicly disposed of, and also, what is the character of the new man and of his activities? Will you let me know as to this?

T. D

1. Samuel Ornitz. See Dreiser to Yvette Szekely, Friday-After Thanksgiving, (25 November 1932), n. 4. The movement Dreiser refers to was Ornitz's attempt to organize opposition to the anti-communist activities of William F. Hynes (see note 3 below).

2. Thomas Mooney. See Dreiser to Yvette Szekely, Friday-After Thanksgiving (25 November 1932), n. 1.

3. Captain William F. Hynes was the head of the Intelligence Bureau in Los Angeles and also in charge of an anti-red police squad. Dreiser is referring here to the news from McCoy that Hynes, because of marital difficulties, had recently offered his resignation—which was subsequently rejected by the local authorities.

To Esther McCoy [TS-DPUP]

Theodore Dreiser
The American Spectator

As the Depression of the 1930s worsened, Dreiser became increasingly involved in social causes. He tried to consolidate his point of view in Tragic America *(1931), which caught the attention of a number of leftist groups.*

April 11, 1933.

Dear Esther:

I have sent the suggested letter to the movie people, with one exception.[1] If any replies come here, I'll see that you get whatever information they contain at once.

I have sent a wire to Mary Campbell, as you suggested, approving the use of my name in connection with the endorsement for Leo Gallagher.[2]

There has been no communication from Ornitz about the Hynes meeting which it was proposed I conduct.[3]

Yes, if you finish the article on Leo Gallagher, let me see it. I don't know that it would do for The Spectator, but there is a new magazine here called COMMON SENSE,[4] and I might ask you to let me send it to that.

I will send you a copy of the excerpt tomorrow. It is not available at the moment.

As to the letter for Shubert Sebree,[5] (and two others which I am enclosing) there is little I can say, for this is a spontaneous growth. Evidently they felt that the clubs would be more prosperous if the book was sold at a lower price. Very shortly, the price will be reduced to $1.00. If you wish to determine just how the Indiana people are going about it, why not correspond with Sebree, and give his name and address to anyone who asks for information? I am very much pleased that some university students are interested, and of course approve of this connection.

I do not see, really, why organizations of this sort could not use TRAGIC AMERICA[6] as a kind of Bible, for certainly the book represents my analysis of our present system and my recommendations for change, and, outside of the revelations in every daily newspaper which support my charges, I do not see that there is anything for me to add to it. Let me know what progress is made, won't you?

T. D.

1. Unidentified.

2. Leo Gallagher (1887–1963), a Los Angeles lawyer who specialized in labor law. Throughout his career he was involved in progressive politics. Dreiser supported his losing 1933 run in the Democratic primary for a seat on the Los Angeles Municipal Court bench, a campaign for which McCoy worked.

3. See Dreiser to Esther McCoy, 17 February 1933, nn. 1, 3.

4. *Common Sense* was founded in 1932 by Alfred Bingham (1904–98). Leftist but anti-communist, its aim was to develop a radicalism native to America, and its editorial policy was to support "all movements that promise intelligent, courageous action, whether among labor organizations, unemployed councils, student leagues, or political groups."

5. Milton Shubert Sebree, a political socialist from Indiana and a champion of the socialist leader Eugene Debs; he had narrated a documentary on Debs. Along with others, Sebree advocated the establishment of "Dreiser clubs" to discuss the social and economic problems of the day, using Dreiser's *Tragic America* as a central point of reference.

6. *Tragic America* (1931) was Dreiser's manifesto for reform. He believed in the possibility of an American version of Communism. Critics of the book point to its factual errors, loose organization, and over-generalized analysis in dealing with the social, political, and economic problems facing the country at the time. Others argue that as a social jeremiad it expresses a sincere, passionate, and coherent reaction to the calamity of the Great Depression. While it sold poorly in the United States, it was published in England and in translation in France, Germany, Hungary, and Russia. Dreiser here imagines, somewhat grandiosely, that the clubs named after him might use the book "as a kind of Bible."

To Alma Clayburgh [TS-DPUP]

A long-time acquaintance of Dreiser, Alma Lachenbruch Clayburgh (1882–1958) was a concert singer, patron of the arts, philanthropist, and social activist who was deeply influenced by the controversial prison reformer and author Thomas Mott Osborne (1859–1926).

THEODORE DREISER[1]
The American Spectator, Inc.

May 31, 1933

Dear Alma:

I want to explain about Monday. I enjoyed the police trip immensely; not only that, but I found it of great sociological and economic value.[2]

Though I may have appeared a little crusty toward the end of the visit to the police training school across the street, the intellectual results to me were enormous.

Thinking it over, I would not have missed examining that crime history room for anything, because it has clarified an idea of mine in regard to why people commit crime. That is, because they are of meager intelligence, and are defrauded by an economic system that raises the value of money beyond all reason—so high, indeed, as to make the capture of a hundred dollars the reason for a terrible crime.

Never mind how I acted; such are the results.

Thank you very much.

T. D.

Mme. Alma Clayburgh
50 East 72nd Street
New York City

1. This letter was originally pasted in a copy of *Dreiser Looks at Russia* (1928), which was inscribed by Dreiser to Clayburgh.

2. There is no other record of the tour Dreiser describes here.

1934

To Clare Kummer [TS-DPUP]

Clare Kummer [née Clare Rodman Bacher] (1873–1958), now remembered mainly for her popular plays, had known Dreiser since 1909, when he had published her work in The Delineator *and* Bohemian Magazine. *She became one of Dreiser's inner circle of friends after her marriage to his old friend Arthur Henry,*[1] *who had recently died.*

Hotel Ansonia,
New York, N.Y.

June 28, 1934

Dear Clare:

When Arthur died there were notices here in the New York papers, but I did not see them. The first news I had was from Will Lengel[2] of Liberty Magazine, who knew of our friendship and called up to say that Arthur was dead. When I asked for details he said that the body was at his home in Naragansett Pier and that according to the paper his daughter Mrs. Van Auken was in charge. From that I assumed that you were in Hollywood or elsewhere and in my hurry to say something I addressed my telegram to her.

Since then the long notice in the Times has been put in my hands and I see that you were there. I don't think I need to explain or say anything more to you. As I said, Hen's death struck close to me.

I think of you so often. I wanted to see the play that you had on here,[3] but my work has been such that about one play in six months is my average. Are you going to be in New York before returning to the coast? If you are let me know, as I would like so much to have another talk with you.

Affectionately,
T. D.

Mrs. Arthur Henry
Naragansett Pier, R. I.

1. Arthur Henry. See Dreiser to Helen Richardson, 21 April 1924, n. 2.

2. William Charles Lengel. See Dreiser to Kirah Markham, 18 February 1914, n. 10. At this time, Lengel was editor of *Liberty* magazine.

3. Kummer's *Her Master's Voice* had a few weeks before ended a run of 224 performances at the Plymouth Theatre in New York.

To Louise Campbell [H-DPUP]

Tuesday [24 July 1934]

Dear Louise:

Ok for that sketch of yours truly.[1] It's almost painfully accurate, but I like it just the same. Always, in thinking of your short stories I feel that they should be just what they are—good naturedly ironic—not poignant—since you do not run to poignant studies of this earthly scene—and that there should be a market for them. Also I have more than once thought that if you had lived & written in & about London you would have found a market there. Over here, I dont know. A friendly leisurely thing, however accurate, doesn't seem to get so very far. Just the same I liked all of the things of yours that I have read.

About the Hedgerow. I went over at Anderson's & Wharton's request.[2] His play was interesting but somehow I question popularity for it unless it is pulled together more. But it has very human material. Libby Holman[3] was an incident. She was here & Esherick was determined that I should talk to her. She's clever. But hard & horribly cynical. I'm sure she's half Jewish.

Give me an idea for a movie for Anna Sten & another for Mae West.[4] If I put them over I'll pay you commission. I understand that $25,000 is now *top* for almost any picture.

I never knew until two weeks ago that *Back Street* was a complete swipe of Jennie—and a better movie of the book than by Paramount.[5] Paramount even took material from Back Street to make the "*great original*" they showed me.

Love—
T. D

1. Campbell had been trying to write familiar essays and stories for the magazines.

2. The Hedgerow Theatre in Pennsylvania was a repertory company founded by Jasper Deeter in 1923 as part of the Rose Valley Arts and Crafts Community. Dreiser went there in late June to see the premiere of the dramatized version of Sherwood Anderson's *Winesburg, Ohio*. Wharton Esherick did the set design and construction for the production. (For Esherick, see Dreiser to Kirah Markham, 30 December 1928, n. 5.)

3. Libby Holman (1904–71), a sensational and often scandalous star on Broadway in the 1920s and 1930s. Known as the smokiest of torch singers (she is credited with the invention of the strapless evening dress), she was a revolutionary not only as a performer but also in social and political arenas, in which she fought against racism and poverty.

4. Anna Sten (1908–93), Russian-born actress Anjuchka Stenska, who was discovered in her early teens by the celebrated Russian director and acting instructor,

Konstantin Stanislavsky. The American movie magnate Samuel Goldwyn brought her to the United States and attempted, unsuccessfully, to promote her as another Greta Garbo.

Mae West (1893–1980), vaudevillian, actress, singer, playwright, and screenwriter. Famous for her double entendres and openly sexual persona, West encountered censorship as well as wide popular fame during her long career.

5. Dreiser is referring to the film *Back Street* (1932), based on the popular novel of the same name by Fannie Hurst. The story of a girl who becomes a kept woman, the film has similarities to Dreiser's novel *Jennie Gerhardt* (1911), which was made into a movie in 1933. Dreiser contemplated a lawsuit against Universal Studio but never took the case to court.

To Esther McCoy [TC-DPUP]

Dreiser was fascinated with the psychology of criminal cases in which an attraction existed between the accused and the accuser, and at times thought of writing a novel centered on such an episode. (For a later such instance, see Dreiser to Thelma Cudlipp, 1 August 1942.)

Hotel Ansonia,
New York City.

August 1, 1934

Dear Esther:

Back in 1921 in Los Angeles, a woman by the name of Madalynne Obenchain was tried for instigating murder, and there was a fellow by the name of Birch who was also tried. He was the man who she instigated to kill a young man by the name of Kennedy, and Birch was convicted. I don't know whether eventually she was let loose or not.[1]

The murder was committed, I think in the summer of 1921 and ran through that fall. Now this is what I want:

I want you, if you have the time, to go through the files of the Times and the Examiner of that period from the beginning of the case to the end and copy out for me the data. I am particularly interested in all the data that relates to Madalynne Obenchain and also everything that relates to the District attorney—Woolwine, who was the prosecutor. I don't know whether it appeared in the papers there or not, but I heard from newspaper men that after Birch was convicted and at the time when Woolwine was getting ready to prosecute her, he fell in love with her while she was in jail and threw the case over, that is, he decided not to conduct the prosecution himself but appointed his assistant Keyes to do the prosecuting, and I think she got off. The same data in regard to that, his making love to her, or her seducing him, got out and he was finished as District Attorney and also as candidate for Governor, because I believe the Republicans were planning to run him for Governor.

Then she came down, so I heard, to Staten Island here in New York and he followed her and tried to get her to marry him or to live with him, and when he found that she had double-crossed him he took to drinking and was finished politically and in every other way, so far as I know. After that I could never find anything out about her, where she went, what she did. But now this work, as I know from personal experience may take weeks of your time. As you know, I am perfectly willing to pay for it. I want you to tell me how much time you can give to it; what you want a week and anyhow let me know whether you can or can't do it.

If you can't do it, I have my friend George Douglas[2] on the Examiner who probably could get the work done, or maybe you know some thorough-going person, as thorough-going as yourself who could give the time to it. Let me know.

Of course it is understood that you are not to mention this to any one. This is personal and private between ourselves.

Affectionately,
TD

1. The Obenchain litigation was one of the more sensational murder cases in the history of Los Angeles County. The victim was J. Benton Kennedy, and it was alleged that Arthur C. Burch (not Birch, as Dreiser has it) was implicated with Obenchain. The district attorney, Thomas Woolwine, made news when he withdrew from the case, claiming that he wanted to take personal charge of the investigation of another celebrated case, the unsolved murder of the Paramount director William Desmond Taylor. Dreiser and others speculated that a personal relationship between the prosecutor and Obenchain had developed and was the real reason for Woolwine's withdrawal from the case. In a letter to McCoy on 9 August 1934 (DPUP), Dreiser outlines more specifically his interests in the data of this case:

> A great thing would be to selectively condense the material before you, presenting, of course, all the important thoughts and actions of Birch, Madalynne, the District Attorney, his Assistant Keyes, interpretations of the mood of the public at the time as it is reflected in the comments by the newspaper critics said to psychologize the trial. I would be glad, after you have examined the material if you would psychologize the case yourself and give me your interpretation of the motives of the different people. Above all things, if there are touches of character or procedure of any kind in connection with the District Attorney, and the inmates of the jail, I would like those pointed out, and if they are good incidents, copied out, because what I want is the character of the life in jail and how that surrounded Madalynne, Birch and whoever else was connected with it at that time.

2. George Douglas (?–1936), Australian born journalist and critic. During his career he worked for several newspapers including the *San Francisco Bulletin*, the *San*

Francisco Chronicle, and the *Los Angeles Examiner*. Dreiser had a special affection for his company and conversation, claiming there was a kind of "psychic osmosis" between them.

To Louise Campbell [H-DPUP]

[10 December 1934]

Dear Louise:

You remember Miss Clark of Philly? Well, she's written a novel.[1] She sent it to me to read & I gave it to someone else for an opinion. The opinion was favorable. Then I sent it to Knopf[2] who rejected it. However, even there he said that one of his readers liked it. But he also said it was diffuse. I so notified Clara & then she suggested—having heard me speak of your editing—that I inquire as to whether you would read it and if you thought it worth while ask how much you would charge her to edit it—but *only* if you thought it worth while. Not otherwise. If you say the book is not much I think she will lay it aside & try some other theme. If however you like it & decide to edit it, I am [word missing] she would like to try another publisher. She hasn't much money. I think $35 or $40 would be high for her but if she felt it worth while she would pay it. Tell me what you think. The ms has been lying here for some days.

How are you? I'm still plugging along. Mencken was over to see me the other day & we patched up a tentative armed peace.[3] He wants me to take a trip with him somewhere—Helen is reading Powys book[4] & is fascinated. I skimmed it & found out what I want to know. You see I know Jack this long while now & much that he says I have heard in conversations with him.

Love—
T. D

Let me know about the book. But don't encourage her unless you honestly can.

1. Clara Clark's novel *Too Many Women* was never published (Clara Jaeger to Riggio, 23 May 2005).

2. The publisher Alfred A. Knopf (1892–1984).

3. Dreiser and H. L. Mencken had been estranged since Mencken's negative review of *An American Tragedy* in 1926. For a brief summary of the complex factors involved in the breakup, see Riggio, *Dreiser-Mencken Letters*, II, 506–10.

4. Probably *Weymouth Sands* (1934) by John Cowper Powys (1872–1963).

1935

To Thelma Cudlipp [HP-DPUP]

After the storm of their earlier, aborted relationship had calmed, Dreiser and Thelma Cudlipp became friends who saw each other socially and corresponded occasionally. In 1918 she had married Edwin Grosvenor, a cousin of former president William Howard Taft. Cudlipp continued her work as an illustrator of mainstream magazines, many of which also published Dreiser's writing.

THEODORE DREISER
Mt. Kisco

Jan 2–[Undated, after 1934]

Thelma Dearest:

Does it seem so long since Anne sung here?[1] The thought has its pleasing side. And the poem. I'd like to talk to Anne about that—particularly the "grotesque and awful store of nothingness." Maybe sixteen sees the leafless tree that way. And misses the "*flush*" of life. But I see an otherwise operating force (the leafless tree itself, no less) wholly artful and lovely in its bareness—and so forceful. And unless change is death there is none—to me.

Why don't you come out some Sunday—or be at home. One or both of us[2] are usually in N.Y. Saturdays and Sundays.

I hope all is well with you.

T.D

1. Anne Grosvenor was Cudlipp's daughter, who delighted Dreiser with her singing.
2. Dreiser is referring to Helen Richardson and himself.

To Kirah Markham [H-DPUP]

Theodore Dreiser

Markham's chances to work in theater practically disappeared in the Depression of the 1930s, and her painting and work for the WPA (Works Progress Administration) did not relieve her financial needs.

Feb. 5–1935

Dear Kirah:

I think your lithograph, *Elaine and Maria* is beautiful. Very. I feel you should exhibit a group of these. Why not the Rehn Gallery[1] in New York?

Why not apply to the Guggenheim Foundation[2] for an award—and refer to me? I'll be glad to testify and persuade. Meanwhile the enclosed 10^{00} is nothing more than a tribute to your aesthetic earnestness and its achievements—including *Elaine and Maria*.

I'm sorry about the Nordfeldt portrait[3] of you. But if it's gone it's gone.

Some day when your coming to town, come and see me—But give me previous notice. I'd like to take you to lunch or dinner.

Just now—far from well.

Affectionately,
T. D

1. The Frank Rehn Gallery, at 665 Madison Avenue, was one of the more prestigious showplaces in New York.

2. The John Simon Guggenheim Memorial Foundation, established in 1925, provides individual fellowships with stipends in all fields, including the creative arts.

3. Bror Nordfeldt. See Dreiser to Kirah Markham, 12 May 1913, n. 3. Markham had lost track of Nordfeldt's portrait of her that she left in Dreiser's apartment after they had separated in 1916.

To Yvette Szekely [H-DPUP]

During the summer of 1935 Dreiser occupied a suite in the California home of his friend the Australian-born journalist George Douglas (?–1936). The two men shared interests in science and philosophy, and they spent days talking, visiting various scientific centers, and entertaining scientists and researchers—activities contributing to Dreiser's ongoing but never realized philosophical-scientific treatise that he often referred to as "The Formula Called Man."

June 3rd 1935

Dear Yvette

Yesterday afternoon I sat in a garden where roses climbed a wall to the sun and a pink marble bowl sunk in dark green grass reflected some leaves of a eucalyptus towering high above. The table was of clear glass and about it sat besides Douglas & myself two physicists—members of the California Institute of Technology. And explaining research methods. These related to neutrons and deuterons, and cosmic rays and space-time. But as I looked at the roses in the sun, the forms of the leaves reflected in the crystal water, the rich green grass & felt the warmth & the light soft *air*, I could not help thinking, suppose I knew all—or at least more about grass, light, roses, leaves or the shadows of them in clear water, would my enjoyment of life be greater—or less. Incidentally, seeing them so I felt as though the scene was not a setting for analysis or research but rather one for lovely sensuous enjoyment in which human beauty & human love would add to the beauty and where analysis would not detract from it. It made me very sad and very lonely. And so am I today—24 hours later.

T.D.

I will answer your latest letter when I am not so blue.

To Yvette Szekely [H-DPUP]

4922 Rosewood Ave.
Los Angeles.

Aug 15–'35

Yvette Dear:

Please note the new address. But don't send mail here yet. Continue to send it to 232 So. Westmoreland, and I will have it forwarded from there in a new envelope. Helen is here with me. She grew suddenly very desolate & I compromised on this. But one day she saw one of your gray envelope letters—properly typed and all—and mailed in New York. But she recognized it and raged. I settled that by warning her not to bother in any way since this relationship was not to be disturbed. She dropped the matter, but not without telling me that a constant visitor of yours at Kisco—one whom you slept with there nights and regularly, was a young Jew—the same one I judge rang the bell in Perry Street.[1] I allowed for rage & so forth, but not for the description. And Helen does not lie. She asserts what she knows. I know that. Curiously though—just before I wrote the "*diluted*" letter, some one else who is at Mt. Kisco and whom you know by sight anyhow wrote and asked me if you had a brother—that *she or he*—(you will have to guess whether male or female) saw a young man about the cabin with you quite frequently. So you see. I have nothing to say. Your emotions and necessities are your own. But when you write me vehemently of love and devotion I cannot accept it undiluted. I have to think that you care for others. Naturally you would conceal knowledge of the others so as not to hurt me. Wont that explain the last letter?[2]

The other night—for the first time—I saw "Escape Me Never."[3] I truly liked it very much,—thought it beautiful. And in many ways Gemma[4]—or whatever her name was reminded me of you—your spirit and wisdom and gift of feeling and romance. Also your sly cleverness. But after all—as Gemma said of her artist-god—I would not change you. You are as you are. And if I value your friendship and your diluted affection I will have to make the best of it. I cannot help liking you. You have genius of mind and skill at living. You are kind & forgiving and understanding and ready to help all who need help. I cannot change or make you into anything and do not wish to. I try to understand & endure as you understand and endure. In real life I fancy Gemma was not better than yourself if as good.

I'm sorry about the Perry street room. I liked it so much—until—and still like it in a way—because I know that another place wherever it may be will not be any more sacred. Certainly I will come to see you when I get back—but don't you think you should do the picking? I notice that whatever you choose and wherever you are you create a loveliness especial & peculiar to you. And it is soothing to me.

But, ah, Yvette—I am really lonely. I cannot tell you why. Some essential thing is wrong. I know that I am liked well enough. A to-do is made. Here & there a girl will frantically seek me out—and many men. But just the same. In your little rooms though I have been happy. And for the most part in your presence this almost crushing despair has fled. I wish it would go forever.

T.D

1. Szekely had lived in Perry Street in Manhattan. She often stayed at Iroki, Dreiser's country home at Mt. Kisco.

2. Most of Szekely's letters to Dreiser are not among his papers.

3. *Escape Me Never* (1935), directed by Paul Czinner, is a film adaptation of the 1930 novel and play written by English novelist Margaret Kennedy. It tells the story of a poor composer and his brother who get involved with an heiress and an itinerant waif.

4. The name of the waif in *Escape Me Never*.

To Kirah Markham [H-DPUP]

4922 Rosewood Ave.
Los Angeles.

Oct. 7–1935

Kirah Dear:

It was nice—very—to get your letter and when I'm next in New York, I'll stop in. I know how wretched the place looks. But I also know how charming it will be after you play with it awhile. But when it is beautiful as it will be, I hope you can keep it. Never show it to the landlord. He will raise the rent, because instantly he will realize that he can sell what you have done for more money.

I got quite sick last winter and had to leave. For a while I thought I was going to have a breakdown. Went to bed & stayed there for weeks. Then in May I came out here. Later Helen came & we have been living in one of those floral bungalows that make the town. Slowly I picked up, took up my work and now am normal again. I dont feel that I owe it all to L.A. I got better at Mt. Kisco and getting out of N.Y. helped. But I'll be back—for a time anyhow. This pleasant land of drowsy heads helps everyone for a time,—I think. Beside its not so hicky as it once was. 2,400,000 people make a city, regardless. There are great avenues and the old business heart is something of a back number. New centers have sprung up. Hollywood Boul is a second rate street. And Hollywood itself is no longer swank. Instead cheap. The smart areas are elsewhere. And the movies do not dominate the atmosphere. They are important. But so is oil, the fruit industry, the shipping business, the aero-plane factories and other such things. You wouldn't know it. The L.A. of 1914–1919 is dimly imbedded in a huge world that seems to be looking south to Mexico and west across the Pacific. 40 hours to Chicago by train makes everything less remote. But I'll be seeing you one of these days. Regards to David[1] & luck to both of you.

T.D

Howard Scott[2] is in town. He spoke at the Bowl yesterday to about 9000 people & is touring the west coast. He was here last night for dinner & we sat around & talked. He is something like a rock that changes little and as positive & defiant as ever.[3]

1. David Gaiter, Markham's husband.
2. See Dreiser to Kirah Markham, 7 August 1922, n. 2.
3. This last paragraph was written sideways in the left hand margin of the second page.

To Louise Campbell [TC-DPUP]

There were plans being made by Milton Shubert to produce The Case of Clyde Griffiths, *an English version of the German dramatization of* An American Tragedy *by Erwin Piscator. Campbell had done the translation from the German, and the play had been produced at the Hedgerow Theatre in April 1935. For the new production, Shubert suggested a number of structural changes, and Dreiser turned to Campbell to help with the revisions.*

Mount Kisco,
New York

November 26, 1935

Dear Louise:

There is no news concerning the play as yet. It appears that I personally am not to be asked to change anything. The hitch if any lies between Shubert and Piscator. Shubert wants him to come this year and sign up for three years. Piscator, with an eye on Hollywood or such, refuses to sign for more than two years. All other matters have been adjusted, so far as I know.

It occurred to me that in revising some of the lines for Shubert you might like to look at the Patrick Kearney version, or at a recently completed French version which is far superior to the Kearney version and which is a very moving redramatization.[1] I can let you have it in case you think you really need it. Otherwise, I would prefer to keep it here.

Thanks for the word about *Africa Dances*.[2] As you see, Fort[3] is certain to come into his own. I am always anxious for the time to come when I can write a picture of him; and in connection with that, the appreciation of this man and others will help. If you see anything more about him let me know. I enjoyed the last visit so much, and one of these weeks you will have to come over again. Incidentally, I want to get over to see Wharton at Paoli,[4] and if we do we will look in on you.

Regards,
Th.D.

1. Patrick Kearney (1893–1933) had written a dramatization of *An American Tragedy* that opened at the Longacre Theatre on 11 October 1926 and ran for 216 performances. It was revived five years later, when it opened at the Waldorf Theatre on 20 February 1931 and ran for 137 performances. Kearney's version was straightforward and structurally conventional; the Piscator adaptation dramatized the class struggle in the book by staging the action on two levels, representing labor and capital, with a stage manager who asked questions of the two groups that provoked debate on social and philosophical issues. The French dramatization of the novel was never produced. (Also see Dreiser to Lena Goldschmidt, 27 April 1929, n. 1.)

2. *Africa Dances: A Book about West African Negroes* (1935), by Geoffrey Gorer.

3. Charles Fort. See Dreiser to Helen Richardson, 18 June 1924, n. 6. Fort was mentioned favorably in Gorer's book. Dreiser never did write the character sketch of Fort mentioned here.

4. Wharton Esherick. See Dreiser to Kirah Markham, 30 December 1928, n. 5. Esherick lived in Paoli, Pennsylvania, northwest of Philadelphia.

1936

To Esther McCoy [H-DPUP]

Hotel Chelsea
New York

Feb. 26–'36

Dear Esther:

This package contains *Man, the Unknown*[1] by Carrel and the latest survey of scientific achievements. Look through both with an eye to The Mechanism Called Man, Myth of Free Will, Good & Evil, The Wisdom of the So-called Unconscious, The Myth of Individual Thinking, etc.[2] Return books & copied quotes to me at Ansonia—but notify me when you leave them there.

So that you will have something to go on I am enclosing my check for 15^{00}. Let me know when you get these.

T.D.

1. *Man the Unknown* (1935), by Dr. Alexis Carrel (1873–1944), was a best seller in its time and his first popular book. Carrel, a biologist and surgeon, won the 1912 Nobel Prize in Medicine for his pioneering vessel-suturing work. Carrel is sometimes called the "Father of Transplantation" because his research brought medical science a step closer to the reality of organ transplants.

2. The titles Dreiser lists here are chapter titles for a book he variously called "The Mechanism Called Man" or "The Formula Called Man." It was a work in progress that he never finished, an attempt to synthesize his thinking on the nature of human life based on modern scientific data. Dreiser's method was to have knowledgeable researchers like McCoy go through books and articles that he had discovered and perused and provide him with pages and paragraphs relating to certain themes that were the subjects of his chapters. Marguerite Tjader and John J. McAleer published a portion of the manuscript notes, fragments, and chapters as *Notes on Life* (1974).

To May Calvert Baker [T-DPUP]

Mount Kisco, New York

March 7–1936

Dear Teacher:

So glad to hear from you, and all my love to you. I, too, read in the papers that the Paul Dresser Memorial Committee of Terre Haute has secured a federal grant to help buy and landscape a park which is to be named after Paul. Back in 1924 they raised $35,000 for that purpose by a public subscription, and they still have that money.[1] However, apart from helping on the original publicity, I have never been invited to participate in any way. It is possible that I may receive an invitation to the dedication ceremony, but as yet I have had no word. If I do go to Terre Haute, I will most certainly come over to Indianapolis; and if you have a hall bedroom out on the lot somewhere, I will be glad to occupy it.

I never enjoyed a visit more than the one I paid to you back in 1917.[2] And I am delighted to know that you are in good health and spirits, and able to invite me again. You will always be May Calvert to me—the teacher that made the public school a sort of Paradise.

Affectionately,
TD

1. Talk of a memorial for Paul Dresser went back as far as 1920 (see Dreiser to Mencken, 25 October, 14 November, 20 December 1920 in Riggio, *Dreiser-Mencken Letters*, II, 403, 405–6, 417). The Paul Dresser Memorial Committee was founded in 1922, plans for a Paul Dresser memorial in Terre Haute were approved in 1923, and a national fundraiser took place in 1924. There were plans, some grandiose, at various times to build monuments to Dresser, but most were either abandoned or begun and left incomplete. For a summary of these enterprises, see Henderson *On the Banks of the Wabash*, 324–28. See also Dreiser to Robert D. Heinl, 30 September 1924, in Pizer, *New Letters*.

2. Dreiser means 1919. See Dreiser to May Calvert Baker, 23 July 1917, n. 4.

To Esther McCoy [TC-DPUP]

Mount Kisco, New York

April 3, 1936

Dear Esther,

I tried to get in touch with you yesterday by phone to explain what I want you to do in connection with the material on color in relation to emotion.[1] I do not want you to spend too much time on it. Briefly, here are the questions which interest me with regard to it: What colors seem to be consistently with what emotions—for example, love and hate, sorrow and joy? Is there anything inherent in color and unconnected with color values by association that seems to be able to arouse emotion, or, on the other hand, is it purely because of the connection in experience of certain colors with certain emotions that colors have the power to arouse emotion? For example, has color the power of arousing emotion in the same way that a bell can cause evidence of hunger to appear in a dog who has been trained to associate the bell with its feeding time, or could color arouse emotion without any previous association? Also, does the intensity of color have any connection with intense emotional stress, irrespective of the particular color or emotion?

Does color have more connection with emotion than other sensory relations? Is there an analogical connection between all the various sensory reactions, sound, color, smell, etc. and emotion? For example, could red be connected with certain chord relations, and certain odors, and all of these with certain emotional states?

I think you might find some material on the color organ useful in this connection.

But remember, I do not want very much material on this.

As ever,
T.D

1. Dreiser's request for data on the nature of color was for his philosophical-scientific treatise, "The Formula Called Man." See Dreiser to Esther McCoy, 26 February 1936, n. 2.

To Esther McCoy [H-DPUP]

In mid-May Dreiser, McCoy, and Helen Richardson had driven together from New York to West Lafayette, Indiana, where he was to speak at Purdue University. Dreiser returned to New York, but Richardson drove McCoy to her hometown in Kansas, and continued on to visit her family in Portland, Oregon. McCoy wrote him, discussing the mental strain on Richardson, who was then separating from Dreiser, as she often had in the past. By the time this letter was written Richardson was in Los Angeles.

Mount Kisco, N. Y.

June 22nd 1936

Dear Esther

Thanks for your nice letter although the part about Helen makes me very sad. I care for her truly although often enough we dont get along. But the drift of her temperament is truly lovely and she suffers keenly through her reactions to the beautiful and the dreams and ideals evoked in her by the illusive phantom of beauty in life. So often I wish, I wish I could make her wholly happy and when she leaves me I am sorrowful and grieve for her and myself. I know she is sick. Have written her to rest & take medical aid. I will always look after her to the best of my ability, as she knows.

In regard to your letter—didn't you write me a short note from Coffeyville about two weeks ago apologizing for something. I thought it related to some imaginary something when we were in Cleveland. But I didn't understand clearly and tore it up but not before writing you. As I read the letter it seemed to indicate that you felt that I might be thinking you had been distant or critical or something but *I didnt think so*. Hence my note.

So your going on to L.A. I wish you every good thing. If you see Helen again try to make clear to her that I care for her & that I have my troubles & strains plenty. I want her to get well & I want to pull myself together & then maybe we can make a go of it out there.

Love & all good wishes
T.D

1937

To Clara Clark [H-RIG]

At the time of this letter Dreiser and Clara Clark had not seen each other for nearly three years. She had developed what turned out to be a life-long involvement in social and religious activities.

Hotel Park Plaza
50 W. 77th St.
NYC

Jan. 15–'37

Click[1] Dear:

I was so pleased to hear from you. I've thought of you plenty—just as though nothing had ever changed, and so I'll continue to think. I'm interested by and sympathetic toward what you tell me of the Oxford Movement.[2] I've read of it of course and know some people,—you among them—who are gripped by it. Alas, honey, I'm one of the irreconcilables, as you know. I was brought up in the Catholic faith, but it meant nothing to me. My sister Sylvia is a C. S.[3] healer with patients, but somehow—well, I could

Clara Clark and Dreiser (ca. 1932).

argue about it for years. What I did love in you was your enthusiasm for the universe with all it contained—good and evil—and your poetic rhapsodies anent *that* still run in my mind. You were, and I suppose will always remain, something like a fresh wind, blowing here and there, in the alleys as well as the gardens of life, and remaining sweet of heart. You used to accuse me of roaring violently against this and that but with no enduring rage or evil intent, and I often think you're a piece of cloth off the same bolt. I insist there's no real badness in you. Anyhow, I hope not. I used to denounce you to your teeth—but not elsewhere, as you know, and yet I never really believed that I was justified in so doing. Rather you were colorful & erratic, and gay & wistful and courageous enough as life goes—and I wish so much that you could remain so. If I were anything but *lunacy personified* I could keep you content with life, I know—partially so, anyhow. But being what I am—Ah—the devil.

Dear, I hope that you are a little happy. How much I wish that. And you'll never be anything but what your entitled to be by reason of youthfulness of heart, sweetness of mind and the right we all have to dream—if we can. Write me again. I think of you so often in that Quaker dress you put on once. *Lovely* was the word for *Click* in that.

Give my regards to all, please.

T. D

I've been sick. Flu, a little. Now I'm up again.

1. Click: Dreiser's nickname for her.
2. The Oxford Movement had its roots in the religious reformation of the Anglican Church that took place at Oxford University in the first decades of the nineteenth century. By the time Clara Clark encountered the movement, it had shifted its focus to social concerns. She became involved in the "Oxford Group" founded by Frank N. D. Buchman (1878–1961), a small but worldwide society that advocated personal spiritual growth as a way of building a better society. There she met her future husband, William Jaeger, who became known for his work with the Moral Re-Armament Association, which expanded the mission of the Oxford Group by focusing attention on the international labor union movement. For a full treatment of her participation in the group, see Clara Jaeger *Never to Lose My Vision: The Story of Bill Jaeger* (London: Grosvenor Books, 1995).
3. Christian Science.

To Helen Richardson [H-DPUP]

In October of 1937, Dreiser had moved to a second-floor apartment in the Rhinelander Gardens complex on 11th Street in New York City, where he had lived with his sister Mame in 1924. His investments had diminished after the 1929 crash of the stock market; but 1937 was the start of a particularly strained three years, in which his income was not keeping up with his expenses. He could make no headway on the novel at hand, The Stoic; *and his attempts to sell the film rights to one of his novels to Hollywood were coming up against the demands of the censors at the Hays office. Moreover, relations with Helen had deteriorated, and she once again had gone to Oregon to stay with her family.*

116 W. 11th St

Dec 7–37

Dear Helen:

I have been really sick in bed for the last three days or I would have written you before, particularly since this last letter of yours is the only one in heaven knows how long that has not confirmed me in my desire to close the account between us. This letter doesnt tell me much of anything that I didnt know but it acknowledges a lot that I do. And the absence of that acknowledgement, coupled with the constant assertion of worthlessness, and intense cruelty and what I owe you for what you have done for me, has about broken up the alliance. For as this letter of yours shows you were getting something—(a quite considerable thing) even though you were not getting all of what you wanted or needed.

But of that it all comes down to what human beings are entitled to ask of each other *in return for what*. The quick answer is 50–50 and it sounds fine. But who is to say that the 50 that one person sees as his contribution is the exact duplicate of the 50 that the other person sees as his contribution. And since there are so many differences of opinion there have come into being the endless courts with their judges, juries, jails, fines and public arguments. But when all is said & done who is to say that all of the agents or any of them have given the correct answers to the 50–50 question.

You have your needs. I have mine. You want your needs fulfilled, I want mine & you charge me with cruelty in refusing or failing to supply what you need or needed. I sit back & consider my needs & then place opposite them the things I havent, that I might have or might have had. No one can go with us into our deepest selves. To make things come out at all large sacrifices have to be made, I suppose, but who makes them—or makes them understandingly.

You ask am I going to leave you. What springs in my mind immediately is could we ever live happily & profitably together. My thought without alteration is on my work. Mentally I never leave it & mostly as at Cold Spring Harbor,[1] I find myself happiest talking to those who can throw a light on it. It is true, on the other hand, that you do and always have represented a certain untutored and uncontaminated emotional response to beauty which is very moving. Except for your singing and some of your worded comments on nature it is voiceless. You rarely read a book. Your poetry does not take form on paper—only in song. Yet I read your silent moods. Most of my deepest and tenderest reactions to you have been at these times.

Despite all this you are not an easy person to live with—any more so than am I. Mostly, as I have seen over so long a time you live within yourself—contemplative & silent. I used to wonder as to this—even in Glendale.[2] You insist you supply an atmosphere—an artistic and poetic one. It is true for such times as your broodings over and interests in things which do not coincide with my interests or moods. But those times were very numerous. And mostly I have found that I could not go to you with my intellectual or emotional interests. Perhaps mine were too definitely in one key or vein—yours in another. Largely I have gone abroad for intellectual and emotional reactions which I felt necessary for me at the time. Add to this the natural resentments and quarrels on both sides and you can see to what we would come.

So when you say am I going to leave you I scarcely know what to say. If I only knew or could believe that we could go on in some helpful constructive way. But I cant help feeling that it is likely to come to nothing. At the same time just now I am in the midst of so many financial ills that I scarcely see how I can go on. If anything comes through I would be the last person to throw you on your own, even though I feel that if you had some task of some kind, it would be good for you, and would, in your case, lead to some development favorable to you. The idea of uncreatively dreaming whether in marriage or out of it, seems self destructive and dangerous to me. Everybody ought to be made to work at something.

I have several bits of news. Through Mr. Gredlev I found a caretaker at 10^{00} for the winter.[3] His name is Gandineir (Henry L.), and he lives in that little white house up the road. He works for the Reiglemans and is their caretaker in the winter. About a week ago he repaired several broken windows in the big house. Last week two boys whom his wife saw but could not identify broke into our place & the Reiglemans. From the Reiglemans they stole silverware and from our two houses they took my radio in the guest house & that elephant lamp in the dining room of the big house—nothing else that I can see. The police took some finger prints from both houses & are looking for the thieves. They also said that from now on, until spring, the state police would patrol the road at least once a day (!) This Gandineir seems to be a bright fellow. He asked me, when I went up, if I wanted to sell that corner of land—from the blue road door to his place. I told him yes but not before asking Cox how land prices there should run. He said that parcels of land (2 or more acres) from the Reiglemans on to

Katonah were selling from 650 to 800 an acre, according to location. I told Gandineir if he could find someone who would take the whole corner at 750 an acre that I'd part with it. There should be four acres in there any of which would bring $3000. The way things are now we'd be lucky to get that. Or do you think so.

I have had no word from Kertesz[4] & now I doubt if he represents Piscator[5] although he says he does. Anyhow I had some copies of The Case of Clyde Griffiths made & I am sending it on.[6] You can see if anyone is interested, & by that time since Goldschmidt[7] wants to do it, it probably can be arranged. Meanwhile let me know how things are. This cold hanging on keeps me weak. Otherwise when I'm up I work well enough.

T.D

1. Cold Spring Harbor is a town on the northwest coast of Long Island that was the site of the Carnegie Biological Laboratory. Dreiser's interest in biochemical phenomena led him there in the summer of 1937 to visit his friend Calvin Bridges (1889–1937), a scientist who pioneered in genetics. At the time, Dreiser was collecting scientific data for an ambitious study he planned to write on the scientific and philosophical nature of key aspects of human life. See Dreiser to Esther McCoy, 26 February 1936, n. 2.

2. Soon after they first met in 1919, Dreiser and Helen moved to California. They lived in six different places in the Los Angeles area until August 1921, when they bought a small bungalow in Glendale. They lived there until October 1922, when they returned to New York.

3. Dreiser is talking about a caretaker for Iroki, a thirty-seven acre parcel of land on which in 1928 he had built a home outside the town of Mount Kisco in Westchester County, New York. The neighbors he refers to in this paragraph helped him find Gandineir as caretaker. Cox was a local real estate agent.

4. Andrew Kertesz, Erwin Piscator's agent.

5. Erwin Piscator. See Dreiser to Lena Goldschmidt, 27 April 1929, n. 1.

6. *The Case of Clyde Griffiths*, a dramatic version of *An American Tragedy* that Dreiser is suggesting Helen try to sell in Hollywood. It was Louise Campbell's translation of Piscator's German adaptation of the novel. Campbell's version had a successful run at Jasper Deeter's Hedgerow Theater in 1935. On 13 March 1936, it had opened at the Ethel Barrymore Theatre in New York. It ran for only nineteen performances, despite the fact that it was produced by Milton Shubert, directed by Lee Strasberg, and had a cast that included Morris Carnovsky, Alexander Kirkland, Elia Kazan, and John Garfield.

7. This is a reference to Lina Goldschmidt's husband, Alfons (1879–1940), who was a journalist, editor, economist, and political scientist. After his wife's death in 1935 he negotiated—on the basis of her work on the text—for an active role (and share) in the production of the Piscator play or in any adaptation of it such as *The Case of Clyde Griffiths*.

1938

To Helen Richardson [H-DPUP]

Feb. 27 [1938]

Helen,

I have been looking over your poems again. The two that I like so far are *Twilight Nostalgia* and *The Blue Heron*. [word unintelligible] is not clear to me. I cannot interpret the similes. And *Another Spring* is too much like a catalogue of flower names. But the first two are good. They derive from a mood whose significance or meaning is clear and moving to you. If I were naming *Twilight Nostalgia* I would reverse the words thus—*Nostalgia: Twilight*. I feel that the desire to write poetry is the loveliest instinct anyone can have—the desire to express the feeling of life, and in the above two poems that desire is plain. If you were to study the dictionary—reading and meditating over the definitions—you would see how quickly you would profit and how inspirational so many words are. I have always known that you are deeply responsive to beauty and that your moods reflect your love of life and beauty. So, most naturally, I sense that should you ever find the words that appeal most to you, you will write beautiful verse or—which is just as well—beautifully express your moods or reactions to life.

I have been in a very bad state mentally of late as you have seen. So many things have combined to make bad days and months. Pretty soon I must decide on some new way of living. I have too many cares that come with money—that I never had before. And now how I regret so much of it. The stupidness of show.

Mame telephoned today that Frank Thomas[1] was better. He has passed the crisis, but is pretty weak. She stirs me up so. This is Sunday. Tomorrow I will get your check ready & mail it. I never have been able to reach Piscator.[2] He is determined I think not to let the Griffiths play go on.[3] He wants to forget communism, I think. But things are getting so bad I think it may yet be popular. Any day now I expect to hear from Hume[4] as to the result. Also from Rosen[5] as to the house. If he takes it, I may come out there. What do you do with your time?

Love
T.D.

1. Frank Thomas was the companion of Dreiser's sister Mame.
2. See Dreiser to Lena Goldschmidt, 27 April 1929, n. 1.

3. *The Case of Clyde Griffiths*. See Dreiser to Helen Richardson, 7 December 1937, n. 6.
4. Arthur Carter Hume (1869–1942), Dreiser's New York attorney, was handling the negotiations over *The Case of Clyde Griffiths*.
5. Dreiser was negotiating with Mr. and Mrs. Rosen to rent the house at Mt. Kisco.

To Ruth Kennell [H-DPUP]

Throughout their relationship, Dreiser took Kennell's advice on political matters seriously, and she often influenced his actions as well as his opinions. Here Dreiser is responding to her plea for him to write to President Roosevelt personally about aiding the Loyalist military cause in Spain. The Loyalists had been attacked by General Franco's coalition, supported by the Monarchists and the Catholic CEDA—as well as by foreign forces, including Nazi air force bombers and troops from Italy and Portugal. Kennell wrote that it would be "a tragic mistake for Roosevelt to interpret the Neutrality Act in such a way that the recognized government of Spain is denied its legal right to purchase arms from us with which to defend itself against rebellion and invasion. We know that lifting the embargo will enormously help the Loyalists to withstand the mechanized forces of Germany and Italy. Your name should carry great weight with him" (21 April 1938 [DPUP]).

Mt. Kisco, N.Y.

April 26–'38

Dear Ruth:

Thanks for your letter and I'll do as you say.[1] Dont think though I haven't done things for the Loyalists. I've contributed regularly to the Loyalist funds, written articles and talked long and fiercely on various occasions. I think we'll pay for our indifference if Spain goes fascist. I think Cordell Hull[2] is an enemy of labor and the mass generally. Why does Roosevelt select enemies to his aims and place them in high positions. He is constantly being bitten by once frozen snakes he has chosen to warm at his fireside.

I'm glad your so rampant. You sound like your real self. I meant to write & say come & bring your friend or call me up when in town. But I had 3 connecting cases of grippe running over 6 weeks—up and down. Then I moved out here. I now feel better. If your ever over this way stop in & if I pass through Bridgeport[3] Ill see you there. But I'm wanting to sell as well as rent this place & if I do I'll move somewhat nearer to N.Y. or maybe back into it.

Affectionately
T.D

1. Dreiser did write to Roosevelt, and after his visit to Spain later in the year met with him. At that time Roosevelt agreed with the need to provide aid, but said that Americans were largely against lifting the embargo on food and arms sales to Spain. He suggested Dreiser form a committee of prominent citizens (made up of Protestants, Jews, and Catholics) to help change public opinion.

2. Cordell Hull (1871–1955), a former congressman and senator from Tennessee, was appointed secretary of state by Franklin D. Roosevelt in 1933.

3. Kennell was living in Bridgeport, Connecticut.

To Helen Richardson [H-DPUP]

June 21—the longest day [1938]

Dear Helen,

Your selection of love poems is delicately percieving and very sensitive. I never read Sir Philip Sidney's *My True Love Hath my Heart* but it is one of the best. I'll keep it in my collection. And Edna Millays *Euclid Alone Has Looked*. All the others are excellent. You seem to be turning to poetry. If so I think you may prove one of its best critics and interpreters. Phases of your temperament are certain to be accurately and comfortingly reflected in poetry, painting, as already they are in music. Sometime you should read Thoreau's Journal. It is very long—19 fair sized volumes but full of things that will certainly help you to live. Above all things read first his life by Leon Bazalgette. It was translated from the French in 1922 (Harcourt Brace.)[1] I read *Walden* and *Voyage on the Concord & Merrimac Rivers* years ago. But only recently I read his life and it is *something*. From time to time I have read volumes of his journal & they contain marvelous bits all through.

I've been worrying about money again—damn it. I have not heard from the trial but Rossett was telling me that if the stocks I put up do not cover the loss I may be sued.[2] That house took so much up there, that although now it is in good condition, my total clearance, insurance money & all will be 180^{000}r 185.[3] The last thing that happened was that the northwest corner gave way making a channel & pool further southwest. It had to be drained, the wall and gate fixed & the whole pool cleaned—18 inches of muck—and a pile of sand in the place and large pile of muck in another. One of the steps was broken and had to be reset. The Rosens[4] asserted that they would not keep the place if it was not fixed. To avoid argument I had it done—\$$96^{00}$. I am selling an occasional article, but with so many things to meet I just nervously sink down at certain times. One thing I've been thinking I ought to do is take out some group sickness insurance. For 3 cents a day—11^{00} a year per person in advance you get a semi-private room in any hospital—a nurse, your food, operating room, anesthetist, X ray and other things—all you need—except your doctors bill. That you have to pay.

But with all these other charges out they say his bill can only be so much a visit. If you take the intern instead of an outside doctor its $\$15^{00}$ I hear. For a group of four, they charge (I hear) only $\$25^{00}$ a year. And you can enter any hospital anywhere. It's national. So then if Mame or Rome[5] broke down I would come off better—get better service. And I myself might profit by it. I'm looking into it.

The 1st will soon be here & I'm looking round now. May go to the Chelsea where Masters[6] is for a little while. $\$15^{00}$ a week I hear. I have to arrange about my things in storage & so on. Since Germany took Austria I hear my books are not to be found there. All I have left now is Scandanavia, England & Checko-Slovakia. France has never yeilded me a cent. Russia has stopped. Why I don't know. Poor Dinamov[7] has disappeared. Why I don't know. Still I'm having to turn something. Somehow I wish the Communists or Socialists would take everything & find each person a job.

About going to Portland—I'll see where I stand financially by July 15th. If things look no better than now I'll go direct to L.A. Lill[8] is out there. Goldwyn took a protégé of hers into the movies. Eddie Cantor[9] has hired her protege for his program for 16 weeks. She says she may get an inside job at Goldwyns looking after voices of singers in such movies as are being done. She thinks now she may interest him in Carrie.[10] Well we'll see.

Love,
T.D.

1. *Henry Thoreau, Bachelor of Nature* by Léon Bazalgette was translated by Van Wyck Brooks in 1924.

2. Leo Rossett, Sara White Dreiser's lawyer. Dreiser now owed her back payments for support, and she was threatening to sue him for it.

3. On 13 May 1938 the roof of the main house at Dreiser's home at Mt. Kisco, New York, caught fire from a chimney spark. Although the fire department saved the main building, there was extensive water damage. The fire placed another strain on Dreiser's diminished income.

4. See Dreiser to Helen Richardson, 27 February 1938, n. 5.

5. Dreiser's sister Mame and brother Rome were dependent on him for support. See Dreiser to Kirah Markham, 10 June 1932, n. 2.

6. Edgar Lee Masters. See Dreiser to Kirah Markham, 5 March 1915, n. 8. Dreiser was forced to move because the living arrangement at the Rhinelander apartments managed by Mame was coming to an end.

7. Sergei Dinamov. See Dreiser to Ruth Kennell, 24 February 1928, n. 4. Dreiser was unaware that Dinamov had been arrested and would die within a year.

8. Lillian Rosenthal (1887–1972) was the daughter of Elias Rosenthal, a prominent lawyer, in whose home Dreiser stayed after the breakup of his marriage to Sara White Dreiser in 1910. Shortly after, she and Dreiser had become lovers. She married Mark Goodman in 1922 and became a successful vaudevillian, singer, composer, a well-known vocal teacher, and theatrical agent under the name of Lillian Rosedale

Goodman. In later years both she and her husband retained a close friendship with Dreiser.

9. Eddie Cantor (1892–1964) was an immensely popular star in vaudeville, radio, film, and later in television. In the 1930s Cantor was considered the second most recognizable person in America, following only President Roosevelt.

10. Financial necessity made Dreiser eager to sell the rights to *Sister Carrie* to a Hollywood film studio. However, the process proved frustrating as several deals fell through before RKO bought *Sister Carrie* for $40,000 in 1940.

To Helen Richardson [H-DPUP]

At this time Helen was staying with her family in Oregon and Dreiser was on his way to attend the Rassemblement Universal pour la Paix, or the International Peace Campaign, which was held in Paris on July 21–23. One of the stated concerns of the convention, which was attended by 1,100 delegates from forty-two countries, was how to aid the civilian casualties of war in Ethiopia, Spain, and China.

French Line
à bord le Normandie

July 14–38

Helen Dear:

You got my letter from N.Y. I enclosed a check for $150^oo^. This trip is just one of those strokes of lightening that penetrate my life every so often. As late as last Sunday—July 10—telegrams, telephones, cables began to arrive at Noroton.[1] Also representatives of the League of American Writers and the American League for Peace and Democracy.[2] It appeared that an International Conference Concerning Peace (how to get it) (will you tell me) was going to be held in Paris this coming July 21–22–23. American delegates had already been picked by their organizations (4–two each) but evidently on Saturday a prominent French Peace Avocate, Louis Aragon[3] who owns a big newspaper in Paris wired them to get me and that he would pay my passage & all expenses and meet me at Havre when the boat lands. Also a Lord Cecil,[4] who represents an English League for Peace with 500,000 members joined in this. All I am supposed to do—as I understand it is to say I represent the two American Leagues, say I'm for peace and confer with these two & some other men—maybe I don't even need to speak unless I am willing to and of course what I now know is that I would never have been sent by these two American leagues if it hadn't been for this Frenchman—and possibly Cecil. Since it don't cost me nothing, here I am. And trying to think how to help as I ride.

I had so much trouble getting ready—my money, ticket, passport, clothes that I just fell on the boat. Terrible crowd at the dock. Had to leave the taxi a block away & walk. At that I forgot my dress suit! Just found it out this morning. I'll have to rent one I guess in Paris! And who should be on board here but Alma Clayburgh[5] first class—going to Paris to meet Alma Jr. whose coming up through Italy. I had to take dinner with her last night & be introduced to all the gold sticks on board. But down in the tourist section where I am because I wanted to be with the other delegates is Marian Powys and *Peter.*[6] They have a little cabin right around the corner from me & we had tea together at 4^{30}. Peter is nearly 6 feet tall and handsome and so really nice. And Marian is fat and as happy as any creature alive I guess. They're going to see Llewellyn at Davos in Switzerland. He's bad again[7] but getting better. Then they're going to see Jack & Phyllis in Wales, then Theodore the novelist—and the African brother who is now over there (in England). Then they're coming back in Sept (15th) and in 2 years Peter is going to enter Harvard for 4 years. Every year they're going somewhere she says—West Indies, Canada, the Southwest and so. She still has her store, a good business & money enough to educate Peter. He's very American in his ideas—hasn't been converted to England yet.

After the 23rd I am taking this boat back at Havre or go to London or catch it at Plymouth. Since I want to see Kyllman,[8] if I can, & some people who want to do the Hand of the Potter I'll do that,[9] if it don't delay me too much. Anything important can be cabled to me c/o E.C. Llewellyn, 18 Place Vendome, Paris. If I go to England a cable to me c/o Constable & Co. 10–12 Orange St. London will get me. I hope to get back to N.Y. by August, because I have some articles to wind up there. If you go to Los Angeles let me know. I plan to come out just as soon as I can make it.

Love
T.D.

Alma & Marian & Peter all asked after you & said they were going to write. Alma still weeps over her daughter—says she doesn't want to see her much!

1. From 1 June 1938 until his departure for Europe, Dreiser lived and worked at a beach cabin rented by Marguerite Tjader Harris off Noroton Bay on Pratt's Island, Connecticut.

2. In early July, the League of American Writers sent Dreiser a telegram asking him to attend, all expenses paid, the International Peace Campaign. Dreiser's letter notes that he received a similar invitation from the American League for Peace and Democracy. However, on the eve of his departure for the conference, he refused to become a member of either organization and decided to speak before the committee as a private citizen. Perhaps because of his intransigence on this matter, the mission proved disappointing to Dreiser, who was discouraged from speaking, though he managed to impose his will on the assembly and gave a speech called "Equity

between Nations" (published in *Direction* [September-October, 1938]; repub. Tjader, *Love* [1998], 117–20). He came to believe that the unstated aim of the conference was to gain support for England, not to aid the civilian victims of the war.

3. Louis Aragon (1897–1982), poet, novelist, journalist, editor, and political activist, broke with the Dada and Surrealist movements in 1931 to join the Communist Party. At this time he was the editor of the newspaper *Ce Soir*.

4. Lord Robert Cecil (Edgar Algernon Robert Gascoyne-Cecil, 1st Viscount Cecil of Chelwood [1864–1958]), British statesman and winner of the Nobel Prize for Peace in 1937, was co-chair (with Georges Bonnet, finance minister of France) of this conference. He was one of the architects of the League of Nations and in March 1936 founded, with French politician Pierre Cot, the Rassemblement Universal pour la Paix.

5. Alma (Lachenbruch) Clayburgh. See Dreiser to Alma Clayburgh, 31 May 1933, headnote.

6. Marian Powys Grey (see Dreiser to Kirah Markham, 25 October 1916, n. 15). Other Powys siblings noted here are the writers Llewelyn (see Dreiser to Helen Richardson, 2 April 1924, n. 3) and Theodore Francis Powys (see Dreiser to Harriet Bissell, 5 August 1938, n. 4). Peter was Marian's son. Before returning home Dreiser visited the Powys family in Wales.

7. Llewelyn had tuberculosis.

8. Otto Kyllmann. See Dreiser to Ruth Kennell, 24 February 1928, n. 3.

9. See Dreiser to Kirah Markham, 25 October 1916, n. 1. Although a private club in London showed some interest in the play, nothing came of this idea.

To Harriet Bissell [H-DPUP]

Upon graduation from Smith College in 1935, Harriet Bissell (1914–2006) took a job as Dreiser's secretary and research assistant. Among her duties were managing Dreiser's finances and legal records, representing him before publishers, taking dictation of his writing, and doing research on his scientific and philosophical projects. Dreiser is here writing to her from aboard the Normandie on his way to Paris to attend the Rassemblement Universal pour la Paix.

French Line
S.S. NORMANDIE

July 15–'38

Dear Harriet:

Here I am. Friday. So far so good. Absolutely quiet, as to sea—but hot. And muggy. I wish today that I had not come. This is truly the snob boat of the seas—stuffed with would-bes of all nationalities—French, English, Americans, Japanese. Each one studying the other to discern, if possible, the exact social weight as to money, clothes, taste, whether anything is to be had out of them and are they to be shunned for fear of loss or contamination. The *on guard* factor, present in all nature, but a special measure of it crowded into one ship and pressed upon me and probably others. It irritates me almost beyond enduring. Just to see the show and tinsel—to be unable not to see it if one walks out anywhere—!! Not that physically I have been treated badly. From out of nowhere—in so far as I know—comes an order to remove me from the *three-bed* room which you saw—(no toilet; no bath) to a large single room with toilet and bath & shower—and a most comfortable centered bed—private writing desk, table, a chair or two and so on. I have been invited to cocktails with the purser, joined by people whom I know of, as well as knew in New York. Yet the air of the whole ship is none the less painful to me. It is built almost exclusively for the 1st class world and the rays that emanate from these same irritate like mosquito bites. You must be known for something—money, friends, clothes—the size of your suite—or. Hence I have eaten my meals quietly, breakfast in my room, read Left papers delivered to me, read Thoreau.[1] But truly I do not belong here. Either I am sick or this ship is—(a sick idea)—or Life is a sick idea.

I was so sorry that there was a jam at the boat, that I had such a difficult time getting my ticket and causing you so much trouble & then not seeing you after all. You know, after you left I tried finding a place at the rail, hoping that I might see you, but I could not (not on the main deck). So I tried finding another one, got lost & when I got placed at last the boat was out in the middle of the Hudson. I sent you a telegram and decided to cable later—but gave it up after discovering the wireless charges. Then when I unpacked and went into dinner I found dinner jackets & white shirts & black ties in great number (even tourist) and I foresaw what was coming should I be invited to the 1st class dining room and so it made me go look for a dress suit—trousers & dinner jacket. But no dress suit or shoes. Then I tried the green suit with brown shirt & brown shoes and it seemed to me less conspicuous. Later in searching for a tie for my green shirt I was up a tree. And as for a pair of cuff links for my newest grey brown shirt—no cuff links. So I'm looking for a piece of brown string.

All sorts of people that I know are on board—Jack Cosgrave & his wife.[2] He used to edit Everybody's when it was alive & had a million circulation. His wife owns the Finch School in N.Y. Also Reginald Wright Kaufman who wrote one pretty good novel[3] 30 years ago—and his wife. Marian Powys (Jacks sister) and her boy Peter,[4] Alma Clayburgh,[5] going to join her daughter, J.H. Conway, an engineer, formerly of St. Louis and then a number who have introduced themselves. But I'm planning to keep off decks or find some obscure corner and read.

I've been—and am worrying about you. You are so mercurial. You torture yourself—or you are tortured by so many things that you think you are denied or that you are denied—maybe. But I always see you as so much better equipped than thousends to make your way, affectionally or practically, although you fly in a rage at the mere suggestion of it. Your thought I think, at times, is to dominate everyone that you are convinced that you can outwit and move in quick circles about everyone—and that sensing this in some way—directly or indirectly many fear you. I know from my own experiences how you do and are and as you know I am often at the edge of all that I can take. Now that I am alone I feel you as strongly as though you are here and curiously there are hours when I am fighting you—at other times living in the utmost peace thinking of the better times—the happier hours. Then I love you & wish that I might remain in just that relationship. But the weather changes, an ill wind blows from somewhere and there I am tortured, angry, feeling heavens knows what. But enough of that.

The reformers on board are fairly interesting, as practical people with definite objects always are—but no more than that. I find I cannot even suggest some of the difficulties I sense and so have to be less than frank. What good I am to do over here, God only knows. I'll probably speak my mind frankly & get in bad.

As for other things of course I wish I knew about Hume,[6] the loan, etc. Also whether you are able to work, or have dropped everything. That may well be. This wretched boat, as I say, irritates me by its grandeur—the number of people I know, these leftists who want to talk but have nothing except money raising & resolutions on their mind. Of all people on board I have found one—a small, intense Jew[7] driven out of Germany who is a natural thinker and of course shrewd. He has introduced me to an English version (condensed) of the Talmud,[8] and now I see that if it were fully condensed & expressed it would—should every Christian be able to read it—make clear that Christ must be a myth since all that he said is said quite clearly there and thousends of years before. No wonder they could never be converted. Even his "love one another" is put in a more practical & possible way. Their strange dietary laws are now clear to me. And much of their shrewdness seems to be ordered by this book. Thus & so must they do—or fail & be unworthy of their Lord! Well, I stand illuminated as to that at last.

Love—
And more another day
D—

1. Dreiser was reading Thoreau's writing (large selections of which Bissell had culled from the transcendentalist's writings) and attempting to write the introductory essay for an edition that was published as *The Living Thoughts of Thoreau* (1939).

2. John O'Hara Cosgrave, editor and illustrator, was Dreiser's former colleague at the Butterick Publishing Company.

3. Reginald Wright Kaufman (1877–1959), American-born drama critic, editor, poet, and novelist. Dreiser is probably referring to *The House of Bondage* (1910).
4. Peter Powys Grey, see Dreiser to Helen Richardson, 14 July 1938, n. 6.
5. See Dreiser to Alma Clayburgh, 31 May 1933, headnote.
6. Arthur Carter Hume. See Dreiser to Helen Richardson, 27 February 1938, n. 4.
7. Samuel Groskopf, a merchant living in Paris whom Dreiser had known in California.
8. The *Talmud* is a body of Judaic religious-legal literature consisting of laws, legends, and arguments that grew out of commentaries ("Oral Law") on the "Written Law" purportedly transmitted to Moses in the Bible. It includes laws governing liturgy and agriculture; feast days; the role of women; marriage and divorce; civil and criminal law; laws of temple service; and laws of ritual purity.

To Harriet Bissell [H-DPUP]

THEODORE DREISER

July 20–1938

Harriet Dear:

I got your cable on arrival of course. But no mail yet. As you can guess I'm in a rush of things. I was met at the boat & brought to this hotel (Hotel Lutetia, Boul. Raspail at Rue Sevres) which is about 10 minutes from the heart of Paris. I was so sick of that damned upstagy boat. Terrible. I have never seen rich Americans at this icy height or depth before. The limit. It would make a swell left article. Wonderful. Once here I have had meeting after meeting at which French radicals gather. This is Wed. There is one more today—4^{30} to 7^{30}. Aragon[1] is one of these parlor radicals who is crazy to meet celebrities—left or right. Paul Blech[2] is much better—much more severe and sincere. I am trying to look up real people—Henri Lenormand,[3] Andre Gide[4] & others, my 2 playwrights,[5] Leon Bazalgette[6]—but with all committee stuff its hard. I always like Paris. Its clean, intelligent, practical, gay. There's little nonsense about the French. They practiced this business of living until they have succeeded in making an art of it—almost. The family is the unit. *It* sticks together—runs a business, employs the family, arranges the marriages, talks almost everything up. Our American families blow up like the seed pods of so many weeds & flowers and the members float away on the wind.

But really I haven't time for this. Only I do wish you were here. I see now clearly that one can live here cheaply and well. All the world is here—quite every tribe. They cant help liking it, because everyone is really welcome. And they do their best to make themselves & the stranger comfortable. Compared to life in New York here it is easy—more "*we live but once*." Why hurry so. But I must quit. I miss you—when I have time to. But by 1 AM I am so tired—and by 9 AM I have so much to do. Already I could write an article on radicals. They make me laugh. The English papers (delivered here every day) are better than ours—full of intelligent things—even the "Mirrors" and "Looks." Well I must go. I love you when I don't want to have you arrested.

I had a strange, pathetic talk with a street walker at 1 P.M[7] last night. She wanted me to give her 10 francs which I did—and then a cigarette—of which I had none. But the interesting part (put over as kindly as I could) was why I did not wish to do more than talk with a streetwalker. At first she became angry—then friendly & finally borrowed—I mean begged the 30^{cts}! Oh, Lord.

Love
T.D.

1. Louis Aragon: see Dreiser to Helen Richardson, 14 July 1938, n. 3.
2. Paul Blech, an associate of Louis Aragon on *Commune*, and secretary of the International Association of Writers.
3. Henri Lenormand (1882–1951), French dramatist who wrote plays in which he explored subconscious instincts and motivations.
4. André Gide (1869–1951), renowned French critic, essayist, novelist.
5. Dreiser is referring to George Jamin and Jean Servais, who had dramatized *An American Tragedy* several years earlier.
6. Léon Bazalgette (1875–1929), writer, literary historian, and translator who wrote *Henry Thoreau, Bachelor of Nature*, which Dreiser thought was one of the best books on Thoreau. Bazalgette also translated Dreiser's works (see, Elias, *Letters*, III, 804, n. 12). Dreiser was unaware that Bazalgette had died in 1929.
7. Dreiser meant to write "A.M."

To Helen Richardson [H-DPUP]

[25 July 1938]

Helen Dear:

I have not heard from you yet. (This is July 25–'38 Monday) but if a letter comes before Wednesday night, I will get it. Otherwise it will be forwarded to me in London, where I want to see Kyllmann about my books and "*The Hand of the Potter.*"[1] A private club wants to present it once a month I hear. My visit here has been rather successful. I was permitted to speak at the meeting of the International League[2] for direct financial aid to Spain—Hospitals, nursing homes and Spanish children. It was held at this hotel. Then Saturday at the Conference for Action on the Bombardment of open towns & the Restoration of Peace. I spoke 15 minutes. The talk was reported rather well in the Paris Herald-Tribune.[3] I also had a telegram from Moscow for a copy of it. Today I am chairman of the International League of Writers of All Countries, a sort of farewell meeting, and I also speak at that. Then I am invited by the League of English Writers to come to London as their guest. As I want to see Kyllmann I may accept.—This all sounds very silly for me & from one point of view is. I am being put forward as a front as I was in Kentucky.[4] On the other hand it is good, for I needed a change of a drastic kind & this is it, Paris: these radicals from all over the world, my expenses paid. Last Saturday I lunched with Mr. Bonnet,[5] the French Foreign Minister—a Jew who looks like Richelieu[6] and we soon got into an argument—himself, myself, and Lord Cecil[7] the pro-Loyalist leader of England. I gathered from what I heard that at bottom they do not want the Loyalists to win and we had it out. As a result, I was almost shelved as a speaker—but finally was allowed to go on at 6 oclock in the evening. And so I work, work, work, running here & there. But the sight of Paris in between is really refreshing—such a change from N.Y. & America. They live so differently—so practically. The food is so good—the wines so cheap. I have been interviewed & interviewed—Russia, Holland, England, Denmark, Sweden—and there are more to come. Five French papers have had articles. I have heard from Claude Bowers[8] down on the Spanish border. They have given us the worlds homeliest secretary—a woman or "girl" of 40—French-Jewish, who runs here & there bringing me the news. I have met French actors, playwrights—poets—the movie man who did Maternelle[9] and the other one who did Under the Roofs of Paris.[10] It is said that I am to meet ex-Premier Blum[11] before I leave. I would like to—But the change. It is a relief. I hated the Normandie with posy rich Americans—but here you feel differently and can live simply. I can get a hotel room for 35 francs a week—1^{00} (!) I can get a fine meal with wine for 15 francs (45 cents) or a marvellous one for 35 francs (1^{00})! Taxis carry you really anywhere for 10 francs—30^{cts} most places for 6 or 8 cents. Clothes though are high & not so good.

But now I cannot stay here. Have to go on this week. I will arrange it so that I will spend three or four days in England—then catch a French boat for which they give me a ticket at Southampton or Plymouth. In N.Y. I must furnish an article about Thoreau,[12] see Golden[13] about a play he wants me to collaborate on, and about that Radio deal,—then I'll pack my things & depart for Los Angeles. I hope when I get out of here I get a chance to rest. Here is no rest. I think of you here and being on the West Bank & going here & there to see things in Paris. It really has not changed. In fact it is much more cheerful & gayer than in '26 or '27[14]—much. But I'll be seeing you—most likely before Aug 27. I wonder where you are.

T. D.

1. Otto Kyllmann: See Dreiser to Ruth Kennell, 24 February 1928, n. 3.
The Hand of the Potter: See Dreiser to Kirah Markham, 25 October 1916, n. 1.
2. Dreiser spoke at a session that addressed the issue of "The Bombing of Open Cities."
3. The Paris edition of the *New York Herald Tribune*, 24 July 1938.
4. In 1931–32 a series of strikes occurred in the eastern coalfields of Harlan County, Kentucky. Troubled by the use of National Guardsmen to support unorthodox strikebreaking tactics, the blacklisting of union leaders, and the general violation of striker's civil rights, Dreiser made a much-publicized trip to the area in early November 1931.
5. Georges Bonnet (1889–1973), the French ambassador to the United States (1937) who later served as France's foreign minister (1938–39).
6. Cardinal Richelieu (1585–1642), a French statesman and prelate who served as chief minister under Louis XIII.
7. Lord Cecil. See Dreiser to Helen Richardson, 14 July 1938, n. 4.
8. Claude Bowers. See Dreiser to Helen Richardson, 3 July 1924, n. 15.
9. *La Maternelle* (1933), French film directed by Jean Benoit-Levy, is the story of poor Parisian children seeking refuge from their unhappy homes at a neighborhood children's center.
10. "Under the Roofs of Paris" (*Sous les toits de Paris*, 1929), French film directed by René Clair: a simple love story about a street singer and a young girl.
11. Léon Blum (1872–1950), the prime minister of France three times: 1936 to 1937; one month in 1938; December 1946 to January 1947.
12. Dreiser is referring to the introduction for *The Living Thoughts of Thoreau* (1939).
13. John Golden (1874–1955), then considered the dean of Broadway producers.
14. Dreiser had been in Paris in 1912 and again in October 1927, when en route to Russia for the celebration of the tenth anniversary of the revolution; in January 1928 Helen met him in Paris after he had completed his Russian tour.

To Harriet Bissell [H-DPUP]

HOTEL LUTÉTIA
PARIS

July 26–'38

Tuesday.
Harriet Dear:

Only today every letter save the first one written by you arrived *in one bundle* and I have been so troubled about not writing every day. But if you could see the cards, the telephoned messages—the slips saying Mr. So & So is calling at such and such an hour! I have them all & can show them. There has been a group or League[1] meeting every day beginning Tuesday July 19—the morning after the evening I arrived here. We arrived at (off) Southampton, England at 8[30] Monday morning & at Havre at 2 [PM] the same day. But just the same what with having passports examined, baggage examined, and seats found in the Havre-Paris Express we did not arrive in Paris until 7^{30}! At 8^{30} I was placed in this hotel—and at 9^{30} called to go with Louis Aragon, his wife and a Frenchman named Blech[2] to see Paris which was decorated for the arrival of the King & Queen of England. I didn't know this was ahead of me until Saturday July 16. But this trip around the town dumbfounded me. The place was literally covered with British flags. The trees in the Bois, the Avenue of the Army etc. were trimmed Xmas tree wise with glittering bulbs. They looked like green glass trees hung with diamonds. The streets were packed. The restaurants stuffed, a Zeigfield like ballet—only better. Entertained 1500 people in a hall the admission to which was a hundred francs! 3^{00}. I had to go there at 11^{00} & was brought back here at 3^{AM}—so judge. Next day newspaper men & women. A get together meeting of celebrities at 3^{30}. I met the man who directed *Maternelle*.[3] Also the man who wrote Under the Roofs of Paris.[4] At 7^{30} to dinner with three members of the French League of Writers. I only recall M. Blech. Then back to the hotel. But en route we had to see a part of the military parade—the King & Queen riding by. They arrived at 6^{30}. He looks like a poor, confused luny—scarcely able to endure the nervous strain. (I think the world is crazy). After dinner more Paris. Crowds laughing, pushing—like N.Y. at Times Square. I got home I think at 2^{30}. Then more meetings. Three days of reports and resolutions of the—(some International Group for Aid to Spain). I spoke one afternoon. In between luncheons—one given by M. Bonnet the French Foreign Minister and Lord Cecil[5] at a beautiful restaurant in an old palace at Rue 21–Casimir-Perrier. Before I was through I had an argument with M. Bonnet & Lord Cecil about America—its duties to France & England and I could see the atmosphere chilling. The 40 odd guests were troubled. But I came out ok. But at a great International meeting for Peace and the Bombing of open cities, at which I was listed as the 1st speaker of the afternoon, I was given the very last speech or place—after even committee reports were permitted! But it caught on. Whereas the many speeches that preceded me were given paragraphs—mine got space (see the Paris-Herald-Tribune).[6] Also a cable from Moscow for a copy. Also requests for copies until finally Lord Cecil's committee decided to mimeograph 50 and sent me 12. They asked today for leave to print.

Otherwise I've been lonely. In between every talk or trip with anyone any where (this constant running & shaking hands) I've had time to think where I am—to feel how far away from America and how long it will be till I get back. It's not that Paris isnt interesting but I've seen it before & it hasn't changed very much. Priests, nuns, churches, palaces, police, soldiers and the ordinary Parisian riding in his taxicabs or sitting in chair outside one of his 10,000 Brasseries! Besides I don't sleep well. My morning depressions are stupendous. I see a Rabbi has been seized here with $37,000 worth of cocaine pressed into leaf form—book-leaves and labeled *Holy Bible*! But I don't wonder. All I have to remember is how I feel in the morning. Besides I worry about Thoreau[7] & how that ought to be done by now. On the boat I read a lot of his paragraphs and made notes but, writing the essay, no. I have too much to do. And they want me to go to Spain this week. Fly. And then back here to catch the boat—or to England to catch it at Southampton. I've seen Messrs Jamin and Servais.[8] Both are actors. But M. Jamin is also a playwright—Jewish-French who also borrows money & puts on his own plays. The two have had a row. Jamin accuses Servais of wanting to play a part which he can not do. Anyhow they could not get the money & the play was not done. They want to try their hand on The "Genius." I wanted to see Bradley[9] but he is not in town. Everybody here says that French publishers never pay anybody. A hundred or two hundred dollars and publication of the book is considered a full reward! I begin to think its true.

You write very gloomily and always a little threateningly and I feel that things are not going right. I don't think you are working on Thoreau and I can never feel that you connect love with sexual faithfulness any more than you connect air with stars. Love is one thing—sex another. But when it comes to me you want them connected. Well, in so far as this trip is concerned you are having your wish. I am wholly too miserable to think of anything except dying or finding some soothing drug. All this detail of living begins to pall on me. When I get enough whisky in me I'm all right for a little while, but then come the blues again—the blue devils. I feel alone.

How in Gods name am I to do, really. There is no true worth in life—not any fixed thing that one can hold to—just rival conflicting wants. We shake hands, we smile, we kiss, we praise, we long to see some one, but the least variation in the quantity of satisfaction we desire—the merest feather's weight and in rushes anger, hate, sorrow, despair, revenge . . . the devils of greed & jealousy in full armor. Richard the III it was who screamed A horse! A horse, my kingdom for a horse.[10] I would make it a drug. If I could only find one that would pull me through.

And yet I have been as happy with you as anyone. You are wild & unreliable and hateful and gloomy but at least you are alive & have the courage to live. I'm losing that I fear. Just the same I miss you. Call it love or a great need. So what. Love is a great need. A hell of a need.

Did the Rosens pay their rent?[11] Are you & [word unintelligible] living together? He is not hanging around for nothing I know. As for Libby[12] she seems to choose lust. It's a practical choice and enough for some. I shall go to Spain I think this week by air. I have no fear. And to England by air. Cant you see from the letter that I have not changed?

Dee—

1. The short-lived League of American Writers, founded during the tense, prewar period of the mid 1930s, sought to promote intellectual and political freedom through four congresses of national writers, the establishment of schools for writers, and campaigns for the rights of African Americans, the foreign-born, and labor. Considered by the FBI to be, in the later jargon of the Cold War, a "Communist-front organization," it had at its peak more than eight hundred members, including many of the most important literary figures of the time: Dashiell Hammett, Lillian Hellman, Langston Hughes, Ralph Ellison, Ernest Hemingway, Richard Wright, Malcolm Cowley, Ring Lardner Jr., Archibald MacLeish, Thomas Mann, Dorothy Parker, Upton Sinclair, John Steinbeck, and William Carlos Williams. Dreiser's ambivalence about the League reflects some of the larger internal conflicts and external pressures that preceded its demise in 1942.

2. Louis Aragon. See Dreiser to Helen Richardson, 14 July 1938, n. 3.

Paul Blech. See Dreiser to Harriett Bissell 20 July 1938, n. 2.

3. *La Maternelle* (1933). See Dreiser to Helen Richardson, 25 July 1938, n. 9. Dreiser is probably not referring to the director, Jean Benoit-Levy, but to the author, Léon Frapieé, who wrote the novel upon which the movie is based and who was active at the meetings of the Bureau de l'Association Internationale des Écrivains that Dreiser attended.

4. *Under the Roofs of Paris*. See Dreiser to Helen Richardson, 25 July 1938, n. 10.

5. Georges Bonnet. See Dreiser to Helen Richardson, 25 July 1938, n. 5.

Lord Cecil. See Dreiser to Helen Richardson, 14 July 1938, n. 4.

6. "Americans Favor U. S. Action to End Bombing Civilians, Dreiser Says," *New York Herald Tribune*, Paris, 27 July 1938.

7. Thoreau: see Dreiser to Harriet Bissell, 15 July 1938, n. 1.

8. George Jamin and Jean Servais. See Dreiser to Harriet Bissell, 20 July 1938, n. 5.

9. William A. Bradley (1878–1939), American literary agent working in Paris.

10. Shakespeare's *Richard III*, act 5, scene 4,1. 7.

11. Rosen: see Dreiser to Helen Richardson, 27 February 1938, n. 5.

12. Libby Fisher, Bissell's friend and former college roommate (Harriet Bissell to Riggio, 12 May 2005).

To Harriet Bissell [H-DPUP]

At the conclusion of the peace conference, Dreiser was invited by Spanish Loyalists to visit war-torn Spain. He arrived in Barcelona at the end of July.

Barcelona[1]

Tuesday—
Aug 2–38

Harriet Dear:

Only one long letter from you at Paris the day I left for here. No proxies ever came to me. I never heard whether Rosen[2] paid that $500 or not: I am here in a dangerous atmosphere. They are expecting a big push from Franco & more intensive bombings every hour.[3] Strange—sitting in a hotel room

& being ready any moment to hear sirens all over the city & to have to grab your bag & make for an underground shelter (There are about 2 miles of them here—dug in sections in different parts of the city. There was a raid here the day before I came. Friday August[4] 28th 30 people killed.).

Some war planes were sighted off the coast here (Mediterranean East) but turned they said about five miles out & went away again. They were looking for cargo vessels trying to bring food in here to these people. No milk, no butter, little bread, almost no meat. Vegetables & fresh fruit now. I was warned to bring a little hard sausage, cheese & whiskey from Paris. Also cigarettes, but I've given nearly all of it away. Have dined with the President & foreign minister[5] (Last night). Have a private message or proposition to put to Roosevelt for the President of the Loyalists.[6] Have worked hard & seen much. Admire these people. Their courage. They have so little to go on—their desire for their own type of Govt. Interviewed 2 captured Moors and six captured Franco Italians. Have seen hospitals, camps, military training schools. (The poor, almost ragged small boys) But they're a great people. The courage of them. The pride. They won't beg! And their looks—how handsome the men & women even in poor clothes. Marvellous.

Well, I can't write a history. Gave an interview to 20 foreign correspondents in one group last night.[7] They came to this hotel *The Ritz* (once). You should see how it is run now. No food—but the grand manner in which plain water is served!

Love—So long
T. D.

1. The letter was written in Barcelona, but the Paris postmark indicates that Dreiser waited until he returned to France to mail it.

2. See Dreiser to Helen Richardson, 27 February 1938, n. 5.

3. On 9 March 1938 Franco had launched a major attack centered on the regions of Levante and Catalonia that proved to be the turning point in the civil war. The Republican army was forced to retreat, and by mid-April Franco had reached the Mediterranean and had effectively cut the Republican forces in half. In July of 1938 the Loyalists mounted a final campaign to cross the Ebro and regain these lost territories. After some initial success the campaign failed, and despite the continued resistance and conflict that Dreiser witnessed, the war was essentially over at this time.

4. Dreiser means July.

5. Manuel Azaña (1880–1940).

6. See Dreiser to Ruth Kennell, 26 April 1938, n.1. Dreiser met with President Roosevelt and petitioned for aid to the people, mainly in the form of food to the children and needy civilians of Spain. Roosevelt told Dreiser that the United States would remain neutral in regard to the Spanish Civil War and that a committee of private citizens could best address the issue.

7. Unidentified.

To Harriet Bissell [H-DPUP]

London

Friday Aug 5–'38

Listen, Harriet I cannot write you very much. The travel I have to do—the people I have to see, the arrangements I have had to make to get in & out of Spain, the interviews I have had to give, the notes put down, make a hash of every day. Here I am in London now, with requests from Spain—and the different convention groups to do this & that. And tired! I have seen much but, almost it seems I have worked so hard in seeing that clarity as to all of it has escaped. Perhaps it will come back but Lord how tired I am. You complain of no letters & mine from you have come days & days apart. I got 4 in one mail—four in another—and the hat & address book you sent me just as I was leaving Paris yesterday (Aug 4) and you had been writing concerning them how long before? I did write Masters[1] on the boat. But on the same day I wrote you a long letter—not very happy—very grim & angry really because life was torturing me so—thought about your insurgent, heartless realism, your violent hatreds & purposeful revenges. I cannot see but a fraction of peace or constructive energy in you and I grow violent myself. I dream & imagine all sorts of things. Faith becomes a joke—love a rat-trap—romance, poetry, mere marsh-fire—a will-o-the-wisp, leading to the slough of despond. When your letters come I read them, but feel & say to myself how much of anything is told here. A letter is one thing & the actual scene at the moment another. One can lie in bed with one man & dream of another; arise after an orgy and write of ones despondent lonliness. So without faith—with treachery counted upon,—compelled in some temperaments—as hunger & thirst are compelled—I recall your saying let those do it who can do it. Why bother with others.

But you write so beautifully when your mood is toward me—perhaps toward anyone. The lines! The thoughts. They have the ache of reality—just as your rages have. But, God, how is one to live without faith? Hell is that lack of faith that breeds lack of hope. And yet when I read *you to me*—how I wish to see you (Like I did when you were in Mississippi.[2] Ha!). Yet I have written a number of letters in the time I have been away and have always wished that I might believe that something could come of this. But! It is your curse and mine that we can have no faith in each other. The result is the endless quarrels that take up time—waste it and bathe one in pain. So actually your letters at this distance make me sad, terribly so—and I know mine do you. So what will seeing each other do? If I were only one who could love without suspicion—or you were. Starr Faithful[3] (that name!)

leaped into the sea, harried by her inability to be true or to stop giving pain. There are hours when I could do so—so often I am tortured to the acting point. And you.

I am only going to be here in London until Tuesday. Then I am going to run up to Corwen, in Wales to see Jack & his brother, Theodore.[4] From there it is only 50 miles to Liverpool. And I take the Lucania on Saturday. Then we'll meet & talk, and hate each other again. Imagine!

The stock certificates came just now from Kyllmann's office[5]—having been sent on from Paris. I'll bring them with me. In several letters I've asked about the *Rosen* check. No answer. England, France, Spain, Czecho-Slovakia, and all the little states are enduring fear—pitiable unrest. I feel as though I would like to find a hole in a mountain and stay hidden & alone for good. It is truly dreadful.

TD.

Can this be love

1. Edgar Lee Masters. See Dreiser to Kirah Markham, 5 March 1915, n. 8. The letter Dreiser mentions here is Dreiser to Masters, 16 July 1938 (in Pizer, *Letters*).

2. In the spring of 1938, Bissell had been sick and left New York to recover, spending some of her time in Nachez, Mississippi, with a male companion. The illness was diagnosed as an ovarian cyst, and Dreiser paid for the operation and the hospital bill.

3. Starr Faithful was a young socialite who was found drowned on the shore at Long Beach, Long Island, on 5 June 1930. It could not be determined whether it was an accident, suicide, or murder.

4. John Cowper Powys. See Dreiser to Kirah Markham, 22 December 1914, n. 3. Theodore Francis Powys (1875–1953), novelist, short-story writer.

5. Otto Kyllmann. See Dreiser to Ruth Kennell, 24 February 1928, n. 3.

To Helen Richardson [H-DPUP]

Having been separated from Richardson since May 1937, Dreiser was attempting to finish his business in New York so they could meet in Portland, Oregon, and then travel back to Los Angeles together.

N.Y. Sat. Nov. 19–38

Dear Helen,

I'm winding up here as fast as possible. I had to go through the storage warehouse stuff and recheck it so that if there is something I need to get out I could find it in my storage list. I've had to have the car fixed so that I can use it in getting things in and out of Mt. Kisco. I have had a lot of things underway here—attempts to get things on the radio, the stage etc.

that I've had to clean up, besides the reading and writing I've been doing on The Bulwark. Also those lecture trips.[1] I have to go up to Boston tomorrow & will get back late tomorrow night or early Monday a.m. Then I close up my various boxes & take them to the freight office. Pack my trunk & start for Portland. I'm selling my few remaining stocks Monday because I fear prices are going to fall & to live this winter I'll have to have ready cash. I thought I might get the Nobel Prize but it went to Pearl Buck—who like Eugene O'Neill a year or so ago said I should have had it.[2] What the feeling over there against me is I don't know.

In L.A. if possible I want to sell that property. The taxes are terrible. \$150^{00} this year for streets & sidewalks again & 150 for those dinky lots and the house. Then it will be 388 on the Kisco place plus insurance on everything & so it goes. This winter I cant help Mame[3] & I certainly wont pay Mrs. D.[4] I cant live & do it. I have some lectures on the coast that may net me \$1000. But no more, and I wont have 2,000 in cash when I get out there. Nothing worth anything has come through so far. I'm sorry I cant be there for Thanksgiving but I'll probably be on route—New York Central & Great Northern—I guess. I would fly if it didn't cost me more.

One thing, I'm tired. But when I get this wound up & rest a little maybe I'll feel better. Rosen[5] hints that he & someone else may buy the house next year if it can be had for 26,000 or 30,000 on time. It may have to go.

It's been lovely weather here so far (cold & rainy today). Even leaves came out on the trees. I've written a poem or two myself and I have an idea for a fine story about Oscar Wilde.[6]

Will you be on hand when I get there. Better wire me. Night letter. I'm writing the Post Master down there to hold all mail until I come. No use sending any to Portland. Are you all right? My nerves are so very much strained that sometimes I wonder that I get anything packed & shipped at all.

Love
T.D.

I'll be here at the hotel till I leave.

1. Dreiser had undertaken a lecture tour earlier in the month that took him to several cities, including Indianapolis, where he visited with his ailing teacher May Calvert Baker on 12–13 November.

2. Pearl S. Buck (1892–1973) was an American novelist who won the Nobel Prize in 1938, the first American woman to do so. When she was contacted about having received the award, she said, "That's ridiculous. It should have gone to Dreiser" (quoted in Conn, *Pearl Buck*, 208). Upon receiving Dreiser's congratulations for winning the 1937 Nobel Prize, O'Neill wrote him that "I have a sneaking

feeling of guilt—as if I had pinched something which I knew damned well should, in justice, be yours" (Eugene O'Neill to Dreiser, 3 December 1936 [DPUP]). For a detailed analysis of the attitudes toward Dreiser of various Nobel Prize committees, see Rolf Lunden, "Theodore Dreiser and the Nobel Prize," *American Literature*, 50, no. 2 (May 1978), 216–29.

3. Dreiser was helping to support his sister Mame.
4. Sara White Dreiser. See Dreiser to Helen Richardson, 21 June 1938, n.2.
5. See Dreiser to Helen Richardson, 27 February 1938, n. 5.
6. No evidence of this story has been located.

To Harriet Bissell [H-DPUP]

Dreiser had joined Helen Richardson in Oregon in November of 1938. Bissell remained in New York and continued her administrative duties, not the least of which was managing Dreiser's finances, including his extensive financial support of his siblings. The Depression had cut into his available funds, which made negotiating with his relatives an ordeal.

Friday, Dec. 2 [1938]

Dearest:

Your letter about Mame[1] just arrived (Friday AM). At the same time I'm leaving for L.A—in about an hour. So far my mind is just as much disturbed & puzzled here as it was there. But this explanation will have to wait till I get to L.A. Will be there Sunday night. Don't think I'll stay at or with McCord.[2] For immediate purposes he's too far out. I'll wire you. As for Mame I sent her $10 Wednesday—the morning I got here. Her belly-aching about Rome[3] being put on her is a scream. Eight years ago I brought him to N.Y. (to her in Astoria) and paid her 40^{oo} a month to look after him. And I furnished suits, underwear, shoes, hats. Later I induced Sylvia[4] whom I was carrying to move in with her and paid the two of them $75^{oo}. This kept up just this way until 1934 when I had to reduce it to $60. In 1935 she was getting 50^{oo} and she had with her Frank[5] who was paying $10 so he once said to me & Syl who was paying whatever she could—maybe five. But in addition she had Carmel (Brennan's[6] neice). Also Gertie[7] who gave her 5^{oo} a week to take care of Emma & I gave Emma 5^{oo} (a week) all going to Mame. I know that right now they live better than she says. Her real desire is to get rid of Rome & probably live with Carmel who makes money but who has no one to live with. I can't afford to give her 20^{oo} right now and I know from what I've seen that they have been living very well. Besides for the last two months I have been sending her 20^{oo}. So for her to talk of my throwing Rome in her hands and then walking is one of those nasty, ungrateful things which should be pointed out to her. Besides what

I have been giving her Rome has had a pension for at least 2 years. Mame the same. Actually I have kept them all together—made it possible for them so to do when all of them were on the rocks. And then I'm packing Rome off on her & walking off. She has been getting away with murder & she is as inequitable as it is possible for a person to be.

I wish you could get them into a cheaper apartment. She told me she was paying $55^{oo}. Besides she ought to rent a room. Also I think it would be most helpful if you would go & see Ed.[8] He has done nothing but again he dislikes Mame & Syl & Rome—and so does his wife. One thing I would like to know is this—in case Mame dies is there some institution where I can put Rome reasonably. It seems odd that with all the others around I should be looked upon as the one who is solely responsible, but so it is. Except for his pension they would let him die. With his pension & maybe something from me, he might make out. If Mame talks too rough about it why not suggest that with his pension & a little help from me he might be taken elsewhere. I doubt then whether she will talk quite so loud.

In more than one way I think it good that I came out here. There are certain things I see & can point out that may bring about a working change, really cause H.[9] to take hold for herself. I will see—soon. There is no other consideration as important as this at this time.

I feel so keenly about you—so sad at heart too. At the same time I feel that you and I must reach a more peaceable level. The other is too strenuous. Perhaps this current separation will show us both how to do. You may teach me something & I you. Let us see.

But I love you just the same.

T.D.

1. Dreiser's sister. See Dreiser to Sara O. White, 26 December 1896 n. 3.

2. Donald McCord, a retired army doctor and the brother of Dreiser's good friend Peter McCord (see "Peter" in *Twelve Men* [1919]), had invited Dreiser to live with him at his home in San Diego.

3. Dreiser's brother. For more on Dreiser's support of Rome, see Dreiser to Kirah Markham, 10 June 1932, n. 2. Also see Dreiser to Edward M. Dreiser, 16 April 1938 (in Pizer, *New Letters*).

4. Dreiser's sister.

5. Frank Thomas. See Dreiser to Helen Richardson, 27 February 1938, n. 1.

6. Austin Brennan. See Dreiser to Sara O. White, 26 December 1896, n. 3.

7. Gertrude Nelson. See Dreiser to Sallie Kusell, 4 August 1923, n. 2.

8. Ed Dreiser. See Dreiser to Sara O. White, 26 December 1896, n. 2.

9. Helen Richardson.

To Harriet Bissell [H-DPUP]

253a Loraine St. West
Glendale.

Monday, Dec 12 [1938]

Dearest:

This is Monday. I've been wanting so much to have a letter, but it seems that they assemble them somewhere until they have three and then deliver them. Three came this a.m. & reading them really hurts since I cannot hear your voice nor see you. Except as one sees with the mind—wraith wise. And there are so many things I want to ask you. And you are so far away. Truly I can see nothing in this change I have made except silence and work. Being with you has insulated me almost wholly against the ordinary run of mind. I find that I have nothing but work and this strange climate to comfort me if a climate anywhere could ever comfort the solitary heart. Helen is a person of emotional resources of a given variety, but the mental grip on problems that interest me are wanting. Impractical, meditative, sad. Wanting some dyke or stay against the inevitable inroads of time. I would like to find one for her, and for myself the only one I know of is you—and because of strains between us, and the necessity to rid myself of this feeling of a possible injustice to Helen (done in the past) I have undertaken this adventure.

And yet that, as you know, if you know anything, is as much your fault as mine. To be watched over and investigated at every turn when, for so long, I was used to going my own way and particularly when I was uncertain, as I was for so long, as to whether you really cared, except in a selective, assorting way—picking me as a fairly agreeable means to an ultimate varietistic end. (In how many horrible rows have we had that out)

But more recently I find myself believing, and liking to—that all this was more real than I had hoped for. And, when storms were not too numerous, looking toward it as something permanent,—as permanent as the age limit of man can ever permit. But then, as you know, there was Helen. As much as I realized her follies—(and weighed in the scale against your worst traits, there was something to be subtracted from them), I felt, past this, that if I came here and by my presence and natural actions—more particularly my honest reactions to her and her various defects or virtues I could make her see that the relationship other than it might be of practical value to her had none for me. For, until that was proved to my satisfaction even if not to hers—I felt that I could not be, unreservedly, restful with you.

Well—the experiment is on. I have been studying her as she has been studying me. I begin to see clearly the incurable difficulty of the relationship. It involves sacrifices—a variety of them. No doubt all relationships do. But some of these, after you, and by reason of kind and degree, are really impossible. That they may be endured is possible. What is not endured at times? But probable? No. She herself, after experiences of various kinds is not, as I can see, ready to accept such a provisional setting. There are too many things to be endured by her. They are inescapable since love will not go where it will not go. No patience either. What is needed and what now is—is a factual demonstration of what is wanting, and some financial adjustment which is final.

But, on the other hand, here are you. And you have repeated and repeated that you are young and entitled to the full active life of youth & to go places, meet people, do, be. I note that alone you are going already. I know you can at once ask, have I had that since I have known you? No. Or at best in a very slight measure. But if you insist no—then of course it is no for you. But such being the case, how much of that can you possibly hope to enjoy through me? More and more, I tend to sit and think. The problem of this strange and, except for love & lust, pointless activity called life, engrosses me. I stare at every seeking thing from microbe to Man, asking, why? Physically, as you know, it almost stops me. I can almost say that I am done with the common aspirations of life. Now they seem to be—(actually I know they are) mechanistic, and mechanistically, lead to a set of petty achievements, contacts, how-do-you-dos, envies, jalousies, asinine glories & fantastic despairs which in the end—inevitably—melt into the common or factory or cosmic laboratory forces that have produced them—like Dr. Ford[1] produces Fords. Great Jesus!

But since you want them or some portion of them what the hell does my rheumatic conclusion amount to? Old age against youth; senility against virility; April against November. Take it away. And why shouldn't you say so? What is youth for? The young moon is not for me. It is for you. Dance out where its light is and live. What a fool you to do less than that.

Just the same as Thoreau said, "I live & have my thoughts."[2] Just now they are of you. Just as sure as I am at this table, & write you, one of these hours I will be done with all this. I will put on my hat and go. But where? To you? If you truly loved me I suppose to you. If not—

Doors open and doors close.

There have never been any happier hours than some I have spent with you.

Love—love
T.D.

PS I like the corrections[3]—will advise. Clever. Very.

As for jobs, I know you can get them. In that direction Bissellburg.[4]

In a supplementary letter, I'll make some practical inquiries.

1. Henry Ford (1863–1947).
2. The quotation has not been identified.
3. Dreiser had asked her to edit a draft of the introduction to his edition of Thoreau.
4. A fantasy town they joked about in which everything is run by Bissell.

To Harriet Bissell [H-DPUP]

Glendale.

Dec. 30–'38

Harriet Dear

Yes it ok about Masters and Emerson.[1] I wish they would get him to do it. He seems to believe that Emerson is the greatest and cleanest philosophic thinker, which should make his study of him interesting to people and important. I would like to read his study of him. Will the publishers write me or shall I write someone there.

In a letter to me Masters said he was thinking of writing Rupert Hughes[2] to get him to help have The Spoon River Anthology done in the movies. I do not think Hughes has sufficient influence to help him much. I am in touch with Willy Pogany[3] here who has considerable influence just now with MGM. Also there is Wanger.[4] I plan to speak to both this coming week. I'm afraid Gertz[5] is much more of a talker than a doer. He seems to say anything and then trust to luck. I am seeing Cohen[6] of Columbia next week but due to my own efforts, not his. Still, I am not saying anything—remaining wholly friendly.

I'm glad you are using your personality to enter the literary or rather publishing world. To my way of thinking you are certain to go as far as you choose or bother to go. I am troubled by the change I have made even though I feel that I was psychologically forced. But, what is to be is to be. I have passed through and endured really terrific things—sometimes for the worse, sometimes the better. Don't mind my gloom. I will come out of it—must. Anyhow endure it. Your last two letters were very optimistic and gay. I'm glad of it for both our sakes. Perhaps I have not reason for complaint. And yet so often in the very center of quite heavenly sunshine I am so dark in mood as to wish for unconsciousness—prolonged and secure. Once it was called hypochondria I believe. Nathan wrote me to send him a six week exclusive radio agreement.[7] I will do it if you say so. Or you can give him my word. I have no other offers of any kind anyhow.

Bridges funeral[8] was made nothing of by that stupid & I think jealous Morgan.[9]

I sensed, I think, real opposition to any comment on his worth. No one said a word.

I wanted to but was almost frozen by a stiff priestly crowd—the new and pretentious royalty of science.

Love
T. D

If you have time will you cut out and mail me any scientific data you run across?

The Los Angeles papers are almost worthless.

I have a laughing picture of me made by Van Vechten.[10] Would you like it.[11]

1. Dreiser was urging Edgar Lee Masters to edit a volume of Ralph Waldo Emerson's central thoughts for the Living Thoughts Library series published by Longman, Green, and Company of New York. Dreiser had recently completed *The Living Thoughts of Thoreau* (1939) for the series.

2. Rupert Hughes (1872–1956), playwright, novelist, and long-time screenwriter who had been adapting plays and novels since 1914 for the movies.

3. William Andrew Pogany (1882–1955), Hungarian-born sculptor, painter, and book illustrator who had become an art director for motion pictures.

4. Walter Wanger (1894–1968), Hollywood producer for Paramount, Columbia, and MGM before becoming an independent producer and founding the Society of Independent Motion Picture Producers.

5. Mitchell Gertz, Hollywood theatrical agent and producer.

6. Harry Cohen (1891–1958), founder of Columbia Pictures.

7. Unidentified.

8. Dreiser had attended the funeral of his close friend Calvin Bridges, a scientist who shared many of Dreiser's intellectual preoccupations, as well as his interest in women. See Dreiser to Helen Richardson, 7 December 1937, n. 1.

9. Unidentified.

10. Carl Van Vechten. See Dreiser to Helen Richardson, 16 April 1924, n. 6.

11. Dreiser wrote these comments in the left-hand margin of the letter.

1939

To Harriet Bissell [H-DPUP]

Dreiser was looking for projects to supplement his dwindling income, and Bissell was helping him by providing advice, preparing manuscripts, and making contacts in the radio and film industry.

253 W. Loraine

Friday-Jan 6–'39

Harriet Dearest:

I have your latest letter about the radio program—that is, Gertz[1] getting a master script writer out here to take the stories I told Helen recently and Radio-ize them. I immediately called him up but he said he had no letter from Watters.[2] I called him again to day—Friday—this morning & he had no writer. If when the letter comes he gets me a writer I'll do as you say & dictate those stories. But he didn't seem to think it amounted to much.

As for a short story for Orson Welles[3]—*Yes*. I suggest *The Hand*[4] which he could do. Or my one act plays—particularly *Laughing Gas* or In The Dark or The Blue Sphere. I think too the story called *Tabloid* might interest him. One of the scenes from An American Tragedy. Clyde trying to escape from the picnic party on Third Lake and meeting the sheriff and his officers in the woods. It's so sad. Or the scene with Roberta on Big Bittern—where she is accidentally struck by him & the boat overturns.

As I wrote you I saw Cohen[5] and Marx[6] of Columbia. Very friendly. They have agreed to buy Sister Carrie for $35,000 if I—or they with me—Marx, Cohen and [word unintelligible], their master script writer can get it past Breen[7]—the Catholic half of Will Hays office.[8] But please don't mention this—don't tell Watters or anyone for it may fall through and I don't want to publicize another flop or get any bad publicity. I'll let you know as soon as there is anything real. Besides Wanger[9] is now friendly to me, and if he stays so he may take something, but bad publicity wont help me.

I'll write you as soon as can fix it. I love you but I cannot help wondering who you are with and how you do. I work all of 10 hours a day now. My one recourse is work. I have no love life & no sexual—as you so carefully distinguish them. And I see you have moved. I'm glad if its better and your less lonely. But as for me!

T.D

1. See Dreiser to Harriet Bissell, 30 December 1938, n.5.
2. William Watters, theatrical agent and director.

3. Orson Welles (1915–85), American motion-picture actor, director, producer, and writer. Dreiser is considering the possibility of providing a story or play to be scripted for Welles's radio program called *The Mercury Theatre on the Air*.

4. A short story that in this period Dreiser also attempted to convince Charles Laughton and others to turn into a film.

5. Lester Cohen (1901–63), novelist and screenwriter.

6. Unidentified.

7. Joseph Breen, a devout Catholic, was the head of the new Production Code Administration. Although the film industry had instituted a code of ethical standards as early as 1922, the Motion Picture Association of America had responded to recent criticism of the racy and violent films of the early 1930s by creating a stronger self-regulatory code of ethics. An amendment to the old code, adopted on 13 June 1934, strengthened it by establishing the Production Code Administration, which required each film to obtain certification that it was morally acceptable before being released.

8. William Harrison Hays (1879–1954), president of the Motion Picture Producers and Distributors of America from 1922 to 1945. One of his duties was to administer the motion picture Production Code (often called the "Hays Code").

9. Walter Wanger. See Dreiser to Harriet Bissell, 30 December 1938, n. 4.

To Harriet Bissell [H-DPUP]

Glendale

Feb. 6–'39

Harriet Dear

I have had so many things hanging over me—so much to do, that along with your nervous depressions which come as straight as radio waves to me, I had to go to bed.[1] I couldn't work and just gave up for two days straight until the psychic depression—or what is truer the dissipation of nervous energy ceased. I could feel it going until I had scarcely enough to live on—keep the body functional. It is all too sad these emotional compulsions and entanglements which leave some for dead. You constitute the worst experience for me—and by equation, the best. I miss so much your buoyant force, when it is buoyant, but I know so well how completely the reverse of that is implied. You wonder how I can miss you so horribly at times and yet not want you to come immediately. But having suffered through days and days of your savage psychic assaults—and then slipped into humdrum and stillness—no flashes of news or lightnings of thought—no machine gun fire of ideas—fired for the firing so often—nothing more (but always exciting). Well, with a lot of work to do, it was easy to feel it as work like. For all day here there is not so much as a disturbing word—no discussion, no quarrels, nothing. For 10^{00} a week H does all the work—marketing & whatsoever, and typing besides. Of course there is extra money—some paid to Esther McCoy[2] but all told not above 20^{00}. And rent and all else is cheap. My chief worries as you know are taxes, repairs, and gifts of cash which have to be met. For instance I have to put a new roof on the Montrose house—(estimated 175^{00}) and it has to be painted—needs it badly (estimated $160). Painters & roofers get $8^{00} a day out here. WPA workers $40^{00} a month. $10^{00} a week for 3 days! You snarled at my mention of getting a $1000 for my lectures—making that clear—but with things like this—and this new roof on the porch you spoke of—and this painting in the spring—well—sneering at my hanging around studios (wasting my time) seems more like a determination not to understand at the moment than any thing else.

I could take this thousand and wire you to come and spend it or most of it, idling up and down this coast for a month. And how I would like to do it. But instead H is going to Portland by train (bus & train fare are the same out here except for Pullmans) and I am going by bus and alone over the whole route. I will get in touch with her after this trip, and will then see what to do. But unless I can make some real money somewhere it looks to me as though presently I will have to reduce my expenses, not add to them in any way.

And I didn't say that I intend to *complete* two books before sending for you. I said I was working on two and I meant that I wanted to be far enough along so as to feel sure of my ability to complete them—the novel in particular.[3] I have all the data I want in this philosophy[4]—have finally psychologized it—the remaining most points—to suit me and having been wanting to get my complete files of it here, so to select the data for three chapters and sell those as I am sure I can. You said in your letter, "the philosophy material is on the train." Yes but where are the way bills or claim slips. Now I have to leave Wednesday at 8^{00} and here it is Monday afternoon. If the claim slips come after I'm gone and the stuff lies here I will be charged so much a day storage—and I'll probably be gone 3 weeks. Why, if the goods really went, didn't you send me the slips? Don't you really care whether I am put to trouble and expense and delay—or not.

Another thing. In that trunk of mine, when I put it in the storehouse last May were two overcoats—an old light colored English winter coat and a much handsomer and more expensive one that was made in New York—a somewhat darker hue. It cost me 75^{00} and it did not come in the trunk. I meant to speak of it but over looked it until now—when I need it. Did Frank[5] take it or who, or do you know where it is? If it is lost, just one thing lost it—smashing that lock of the trunk, and leaving it smashed. While I had the key it was there. Can you possibly trace it? If not, I am out a swell coat. That is all.

As for fixing the garage roof now. If you will undertake to look after it, that will be fine. I would like to know though how much it is to cost?

Also when, exactly, the Rosens[6] intend to leave. It may be that it is going to be hard to rent this year, but real estate agent inquiries are much more numerous right now. Their comment is that the Worlds Fair[7] is going to bring residents (visitors) to Westchester. I thought to refer all inquiries to Cox,[8] since he said he would look after it.

With all of your prospects and your real abilities you should connect with a good job in some field. I can never understand why anyone with real brains wouldn't see your value clearly. It must be that it is your love or sex emotions or the two together that prevent you from coolly concentrating. You say you pass off into a psychic slump, like myself—but unless those things last too long at a time—or are principally present, one can get by. An errant dreamy romantic mood used to drive me from job to job—and city to city but not to the final detriment of failing to get a job which I always needed. So I know it can be with you, if you are not fully determined never to work at a *job* of any kind. I used to determine that way—but it never worked out.

All this is nothing other than an attempt to put down an explanation of a condition that is almost impossible for me to decide,—that is rightly. I want to work. And I wish, how much, I might see & be with you without another fight or insult. A part of this thing I am convinced that it is folly to dream of adjusting two such temperaments—that we are best 3000 miles apart. That is when I am enraged, as so often I am. At other times I am ready to assume that the worst is not too much to endure. But when I begin to plan up spring the practical considerations—and the memory of certain things which I insist I can never forget nor forgive. And so it goes. All day Friday & Saturday I was in bed sick. Now I am up and writing this. Wednesday AM—at 8^{30} I take the bus and will be in Portland at 8^{40} PM. The next day I speak—but I want to use the day to see a doctor about my kidneys and thyroid. Something seems to be wrong. Not too much so—but enough. You have all my dates & can write or wire. Anyhow I'll write you.

Mornings & at night, so often, I lie and wonder Where you are. What doing! The ease with which you go to live with another man for companionship and sex! could go if I would. Somehow, just now, the whole life game is not worth rising for, although sinking to rest, if it ended so, would be OK indeed.

T.D

Please mail the railroad claim slips to me at San Francisco, either the club or the Clift Hotel.

1. Dreiser believed in psychic transference via brain waves between individuals who were emotionally in tune with each other. See Dreiser to Kirah Markham, 9 February 1914, n. 1.

2. At this time Esther McCoy did occasional research for Dreiser.
3. *The Stoic*.
4. His philosophical-scientific work in progress, "The Formula Called Man."
5. Frank Thomas, the companion of Dreiser's sister Mame.
6. The Rosens were a couple who were renting a section of Dreiser's country home at Mt. Kisco, New York.
7. The 1939–40 New York World's Fair, "The World of Tomorrow," opened on 30 April 1939 at Flushing Meadows-Corona Park and closed on 27 October 1940. The fair attracted over forty-five million visitors but was, in the end, an economic failure.
8. Cox was a local real estate agent in Westchester County.

To Harriet Bissell [H-DPUP]

Dreiser had just returned from an arduous lecture tour that took him from San Francisco to Salt Lake City and back to Glendale in the Los Angeles area. The psychic and physical strains are apparent in his despondent mood.

Monday-Feb. 27 [1939]

Harriet:

Back in Glendale. And from the point of crowds and public interest and newspaper publicity and entertainment—("attention" covers most of it), the trip was a success. But at the heart of me, how dreary, how lonely, and how puzzled sometimes I feel as though I cannot stand much more of anything. Nothing straight. Nothing simple. One compulsion driving out another. One problem confronting and non-plussing another. Wishing so to be loved in some simple, uncomplicated, satisfied way. Although knowing myself for the most part unworthy of it. Hating to think that anyone ideally valuable to me could be even more so to another; hating to feel that one can love deeply—tortureful—and yet be counted 2nd 3rd—10th in the desires of the one most loved; knowing that day by day the remaining days are numbered against one . . . one less, one less, one less. Brooding over the frail little plants of life that spring and die at the feet of the giant mountains of time. Puzzling, sighing, wishing so vainly and of a sudden or at long (brief) last dying. Truly, truly, the very heart of me is sick and never, never will be well. Never.

> "What is man that thou art mindful of him
> He cometh up as a flower and is cut down
> He fleeth as a shadow and continueth not"[1]

What sad, sad heart like my own wrote that? One likely as not, that had everything—and nothing! One that like myself now, looked at a sinking sun and saw nothing to live for. How impossible! How horrible really! I feel so truly that I could shut my eyes and die—gladly.

But you must know why! I brood over you so. The wrong & the right of you. And over the seeming impossibility of making anything of a relationship that should be perfect—and is not. Someone writes me of you—of your life optimism ("incurable"!) and yet of an undertone of sadness—as of some one *bearing up*. Of Mr. Fowler.[2] Of your seeking to make the best of a change and bearing up—running briskly here and there—and giving everything for a little surcease. And that process of obtaining it. That life should be so! Emotions all mixed. And I coming to this point of torture and yet feeling that emotions so mixed offer so little refuge to other emotions—equally mixed. Imagine sorrow, pity, a desire not to be too harsh at one point confronting a strong yearning for a true companionship with another, at another point—and yet feeling that mixed emotions there offer no true refuge!

How dreary the mountains! How dead the clear sunlight. I am reminded of Pavlov's dog confronted by the symbol of food & the symbol of pain—hunger and fear—now slowly, now quickly—now more slowly, now more quickly, until at last, beaten as by hammers, growing weak, confused, at last wholly mad. (The tortures with which life can confront one.)

Yes, I care so. I need so much to do something to straighten all this out. Not to go wholly mad.

Do I seem to rave? It is all so real and cruel to both—a trick, a plot on the part of life. Are you not really as sorry for me as I am for you, for myself as for yourself. How pathetic to be able to forgive! To accept leftovers from Life.

To have the dainty dish held up and then spit on—and then offered!

What a noble creator of a noble world!

By God-
D.

1. Dreiser combined two quotations from different books of the Old Testament:

> "What is man, that thou art mindful of him" (Psalm 8.4).
> "He cometh forth like a flower, and is cut down: he fleeth also as a shadow and continueth not." (Job 14.2)

2. Bissell's future husband.

To Ruth Kennell [H-DPUP]

Kennell had been residing in the San Francisco area for several months, but she and Dreiser had not found the time to have a reunion.

THEODORE DREISER
253 W. Loraine-Glendale

April 11–'39

Dear Ruth:

Well, thanks. And I feel much more comfortable. Are you going back East without seeing me? Why not take a bus and come down for a day or two. There's plenty to entertain you and if we dont do anything else we can discuss the dear English.

Incidentally your all wrong about the importance of fatherhood identification or motherhood identification either.[1] From a capitalistic point—or Royal primo-generative point of view it's important. But from the point of view of two people truly in love it need not be emphasized. True love would take care of that. And if true love was wanting—what difference to the participants. As to society at large—what difference? Who truly knows who his father was. If he's strong and creative—what difference? But come down & talk to me.

Love
T.D

I am sure our American financiers, trust and corporation magnates are in league with all others of that ilk in England, Japan and elsewhere. The object is dictatorship. Observe Dr. J. P. Morgan sculling the retroactive fascist Archbishop of Canterbury around in his Yacht, the Corsair. Morgan & Company are English-American bankers—not American Bankers. J. P. Morgan before 1929 had organized America Incorporated—167 Corporations[2]—which was to control the U.S. and appoint its Secretary to be president. Dwight Morrow[3] was to be the 1st secretary—acting as President of the U.S. at Washington. Congress exposed all this. Roosevelt suppressed the general advertising of the fact. Why? The argument was it would cause the rank and file of Americans to lose faith in their government. Write any radical congressman for the data. Pascelli—now Pope[4]—was in on this. He came over to see Morgan, Morrow, et al.

1. Kennell argued that the success of relationships between couples was often determined by their early experiences with their parents.

2. With the stock market crash of 1929, J. P. Morgan & Company formed a group of leading private banking institutions to pool resources to withstand the effects

of the crisis. When in 1933 a Senate subcommittee of the Banking Committee investigated the firm, it revealed that the partners in the House of Morgan held 167 directorships in 89 corporations with assets of about twenty billion dollars. It was shown that the younger J. P. Morgan held virtual veto power over the actions of his partners in matters of policy and practice. These complex dealings were overshadowed in the public mind by revelations that Morgan and his twenty partners had not paid income tax for 1931 and 1933 and only a total of $48,000 in 1930.

3. Dwight Morrow (1873–1931) was a partner at the Morgan bank; he was appointed ambassador to Mexico by president Coolidge and elected as a Republican senator from New Jersey in 1930.

4. Eugenio Pascelli (1876–1958) had become Pope Pius XII on 2 March 1939.

To Harriet Bissell [H-DPUP]

Glendale

May 6–39

Dearest:

What a lovely, loving letter. When you stop contemplating my (as I well know) innumerable faults and consider only the remnants of virtue still available, your bias toward the ideal man I might be caused your pent up affection for that to gush fountain wise and I am bathed in glistening superial spray. Aladdin—or rather his Genii could do no more. If I want to cheer myself up, as so often I need to do, all that is required is for me to get out your *good* letters—the blind ones—and read how real swell I am. Then the dark clouds part and there I am,—an angel of light, shining in the sun, not a flaw. As Father Divine[1] says, "it's wonderful!" and if I could only believe it. All my troubles would be over. But I know me. All I can do is promise to live up to it—try as it were. "If at first you don't succeed"—flee as a bird to the mountains.

But this last week has been a hard one for me—very. Two of those fillings put in by that dentist Evans last summer came out and I have been having them exrayed, rebored and refilled. Charges!—I don't know what yet. But pain—and running every other [word missing] regularly. And not eating with them more than I can help. In between—trouble about Sister Carrie. Apparently he is not going to be allowed to commit suicide—not exactly immoral but irreligious, a cowards escape—and a bad example—as well as a reducing one for the youth of America.[2] What is to be emphasized is "You Can" "Its Yours" (what's left) "Live and build a better world." Else it or rather *I* wont get past the Hays office.[3]

More, a happy ending is looming. *Ames* (the one "decent, upright" character) is coming back, I fear. And after I was told that this book is a classic and will be done as a classic. (Brave talk because of box office returns on

Wuthering Heights.)[4] For now talk as to how hard it will be to get one of the *Big Eight*[5] to release it—*unless*. So, talk of a closing scene with Ames and Carrie seated on a small town front porch deciding that, well, maybe a town like this would be best! Smack, smack! RKO might back that. And I may have to face the music or—. And even so it isn't sure that a big release can be had for me. Under the circumstances I suggest that you do not resign your job just yet for I may have to come back to N.Y. and simplify my life still more.

By the way you didn't answer my question as to Irving Levi,[6] in the Log Cabin. He wants it for another year. And wants an answer. Do you think I should rent the place minus the log Cabin? I ought to write him . . . The funny thing is that because of agent publicity in regard to this very tentative approach toward a sale, I am getting letters from writers & newspapermen in New Your asking me (now that I'm in!) to use my influence with powers to get them taken on as script writers! And—oh, well.

By the way I read that a play by some one named Kandel is catching on in N.Y. Is that Libby Kandel?[7]

Just the same I have my moments of better feelings—particularly when I get no depressing waves from you. Talk about television and radio. You are the high powered station.[8] They come through straight, I think,—good or bad. And the bad ones are the limit. But as you say, maybe now that you are doing these practical things so successfully and obtaining insight into the many things you can do, it will make you self reliant. End brooding, which is the curse of the sensitive. I can see you on the job, putting things over—and in one way, for your own sake I wish you could continue with it. A year might effect a psychologic turnover that would last and make everything better. But how would that effect me I wonder? (Imagine my daring to ask, as you would say.)

Anyhow here's love. I think of you all of the time. But as to the situation here—don't give up anything until I can see which way this thing is going to go.

T.D.

Have you figured the cost of putting the place in order yet.

1. Reverend General Jealous Divine (1880–1965), who began life as George Baker, was an African American religious leader who founded the International Peace Mission movement. He developed its doctrine, and oversaw its growth from a small, predominantly black congregation into a multiracial, international church.

2. The censor objected to including Hurstwood's suicide in the film. Dreiser goes on to speculate that the finale would include a union between Carrie and Robert

Ames, a minor and very idealistic character. When the film, entitled *Carrie*, was finally produced in 1952, Ames did not appear. Hurstwood (played by Lawrence Olivier) was not allowed to commit suicide, but the final scene hints at it, when the character eyes a stovetop in Carrie's theater dressing room and switches the gas handle off and on before departing.

3. See Dreiser to Bissell, 6 January 1939, n. 8.

4. *Wuthering Heights* (1939), directed by William Wyler and starring Merle Oberon and Laurence Olivier, was a box-office success.

5. The major film studios.

6. Levi was a renter at Dreiser's summer home at Mt. Kisco, New York.

7. Libby Kandel was the married name of Bissell's good friend and former college roommate Libby Fischer. Dreiser is probably thinking of a play by the dramatist and screenwriter Aben Kandel.

8. For Dreiser's belief in "wireless" communication between individuals, see Dreiser to Kirah Markham, 9 February 1914, n. 1.

To Harriet Bissell [H-DPUP]

1426 North Hayworth
Hollywood, Calif

May 15–1939

I haven't really anything in the way of good news to report. Although the columnists report the sale or imminent sale of S-C-, still it is not sold[1] The Hays office is raising objection, due I hear to the Catholic Side of the office and unless these can be overcome there can be no sale. The producers say that the church, attacking in the small towns—banning it to their parishioners and stirring up Protestant moralists can cause any picture to lose money—also any theatre! So.

Next, I had to leave Glendale & come over here to Hollywood. The distances here are enormous and running from there to here (Hollywood) on this conference stuff has taken days & days of time and gasoline money. Even so I might have stuck it out. But suddenly trucks & cars appeared & they began building a really huge court next door. So with hammering & sawing for months ahead I gave up. The litter of lumber and cement bags & what not proved a little too much.

Lately I had a real shock. For some reason my bladder trouble became so bad that I had to consult a doctor. He suggested a surgical operation to remove the prostate. We all know what that means. Meanwhile I was given medicine to remove the strain which comes from the lack of passage for even urine. That worked fairly well. Later I consulted another surgeon who decided that the prostate need not be cut out but burned out—internally—with an electric needle. That would clear the urethra—open the passage for urine, but effect partial and possibly complete impotence. So, here I stand, this side of the Rubicon, as it were, wondering if I must cross. Its not a pleasant scene ahead. Meanwhile I am taking the temporary relief medicine—Buchu, Mullein,[2] and *gin* (!)—a tablespoonful 3 times a day. Judge for yourself.

I had your letter about the probable costs of repairs[3]—$150 ^{00}. But what must be must be. Also I know that some one is writing Helen concerning you and your life in N.Y. for I saw reference to your actions—not very complimentary. Since it was type written and not signed—not the page I saw, I cannot say who. I expect that I will learn whether I wish to or not for I fancy the page was intended for my eye.

Regardless of that my immediate outlook is not bright. If I have to undergo that operation I am not going to feel particularly gay about life in general. I can go on with my work, of course, but—Incidentally this surgeon said (I. A. Westphal of Glendale) that prolonged abstinence sexually was not favorable to the continuance of the ability to perform the act. For a period of time yes, for a year or more, no!

All told I am in a blue funk. Which way to go! What to do? How to make a life in case—Except for companionship what woman would endure me? What would I need. The presence of the other half—without anything more than the reminder of what was but could not be—really. Well. I am thinking.

But I wont write more today. But I wish you would write me. I feel nothing of the old time mood on your part. The waves[4] that used to reach me and in one of your first letters—When this latest correspondence was resumed you said you would write every day. With your present work that is too much too ask, I know. But a brief letter will do. Your latest letters have been brief enough. You had best keep your job and study your Spanish. I will not be a happy companion for anyone that I know if this thing has to be.

To top it all there has been a solid week of gray, sunless days.

Love
T.D.

Will I have to send you money to make the repairs—or can they be paid out of the first rental money? Ill pay if need be.

T.D

1. Dreiser was having a hard time selling *Sister Carrie* to the film companies. See Dreiser to Harriet Bissell, 6 January 1939, n. 8 and 6 May 1939, n. 2.

2. Buchu and mullein are common medicinal herbs used for various respiratory and urinary disorders.

3. Dreiser is discussing repairs to Iroki, his thirty-seven-acre estate at Mt. Kisco, New York, which he was renting at this time.

4. Telepathic "waves." See Dreiser to Kirah Markham 9 February 1914, n. 1 and Dreiser to Harriet Bissell, 6 February 1939, n. 1.

To Harriet Bissell [H-DPUP]

July 5–'39

Harriet Dear:

Your letter sounds more contented than usual. I'm glad in one way because your moods can be so dark—or—you can make other people feel that they are—which is a dark indictment indeed. You are always able to affect me. But don't take my comment ill. I shall think that most of your darkest moods must be real, and they have imprinted themselves indelibly on me.

Its so nice here from a weather point of view. Perfect sunshine—not too hot. Nights always cool enough for blankets. The side of the city is sea shore—mostly bathing beaches. From the Mexican line almost to San Francisco beach after beach after beach. Some day the coast south of San Francisco will be a western Riviera. It is so truly beautiful.

But there's poverty here. Lots of it. And California is uniformly cruel to labor. Stingy & hardboiled. There are no effective unions—except company unions. Most people work for very little. What keeps them fairly content is sunshine—warmth, no flies to speak of, no mosquitoes—Lovely lawns with grass & flowers all winter long. And daily more pour in—150,000 this last year. The building is simply enormous—If only I had a little luck I could sell my lots in Montrose, one or two anyhow and I think they will move soon.[1] Meantime I have to wait for the S-C- thing which drags along.[2]

You say why don't I send for you. I would today if I knew how to manage. But what would happen after with us I dont know. All you write seems to point to growing content with yourself and that means what? Good conduct? Sweetness of April? Or just rough playgirl stuff leading a crowd in a hectic dance? Your last words seem to indicate that. Anyhow I'm not out of the woods. The long threatening letter from Rosset.[3] The old stuff. (I owe $4000). Bills, bills, bills. But living here is certainly inexpensive and if I don't think of the movie crowd or mingle with them I do very well. You will never know until you see it. The amount of painstaking work I've done and the scope of my data—and its lonely.

But nevertheless, when not lost in work I lean to the regretful side. I like life too much—miss the lovely moments that never require means—only sensitivity, I suppose. And the more I study the more exquisite—and profound—(staggering really) the architectural, engineering, social and art knowledge or wisdom that underlies and at the same time inhabits life. I hang over the markings & colorings and formation of a flower or an insect or a worm or snail and at such times, and only so, seem to *see* and *know* something of the instincts, and intents as well as powers of the sublime creative force that permits and maintains us all. Then the only other question is *Why*?

Oh, no! I sigh as you do. And here is a kind of peace and rest. For—be life what it will—this aesthetic skill with its suggestion of intention seems so not only respectable but awesome. I *admire* until I border on affection—maybe love. And that as you will admit is *saving*. It counteracts—at times even overcomes—loneliness. And I understand Thoreau better. I think he sensed and was comforted by the presence of not an *invisible* but a visible personality. One so wholly and so magnificently mental. And so wholly beyond all good or evil as man senses those things.

Do you care for me enough not to quarrel or hate or rage?

Love
Dee

This is not much of a business letter—is it?
Would have gotten this up before but had to get up a new outline of *The Financier*.[4]

1. During their first stay in California, Dreiser and Helen had bought lots in Montrose, a town ten miles north of Los Angeles.
2. On the difficulties of selling the film rights to *Sister Carrie*, see Dreiser to Harriet Bissell, 6 January 1939, n. 8 and 6 May 1939, n. 2.
3. Leo Rossett was the lawyer for Sarah White Dreiser. He was threatening to sue for the $4000 in back payments for support owed by Dreiser.
4. Dreiser was attempting to develop an outline for a screenplay of *The Financier*.

To Clara Clark [H-RIG]

On a recent trip to San Francisco Dreiser had missed seeing Clark.

Oct. 4–'39

Theodore Dreiser
1426 North Hayworth,
Hollywood, Calif

Dear Click:

I was on the spot, so to speak at San Francisco—just a few days to stay. Elizabeth Kearney[1] and other friends on my trail. I was hoping you'd return to L. A. However I may be in New York this fall and if I am I'll come around. I always wonder about you. Why don't the Oxford crowd get up a real dramatic movie—a modern Pilgrim's Progress.[2] Anyhow write me. Regards to Warner.[3]

Love
T. D

1. Elizabeth Kearney was the maiden name of Elizabeth Coakley: see Dreiser to Elizabeth Coakley, 28 June 1940, headnote.
2. For Clark's involvement with the Oxford Movement, see Dreiser to Clara Clark, 15 January 1937, n. 2. Dreiser's reference is to John Bunyan's *The Pilgrim's Progress* (1678; 1684).
3. Warner Clark, her brother.

To Ruth Kennell [H-DPUP]

Kennell had been writing letters to Dreiser condemning the liberal press in America for its hostility to the Nazi-Soviet pact signed in August 1939. Their exchange reflects the uncertainties about what was happening in Europe. Like many others, Kennell had initially "hoped for an alliance with Britain and France to stop Hitler," but with Prime Minister Neville Chamberlain's 1938 agreement at Munich to partition Czechoslovakia with Germany, France and Italy, she felt she could "not trust that England and France are waging a real war against Hitler—I'll suspect that they are secretly plotting with their old pal, Hitler" (Kennell to Dreiser, 20 September 1939 [DPUP]). With Chamberlain in power, there was a growing sense among supporters of Russia such as Dreiser and Kennell that England and France were plotting against the USSR—a position widely taken by more doctrinaire Marxists and communists of the time.

THEODORE DREISER

Oct. 31–39

Dear Ruth:

Yours is a discouraged letter.[1] And I myself do not know what to make of the European situation. It is seemingly too complicated to follow. My personal deduction, at first, was that Hitler had truly split with England & France and that Russia has come to some workable understanding with Hitler that would permit of both going ahead on a social-democratic base.[2] But when I heard that Poland (its executives) would not allow the Russian Army to aid the Poles, I began to doubt. I had not forgotten Hitler's share in the destruction of Democratic Spain—nor England's. Nor France's. Nor Italy's. I know for a fact though that Russia would not aid Negrin & Del Vayo[3] because they could not be sure that if successful they would completely communize the country. He would not accept a democratic Spain & so threw the country to Mussolini and Hitler or Franco & the Catholics! Just the same, if Russia is not to sweep Europe soon, I would prefer to see a strong

German State to the rotten financial dictatorship now holding in France and England and Hungary and the Balkans and elsewhere. I know England's Egypt. And it is terrible. They are colony blood suckers, not developers. And I was told by French radicals that Germany's African colonies were better developed—their natives better treated and trained practically than are the natives of the French Mondales.

Anyhow I wrote *The Dawn is in the East*[4] in good faith and sent a copy to Russia. Apletin[5] cabled me afterward that it was published in Pravda *in full*. That means with the personal approval of Stalin. If he objected to the comments on Germany he did not order them cut out.[6] But yesterday again, I saw the enclosed clipping and cut it out for *you* to see. True? Or False? *Your article is excellent*.[7] I intend to send it on to others but it will not make them happy—not if England, France & Germany are to combine against Russia. But if so why did they let Russia take a part of Poland & then to offset that tie up with Turkey!! It seems lunatic—or maybe it is just too ably crafty for me to grasp. As far as Dawn is in the East—that is done and over with. I will have to wait and try to sense what really is afoot—if anything good is afoot.

Out here there appears to be a real fear that Ham and Eggs[8] will win. I dont know, but if I could I would vote for it as a protest. This state—the money crowd—is so savagely fascist. It would like a money dictator. Their cruelty to labor & poverty is really infuriating. Because of it I have taken up with all radical protests and speak to CIO,[9] Newspaper Guild & other groups whenever asked. I have even devised a technical worker-leader procedure which might help labor defeat capital. It has already been endorsed by the local Newspaper Guild.

But your busy—I can see that and I wont take up more of your time. Not strange to say I cant learn to like Los Angeles. It is too luxury conscious; too greedy for a petty little measure of social precedence. Its so-called radicals are soft and lazy. I'll get out presently & go back to Manhattan Island or Connecticut—near Stamford or maybe Old Bedford. I like it there.

Love & good luck

D.

1. In her letter of 26 October, Kennell had criticized Dreiser's article "Civilization—Where? What?" for its "failure to discriminate sharply between Nazi Germany and Socialist Russia. It seems to me that such a point of view is quite as dangerous as those of Westbrook Pegler and Congressman Martin Dies, who say nazism and communism are similar ideologies" (DPUP).

2. Dreiser is referring to the Russian-German non-aggression agreement of August 1939, which was followed by the invasion of Poland by both powers. Dreiser and other supporters of Russia initially found themselves hard-pressed to defend Russia's alliance with the fascist regime in Germany. Kennell's original line of reasoning—that the pact was an indirect method of controlling Hitler—is echoed

here by Dreiser. A number of factors influenced his positions in this period: his hatred of the British class system and its colonial rule; his belief that Russia represented the best hope for democratic equality (and consequently his espousal of the communist anti-capitalist ideal of economic parity for all classes); an assumed equation between British and German imperialism; and an acute sense of the failure of western "democracies" to help democratic Spain. Such convictions led him to denounce any of the ideological enemies—notably England and France—of the Soviet Union. Dreiser opposed American involvement in the European conflict as long as Russia remained neutral. The subsequent attack on Russia by Germany changed his position. The hostilities should have come as no surprise to Dreiser, however, since one of the major causes for the rise of the Nationalist Socialist Party (Nazis) was the reaction to the German Communist Party, whose members were among the first to be persecuted after the Nazis came to power.

3. Juan Negrin (1892–1956), a member of the Socialist party, became minister of finance in Spain in 1936. He transferred Spanish Gold Reserves to the Soviet Union in return for arms. He took over as Spanish minister of defense in 1938 and eventually appointed communists to high-ranking army posts.

Julio Alverez del Vayo (1891–1974), also a member of the Socialist party in Spain, sought support from foreign governments for the Republican Army, and was instrumental in getting the support of Joseph Stalin.

Dreiser had met with del Vayo and Negrin in Barcelona in July 1938. They collectively regarded the refusal to help democratic Spain as a sign of England and France's duplicitous and imperialistic aims, a position reflected in Dreiser's views in this letter. Dreiser also reported del Vayo as saying that "they [the Spanish] had ceased to look for equality in foreign lands. Russia had helped them to some extent. But not enough to make a decisive difference" ("Loyalists Tell Dreiser They Will Not Surrender," North American Newspaper Alliance press lease [DPUP]). Dreiser also discussed his meeting with del Vayo and Negrin in speeches to the League of American Writers (24 August 1938 [DPUP]) and to the League's National Council (15 September 1938 [DPUP]). For Dreiser's discussions with del Vayo and Negrin on the question of American aid for the needy in Spain, see Dreiser to Caroline Slade, 28 September 1938 (in Pizer, *New Letters*).

4. "The Dawn is in the East" was published in *Common Sense* in December 1939. Dreiser argued that the Nazi-Soviet pact safeguarded Russia and was a threat only to England and, above all, to Western capitalism.

5. Mikhail Apletin headed the Foreign Commission of the Soviet Writer's Union, which promoted exchanges between the USSR and writers in Europe and America.

6. Despite his defense of the Nazi-Soviet agreement, Dreiser warned that Nazi aggression could mean the "death of civilization."

7. The clipping Dreiser mentions has not survived in his papers. As to Kennell's "article," a marginal note in Kennell's hand reads "In Nation, defending the Soviet-Nazi pact. R. K." In fact, the editors of *The Nation* asked her to turn the article she had submitted into a letter, which she did. It was published on 4 November.

8. The Ham and Eggs Retirement Life Payments Association urged a recall of California governor Culbert Olson who had backed out of a campaign promise to support a pension program.

9. The Congress of Industrial Organizations (CIO) originated in 1935 when eight unions broke with the American Federation of Labor over the issue of unionizing

unskilled workers as well as the skilled laborers maintained by the AFL. In this period Dreiser actively supported the CIO and other progressive labor organizations such as the Newspaper Guild.

To Esther McCoy [H-DPUP]

Although the urgencies of the political scene led Dreiser to question himself at times about expending energy on "mere literary" endeavor, he continued to support the writing of others.

Theodore Dreiser

Nov. 14–'39

Dear Esther:

St. Bernard is a fine piece of writing: Also a corking good short story,— moving and illuminating. I would like to see you sell it. Do you want me

Esther McCoy.

to send it to George Bye or William C. Lengel—both good agents.[1] Or you can do it yourself. George Bye's address is 535 Fifth Ave. New York. William Lengel's is 654 Madison Ave. New York.

Ask 150^{oo}.

If you can do this you can do others.

To work! To work!

How doth the busy bee.

Go to the gut. Thou slug—hard[2]

Love
T.D.

1. George T. Bye (1887–1957) and William C. Lengel were highly respected literary agents with famous clients, including Dreiser. For Lengel see Dreiser to Kirah Markham, 18 February 1914, n. 10.

2. Dreiser is recalling popular Victorian rhymes such as "How doth the busy bee," which originated in the first stanza of "Against Idleness and Mischief," a hymn by Isaac Watts (1674–1748):

> How doth the little busy bee
> Improve each shining hour,
> And gather honey all the day
> From every opening flower!

1940

To Ruth Kennell [H-DPUP]

1426 N. Hayworth

April 3–'40

Dear Ruth:

Thanks for your letter. I thought, after I mailed you my last note that possibly you had gone East again. When do you go? As for me speaking on the 20th, I have not surety, as yet, that I will feel strong enough to do anything as strenuous as that. I was in bed for 6 weeks and seem to be pulling back not so fast—although I'm up and around. I write well enough at a desk but walking out is not the stimulating thing it was before I went down.

I'm so glad you liked the *Dives & Lazarus*[1] thing. It will be in this months (April) Soviet Russia Today. But I've had calls for it from individuals here and there—calls for fifties and twenty-fives. Just today the *Book of the Day Shop* here—a sort of left center book store, called for 1,000 of it and 500 of this thing on *War*[2] that I am enclosing. It is paying the printer for them! The Manager of the place said he hung a copy of Dives & Lazarus & there was such a crowd around it all the time, trying to read it, that rather than have his aisle blocked he decided to give it away—have its readers go outside. The newspapers are so completely closed to any but the corporation side that the public has no place to go to learn what they want to know. If only I had one or two hundred such left center book stores or meeting places over the country I might win a large number of people to our way of thinking. If you know any names or places to send any & will furnish me the list, I'll send them or, I'll furnish you copies & the money for stamps & envelopes, & you send them.

This war is such a trying affair. It has so many people stirred up & worrying. And now the capitalistic gangsters are taking over the KKK & turning it loose on so called *Reds*. Next comes a good beating or burning for some of us. But heres luck and that we dont go under.

And Roosevelt! And his promising to bring this country into the war on the Allies side!

Well, love and best wishes. If I can possibly come up I'll let you know. But I doubt it. I'd be so glad to see you.

T.D

P.S. I'll send you any number of copies you want at anytime.

1. Dreiser is referring to a piece he wrote in response to the Russian-Finnish War, which had resulted in the invasion and defeat of Finland. Responding to those that deplored this action, Dreiser's answer was "The Soviet-Finnish Treaty and World Peace," in *Soviet Russia Today* 8 (April 1940): 8–9. In March it was published as a broadside, *Concerning Dives and Lazarus*. In it Dreiser defends "this recent development in Organized Labor, Russia," which he describes as the embodiment of a "non-profit system"; and he sees as its chief enemy "England, which represents the Capitalist System [that] wishes to destroy the non-profit system" (repub. in Pizer, *Uncollected Prose*, 321).

2. Dreiser is referring to "Theodore Dreiser Condemns War," published in *People's World* (San Francisco) 6 April 1940, 7.

To Elizabeth Coakley [H-UCLA]

Dreiser met Elizabeth Kearney Coakley (1903–85) at the funeral of her twin brother, Patrick Kearney, an actor and dramatist who had adapted An American Tragedy *for a stage production. A widow with three young children, Coakley moved to Hollywood in 1938, with the intention of writing for the films. She became Dreiser's companion and secretary—a situation that increased tensions between Dreiser and Helen Richardson. Coakley continued her writing and also collaborated with Dreiser on several projects, including writing screenplays, some adapted from his stories. At the time of this letter, Helen's mother was ailing and Dreiser was visiting the family in Oregon.*

1856 S. E. Yamhill St.

June 28–'40

Dearest:

I went Thursday to the State Capital here—to see the leader or rather ex-leader of the Oregon Branch of "*Technocracy*"[1]—A. C. Dahlberg.[2] I wanted to learn about labor & reform here in the Northwest (and I got an ear-full)—how tightly & savagely the money bunch is united against the masses. It is a cruel picture—a completely money & bank & business dominated press. Also political party (Republican), also all law firms of any impact, all judges & their courts, all office holders etc. They want to see if they cannot defeat Roosevelt (as bad as he is) and at the same time use American money & men to help England because England stands with the corporations. They hate Hitler & Russia. I didnt take Helen with me on this trip & I did not come back until this Saturday a.m. But, alas, only to learn that Los Angeles had been on the wire! Did you call me? If not I dont know who could have unless it was one of my agents. I gave no others (except you) this address.

Today I did get an air mail special dated Tuesday which reads as though you were at once angry, cynical and contemptuous—a development I scarcely expected in you. It doesnt sound like a person who is willing to make allowances for anything and that does not sound like you. I thought I was dealing with a much more tolerant and diplomatic person—one who knew that stresses & strains are never to be wholly escaped in this life—that no one of us can have everything. Certainly I have never had my own way much more than 50–50. And I certainly felt that you believed that I cared for you enough to want you and no other girl at the same time. And that is true. But I did not expect that you would begin looking on Helen as the other girl or another girl, since she was with me from the first & if I had preferred her I certainly would not have begun to devote myself to you. But now it begins to look as though you had decided that I must drop H—entirely and have only to do with you, which is not what I meant at the time, since I could not have done that without great difficulty then & still cannot do it without difficulty now. Not that I am not unhappy about it & uncomfortable. I am. At times I am furious. But your situation presents a problem also which is not an easy one to solve for a writer like myself. You have a family and I can see that you are indissolvably linked with it because you are deeply chained by your affections—deep mother love. Your Xmas story showed me that. At the same time that is not a situation which should or would trouble you, once you place yourself as a writer. As a matter of fact as a writer it would be an incentive & so an advantage. But for two writers to work in separate fields and yet at once & the same time to jointly manage a family in the same household, I did not and cannot now see that. I felt and I still feel that you could be better & perhaps most happily placed as the head of your own family group writing—and with me (if you truly wanted me) as not only your friend and companion, but as one who would advise & help in the matter of your development, while privately pursuing my own literary way as best I could. And I really thought that that was what we were doing most happily until that matter of this trip came up & I went off with you first. Since then, or because the trip was ended by Pat's[3] sickness—not by me, all has gone from bad to worse. I did not bring Helen's sister & her husband to L.A. In fact, except for Pat's illness I would not have been there & she would have gone without me. And that would have been ok. Her mothers illness is not of my doing—not hers either. That I came here, particularly since you could not leave L. A. just now seems nothing of any great import. I wanted to go to S. F. as you know & now am going. When I left for Salem (the other day) I sent a wire to Von Sabern[4] my friend in S. F. advising him of my delay & found this telegram along with your letter when I came back today. As for all the bitterness on your part I do not get it. I have assured you I have no passion, love or sexual relation with H—& that is true. At this time it appears she is also undergoing a change of life & is suffering in various ways due to it. That you & I should not go to S.F. or anywhere else a little later for a week or 10 days is nothing which need ever be questioned. I would love it & we can. And I miss you now as much as ever. So why all this temper. If you were called upon to do something away from me I am sure you would go and attend to it & think it perfectly natural & so would I. And I would not think any the less of you. Nor would I write you sharply. Supposing Coakley were alive & it were he you were away with & I in L. A. Do you really feel that I would rage? Or that I ought to—particularly if I felt that you cared for me & believed you had nothing to do with him? I do not feel that I would or should.

However letters dont seem to help. I dont think this will. But it is a very good expression of how I feel & perfectly honest. But if you do not think so, what can I do? Just the same I feel toward you & care about you exactly the same as before this came up—exactly as I felt the morning we left together. Will you really think this is a lie? If so dont write me that. It wont make things any better.

Incidentally write me if you will,—c/o Henry Von Sabern, 1851 Union Street, S.F. & mark it "Hold" although barring accident I'll be there by the time it arrives. All my love & please quit [word unintelligible].

T.D.

1. Technocracy Inc. was a non-profit research group of scientists, architects, and engineers that worked to bring social proposals to the general public. It influenced Dreiser's thinking in the 1930s by impressing him with the significance of technology in achieving a more equitable form of society.
2. Arthur C. Dahlberg, engineer, sociologist, and author, best remembered for *Jobs, Machines, and Capitalism* (1932).
3. Coakley's son.
4. Henry Von Sabern, German-born sculptor and architect.

To Louise Campbell [H-DPUP]

Dreiser had learned of the recent death of Campbell's mother.

Nov. 30th '40

Dear Louise:

I cant feel deeply sorry for you for I know of all the years of pleasure and delight you have had in, with and through your mother. As you know I thought her an exquisite creature, really,—something apart from the crass and so often coarse forces of life.[1] I remember the times you told me you could not stay out here (Los Angeles) or move to New York because of her—

and I understood why. I wish I could help you with a thought as to how you are to do from now on, but all that comes to me is that you have gathered so much of all that was inspiring and comforting in her into yourself—through your love and devotion of course,—that in a very real sense she cannot be very far from you any more,—anymore than my beloved mother—dead these 50 years—is ever far from me.[2] She isn't! I absorbed too much of her, to me, exquisite nature to think of her as dead or unreal. She is not to me and never has been. So, I am sure, it will be with you. She will comfort you all of your days. And you will be proud and happy because of that.

And dont forget, Louise dear, that you too are a spirit of force and comfort to others—and have been for so long. Like myself, others must have looked to you for affection, understanding, sympathy and human and sustaining warmth and recieved it. And you will always know that their thoughts and affections are with you unchangingly—mine are. And will continue to be. I know you are busy and cannot write much. And I seem always blocks behind my work. But my thoughts are quicker. And certainly they must reach you often. I wish you could come out here for a visit with us.

With love and all good wishes
Always,
T.D

1. See Dreiser to Mrs. Heym, 27 February 1930.
2. Dreiser's mother, Sarah Mary Schänäb Dreiser (1833–90), died when he was nineteen.

1941

To Yvette Szekely [H-DPUP]

Dreiser had recently returned to California from a trip to the East Coast, occasioned by a speaking engagement in New York City paid for by the American Council on Soviet Relations.

Mch. 19–'41

Yvette, Sweet

I had to rush off as you know to Newark and then to Philadelphia and then to Washington and then to San Francisco (on a special mission to see J.B. McNamara[1] before he died, only he died just as I got there). But I have been thinking how sweet it was of you to respond to a midnight call and come to me so generously. And I loved being with you. And if only I could endure New York as I once did you would see more of me. Or if ever you managed to move out here.

For there is, for me, something perpetually enticing about your mind as well as your body—a natural and poetic refinement which makes many of your letters dreamily phrased compositions on the contrast and the varying values of life. Naturally you percieve so much—life's meannesses as well as its beauties. But you do not quarrel with it as I do. You are so tolerant and kindly and forgiving! Mayhap you feel you have things in yourself to forgive, but no matter. I doubt if a father confessor could demand much more than a few "Hail Marys"—six or seven at the most, before you could go in peace. As for myself I love your laughter, your desire for love—as you once said "to belong to some one"—your kindly, smiling, amused and amusing accounts of the peccadilloes and little sins of others. But, dearest, belong to whom you choose, you will always belong to me. You cross me at times, as you know, but I get over it. And in due time return in thought as well as in affection and love to the sweet things that make you what you are—my Yvette.

Write me sweet and I will write you. And one of these days we will be meeting and loving as we did—and much more than you think.

With the sweetest memory of your coming and of us together—

T.D.

1015 N. Kings Road,
Hollywood
A long letter from Clark.[2] I fancy you met and you told him about us.

Baddie

1. James B. McNamara (1882–1941) a labor leader who died while serving a life sentence in San Quentin for the 1910 bombing of the Los Angeles Times Building that left twenty-one persons dead. Defended by Clarence Darrow and championed by Eugene Debs, McNamara lost support when he confessed to the bombing in 1911. In 1936 Dreiser was among forty-eight prominent citizens—including John Dewey, Upton Sinclair, Mary C. Woolley, and Emanuel Celler—to petition unsuccessfully for McNamara's release.

2. Szekely would later marry Kenneth S. Clark, a writer and superintendent of the Canadian Press Bureau in Halifax. He had written Dreiser asking for help in placing his stories.

To Alyse Gregory Powys [T-DPUP]

Alyse Gregory Powys was the widow of the writer Llewelyn Powys, the brother of Dreiser's close friend John Cowper Powys.

1015 N. King's Rd.,
Hollywood, Calif.

April 16, 1941.

Dear Alyse:

I have just finished reading Llewellyn's book *Love and Death.*[1] And, as you can believe, I am deeply moved. It is at once so beautiful in wisdom, truth, narrative, poetry and human as well as natural delineation. I am so touched—as always I have been—by Llewellyn's sensitive response to every phase of life that he was permitted to contact either in letters or in life. As I write my mind goes back to personal conversations with him and with you—with him before you and he met. Only now, as I read the book, I am so grateful to chance or fate that he was permitted to enter upon your loving and understanding companionship, your bracing courage, combined with your so sensitive compassion. Truly I am deeply moved, most particularly when I recall your statement to me in one of your letters of your uncontrollable jealousy of the strength of the passing farmers or hinds of your village, when he, who needed a little physical strength so much, lacked it. When I think of you and your devotion, I can only think of Paul's words to the Corinthians,—"though I speak with the tongues of angels and have not love, I am become as sounding brass or a tinkling symbol."[2]

But you had and have love for him, and I sense behind this work the courage and the love and the patience and service that made it possible for him to bring this lovely book into being.

Believe me you have not only my deepest sympathy but my profound admiration for the courage and patience that your obvious love provided, and so made it possible for this lovely thing to be.

I am, as always,
Affectionately,
Theodore Dreiser

We have moved to Los Angeles. All my books and letter files are now here—in a big store room. At the first opourtunity I'll make a search for Llewellyns letters.[3]

1. *Love and Death* is a fictionalized autobiography published posthumously in 1939. Dreiser had written a preface for Powys's earlier autobiographical work, *Ebony and Ivory* (1923).
2. Dreiser is referring to First Corinthians 13:1.
3. The postscript is in Dreiser's hand.

To Elizabeth Coakley [H-UCLA]

Portland, Ore.

June 26–1941

Elizabeth Dear:

Enclosed is The Tithe of the Lord, written in 1934 & sold to Esquire.[1] Now that I read it over I see it is badly written, although the story itself is correctly outlined. It is a true one.

At the time it was published there were several movie inquiries but no takers. Recently Blaustein[2] who found it (a copy) in the files of Paramount suggested that it might be sold. But I do not care to submit it as is. What I wish is to have you read it and see if you can outline it more interestingly in short script form. Before working on it I prefer that you read it & then talk to me about it. My hope is that you can make a few suggestions which will make it more moving and colorful, suggest a few dramatizations of scenes (now not sufficiently dramatized) as may make it structurally as well as emotionally worthwhile from a movie point of view. If it cannot be done it cannot be done but before dropping it I would like your opinion & advice. Will write you about other matters later. Please give this your early attention and let me know—

T.D.

1. "The Tithe of the Lord," *Esquire*, 10 (July 1938), 36–37, 150, 155–58.
2. Julian Blaustein (1913–95), screenwriter and Hollywood producer.

To Elizabeth Coakley [H-UCLA]

Dreiser had gone to Indianapolis to give a talk on what he believed was the unconscionable failure of the British to support the Soviet Union. He was invited to visit the university at Bloomington, where he had been a student for a year in 1889–90. He also took the opportunity to visit for the last time with his old schoolteacher May Calvert Baker, who was now blind and diabetic.

Columbia Club
Indianapolis

Sunday, Nov. 23–41

Dearie,

I have to go to New York today, but just as I was packing yesterday the Dean and also the head of the *law* school of Indiana University descended on me and insisted on my taking the day off to see the University (grounds and buildings). Also the annual foot ball game between Purdue and Indiana. So finally I wired Lengel[1] and went down for the day. And it was surprising enough after 42 years,—a college of four buildings and 500 students grown to 18 imposing ones and 6000 students. There were 22,000 people down to see the game and I sat in the president's box—for once. Only it snowed and drizzled alternately. But it wasn't a bad show at that. I just got back—9 *a.m.* after a 40 mile drive. And tired. But I'm packing just the same and catching a noon train to N.Y. At that I have to run out & see my old school teacher—May Calvert. Also to recieve & thank the people who brought me here. Indianapolis has less than 400,000 people, but the crowd was about a thousand which (they say) is a record here for that hall—largest & best.

I'm sorry about the delay. I didn't expect a book offer from N.Y.[2] (question: is it good enough) or a visit from the University. But I'll waste no more time, for I'm anxious to get back. I would have written on the train but I felt so generally low that I staid in my berth most of the time to feel strong enough to do anything when I got here. Now that the lecture is over I feel somewhat better. But I'll be glad when it's all over and I'm back where I can see you. We'll take the trip as soon as I get there if Im not sick. Only I fancy I'll be ok.

I don't know whether it is advisable to write or even wire me. I expect one conference with Lengel will settle everything. However I think I'll stay the night—Monday night—at the Pennsylvania, since it's right at the depot.

I've been wondering how you are. Your probably short of cash so I'm enclosing $25^{00}. I've been thinking such nice things of you and wishing you could have a better run of days than you have had. Helen wired that she had gone to Portland for a few days. The reason I didn't call back at the depot was because I was seized by three different people—one of them that John Stapp[3] who has some influence with the A. F. of L. union and I wanted to get his help for Eisenberg.[4] Before I got loose they were calling all aboard.[5]

Love
T.D.

1. William Lengel. See Dreiser to Kirah Markham, 18 February 1914, n. 10. Lengel was serving as Dreiser's literary agent at this time.

2. Dreiser was going to New York at Lengel's request to meet with Earle Balch, the vice president of Putnam's, about publishing his long-delayed novel in progress, *The Bulwark*. At the meeting Balch agreed to be his publisher.

3. John Stapp, a Hollywood film agent who would be named in the early 1950s in connection with the House Un-American Activities Committee's probes into communist infiltration of the film industry.

4. Emanuel Eisenberg, a New York theatrical press agent who died in an airplane crash; a Testimonial Committee was established to raise funds to assist Eisenberg's family.

5. Dreiser is excusing his failure to say goodbye to her personally before he boarded the train from Los Angeles.

To Ruth Kennell [H-DPUP]

THEODORE DREISER
1015 N. Kings Road
Hollywood[1]

Dec. [8th]–41[2]

Dear Ruth:

It's nice to get the latest news to date concerning you. I have assumed that you were in Bridgeport. You looked and spoke so well at The Writer's League Meeting that I assumed everything was going fairly well at least. I have been supporting Russia so earnestly that I have been attracting the personal attention of Mr. Dies.[3] Just the other day, because Prof. F. V. Harper of the Indiana University Law School, chose to introduce me at Indianapolis, his committee announced that it would investigate him and seek his removal. I think he is Dean or head of the school. I think he (Dies) has given up on me because I always emphasize our Free Press, Radio, Movies. Also Mr. Dies' right to have his say so whether paid for by the corporations or not.

I can imagine your mother doesn't like Amarillo after the California Bay district. However, I like San Antonio and El Paso, to say nothing of New Mexico which I consider a dream world really.

As I write this I am pausing to listen to Roosevelt's address to the American people calling for war against Japan. Only yesterday came the news of the bombardment of Pearl Harbor and the death of 5000 Americans! I can imagine your reactions & you can imagine mine. I think they expect to drive us out of the Phillipines and Asia & the South Seas, but I hope we pay them out and so help Russia & China. Anyhow, I'm in a troubled and contentious frame of mind.

So I won't see you this winter. Sorry! Better luck next time. I always recall our days in Russia together with so much mental as well as physical pleasure. Write me when your moved to do so. I was in N.Y. City about ten days ago, but only for a day & a half. And I wasn't lecturing—just arranging to move from Simon & Schuster to Putnams.[4]

Love
T.D

1. Dreiser drew an arrow pointing at the address and wrote in the margin, "Note the new address."

2. Dreiser mistakenly wrote "Dec. 3rd-41." In this letter, however, he mentions the bombing of Pearl Harbor as occurring "yesterday" (7 December).

3. The reference is to Martin Dies (1900–1972), the Texas congressman who chaired the House Un-American Activities Committee that was investigating political radicals.

4. Dreiser had signed a contract with Simon & Schuster in 1934 in which the publisher agreed to issue all past as well as new books. The plan did not materialize, and Dreiser became embroiled in legal haggling with the firm over royalties and book rights that was not settled until the fall of 1941. Dreiser did sign an agreement with Putnam to publish *The Bulwark*, but once again the book took so long to complete that he eventually returned an advance and gave up the connection. Doubleday published the novel posthumously in 1946.

1942

To Hazel Godwin [H-DPUP]

In 1936 Dreiser began a correspondence with Hazel Godwin (1903–?), an American living in Toronto with her Canadian husband. She wrote mainly to explain how much his writing meant to her personally. The correspondence was desultory and sporadic, with Dreiser always responding to her initiatives; but when he sent her a Christmas card in 1941, a more intimate exchange began. Among the attractions of Godwin for Dreiser was her Quaker background, particularly as he returned to the writing of The Bulwark. *As he wrote Godwin, "I've always been partial to the Friends—or rather George Fox's interpretation of true religion. Reading his great autobiography I was satisfied that he had conceived a great truth from somewhere.*1 *And as for the Hicksite branch or schism of Quakerism,*[2]*—I prefer that to any other. In fact I have attended many Hicksite Meetings for Worship and look on their Book of Discipline as the finest exemplification of human conduct and proper human awe that I have ever read. It is beautiful" ([Dreiser to Hazel Godwin, 2 April 1942 [DPUP]). He increasingly asked Godwin to supply him with anecdotes of her early years that he might use in his novel about Quakers in the modern world. At this time they had not yet met, and Dreiser based his accounts of her appearance on photos she had sent him.*

March 22–[1942]

Hazel Dear:

You write such subtle, intriguing, provoking and for me exciting letters. It is your gift,—the delightful gift of implying and yet not truly saying, which is that which stirs and yet never quite wholly assures the imagination. Your letters are like your eyes and your smile in the little picture of you—tempting and yet evasive. It truly makes me want to know you,—that is if you care enough. And actually, as to that, paragraph four of your letter is the most ingenious or adroit bit of art craft in writing that I remember reading anywhere, "I think you know as you are too discerning to have missed that." Anyway I "liked you years ago and the affection I have for you increases all the time. *Though no doubt I shouldn't say it.*"

Sweet! You are a gifted darling and no mistake. Such facility and dexterity and felicity in the matter of self-expression. You come *so close* and yet so easily and gracefully. I think now your little picture doesn't do you full justice—couldn't—because your facile, friendly and plainly able mind cannot be photographed nor your eyes either.

Eyes to be understood and appreciated need to be seen in action in real life or in a moving picture. Knowing this and reading your felicitous and discreet letters—only two of them—, I thrill not a little in thinking of what it could mean to be really close to you, to see your eyes and your smile and to hear your voice. For as I told you, or rather want to tell you now,—your physical self in the little picture plus the art of your mind as displayed in these letters combine to evoke a lovely desire to be with you—close to you all of the time,—sick or well. I know that my talking of being sick rather suggests a physical weakling needing constant medical attention and, in addition, nursing. Well it isnt quite as bad as that although on this last trip I did catch a cold and was laid up for a few days.[3] Ordinarily I run along briskly enough and make out quite as well as the next one. However I would gladly stage a sick act if I were sure it would get me close to you.

Sweet, your two letters truly are intriguing and wholly delightful. They do make me want to know you ever so much—wholly. I wish I could say I was coming instanter but the last trip has left me facing a score of things to do. Among others I am writing a novel about a Quaker—The Bulwark—and your saying your grandmother was a Quaker & that you look exactly like her, makes me wonder how much you know about the Quaker Social World and whether I might not find your particular knowledge of that wholly delightful and to me most attractive, respectable and ethically distinguished sect of literary use to me.

You see most people today—editors & writers included—know almost nothing of that remarkable body & its history. I became enormously interested in it years ago when I ran accross & read George Fox's Journal. Later I found & read John Woolman's Journal which moved me as nothing since the Gospel according to Matthew ever moved me.[4] Since then I have read various works—the Hicksite Book of Discipline, The Philadelphia or Orthodox Book of Discipline, A History of Friends in America, etc, etc.[5] But the ordinary conduct & social reactions of Friends of say of sixty or seventy years ago are not so easy to discover. The Quaker novels I have read are silly. Mine happens to be the real life drama of a certain Philadelphia family.[6] And now reading this last letter of yours as well as rereading the first one and finding you so mentally and critically aware causes me to feel that in connection with certain aspects of this book—its probabilities here & there—you might be willing to advise me. Do you think you might.

Anyhow and howsoever Sweet, I'm drawn to you. I'd like to be close enough now to take you in my arms and kiss or have you to kiss me or better both. Your really so gifted—that's plain. Your writing reminds me somehow of artful dancing—rich in delicate, graceful balancing & surprise. How favoring & satisfying to me that you ever thought or troubled to write me. Write me soon again—Sweet.

T. D

1015 N. Kings Rd.

1. George Fox (1624–91) founded the Quakers, or Society of Friends, in the 1650s. In 1694 the original manuscript of his *Journal* was published posthumously in two volumes. Selections from it, edited by Rufus M. Jones with the title *George Fox, An Autobiography*, were published in Philadelphia in 1903.

Fox's approach to religion appealed to Dreiser, who never forgot or forgave his father's scrupulous adherence to the rituals and the clerical hierarchy of Roman Catholicism. Fox maintained that every individual could have a direct, personal relationship with God. Therefore every individual could minister. Priests, churches (or "steeple houses" as he called them), and sanctified rites established by canon and doctrine were all rejected. He believed that revelation had not ended and therefore an individual's insights, when prompted by the guidance of the Holy Spirit, took precedence over the Bible, providing they did not contradict its teachings. He viewed the Bible as a valuable reference point but not necessarily as the last word on spiritual matters. He believed the forms and systems of the established churches of his day had become rigid and static, and therefore he refused to institute a new sect, establish a formal liturgy, or build a ministerial organization.

2. Elias Hicks (1748–1830), born fifty-seven years after George Fox died, and like Fox before him, believed every individual was capable of a direct personal relationship with God. Hicks also distrusted theology, was suspicious of higher education, and discounted the importance of doctrine of any kind. He dismissed the concept of the Trinity, thought the matter of the Virgin Birth irrelevant, and that Christ was more than likely the son of Joseph. For Hicks, however, taking an erroneous position on any of these issues would be among the lesser sins. "In regard to our salvation," he wrote in an 1821 letter to Thomas Willis, "they are . . . non-essentials, and I may further say, I believe it would be a much greater sin in me to smoke tobacco that was the produce of the labour of slaves." It was not until his later years that his teachings came to be regarded as heretical and not in accord with the views held by the Quaker founders. Controversy over his teachings led to a split among the Quakers. A separatist branch formed under Hicks's leadership in 1827. The two branches, commonly known as Hicksite and Orthodox, were reunited in 1955.

3. Because he had been feeling weak when he visited Chicago in February 1942, Dreiser went to the Mudlavia Hotel in Attica, Indiana, to take curative baths.

4. John Woolman (1720–72), a zealous member of the Society of Friends who played an important part in the movement against slavery. His *Journal* was published in 1774.

5. Two of the books Dreiser mentions are in his private library: Allen C. Thomas and Richard H. Thomas, *A History of the Friends in America* (Philadelphia: John C. Winston, 1905) and *Discipline of the Yearly Meeting of Friends* (Philadelphia: W. H. Pile's Sons, 1910). Also in his library are Fox's *Journal* (London: E. P. Dutton, 1924) and *The Journal of John Woolman* (Boston: J. R. Osgood, 1871).

Dreiser probably is referring to the Hicksite Edition of *Rules of Discipline* (1888), but it is not part of his existing personal library.

Other books relating to Quakers in Dreiser's library include *Biographical Sketches and Anecdotes of Members of the Religious Society of Friends* (Philadelphia: Tract Association of Friends, 1871) and three titles by Rufus Matthew Jones: *The Later Periods of Quakerism*, vol. II (London: Macmillan, 1921); *Finding the Trail of Life* (New York: Macmillan, 1927); and *The Trail of Life in the Middle Years* (New York: Macmillan, 1934).

6. *The Bulwark* (1946) had its roots in a story he had heard from Anna P. Tatum (1882–1950) in 1912. Dreiser was intrigued by the figure of Tatum's father, a Quaker who struggled to maintain his religious beliefs in an increasingly secular world and whose children tried to reconcile their religious upbringing with the values of modern society. Dreiser started to write the book in 1914, worked on it intermittently over the next thirty years, and finally finished it in 1945, shortly before his death.

To Yvette Szekely [H-DPUP]

Wed. April 29, 42

Yvette Dear:

I'm sorry I didn't write you, but its not for want of thinking of you. I think of you so very often—our various and varied contacts like that last one, or the one out here. I'm working on The Bulwark and it isn't always easy going. No novel is. But I feel I'll get it done in good form. By the way be sure and see My *Gal Sal*—the movie about my brother Paul which is going to be shown there shortly.[1] Its in technicolor and beautifully done. I wrote the script, and by the way I'm in it for about 10 or 15 seconds as a little boy—only they've taken a little slap at me by showing me crying about something. But the thing is clever—terribly. Its amusing, gay, had delightful songs including My Gal Sal, and On the Banks of the Wabash, and its done in technicolor. Rita Hayworth & Victor Mature[2] are the stars—Mature playing Paul, and while they don't follow my text they borrow enough of it to give the right note: the period & the color of the period—the so called Gay Nineties. You'll love it I'm sure. Its too gay and comic and swift in action for you not to.

How's everybody. You. Sue. Clark.[3] Your mother & Clarks boy. I'm wondering if you'd like to use the upper cabin this summer again.[4] If so your welcome. Mr. Levi[5] is staying in his log cabin until May 31 and maybe longer. If you go, tell me how things look up there.

Right now I'm not as well as I ought to be—*intestinal flu* which I had and from which I'm recovering. I found the cure for it but I lost weight and feel weak. I wish I might see you occasionally but I don't like N.Y. anymore and while this place is growing it doesn't attract all of the people I know, and so I have to make new friends here & there as best I can. And then, of course, the war depresses me not a little but it has to be borne.

I hope you're strong and well & keep your old spirit. You stand up better than most. I know that. If I had the money I'd invite you out here but things are too tough for words and the saving days have certainly come.

Love, of course. And thanks for the letters.

D.

What was that comment of yours on life that I liked so much.

1. In 1941 Dreiser had sold the story of Paul Dresser's life to Twentieth Century-Fox for approximately $50,000; it was made into the film *My Gal Sal* (1942).

2. Rita Hayworth (1918–87); Victor Mature (1915–99).

3. Suzanne Szekely, Yvette's younger sister.

Kenneth S. Clark. See Dreiser to Yvette Szekely, 19 March 1941, n. 2.

4. Dreiser is referring to a cabin at his country home at Mt. Kisco.

5. Levi. See Dreiser to Harriet Bissell, 6 May 1939, n. 6.

To Helen Richardson [H-DPUP]

Richardson was visiting her family in Oregon.

Monday-18th–[May 1942]

Dear Helen:

Thanks for your letter about June and yourself. It is inspiriting and beautiful in its mood. I hope her life continues to be strengthened and colored by this faith. I personally have full faith in the ruling, creative and yet—in so far as man can detect—immaterial force that governs all matter and apparently itself. I have come to believe that only as we are granted wisdom by this immaterial force—Karma, Yoga, The Creative Power, are we permitted to know a way of life and so peace. Other than that I cannot see how life manages to proceed.

I am working here as steadily as I can. This My Gal Sal picture[1] has brought a lot of clippings and interviewers & they have taken not a little of my time. Boutnikoff[2] called. Also Friede.[3] Also Lorna[4] & some others. But this palaver will die down as it always does.

Do you expect to return next week or when. I solved the automobile question through an agency which furnishes good men at 50 cents an hour. They have driving licenses and appear to be OK.[5]

Let me hear from you

D—

1. Dreiser is noting the notoriety and publicity that followed the release of the movie, *My Gal Sal* (1942). See Dreiser to Yvette Szekely, 29 April 1942, n. 1.
2. Ivan Boutnikoff (1893–1972), composer and conductor.
3. Donald Friede (1901–65), who formerly had been vice president at Horace Liveright's publishing house, was now a Hollywood agent; he had handled the sale of *My Gal Sal* to Twentieth Century-Fox in 1941. See Dreiser to Yvette Szekely, 29 April 1942, n. 1.
4. Lorna Dysart Smith (1897–1981) met Dreiser in California and worked as a researcher for him.
5. When Helen was gone Dreiser needed a chauffer service to get around, because his driving skills, particularly as he aged, were less than adequate.

To Hazel Godwin

Dreiser and Godwin were planning for a first meeting in Los Angeles sometime in early July.

[H-DPUP]

Saturday [Before 2 July 1942]

Baby Mine:

The first two lines of Chapter one of The Bulwark consist of a quotation from The Song of Solomon. Chapter II - Verse 12. Here they are:

> "The time of the singing of birds is come,
> And the voice of the turtle is heard in
> our land"[1]

The next eight lines consist of quotations—two—from the Friends Book of Discipline,—that issued by the Yearly Meeting of Friends for Pennsylvania, New Jersey, Delaware and The Eastern Parts of Maryland.[2]

And for obvious reasons in connection with us it strikes me as so appropriate, that is if our dream comes true.[3] For I feel such an urge to take the next train and find you and call you away. Only the fact that I know so little about you—your immediate environment, your obligations or ties, as well as certain matters that I have in hand at the moment but probably may be able to sweep aside—deters me. Because truly I would like to know more about you—all that you wish to confide since the words that you write,—the artful, graceful way in which you indicate or imply your thoughts and desires concerning me and yourself or us as we seek to know and understand one another, intrigue and thrill me as much as you say my words to you do you.

For truly I am interested and charmed and delighted entirely by the lovely way you convey your feelings in regard to us—your and my desire to reach each other in love. It isn't only that you come to me frankly with your love and desire but the art of your mind in doing it. It is essentially esthetic and at the same time so gracefully sensual and impassioned. I feel in you as I read—the fascination, intoxication, ravishment, really. And I so wish, as I read that I could materialize you here in the room and take you in my arms and kiss and pet and play with you.—Oh, Kisses! How lovely they are. And when I look at your face in the little picture you sent me—your eyes and mouth and cute nose about your huddled arms,—I burn with a desire to smother you—to blend our mouths in a long satiating union, and more and more, the while I could caress your body in my seeking love of all of you.

And yet as I write and feel this I am never unconscious of the charm of your mind which draws me as intensely to you in that sense. For you seem to have been seeking me out mentally for so long, and finding what I would most have you find—the essence of so many things in Moods,[4] and in my articles and stories. Think of your having found my little essay on *Change*[5] and reading it so many times. And that other on "Temperaments, Artistic and Otherwise."[6] And most gratifying of all to me being arrested by the particular thought you quote "Imagination is the only door to a reality richer than dreamed of by the seekers after material wealth." For to me that is a deep truth that has caused me to ignore the scrambles of the many for the so often crudely materialized ideas of the materialistic seekers after happiness. And its just this temperamental wisdom in you—your exact understanding of the futility of the unaesthetic that draws me to you—and has from the first & will. For I keep saying to myself here is true loveliness of thought and mood, combined with the lure of body and face—and then I grow intensely seeking—and overcome by a physical as well as mental desire to be close and alone with you—just us and our thoughts and desires and giving each to the other all that we have of love and passion,—in quiet and mutual appreciation of our aloneness.

Oh, Sweet! Oh, baby! I feel so keenly that I have found so much in you. And I'm so eager to know more. Write and tell me of yourself—all that you feel you would like to tell. And I will answer any questions that occur to you. As for that week,—If captivation and admiration and the allure with which you have saturated me mean anything—we will hold each other close hour after hour and find relief and satiation and delight and also loving understanding each of the other.

Oh Baby dear—how sweet of you to come and find me! It seems so like you, period. And you are a darling. How I wish we could be together now. Write me soon.

T.D.

1. This quotation appears in italics as an epigraph at the beginning of the "Introduction" to *The Bulwark*. Dreiser took the passage from the King James Version of the Bible. In subsequent translations, the verse is attributed to a passage spoken

by the Bride or the Beloved, and the word "turtle" is rendered as "turtledove" or simply "dove," the bird traditionally associated with the affection between the mating pairs.

2. The "next eight lines," which Dreiser placed in the body of the "Introduction," are quotations from the Quaker marriage vows as spoken by Solon Barnes and Benecia Wallin.

3. The quotations strike him as "appropriate," apparently because his shared "dream" with Godwin is for a romantic union—or, less euphemistically, for a sexual relationship that in fact did begin on July 2. Dreiser was greatly anticipating the event, though his letters to her reveal that he was anxious about its outcome: "Now that you are truly coming and the time draws near I find myself for the first time a little nervous or shy. I've talked so much of desire and fulfillment that although I feel exactly the same as I wrote I have the strangest sense—particularly when I look at your healthy body and confident & assured smile [in photos]—of having talked too much, of being less vigorous than I myself believe. So maybe I'll visit some lusty Saint of the Church and say a few prayers" (Dreiser to Hazel Godwin, 26 May 1942 [DPUP]).

4. Godwin wrote him earlier of her appreciation of his poems in *Moods: Cadenced and Declaimed* (1926; 1928).

5. Dreiser's essay, "Change" first appeared in *Revolt* in 1916, and was reprinted in, among other places, *Hey Rub-A-Dub-Dub* (1920).

6. "Temperaments—Artistic and Otherwise," *The Golden Book Magazine*, 19 (June 1934), 650–54.

To Hazel Godwin [H-DPUP]

Godwin had recently returned home by train after visiting Dreiser in Los Angeles. They had spent eleven days together, staying at a local hotel. On the way back, she stopped in Chicago to visit the Dreiser family burial plots in St. Boniface Cemetery.

Saturday July 18 [1942]

Baby Mine

It was so loving of you to write me from the train, and from Chicago, and to go out to St. Boniface's Cemetery and tell me about the state of Paul's and my mother's grave.[1] I have read and re-read your descriptions of yourself sitting there and meditating on me as connected with them, and once more I feel so keenly the essential tenderness and artistry of all your moods in regard to life and its masses of people in general and in particular.

How you sympathize with weakness and need and how you sorrow over the cruelty or indifference of the strong or prosperous when & where they meet up with the weak and how ready you are to go to the aid of the latter when and where and how you can. There is for me, something very beautiful in this attitude of yours—the unconsciously kindly or forgiving or helpful emotions you manifest to all who are in need or who are ignorant or mentally or physically unable to do better than they do. Somehow, in so much that you say or think, I find the very essence of the Sermon on the Mount—"Blessed are the merciful for they shall obtain mercy; Blessed are the *pure in heart* for they shall see God. Blessed are the peacemakers for they shall be called the children of God."[2] And you try so hard to make and keep peace.

When you left me crying, I felt so keenly and painfully the sweetness and goodness of your whole being. And I wished so much to keep you for myself alone. And had I been able I would have. And when I said dont cry it was not in complaint or reproach, or rebuke but because your grief hurt me so and I wished so much to be able to console you.

And oh! how glad I am that we had those 11 perfect days—not a moment apart, not a single instance of anything other than love—and on my part deep and loving appreciation of your innate spirit. Truly yours is one of the loveliest temperaments I have ever encountered and I wish so much that we could be together. And as sad as I am now, I still feel that we can & will be. But, oh, if you only knew how intensely I feel your absence and how I wish all of those hours & others like them could be renewed at once. I need so much the sweetness of heart that you bring to life and how I would cherish it.

Please write me soon. I am so eager to hear. And as soon as I have the proper address I will mail the picture and the book.

All my love to my wise, kindly, loving humane sweet heart.

D

Figure some practical way Babe to come back & stay. I am trying to do so now. I want to [word missing] with you or at best or worst near you all the time.

Thanks for the Lengel Article.[3] Lots of exaggerations but interesting. Why dont you write him. Separate letter follows immediately. I love you.

1. The songwriter Paul Dresser (1858–1906) was buried originally in New York in a plot owned by the family of Mai Skelly, wife of Dreiser's brother Ed. A year later, in 1907, Dreiser's sister Mame had the body exhumed and shipped to Chicago so that Paul could be buried in St. Boniface's cemetery next to his parents.

2. Dreiser is quoting the King James Version of Matthew 5:7–9.

3. William Lengel. See Dreiser to Kirah Markham, 18 February 1914, n. 10. Lengel wrote an article about his longtime friend in which he tries to reconcile contradictory aspects of Dreiser's character: "The 'Genius' Himself," *Esquire* 10 (September) 1938: 55, 120, 124, 126.

To Thelma Cudlipp [Whitman][1] [HP-DPUP]

In 1933, Thelma Cudlipp, by then the widow of Edwin Grosvenor, had married Charles Symour Whitman (1868–1947), who had been governor of New York (1915–18). In her letters from her home in Richmond, Virginia, she had confided to Dreiser the details of her problematic marriage to Whitman, telling him of a diary she had kept of her unhappy marital relations. She also discussed the case that propelled Whitman from the District Attorney's office to the governorship: the trial and conviction of police lieutenant Charles Becker for criminal corruption and murder. Her stories interested Dreiser and led him to reflect on his own preoccupation with the psychology of the criminal mind and its representations in literature.

Sat. Aug 1–42

Dear Thelma:

Yours of July 26 is certainly an interesting and revealing letter and the story of the District attorney and his admiration of the criminal he finds himself called upon to prosecute would make a powerful novel and—possibly—an arresting play—but the play is and will remain a limited medium. Often enough, even in a play, a wealth of material can be suggested, but the novel is the *one* medium in which we can set forth the psychology and psychiatry of those very strange and sensitive creatures called humans. In particular, I think it is best for these—their desires and repulsions, their blood instincts often so poorly modified or controlled by inherited inhibitions or environing forces—more often furthered and incited by environing conditions. And these require the novel much more than the play or movie. As I wrote you once, I began a study of the Molineaux case and his prosecuting attorney because I saw just such a temperamental complex as you outline.[2] However, coming accross the Clyde Griffiths case—the social contrasts it illustrated and emphasized, I turned to that and am not sorry.[3] The other may still be done—maybe.

But what you tell me about Whitman & yourself interests me. What illusion drew you to so dark a temperament? One glance and I knew I could never like him. In fact—without data—I sensed the sinister and self-involved. Your diary! That must be interesting. Knowing something of your temperament at 18, I marvel at this illusion of a later period. Obviously an honest diary such as you would keep would be revealing. A second illusion of some kind might be still more startling.

As for Richmond, I stopped there for a time but moved on to Florida—Palm Beach, Miami, Ft. Lauderdale. Of all that I saw I preferred Ft. Lauderdale—its bay, its Everglades River, Harry Thaws housed & forgotten yacht, rotting under the forgotten shelter of a hanger that he built for it. And the money that paid for it taken from deluded slaves trundling iron at 1^{50} a day. I worked for the Pittsburgh Dispatch at the time and saw the ruthless profit system at its peak. The yacht was worth—I hear—$150,000.[4]

No, I'm afraid I can't get to Richmond. Los Angeles is a new and lunatic market, but vivid. I spend nearly 40 years in New York climbing from hall bedrooms to a country place—but it galled at last. Too hot in summer, too raw in winter. Out here I can wear a summer suit the year round. And since weather makes a difference to me I'm afraid—for the time being, I'll have to stick. There are rumors that I'm rich but it just doesn't happen to be so. Besides, as you know—you can be famous & still be poor. Witness one Wm Shakespeare, actor. Also Beethoven—musician.

As to that diary of yours—since you chance to mention it—I wish I might see it. It sounds educational as well as dramatic,—very.

Again I think some one out here—one of these endless script writers would be pleased to dramatize the Becker-Whitman complex.[5] But without your consent I would never mention it. Nor will anyone ever see your letter without your written concent. Even so it would be best—assuming you wished to see the story dramatized,—to first have it redictated and then submitted—the authors name omitted, of course. It's too bad I can't have another personal talk with you. I think we would have an interesting conversation. Anyhow, here's a pleasant month to you in N.Y. And all my good wishes.

Affectionately
T.D

1015 N. King's Rd. Hollywood

1. See Dreiser to Thelma Cudlipp, 21 July 1910, headnote.

2. The case of Roland Burke Molineaux (1866–1917) had once struck Dreiser as the source material for a novel. In 1899 Molineaux, a chemist and a wealthy New Yorker, was put on trial for poisoning his rival for the favors of Mrs. K. J. Adams. He was sentenced to death and spent twenty months in Sing Sing, but he was acquitted on appeal in 1902. He wrote a play in prison called "The Man Inside," which David Belasco produced. Molineaux later had a nervous breakdown and spent the last four years of his life in the New York State Hospital for the Insane. In 1915 Dreiser had begun a novel, "The Rake," based on Molineaux's career; he completed only six chapters before abandoning the project. Dreiser wrote to Cudlipp of this elsewhere: "Speaking of Prosecuting Attorneys and Criminals I once started a novel on that very topic—a celebrated N. Y. murder case—but dropped it to write An American Tragedy. My opinion then—1916—coincided with yours of today. A choice between the two is—to me—difficult" (Dreiser to Thelma Cudlipp, 21 June 1942 [DPUP]). See Kathryn M. Plank, ed., *The "Rake"* in *Papers on Language & Literature*, 27, no. 2 (Spring 1991): 140–73.

3. Dreiser eventually became interested in the 1906 murder of Grace Brown by Chester Gillette, which became the basis for the story of Clyde Griffiths and Roberta Alden in *An American Tragedy*.

4. Dreiser is referring to Harry K. Thaw (1871–1947), the millionaire playboy who in 1906 killed architect Stanford White (1852–1906) for allegedly seducing Thaw's wife. As in the case of Molineaux, Thaw was eventually acquitted and spent the last years of his life following a pattern of commitment to and release from various mental asylums. Dreiser here recalls his time in Pittsburgh as a young reporter when he had become aware of the role men such as Thaw and Andrew Carnegie played in creating terrible living conditions for workers in the steel mills.

5. Whitman revealed to his wife that he had in ways admired Charles Becker (1869–1916), even as he was prosecuting him. The case made headlines in 1915. Herman Rosenthal, a notorious gambler, charged police Lieutenant Becker with blackmailing him for protection. Before Whitman could interrogate Rosenthal, the gambler was killed by gangsters in what is considered one of the first drive-by shootings in America. Whitman went on a crusade to clean up the corruption in the police department and eventually convicted Becker. Elected as governor that year, he refused to stay the execution of Becker, who was subsequently electrocuted.

Dreiser's interest in Charles Becker has a number of literary precedents. In Chapter IV of *The Great Gatsby*, Wolfsheim tells Gatsby and Nick Carraway the story of the night "Rosy Rosenthal" was shot. When Nick says he remembers that four men were electrocuted for the shooting, Wolfsheim responds, "Five, with Becker." Before Fitzgerald, Stephen Crane made news with Becker. In 1896, Crane came to the aid of a prostitute whom Becker was trying to shake down, and the subsequent court case received much attention in the press.

To Hazel Godwin [H-DPUP]

Dreiser was preparing to leave for Canada, where he was scheduled to speak at the Toronto Town Forum on the political aspects of the World War in a speech billed as "Democracy on the Offensive." The theme of the lecture was to be the possibility of an Allied invasion of Europe, which would relieve the German military pressure on the Soviet Union—a measure that Dreiser strongly favored.

Sept. 13–42

Hazel Babe:

I recieved two more lovely letters from you on *Labor Day*—yesterday—in spite of the fact that the PO announced there would be no deliveries. And in them you were entirely unaware that my speaking date, on which I tell the poor Canadians how much I love England, had been changed from November 30th next to *Sept 21st* next Monday evening.[1] I leave here on the same train you did—*Union Pacific* at 8^{05} p.m. and I'll arrive at your Toronto Station (I assume) at the same time you did—three days and some hours later.[2] Anyhow I speak on the evening or night of the 21st. At the train (I assume) Bertha Cowan, Secretary of the *Toronto Town Forum* will meet me.

The Secretary usually does & tells me what room has been engaged at what hotel etc. Also what local newspaper men—if any—are waiting to interview me. Usually—since it is well known that I am a Soviet Scoundrel, trying to wreck our charming and kindly capitalistic system—none. When they are waiting it is with the intention of roasting me—or mis-interpreting what I say. At that, sometimes, I get the best of them. I kid them so that they get sore & in writing me up give themselves away—their bias and private rage. They have no ammunition that worries me. That is why I wonder why I am invited to Toronto for I plan to roast the English beef as I always do. If they want to take me to the border—afterwards and throw me out into the night, that's their business.[3] You'll have to decide whether or not you want me to go alone or not.

Furthermore, Sweet, I see no reason why you shouldn't be at the train—or if you cant make that, at the hall. I'll introduce you as an old friend of the family—not aged but just old enough, like they used to say of "*Ann*." Remember that "How old is Ann" joke? The answer always was—in my day—*old enough*.

Incidentally I have a communication to make. The letter in which you said you were on your knees, praying,—or might be—was opened by the censor.[4] Boy, what a nice job these censors have! And they get paid for it!—When things get tough over here—too bad—no bread in the cupboard, I'm going to try and get a job as a censor. Imagine sitting back & reading hot mail all day. Ah! Is that the life?—Answer—That is the life.

Seriously you must be thinking of how we are to do. I'm willing to go to one standard hotel for an hour or so after I arrive, but after that I'd like an idea for somewhere. I wouldn't mind how humble the cot if only I didn't have to be alone. And I'm willing to pay for the cot. But beyond that, in a strange city, I cant think. Or maybe I can. For instance in Toronto do they have any *Motels*? If so why couldnt we drive to a Motel and sell the poor owner the idea that we wanted a room for the night or the week? In those places you can stay as long as you choose. What about it? Answer at once or tell me when I get there.

You write such soft, coaxing, loving letters. You give me the feeling of real loving—physical and mental. But Babe—I have visitors connected with Warner Brothers & I have to stop. But I'll write more tomorrow. Wont we have a delicious time together when I get there.

Kisses and squeezes. My arms are around you tight.

D

1. As it turned out, the ticket demand was so large that the talk was postponed until the following evening, 22 September.

2. Godwin had taken this route after her July visit to Los Angeles.

3. Dreiser's anti-English comments in fact led to something close to what he had jokingly anticipated. At a press conference on 21 September, reporters interrupted him with references to previous disparaging statements he had made about Winston Churchill and England. He responded angrily and injudiciously. The following morning the *Toronto Evening Telegram* reported him saying that he hoped Germany invaded England to rid the country of "those damn, aristocratic, horse-riding snobs there now." He accused Churchill of sending innocent Canadians to their deaths. The furor was such that the speech was cancelled and, fearing seizure by the authorities, Dreiser boarded a train with Godwin and fled over the border to Michigan.

4. President Roosevelt made use of the War Powers Act of 1941 to sign Executive order 8985, creating the Office of Censorship and conferring on its director the power to censor international communications. These included films and photographs, maps and recordings, as well as the mail. Because Godwin lived in Canada, her letters were subject to the scrutiny of the censors.

To Hazel Godwin [H-DPUP]

Although Godwin was more reluctant to continue corresponding with Dreiser after the Toronto incident, she and Dreiser began discussing the possibility of her coming to live in Los Angeles. The question of how she would support herself was a consideration that led him to investigate wartime employment opportunities in the area.

Tuesday Nov. 17 [1942]

Hi-Baby Darling:

Its so nice to hear from you and to write you. You have a temperament that truly appeals to me. I think I'd have a hard time setting it forth in a book—its so genuinely sweet, and tolerant and understanding and comforting—like a warm electric pad or blanket to a person with a chill. You do not allow your broad sensitive mind to range over many topics either in your letters or your conversation, but when you do I can see range and the force and the sweetness of your understanding—its thorough grasp of so many things. And yet you confine yourself so often to telling how good a housekeeper you are—how everything is kept in order and how good a cook you are. Baby your so frank and unpretending and loving & kind that you'd make any sick man or woman well just by being around them. You mean to do good in the world and you do do good. I can sense it in your brief confessions as to this and that. As for me I'm in the main a bad egg—selfish, self-centered, interested in large problems which concern the welfare of millions but fail to take into consideration the poor failure at his doorstep. And that is very bad. I can see it clearly—the Lone Wolf complex. And yet I love & respect those who, like you, do look after the individual as well as the mass.

And do you know your dear sweet naked body is like that. When I hold it and pet your soft flesh I can feel in my reactions to your delicious reactions to me all the above things that I have been saying about you. They are woven into your flesh & your bone by nature. No wonder I love to draw you close & play with you—your soft breasts and thighs and to turn you this way & that & kiss you and satisfy myself and you hour after hour & day after day. What a play baby. And how happy you are & how happy you make me feel,—sweetie pie.

Well I've been looking into this woman's pay matter for women working for the government. Any woman or girl who applies to Lockheed for work—or most of the other big plants here, gets it: no training is needed *if* a person is capable of being trained to do any one of a score of jobs. Unless the applicant really knows a certain line of work he or she is accepted but subject to six weeks training. The applicant gets 70^{cts} an hour for an 8 hour day. This is around $\$33^{00}$ per week. Once trained she is removed to the branch of the factory which uses the type of labor for which she has been trained. Her pay is jumped to $\$1^{00}$ an hour and he or she can stay on for the duration! I get this from two employees of Lockheed,—a man and a woman. The man needed no training & went to work at 1^{00} an hour. The woman took 6 weeks training and is now getting $\$1^{00}$ an hour. So there you have it. When I get more direct testimony I'll let you know. There are no deductions for the war. You are not compelled to buy or subscribe to anything.

Baby I'm in a hurry today so I'll have to quit. But I wish I had you here where I could play with you as we did at the Mayfair.[1] Remember the table? And your soft warm thighs spread out wide for me in the bed—my hand on your sweet belly.

D.

1. Dreiser and Godwin had stayed at the Mayfair Hotel in Los Angeles during her visit the previous July.

To Hazel Godwin [H-DPUP]

Saturday [After 19 November 1942]

Hazel Sweet—

This is my answer to your letter of the 19th. However there was a letter on the way to you from me when I recieved yours of the 19th so that my wish to write often is fairly well maintained. Anyhow this past week has been income tax week for me—reviewing and reporting all items of income and expenditure which are not large but various—very. And Im

no book-keeper—one of the worst. The best I do is to throw all bills and demands and requests in a box and answer them when I can and pay them when I can. And then after 12 months comes this thing—always a week's work or more for me and no one who understands them or would other than myself and as well as myself. So I actually slave over the damned box from 9 a.m. to six p.m. taking off time for lunch. And calculating—adding up and subtracting figures always gives me a headache. So you know how at least one week has gone for me. I've been trying to be a book-keeper. As for your letters they always give me the feeling that you truly like to write me and tell what's going on with you. And since you took that government job—preparing defense implements—I have been doubly interested because you not only write about your private life but that government work about which I know nothing except what I read in the papers and what Berkley Tobey and his wife occasionally report about Douglas—principally that its hard work.[1] But you write about the human side of everything you do; the men, the women, the nature of some of the work at least. The friends you made, how interested you are to do what you do—so that I could almost make an article out of your letters—and a charming one at that. In fact you unconsciously present yourself for the honest industrious, friendly fair minded person that you are. And all this apart from our personal relationship which comes into the picture somewhat like a frame that holds it all. And so—well that's why I delight so to recieve and read one of yours. Yet how mine affect you I cannot tell.

But, before I forget it—did you ever hear anything more about *A Gallery of Women*.[2] If not I intend to buy and register another set. And here's another thing. Why do you go back to *The "Genius"* written about 1912[3] and covering partially data up to the 35th year of my life to find things to be jealous about? Supposing I were permitted to study the details of your life up to say 30—or 35. Then what? Would I be jealous? And would it benefit me any to be made so? You repeat that you are very jealous. And the last repetition seems to refer to my account of my present relationship. Yet my thought was that—since I presented the case as is,—that you would have no cause for jealousy. For my working life is certainly a thing apart from romance. In fact its more like shop work than anything else in my life—entirely removed from my affections and so requiring for me some one whose affections do not intrude on me. I found that out in the case of my deceased wife and years & years ago in this instance. So much so that one time—1927–32—I took an outside office in a great bank building & removed all my working data—some 8 trunks in order to have to be able to concentrate and not be bothered by anyone.[4] The great depression—climaxing about 1932—forced me to condense my living arrangements—cut expenses to the bone—which necessitated the present & less expensive form of living. But only for that reason. Where & when jealousy should begin I cant see—only the human breast is so doubting always, and will be in this case I assume.

Yet you are living with your husband & I think nothing of that. I did for a while because peoples moods are likely to soften or harden by hours & so—if I permitted myself the irritation it would arouse, I might start thinking of that but I cant because I believe you and will continue to do so because I have the conviction you are truly truthful. Besides I care and that makes—in this instance—not for jealousy but for desire . . . SO.

But Hazel Babe, a visitor—a literary agent no less—is now ringing my door bell, so I stop this letter & write you more Monday—a love letter—not a discourse like this. And your letters are always so loving. Wish I might stay with you tonight.

D.

1. Berkeley Greene Tobey (1877–1962), who had known Dreiser since their Greenwich Village days in 1914, when Tobey was managing editor of the *Masses*. Tobey married Esther McCoy in 1941. (For McCoy see Dreiser to Esther McCoy, 9 July 1924, headnote.) The couple lived in Santa Monica, California, where Douglas Aircraft was building DC-4 airplanes for the military. On the night before Dreiser's death, Helen Dreiser asked McCoy to keep a vigil with her; and McCoy remained there until he died. She wrote about the experience in "The Death of Dreiser," *Grand Street* (Winter 1988): 73–85.

2. Dreiser had sent the two volumes of *A Gallery of Women* (1929), but the set had been lost in the mail. He eventually sent another that reached her.

3. Dreiser finished the first version of *The "Genius"* in 1911 (at the time the title did not contain quotation marks); he revised it in 1914 for the first edition of 1915.

4. Dreiser's wife, Sara White Dreiser, had died recently, on 1 October 1942. In 1927–32, he was living with Helen Richardson in the Rodin Studios at 200 West Fifty-seventh Street. His working office was in the Manufacturer's Trust Building on Columbus Circle.

1943

To Hazel Godwin [H-DPUP]

Feb 16 [1943]

Hazel Babe—

Your last letter, love you as I do, sets me thinking. By the way, *Plays of the Natural and the Supernatural*[1] in 1 volume *are* in the mail (were two days ago)—insured for $\$20^{00}$ so I fancy they'll arrive or I'll collect $\$20^{00}$. But I'd rather you'd read them & tell me what you think of each and every one than collect $\$40^{00}$ or $\$60^{00}$ even. Because you have not only an esthetic reaction that is that of the writer but an honest reaction, which I am sorry to state is by no means common to all writers. (And in connection with that *all* I include myself.) For it requires not only amazing courage but sheer *Genius* to be honest—truly *honest*. And so often, in looking back on myself, my life, my writings, I wonder. Not that I don't desire to be honest (who doesn't?) but to step forward and say for all the world to see—I lied! I stole! I evaded my sworn obligations! I am willing to pay the penalty in a court of law—how many are willing to do that? *I? You? My friend? My lover?* Ah me! Ah me! George Fox, the founder of Quakerism, wrote of "*The Inner Voice*" which guides us all. But how many heed it? And yet Quakerism—the *Society of Friends* is the most beautiful religion in the world to me. To me it is the only honest, self-sacrificial religion. Only read the Friends *Book of Discipline*.[2] It is so beautiful. And yet you & I—or I and you would find it hard to live up to. *It is so Exacting! So difficult. And yet I love it so.* And it struck me at the very first that a descendent of Quakers should write me. And want love and sensual satisfaction—as do I through you. And yet George Fox and John Woolman, how they would frown—these two authors of two of the loveliest and most truthful *Journals*[3] that have ever been written—these and the autobiography of Jean Jacques Rousseau.[4] Get them and read them. Fox and Woolman as set over against Jean Jacques Rousseau. I love them all. I think they constitute great gifts to the world.

As for you—I am unregenerate. I would like to be as I was with you here & in Detroit. George Fox and John Woolman would not approve of us. And they would be beautiful and saintly in their disapproval. Yet, evil as I may be, according to George Fox or John Woolman, how I would like to have you here now—in bed—or in the bath, in the chair—loving and kissing hour after hour—day after day. What the devil is it—a chemic-physical and irresistible pull?—

What I don't understand is why you don't move out here? Your work is so hard. Besides you are gifted. People like you—*fall* for you. I know it. And yet at the risk of your health & strength and although you are American born[5] & really like America—there you stick. And this is your native land! (I'll admit that *in connection with all this* there is a certain element of selfish, sneaky, sensual desire and hope of self gratification but just the same isn't there some of that in you?) Oh, your *magnetic flesh*! Your *shapely thighs*! *Your breasts! Your rich mind and temperament*! And most certainly, if your husband means so little to you, you could do as well here as there. And in a climate of which you could not complain. At this moment I am sitting in a hammock—a folding table in front of me—the sun shining in this court and writing you & you write me concerning the cold, the strain, the this, the that. But each day sees endless ads calling for workers at 90 cents an hour. And you could be near me and I near *you*. Oh Sweet Jesus! Baby! That lovely magnetic sensuality of yours!

And soon the years will be over—the three score years and ten! And that's all—for me & for you.

What about it Babe? Why the devil am I so drawn to you. Tell me that—if we should not be together.

D

1. Dreiser's *Plays of the Natural and the Supernatural* was first published in 1916 by the John Lane Company; but he is probably sending Godwin a copy of the 1926 reprint issued by Boni and Liveright.
2. *Discipline of the Yearly Meeting of Friends*. See Dreiser to Hazel Godwin, 22 March 1942, n. 5.
3. See Dreiser to Hazel Godwin, 22 March 1942, nn. 1 and 5.
4. The *Confessions* (1781; 1788) of Jean Jacques Rousseau (1712–78), French political philosopher and writer.
5. Godwin was born in New Hampshire.

To Thelma Cudlipp [Whitman] [HP-DPUP]

Thelma Cudlipp Whitman had sent Dreiser a personal diary detailing her courtship and unhappy marriage to Charles Seymour Whitman. See Dreiser to Thelma Cudlipp Whitman, 1 August 1942, headnote.

THEODORE DREISER

Feb 23rd–'43

Dear Thelma:

Well I have read the summary of your amazing relationship with CSW. And when I think of the love mood or reaction that ordinarily draws the sexes together and then contemplate a result such as this I marvel that such an error could occur, and if so,—why? For in this instance CSW appears not to have cared for you at all and wasted no time in showing that to be true. On the other hand, without some demonstration of affection on his part I cannot see how you could have gone forward to the altar. Or were you so personally fascinated and intrigued by him as to ignore his obvious indifference?

The manuscript is truly an enigma to me. What a far cry from it to romance—even the shadow of it. The whole approach of the—shall I call him *lover*, it seems so cold and material. And—looking back on youth—imagine material things playing so large and ignominious a role in the field of affections! I still cannot gather how it was that you were drawn to him. Therein—for me—lies the enigma. I can see, of course, your million dollars attracting him and many another. But—kind heaven—what an experience! And what a world! You have, truly, my sympathy and I only hope a divorce will give you freedom from such a pestilential atmosphere.

Regards
Th. D.

I fancy you wish the MS back in your hands & so I am forwarding it—registered.

To Hazel Godwin [H-DPUP]

Sunday May 9–43

Hazel Sweet:

I'm writing because I want to write you. I'm not feeling so very scrum this a.m. although as to sunshine & sky its perfect outside. Inside me, for some reason my sensations dont match that. Rather I feel sickish and glum and yet I know for sure that if right now I were told by you over the telephone from some where around here that I was to meet you in a half or three quarters of an hour to be with you for the day, my internal ills would cease. I would be cured—I'm positive of it. But sitting here and being sure that you wont call me and that I wont be. There will be no miracle.

Just the same Baby—I want to write you. I know your up and around and possibly, having some pleasant contacts—you should have. And I'm glad of that but I miss not seeing you and so the day dont help me any. And wont, I fear, unless something comes up to drive this feeling away.

Last night because of several appeals, I addressed what is known here as *The Severance Club*[1]—agency of intellectuals—architects, scientists, historians, writers, poets—about 150 in all. Its the 1st time I've spoken since I addressed the Business Mens Chambers of Commerce here not long after you left. The Club President suggested an address on a topic I chose—but hating long addresses unless I'm deeply stirred by a particular ill, I worked until I reached the club and ate the dinner it provided and then when called upon to speak I arose and said I couldn't [word missing] of a topic at the moment worthy of a long talk—but if any or all chose to ask a question I'd see what I could do as to that. Fortunately enough they all fell in with the idea. A few even applauded! Then came the questions—political, social, economic, personal—as when one person asked to know why I was thrown out of Canada![2] Well I answered all in turn for about an hour and a half and you never saw a happier or gayer audience. They laughed & even cheered at times—principally because I pulled no punches and said exactly what I felt about Russia, Italy, England, our miserably misused coal miners, our corporations, multimillionaires—our kept—or rather prostitute press, etc. Some even got down to my books! What I thought of them. All hung on so that finally the chairman insisted I had to be released which merely resulted in all swarming and seeking but by no means in all instances succeeding in shaking my hand—for the chairman & one other man helped me get loose. I had to laugh myself truly to see the way they pushed each other around & out of the way. No courtesies at all! What interested me most was to see in the audience here & there Hindus, Chinese, Negroes and Latins from So. America. Also a Burmese woman whose skin was of a very dark walnut shade, and whose head, body, hands were perfectly beautiful and in addition an intellectual of the 1st order as our short conversation proved. She said she had left Burma just before the Japanese invasion and was intending to stay here unless the Japanese were driven out.[3] Her appearance indicated of course that she had money (probably plenty) to do just that. But her features & her mind were really so arresting—I felt beautiful. She gave me her name but I didn't take it down & now I cant remember it—not correctly.

But as for you Sweet, I wished truly you might have been there. It was so interesting & I know you would have liked it. It was not only interesting as to the variety of subjects but the way in which, at times, I had to clarify my statements and then dissipate the denials of some of them by those who fancied that I did not know what I was talking about. Lucky for me was the fact that I did.

But, oh sweet, how I wish you were here today. We could take the car & you could drive me out to the ocean. We might even take shorts & go in bathing. On the beach a pair of shorts for a man and the same for a girl plus of course for the girl a brassiere—is all that is needed. You see them lying about in the sand or on a blanket & hugging & kissing to all but the limit. I think presently public copulation will become common. We certainly are moving in that direction. In that case—Baby—well I fancy we might find the custom irresistible. It is actually common at Blackpool.[4] And I have seen instances of it on the beaches of Staten Island, NY—in June & July. Write me.

Love and Kisses
D.

1. The Los Angeles Severance Club was a cultural conversation group, named in honor of Caroline M. Severance (1820–1914) who worked for women's rights, the abolition of slavery, and educational reform.

2. See Dreiser to Hazel Godwin, 13 September 1942, n. 3.

3. The Japanese invasion of Burma began on 11 December 1941. Conquering Burma had strategic value for the Japanese because it gave them easier access to both China and India.

4. Dreiser is referring to Blackpool Pleasure Beach, an amusement park established in 1896 on the coast of the Irish Sea, located in the town of Blackpool, Lancashire County, England.

To Helen Richardson [H-DPUP]

Helen Richardson was in Portland attending to her ailing mother.

Sunday [23 August 1943]

Dear Helen:

The matter of *Mame* & Sylvia—(the $\$5,000$ & $\$1,000^{oo}$) is all straightened out. I went down to the U.S. Income Department for 1941 as ordered & met a Mr. Smith who looked at my accounts & said he could assure me the government would take no action. I explained the general situation as best I could. He said he felt that Mame was entitled to her $\$5000$; Syl to her $\$1000$—you to your share & I to mine & so that case was closed.[1]

Then he took up the Simon & Schuster affair and when I explained that they had sold my entire stock of old books in order to pay me the advance they made me while exacting a new novel to assure them of a profit on the deal, he declared that the $\$8000^{oo}$ paid them should be written off as in no sense due the government from me.[2] In fact he declared the whole accounting for 1941 correct, said that the share *allotted you* by yourself was correct that I need not contemplate any further bother from the government.[3]

So there you are.

Skelton, the roomer, over the garage has left.[4] He came in this a.m. (Sunday Morning) saying he had to leave at once for duty. Incidentally he handed me a check of $\$8^{oo}$ saying that $\$2.^{oo}$ of it was for a window he broke & which he was told could be replaced for 2^{oo}.

Toby and Esther[5] both phoned Saturday noon—saying they were leaving for *Ensanada* Mexico and that they had arranged with Leo Gallagher[6] to let himself, his wife & child occupy their place pending their return. Esther said I might come out & stay with the Gallaghers & child, occasionally, but I declined.—Edgar Lee Masters writes that he thinks Esther's book is a masterpiece.[7] I have not heard from Mencken, yet. All goes as well as might be expected. I keep the icebox fairly well supplied. Clare Kummer[8] called up to ask where you were & I told her. She said that she had heard that Fox-West Coast was interested in a movie somewhat like yours & wanted *you* to investigate. I told her to write you. An hour later an envelope looking like the one you sent West Coast Fox arrived & I am holding it pending your arrival. As for Putnams and *The Bulwark*, I have decided to stop on that & write,—*instead*—"*A Literary Apprenticeship*"[9] for which I have all the material and which I can write or dictate with ease. If they do not want it I will send back the \$2000[00] advance they made me & offer the book (A Literary Apprenticeship) and the privilege of publishing a complete set of my books to some other firm. You can get up the letter if you choose.

It is very hot here every day. I'm glad that you are where it is cooler and also that your mother is better. I hope she regains her health completely.

Regards to Myrtle,[10] you & your mother. Love to all. This heat keeps me down not a little. The new pool draws not only birds but humming birds—but the gardener says that if I want to have any fish in the pool I will have to shoot the "*fish crane*" which come every day to see if any fish are to be had.

D.

1. In 1941 Dreiser had received money from the sale of the script of *My Gal Sal* to 20th Century Fox, and he had also received royalties from the Paul Dresser estate, which held the copyrights to Paul Dresser's songs. He had to explain to the tax agent that he had split the funds with Helen, and his sisters Mame and Sylvia—and brother Ed, though he is not mentioned here.

2. In the ongoing battle with Simon & Schuster, Dreiser maintained that the firm had sold his works to second-hand bookmen to avoid paying him royalties. He had paid the company over \$8,000 in 1941 (from the profits of his sale of *My Gal Sal*) in order to be released from his contract, and was now claiming this as an expense against his income for the year.

3. Helen was given a share of his earnings because in 1926, with the windfall from *An American Tragedy*, Dreiser had created a holding company called Author Royalties to handle his finances. Helen was president, he was vice president, and each of them drew a salary. The tax-man had presumably judged that individual as well as a corporation tax had been paid.

4. Trying to make ends meet, Dreiser had rented a room above his garage to Mr. Skelton, who had now been called into the armed services.

5. Berkeley Greene Tobey and Esther McCoy. See Dreiser to Hazel Godwin, [(After 19 November 1942), n. 1] .The couple had a cottage in Ensenada, Mexico.

6. Leo Gallagher (1887–1963), a Los Angeles lawyer who specialized in labor law. Throughout his career he was involved in progressive politics and defended the rights of labor unionists, activists, communists, minorities, and the poor.

7. The book that Masters praised is a collection of stories McCoy had sent to H. L. Mencken in 1943, for which both Dreiser and Masters wrote endorsements.

8. Clare Kummer. See Dreiser to Clare Kummer, 28 June 1934, headnote.

9. Dreiser had signed up with Putnam, which wanted to publish *The Bulwark*. Having difficulty writing the novel, Dreiser offered the publisher instead "A Literary Apprenticeship," a book that Dreiser planned to be the third volume of his autobiography, following *Dawn* and *Newspaper Days*. Putnam showed no interest in a memoir of his early days as a writer.

10. Myrtle: Helen's sister.

To Hazel Godwin [H-DPUP]

Sunday-[September 1943]

Hazel Dearest:

Well, I'm up and around after a fashion. But do you know that apart from the chest cold which I had but which is now considerably reduced, and the arthritic pains also—I've developed nerves—things which have never troubled me to speak of in the past. And yet just now they seem to be up and doing. And they evoke a sense of dread or fear in regard to myself as a whole. Suddenly the ability to write or evoke in myself a desire to write, to go on with The Bulwark or in fact anything in the way of work that is before me is up the chimney. I seem to have lost, for the time being anyhow, the creative desire to work even though I am up. And yet I have a lot of things to do if I could—as you know. And I cant even bring myself to think of them. I either lie or sit and think about what might well happen to me if I cant pull myself together and go on. *The Bulwark*, a movie outline of The "Genius" etc. etc. I can sit or lie and think of you all right—the delicious days you were here. But now! Its such a disrupting change. And yet medicine does not seem to do much for me. The best I can do is to write you and even then not so easily. Only not because I dont want to. Its because my right hand is stiff—hard to close and move a pencil easily. And yet I have such nice letters from you. And I wish I could answer them at once, only, as I say—this feeling of weariness! And my aches and pains. My Doctor West now recommends Oreton[1] only I have yet to try it.

Please dont be troubled about my not writing you, for it isnt for not wanting to. But I must get out of this lassitude or else a lot of things that need to be worked on are going to lie just where they are—a situation that can cause me trouble.

But as for you and me,—we're joined in my mind. I go over all the hours. Perhaps I shouldn't, no doubt. I, like many others, expect too much of life.

But I cant fight the desire to dream them over again and meantime please wish me health & strength and that we meet soon again.

I sent the purse of course.[2] And enclosed is the registry slip. Let me know if it doesn't show up. And if it doesn't send the receipt back & I'll trace it here. Oh you! And all those happy bygone hours.

D.

1. A male hormonal drug, probably recommended to treat Dreiser's fatigue and weakness.

2. A gift that he had promised to send her.

To Hazel Godwin [H-DPUP]

Monday Oct. 18/19 [1943]

Babe Dearest:

This morning came your book—that is Hamlin Garland's *40 Years of Psychic Research.*[1] I have begun reading it and find it fascinating. I knew Hamlin Garland in Chicago. Have stopped over at his house and talked over many things. So you can see how interested I am—much because the topic interests me and as much that I get the book through you. Because it is just one more proof of your sturdy intellect—the wide and arresting range of your mental interests. I keep thinking all of the time that because of the evidence you have given me of your mental range that you must write because you will interest people, for one thing is sure—no thinking person could spend a dull hour with you.

As for me Im around and writing but I feel just so-so—and I find I must drive myself to my table. Besides, as things are with me now, I'm more or less lonely—not having the companionship I desire. Not that I don't see people. Various individuals call up and ask to be allowed to stop in around five or five thirty and if I like them well enough I let them come. But still I am not always interested, clever though they be. I like Esther and Toby[2] well enough and they stop in about once every two weeks. Then there are writers & agents like Sam Watters, John Howard Lawson, Donald Friede, Al Manuel[3]—a long list really—but I dont see them much even though I like them. Mainly it requires time & money & just now Im not feeling fit enough. But I do see a few—three or four every week. One of my best bets is Esther & Toby because singly or together both are interesting. Esther is writing a really striking novel which should sell when published.

Oct 19

Last night stopped here for I had to read up on *Banking*—a subject which plays a strong part in my novel.[4] I have three books from the library on the subject. Then this a.m. came your *Company K*[5] which I know—because of the value of all the other things you have sent me—will be good reading just as is Hamlin Garland's book. To me that is really thrilling for I have had psychic experiences of my own—such as seeing a materialized hand operate a typewriter and throw out a score or two of typewritten messages to people who were in the audience but had not given their names. Yet their names were typed on the messages! Also I *saw* the coat of a man whose arms as well as the rest of his chest & back were wound round with a clothes-line turned inside out & put back on him again! I saw that for I was standing not more than 3 feet away from him & the bench on which he was sitting. So Hamlin Garland's book merely confirms what I saw.

Dearest, the exciting dream I had of you and about which I wrote you hasn't been repeated so realistically. But I've thought of the real relations between us over & over & continue to think of them. And they will be repeated when I am on my feet financially & physically. Meanwhile I am loving & playing with you as much as ever. By the way the two sketches have gone to the editor I spoke of.[6] So we'll see what he says. Yet regardless of what he says they are most interesting and entertaining & I wish you'd do two more about 2500 hundred words each.

Meanwhile—love & kisses.

D

I thought afterwards—maybe that last letter was a little too brash. Was it?

1. The novelist Hamlin Garland (1860–1940) had a life-long interest in psychic phenomena, the history of which he recorded in *Forty Years of Psychic Research* (1936). Dreiser's library contains a copy of the book in a 1937 Macmillan edition. For Dreiser's life-long interest in this subject, see Dreiser to Kirah Markham, 9 February 1914, n. 1. Dreiser admired Garland's early realistic fiction set in the rural Midwest, and in 1912–13 the two men had met when Dreiser went to Chicago for research on *The Titan*. Garland's later conservatism and negative response to Dreiser's literary rendering of sexuality cut off any further contact.

2. Esther and Tobey: see Dreiser to Hazel Godwin, Saturday [After 19 November 1942], n. 1.

3. Sam Watters, a literary agent

John Howard Lawson (1894–1977), playwright and screenwriter in Hollywood who was active in the Communist Party and a correspondent for *The Daily Worker*.

Donald Friede. See Dreiser to Helen Richardson, 18 May 1942, n. 3.

Al Manuel, film agent interested in the potential of Dreiser's movie scripts.

4. In *The Bulwark* the main character, Solon Barnes, marries into a banking family and himself becomes a banker. As was his habit, Dreiser thoroughly researched such material while writing.

5. *Company K* by William March (1894–1954), an anti-war novel based on March's experience in World War I.

6. With Dreiser's encouragement, Godwin wrote "unworthy people" sketches, taken from incidents in her life; he edited and then submitted them to his agent Jacques Chambrun.

To Louise Campbell [H-DPUP]

1015 N. Kings Road
Hollywood 46
Los Angeles.

Dec 13–43

Dear Louise:

How art thou? For one reason and another, principally because I care for you so much and always will, I've been thinking of you again and again the past weeks. How are you getting along? With me what between the war and my love of the Russians and my hatred of our cold blooded capitalistic system I'm in a mental stew—depressed or boiling with anger. Did you ever read that book "Sixty Familys"[1] or any portion of it? Its such a damn-ing picture of greed & selfishness, show, folly and amazing waste positively sickening. And this is the crowd that is yelling about labor greed and that terrible country Russia. I've shouted so much about it all that I'm hoarse and incidentally—now and then threatened with prosecution! Dies once sent a man out here to interview me and if possible get some FBI evidence.[2] Needless to say he heard me at my worst or best and left—glad to get out I think. I asked him to ask Mr. Dies to do me a favor and call me before his committee. No call.

And then, now that Im 72 my thoughts go back to the old days in 10th Street and the Village and you. How certain hours stand out! Not only the healthy ones of lust and fulfillment but the really engaging ones of talk in which you described to me your varied experiences—the colorful adventures of your youth which must comfort you some now for truly you can say you have lived and plentifully. At least I hope you think so. As for me I am going on as usual. Just sold a sketch of a woman war plant worker to the Readers Digest, which may interest you when it appears.[3] Also I have an order for a series of studies—6—for Esquire which is either to be called *Unworthy Characters* or *Baa! Baa! Black Sheep!*[4]—only they are not intended by me to be morally critical but rather friendly and where possible amusing pictures of people who just weren't made to conform to social theories—never could and never did. For one I've been thinking of putting in my brother Rome[5] who passed away several years ago. He was a scream. And in that connection I've been thinking that you might have some characters—male or female—who, as described by you, might fit into the series, only and alas they have to be signed by me. And they can only be 2000 words long. The amount offered me is $300 and of that I would see that you got $100[00]. And I would have to retain the privilege of editing the same. Only I have the feeling that I read two or three just short pictures of individuals, anyone of which would do as is. You were always describing someone—verbally or in typewriter type. Does the idea appeal to you.

Everything drags along here as usual. I sold Sister Carrie to R.K.O. two years ago but it has never been produced—and I fear never will be.[6] Hurstwoods finish is too dark. Also I sold *My Gal Sal* to Westcoast Fox which turned out to be successful although they did not pay much for it.[7] Now I work here as best I can—not liking Los Angeles over much but seeing it as better in winter than New York—not so good in summer. And I don't like getting old. With love as ever.

D

By the way give me the names of a few downtown residence streets running between Broad and the Delaware River—to the North of Market. I want to place a character in a decent furnished room there—a room that is a fairly short walking distance from the Broad Street Station.[8]

1. Dreiser is referring to *America's Sixty Families* (1937) by Ferdinand Lundberg, which argues that wealth and power are concentrated in the hands of the richest sixty families in the country and that they constitute the de facto government, exercising enormous control over the general population through the manipulation of markets and media.

2. Martin Dies Jr. See Dreiser to Ruth Kennell, 8 December 1941, n. 3. The FBI was compiling a file on Dreiser.

3. There is no bibliographical record of such a story appearing in *Reader's Digest*.

4. The "Black Sheep" series was eventually completed and sold to *Esquire*. Although all six pieces ran in 1944 and 1945 under Dreiser's byline, number three was written by Hazel Godwin and number four by Louise Campbell, with Dreiser serving mainly as editor.

5. Rome, born Markus Romanus (1860–1940), the second eldest of Dreiser's siblings and the black sheep of the family.

6. In 1940 Dreiser sold *Sister Carrie* to RKO for $40,000, but nothing came of it until 1952, when Paramount released a film with Jennifer Jones as Carrie, Eddie Albert as Drouet, and Laurence Olivier as Hurstwood.

7. In 1941 Dreiser had sold *My Gal Sal* to 20th Century Fox for $50,000, retaining the royalty rights to Paul's songs, which were split among the living Dreiser siblings. See Dreiser to Yvette Szekely, 29 April 1942, nn. 1 and 2.

8. Sites in Philadelphia close to Campbell's residence.

1944

To Louise Campbell [H-DPUP]

Jan. 6–'44

Louise Dear: It was so nice of you to respond to my letter so quickly and to prepare and enclose that sketch. It's quite good, yet I doctored it a little and had it recopied and put with the six sketches to be submitted. Just how Dr. Gingrich[1] will feel about them I don't know. We'll see. But East they'll go pretty soon to Chicago. Now why not do one on *Flora*.[2] Seems to me I once read a study of her by you & thought it good.

But right here I want to tell you how interesting, up to date, wise and snappy your letter reads to me. You talk about getting along in years and never having had quite enough of what it takes to be this or that but judging by this letter of yours, I see no occasion for your deduction. It has the old mental tang which made you the person that you were at 27 or 8 and that was some person.

As for me, well I'm struggling along, as grouchy as usual. We have a rather nice house in West Hollywood—cement blocks all through but snow white on the outside. It has two spare bedrooms so that if you ever blow this way, here you stay. Helen is healthy & busy usually with what to wear? (These wimmin). But Hollywood—or LA has changed so much I scarcely like it anymore—3,500,000 people in the metropolitan area and growing like mad. They calculate—(the boosters) 5,000,000 in two or three years. And now, load after load of writers and would be playwrights as well as scripters of all breeds arriving every hour on the hour and all on the off chance of getting into the movies as assistant screen writers. But somehow even in the face of bright warm winter days it all palls on me. I feel the absence of true wonders and really worthwhile ambitions in so many that are here. They struggle so hard to be something they are not and that makes me look back on good old 10th Street N.Y. and the work shops & studios in N.Y. and sigh. Here so much of it is so showy & so calculating like the girls who break in on Chaplin or Errol Flynn[3] and the men who declaim their special merits to your face. *So you see what a bad mood I'm in*. But *there is* the sunshine—Xmas day like today was like a day in July. Only the second day after it poured & was cold as tomorrow it well may be. But your letter was a ray of sunshine and how I wish I could fill the place of the missing man around your house. You could entertain me while Id sit about and allow you to do it—50–50. You know.

Only please write that Flora sketch. I'll bet money it's lying around somewhere now in one of your desk drawers. Dig it out & let me see it. I wont use it without your written consent.

Meantime love, & all good wishes—no dark hours of any kind. And meanwhile I may be coming down your way this spring, a lecture agent is after me to tell America what's wrong with it! And with Russia as my guide maybe I could.—Helen says to fold in her love, which I hereby do. As for me I, as ever, yours mournfully and yet lovingly.

T.D

1. Arnold Gingrich (1903–76), the founding editor at *Esquire*.
2. A friend of Campbell about whom she wrote years before without ever publishing the sketch.
3. Film stars Charlie Chaplin (1889–1977) and Errol Flynn (1909–59) were known for their numerous and highly publicized romantic affairs.

To Hazel Godwin [H-DPUP]

Tuesday March 7 [1944]

Hazel Sweet:

Just received Miss Cram's little book *Forever*[1] and also finished it. For a person who isn't—as you maintain *Literary*—you certainly recommend the most interesting volumes. You've never sent me one that isn't arresting. And somehow, speaking of *Forever* and having read much concerning spiritualism and materialization and having personally witnessed some amazing materializations I cannot say that there is nothing to it. It may be so. If so—so much the better. We do not die and we may meet on that "Beautiful Shore"[2] of the song. My mother died in my arms and I saw her sick yellowish eyes change to a clear blue grey. Also a look of astonishment creep into them—as though she saw something that was of the utmost interest. A second or later came death—the look of amaze vanished and so to this day I still think that she did see something—just what I wonder.[3] Ditto there was a lawyer in N.Y.—very cynical yet good hearted & helpful to many. And when he died I was standing by. Suddenly—just before his death his opened with that same kind of amaze and wonder in them. Also suddenly he lifted both arms upward as though he were expecting & reaching toward some one and then they fell & he was gone.[4] So *Forever* merely suggests for me that he did see someone or something most pleasing to him. And so Forever doesn't seem so wild to me.

Babe—thanks. Your a fine critic and writer. Write me another sketch of someone. I'll pay you if I can use it.[5]

Love & kisses. I still think I will be East in May. Possibly not but I think so. Could I meet you in Boston if I sent you your fare?

D—

I wish we could get together. I feel better today.

1. *Forever* by Mildred Cram (1889–1985), began as a short story originally published in *Cosmopolitan* (June 1934). Subsequently Alfred A. Knopf published numerous editions of it in book form. Dreiser's reference is to the faith of the young lovers in the story who believe that their bond is so strong that they will find each other after death.

2. "The Beautiful Shore" (1863), a song by Stephen Foster. The phrase "beautiful shore where the loved ones are gone," recurs in the chorus and in the first line of each verse.

3. For a more elaborate version of this experience, see *Dawn*, 512–13.

4. This incident has not been identified.

5. Godwin's response to this request may have been a sketch published in the "Ba! Ba! Black Sheep" series (in *Esquire*, December 1944) under Dreiser's name. See Dreiser to Louise Campbell, 13 December 1943, n. 4.

To Kirah Markham [H-DPUP]

THEODORE DREISER
1015 N. Kings Road
Hollywood, Calif
46

April 22nd–'44

Kirah Dear:

So glad to hear from you. And so glad you have such a lovely rural nook to dwell in and sketch and paint and poetize as you always have and always will. Spiritually you bubble—always—like a sourceful spring *which you are*. As for me, well its true that I haven't finished a novel,—worse luck but I doubt you have seen all of my productions—*Moods, Accented and Declaimed* which I prize highly, also. Also *Thoreau*, the Color of a Great City; Chains, *America is Worth Saving* (suppressed after publication), Epitaph and some short stories and articles.[1] What threw me off the fictional track was philosophy—my desire to analyze this living experience for myself. And because of its intense interest for me I spent five years gathering data. After that I wrote 8 articles or chapters and published them all in various magazines and now have several more which when put in book form will make a fairly arresting volume I think.

However—let that be as it will. I still feel quite fit and May 10th next am leaving here for N.Y. in order to receive the award.[2] For perhaps a week or more after that, I'll be at the *Commodore* and am hoping I'll get to see you—either at the hotel or at Overbrook Lane.[3] Anyhow I'll write you on my arrival. Probably on May 13. Shortly after I have to go to Philadelphia & very likely Baltimore but I'll be back in N.Y. before I leave for out here and I hope to see more of you and David to whom I extend my regards. I have often thought of my interesting visit to both of you at Reading.[4]

Love & best wishes.

T.D.

1. Moods, Accented and Declaimed: the actual title is *Moods, Cadenced and Declaimed*, originally published in 1926 by Boni and Liveright. Another edition with fifteen illustrations or symbols by Hugh Gray Lieber was published in 1928, also by Boni and Liveright. Dreiser's reference is probably to *Moods, Philosophic and Emotional, Cadenced and Declaimed*, published in 1935 by Simon & Schuster. This edition included *Epitaph*.

Thoreau: the complete title is *The Living Thoughts of Thoreau*. It was part of the Living Thoughts Library, edited by Alfred O. Mendel, and published by Longmans, Green and Co. in 1939.

The Color of a Great City with illustrations by C. B. Falls, published by Boni and Liveright in 1923, and again in London by Constable in 1930.

Chains, Lesser Novels and Stories, published by Boni and Liveright in 1927, and again later that year in a signed and limited edition. Constable published it in London in 1928 and again in 1937.

America Is Worth Saving, published in January of 1941 by Modern Age Books. After Hitler attacked Russia in June, Dreiser refused to allow the America First Committee, an isolationist group, to distribute off-prints of an anti-British chapter of the book. After the bombing of Pearl Harbor in December, the debate about America's entry into the war was over. The book was not well received, but historical events, not censorship, seem to be what "suppressed" the book.

Epitaph, a Poem with decorations by Robert Fawcett, published by Heron Press in 1930 in a numbered, limited edition of 1,200.

2. The American Academy of Arts and Letters presented Dreiser with the Award of Merit Medal on 19 May 1944.

3. Markham's address in Pennsylvania.

4. See Dreiser to Kirah Markham, 10 November 1928, nn. 2 and 3.

To Helen Richardson [H-DPUP]

In January 1944 the Academy of Arts and Letters invited Dreiser to receive the Award of Merit Medal and a $1000 prize, and in May he traveled to New York for the ceremony. While there, he met for the final time with his remaining siblings and conducted a round of negotiations with publishers.

THE COMMODORE
42Nd STREET RIGHT AT GRAND CENTRAL TERMINAL NEW YORK CITY

Sunday May-14–'44

Helen Dear:

This has been another full day of running and seeing. Called up Sylvia Saturday and asked about Mame.[1] She did not think that Mame was doing badly at all—that she was more frightened than anything else. But she does not believe in death as anything other than something brought on by mortal thought[2] and so that Mame should exert herself mentally and be better, I decided to go over and talk to Thomas.[3] Found him this AM nervous and desiring to go over and see Mame who is at the Kew Gardens General hospital on Long Island. I decided to go along as he considered her condition grave—and so do I. She is very weak and nervous—cries a great deal. She said—and so did Thomas—that the doctor in charge had diagnosed her case as cancer of the bladder—a small cancer inside the bladder. Also that an operation—a small one must be performed tomorrow—Monday. He says that it will not be hard on her whereas if left untouched it will grow worse and then a 2nd operation will have to be performed later. Incidentally she told us that this doctor will not charge her anything. He is an old friend of hers. Also she told me that she had some time ago put—through Thomas

Dreiser in 1944, with S. S. McClure, Willa Cather, and Paul Robeson.

and Gertie[4]—$784^{oo} in a bank to be held for her but that later Gertie had come to her and borrowed almost 400^{oo} of that money to buy a winter coat—and that she and Thomas had let her have it. Now she (Mame) has only a few hundred dollars—whether enough to pay her funeral expenses I did not ask—but I did ask Thomas. He said that the funeral would cost $250^{oo} and that she might have $200^{oo}(!) but he was not sure. But he did add that Gertie of whom he had asked half did not answer him. And that since she had got the money from Mame she had never been to see her or him & that he believed she would not do anything. I am writing Gertie tonight but whether she will answer I dont know of course.

At Mame's Hospital I met Mrs. Skelly[5] and Ed's daughter Vera.[6] Both were very friendly—invited me over to dinner—but neither appeared hopeful as to Mame. In my talk with Sylvia & Thomas I stated that each of the seven heirs of Paul's Estate should contribute 1/7th of this years song return and so pay Mame's expenses and both agreed. So there you are.

Today has been hard & trying. Syl, Mame & Thomas all look so bad that I feel depressed. And tomorrow I have to meet four or five newspaper interviews singly. They are coming in the afternoon. Incidentally I have to reach Moffat and Balch of Putnam's.[7] Also Random house and Damrosch.[8] Tried Saturday & today to get hold of Madam Clayburgh.[9] Learned from her secretary just now that shes out of town but will be back tomorrow probably by noon. So I can see about her dinner.

Its hot and I made a mistake as to clothes. The overcoat is useless. Lots of men are wearing Hollywood clothes, and I can wear my light color trousers with the brown coat. Really I feel let down by this trip and now I wish I were back in Kings Road with you & I'll be glad to get to Portland. I wish I knew though how your mother is and how you are feeling. I hope you are not too depressed. Mencken is coming over this week but a letter addressed to me here says he will not attend any dinner. He dislikes Damrosch and also the Academy of Arts & Letters. But we'll see the Sister Carrie mss in the Library[10] here & talk over the literary situation as a whole.

Love & all good wishes. I wish now that you had come along. Write me here.

TD

1. Sylvia and Mame, Dreiser's sisters.
2. Sylvia's beliefs were consistent with her practice as a Christian Scientist.
3. Frank Thomas. See Dreiser to Helen Richardson, 27 February 1938, n. 1.
4. Gertrude Nelson. See Dreiser to Sallie Kusell, 4 August 1923, n. 2.
5. Mrs. Skelly was the mother-in-law of Dreiser's brother Ed.
6. Vera Dreiser. See Dreiser to Vera Dreiser, 17 July 1944, headnote.

7. Stanley M. Moffat, an attorney, and Earle H. Balch, vice president, at the Putnam publishing firm.
8. Walter Damrosch (1862–1950), renowned orchestra conductor and the president of the National Academy of Arts and Letters (1940–48).
9. See Dreiser to Alma Clayburgh, 31 May 1933, headnote.
10. In 1914, Dreiser had given Mencken the manuscript of *Sister Carrie*, which was subsequently housed at the New York Public Library. Mencken never went to meet Dreiser in New York. He refused to attend the award ceremony on the grounds that several members of the academy, which he called "that preposterous organization," had been involved in the attempts to suppress *The "Genius"* in 1916 (Mencken to Dreiser, 9 May 1944, in Riggio, *Dreiser-Mencken Letters*, II, 712–13).

To Helen Richardson [H-DPUP]

The Commodore
New York City

May-19–'44.

Helen Dear:

Well this has been a hectic week—interviewer after interviewer after interviewer—publisher after publisher—Random House, Scribners, Putnams and Harpers, but with no result worth talking of except in the case of Scribners—the head of which—Charles Scribner suggested that once the print paper issue were modified it might be a profitable thing for him to issue a set of 18 or 20 of the volumes at 5^{00} a volume.[1] He thought it might sell and he would take it up with me later. Balch[2] on the other hand while very courteous and friendly did not see how he could spend more money to create a demand when he was in so deep already. He did say however that he liked the philosophy idea[3]—and that that might sell in which case he could push the other books but his ruling idea is that a novel that would sell itself would carry all the other books with it, which of course means that I must work on that. Meantime Madame Clayburgh[4] gave her dinner in my honor—that was Wednesday night and she had some 40 people there, generals, publishers, sculptors, musicians, Washington diplomats, etc. It was all very dressy and brisk. She asked me to come up a half hour earlier than the others in order that we might talk and of course I told her all I could about us & Los Angeles. Also I gave her the locket you sent and plainly she was very much pleased & said she was going to write you. Today,—the day of the presentation of the medal etc—she is going to be there along with several friends & I am to go with them. There is nothing to the whole thing except this—that a number of minor gifts or awards are to be made first and last comes mine. I understand the whole business will take about 1 1/2 hours.

As for the rest—Mame was operated on day before yesterday—Wednesday and came through alright. It was said to be cancer of the bladder. I talked over the phone to Vera[5] last night (this early Friday a.m.) and she said that Mame seems to be recovering well enough—no sign of collapse. Gertie[6] was here Wednesday—she & her husband—and I told her what Thomas[7] said about the coat and she insisted that he was lying. None the less she did not know what became of the money although she agreed that at Mame's request she & Thomas had opened a joint account at some bank. She said that she & her husband had invited Sylvia[8] to come & live with them—also Mame but Mame wouldn't come without Thomas! And Syl wouldn't go if Thomas was going to go! They dont get along. So I dont know what to say. I am drawing up a small paper in which—in case of Mames death[9] all agree to allow one sixth of their Paul Dresser estate share[10] to be deducted from this current year in order to meet the cost of the funeral. If all sign it and the undertaker will wait it might be defrayed that way. We will see.

Incidentally I have seen Fabri.[11] He is very well & cheerful & this week-end wants to go with me to Mt. Kisco to see the house. He has given me the keys. Also incidentally Moffat[12] called me up yesterday & said you had an offer of $15000 for the house & 15 acres & that he had advised or was advising you to take it. The shortage of gas (the small allowance he said) was driving people away from the country & would continue to do so. I think he's right and I think its best to sell it.

Well apart from that—going out to the house & seeing two more publishers I am about washed up here. Mencken said he was coming but he hasn't arrived yet.[13] I would like to go to Philadelphia to see Wharton & Louise[14] and will if I dont get too gloomy. Moffat wants me to come out to his place this coming weekend and I may go. Apart from that—nothing.

I see you took the car to Portland. It was the best way I guess. You dont say anything much about your mother so I judge she's doing well enough. I'm so used to the quiet of Kings Road that this is like a mad-house—simply jammed with taxis & people. Wish you were here or I was there

Love
T.D.

Write me.

1. Dreiser was hoping to find a publisher who would print a complete set of his books, but the wartime paper shortage made such a large project riskier than usual.

2. Earle Balch, vice president at G. P. Putnam & Sons. Ridding himself of Simon & Schuster, Dreiser signed on with Putnam, which was anxious to publish *The Bulwark* and gave him an advance on the book.

3. His philosophical-scientific project, "The Formula Called Man." Dreiser never completed this book. See Dreiser to Esther McCoy, 26 February 1936, n. 2.
4. Alma Clayburgh. See Dreiser to Alma Clayburgh, 31 May 1933, headnote.
5. Vera Dreiser. See Dreiser to Vera Dreiser, 17 July 1944, headnote.
6. Gertrude Nelson. See Dreiser to Sallie Kusell, 4 August 1923, n. 2.
7. Frank Thomas. See Dreiser to Helen Richardson, 27 February 1938, n. 1.
8. Dreiser's sister Sylvia.
9. Mame died on 2 June 1944.
10. The Paul Dresser estate received royalties from Paul's songs. Dreiser had arranged to divide the money four ways among his surviving siblings, including himself (and Helen), Mame, Sylvia, and Ed.
11. Ralph Fabri. See Dreiser to Louise Campbell, 27 February 1930, n. 3.
12. Stanley M. Moffat, Dreiser's attorney. The country house, Iroki, was sold later in the year.
13. Mencken: See Dreiser to Helen Richardson, 14 May 1944, n. 10.
14. Wharton Esherick. See Dreiser to Kirah Markham, 30 December 1928, n. 5.

To Marguerite Tjader [H-HRHUT]

Dreiser had met with Tjader during the week of 14 May when he was in New York to accept the Award of Merit Medal from the American Academy of Arts. She had agreed to come west with her young son Hillary to help Dreiser complete his long-overdue novel The Bulwark.

1015 N. Kings Road
Hollywood-46

July 5–'44

Marguerite Dear:

Your letter of July one arrived this a.m.—so different to June 22nd with its school-marmish instructions as to what was expected as to conduct—on my part but with at least one kindly reference as to your own emotional extensions. Naturally that riled me not a little since I did not start this collaboration program. It grew out of instructions on your part as to what I must do to extricate myself from my present literary dilemma—literary and to a degree financial. And sound enough, seeing how pervasive and mentally stimulating as well as physically arousing (and I am not referring to sex but to labor energy) is your personality—apparently from year in to year out. You are a force—a social and intellectual one and that you should find an emotional out in a seemingly endless procession of men is understandable enough. That you should begin to catechize and instruct me as to my emotional conduct for the relatively short period in which you plan to work with me—well as you see that is another story. You struck the wrong note at the wrong time. For that I am drawn to you needs no comment at this time and unless you are drawn to me sensually as well as mentally your letters and various contacts with me over the years were masterpieces of acting and lying—(even your last six letters to me here) to say nothing of your general approach to me in New York.

However that particular aspect of our relationship past and recent need not be quarreled over. I took it that you were drawn to me and that if we decided to try to work together on The Bulwark[1] it would not necessarily follow that a Trappistic self-restraint on my part should reign, seeing that I know full well that no such program governs in your case or ever has. Besides if the work progressed satisfactorily and you still felt this need of restraint on my part I could go else where and you could go your way. Only I also know that any such schoolroom governance on the part of either would develop an atmosphere in which neither of us would be willing or able to work. A creative atmosphere is one in which the emotions thrive even if one works alone. And without the charm that an intellectual and emotional atmosphere usually and beautifully provides I doubt if such work as I plan could be successfully formulated. *So.*

At that (all these things said) I find you one of the most attractive and esthetically stimulating beings I have ever known. It is not a little sad, and I felt it after we first met, that you were not sufficiently drawn to me—(literary fame apart) as to have pulled us into an esthetic and creative union. As it was you were so driven by your own desires as to be compelled to continuously explore all phases of the sex act—almost to the exclusion of the literary creative art. And so—

Well, here we are—80 years older and the act still dominant. You have done something with *Direction*,[2] only I so often think that with your exploring mind—not body entirely—what arresting tales—what revealing emotions you might have set forth for the world to see.

However you are still young and the embodiment of electric force—*So.*

In connection with this trip you are planning. I am enclosing money orders for $200[00]. When you get here I will help you with your search—or Helen will and we will talk over finances. If it does not become too expensive for me, we can work this thing out. And I love you as much as ever.

Th. D.

By the way—do not bother with Appleton-Century. The reason I was turned down there was that it is headed by Morgan Schuster—formerly the head of Simon & Schuster. He is a Jew crook who swindled me out of quite a sum when I mistakenly transferred to him after Liveright died.[3] He hates me because I told to his face what he had done & how my excellent agent Jacques Chambrun[4]—745–Fifth Ave. went to him without knowing my story & so was turned down. I am sorry that he went at all.

P.S. Go to Putnams please—my publishers & get a copy of *Moods*. Take it to Chambrun and ask him if he will show it to one & another publisher with the suggestion that it be reset in smaller type on thin paper and with a [word unintelligible] leather binding so as to weigh about 1/3 of what it weighs now. Schuster who got it after Liveright died and in the face of a personal request had it done in the clumsy heavy form in which it now rests.[5] The book has a following although it was never properly distributed and never advertised at all. Liveright intended to do both of those things but died before he got around to it.

D

I wish you were here today. Say nothing to Helen about the money I forward you.

1. Tjader soon after went to Los Angeles and helped Dreiser to complete *The Bulwark*.

2. She had founded and edited *Direction* (1937–45), a leftist and "antifascist" journal dedicated to new and important writers and artists. The opening number (December 1937) featured Dreiser's picture on the lead page together with a statement about the importance of "new directions" (repub. in Tjader, *Love*, 107). *Direction* published a considerable number of distinguished writers, including Sherwood Anderson, John Dos Passos, Ernest Hemingway, Langston Hughes, Ralph Ellison, Richard Wright, Paul Tillich, Bertolt Brecht, Charlie Chaplin, and Kenneth Burke.

3. By September 1934, Dreiser had finally ended his association with Liveright Publishing, and had joined Simon & Schuster. However, Dreiser had to pay Liveright's successor, Arthur Pell, for his printing plates and for the 13,000 copies of his unsold books. Simon & Schuster gave Dreiser a $5,000 advance and agreed to market his unsold books, paying him his usual 15 percent royalty. However, according to Dreiser, Simon & Schuster took the unsold books and placed them in "old book stores all over New York, where they were sold at 40 to 80 cents." The money they collected from these sales went to Simon & Schuster to recover Dreiser's advance of $5,000. Thus Dreiser felt he was cheated out of the distribution of his books and the 15 percent royalty on sales.

4. Dreiser's literary agent.

5. *Moods: Philosophical and Emotional, Cadenced and Declaimed*, published by Simon & Schuster on 10 June 1935.

To Hazel Godwin [H-DPUP]

Dreiser sent this letter of condolence to Godwin after the death of the daughter of a close friend whom she had mentioned often in her letters to him.

July 15 [1944]

Hazel Dearest:

I was sorry—so sorry to read in your last letter of the death of your little Jane for whom you cared so much and who seemed from time to time to be of such real comfort and also entertainment to you. For you reported to me in one letter and another so many of her pleasing traits. And now she is gone! And you haven't even her to fall back on! And with your affectionate nature—your love of and desire for sympathetic companionship—her passing can only be something that will weigh on you for a period. It always does. I so often think of how I felt when my mother died—quite lost and forsaken for so long a time and then when my brother Paul passed on—that gay and helpful spirit—so generous in his moods and with his means to all in need and that helping lift with his songs as much as his means. Whenever I hear On the Banks of the Wabash—or My Gal Sal or Just Tell Them That You Saw Me,[1] I think of how kind he was to me when I was at my lowest apprenticeship state once—not knowing really what to do next or where to turn. And then how on meeting him accidentally on the street not I but he *cried* because I was truly seeking to avoid his aid. And yet his tears once I saw them were proof good enough to me of the depth & sweetness of his nature and I did accept his aid for a little while—a few months.[2] And he *died.* And how lone and lorn I felt then. I could never express it fully to anyone. His spirit was so truly beautiful.

But here I am writing about Paul & myself and yet feeling so depressed by your condition. For I admire and care for every phase of your character that I have sounded and I know that you are genuine and humane & truly sweet. And it comforts me no little to hear you say you would like to put your arm around me and kiss me—for that is exactly what I wish you could & would do. And also—so much—I wish I were there to take you in my arms and hold you hour after hour as (I/we) did there and here and should do again. For I think of you always as a thoughtful and keenly intelligent and generous spirit—willing and anxious to do your share wherever you are and that touches me. And not only that but it provokes in me a keen admiration which has remained unchanged since your first letters. Actually I was delighted with the prospect of seeing and being with you in New York but when I found myself not only emotionally involved with my sister's illness, but compelled by the nature of the occasion to see really dozens of people—old friends as well as reporters, columnists—the principals of the American Academy of Letters and all who seemed to feel that they had first call on me, I gave up & tried to have the time limit of my round trip ticket extended.[3] But that having proved impossible—not even a possibility before July 5th or later, I gave up and returned here where just now I wish I were not since I wish so much to see you. But I am not tied to this spot. As things stand I may be called back to N.Y. to re-arrange my publishing affairs—move to a new house (The Century-Appleton Co.) in which case if you will be willing to join me there I can arrange to meet you in New York. And we can be together for a week at least. And then! The old loving days all over! Yes? Your arms around me and mine about you—without change I hope except for food—your steady affectionate eyes looking into mine.—Oh, Babe! Remember! The intenseness of it all. The gorgeous thrills—over and over.

Oh sweet—write and tell me that you love me. And how.

D

1. Three of Paul Dresser's most popular songs: "On the Banks of the Wabash" (1895), "My Gal Sal" (ca.1904), "Just Tell Them That You Saw Me" (1898).

2. In 1903, Dreiser was depressed, sick, and homeless. Paul helped him with loans and encouragement, and paid for a six-week stay at a health spa run by a former wrestling champion, William Muldoon. Dreiser describes these experiences in *An Amateur Laborer* and in "My Brother Paul" and "Culhane, The Solid Man" (in *Twelve Men* [1919]).

3. Dreiser is speaking of his time in New York City, where he went to receive an Award of Merit from the American Academy of Letters (See Dreiser to Helen Richardson, 14 May 1944, headnote). Dreiser sought to extend his stay and search for a publisher who would print a complete set of his books, but while he was there his sister Mame died of bladder cancer. He stayed in New York three weeks and was busy with appointments, meetings, visits (including trysts with Marguerite Tjader), and Mame's funeral. Although he does not mention it here, after leaving New York on 5 June, he returned to Los Angeles by way of Stevenson, Washington, where he quietly married Helen Richardson on 13 June 1944.

To Kirah Markham [H-DPUP]

1015 North Kings Road
Hollywood-46
Calif.

July 17–44

Kirah Dear: I was so sorry not to have had time enough to visit you at Overbrook Lane. But my round trip ticket, which it took me five weeks of waiting to get, expired—(the New York end of it) on June 5 and I found that I could not get an extension. And because of that I had to give up my trip to Philadelphia, Baltimore and Paoli Pa to say nothing of a half dozen visits to relations and friends in New York proper. One of the worst and saddest things that happened five days after I arrived was the death of my sister *Mame* who had been suffering for some time with kidney troubles, and that disarranged my entire program. There was so much to attend to. I meant to write you while I was there but every minute was taken up with something—business trips which I had to make or writers & publishers whom I had to receive. And although I have been bad quite all of this time, I'm still not caught up with my letters of explanation and apology, this one to you being ahead of six others that I have still to write.

But I did so want to see your place as well as you and your husband for I have thought of you both times a plenty,—our more recent as well as our old time contacts. And I hope that generally you are all right—healthy and hopeful which is about the best one can be. Personally I am quite able physically, no sickness to speak of and still fairly constructive—so naturally I feel grateful and should, I think.

Do you ever come west? If so will you keep the above address in mind and notify me beforehand of your coming. I'd so much like to see you and go over as many interesting scenes as possible. Life and—or—time slips by so. *And these days—before one knows it—a year has gone*. I try to think that life—*personality*—is indestructible and sometimes think that I can prove it—via energy which is indestructible and of which in toto we are composed. Thus the cell as molecule is something arranged & used by energy—since it is composed of atoms. But atoms are composed of electrons and electrons of ions—and there you are back to eternal energy. Hence the soul is what? Energy or what else, for *all is Energy*,—eternal creative energy. And so a job may be waiting for us. Lets hope so.

Love & all good wishes to both of you. Write when you can. Maybe we'll meet next year, for I have a feeling that I am to be called back to N.Y. for a brief period. If so I'll be seeing you.

D—

To Vera Dreiser [H-DPUP]

When in New York to receive an award from the National Academy of Arts and Letters, Dreiser visited with his family. He traveled to the Far Rockaway home of his brother Ed, where he encountered for the first time in years Ed's daughter Vera. She had received a Ph.D. in psychology, and had become a clinical psychologist and advocate of prison reform. At this time she was married and had recently given birth to a daughter. Although she had written him as early as 1932, the meeting in Far Rockaway resulted in an exchange of letters and a friendship that lasted until his death. In 1976 Dr. Dreiser published My Uncle Theodore, *an account of their relationship which is also a brief memoir of the Dreiser family.*

1015 N. Kings Road
Hollywood-46
Calif.

July 17–'44

Vera Dear:

What a nice brisk, ambitious healthy attractive neice it is that I have fallen heir to—mentally and physically so alive and comprehending and so anxious to be up and doing. Really you are not only charming mentally but physically and I keep wishing that I had such an industrious as well as attractive maiden beside me—at my elbow. For most assuredly you would have me up and doing in connection with the things I should be up and doing about instead of myself complaining of this & that. In fact I think of you all the time,—your thoughtful and energetic and considerate approach toward everything—your friendly and helpful desire to get things done.

I do not wonder that your Dr. Lawton[1] wants you to take charge of his psycho-somatic-research laboratory, for without such a wise and willing and energetic girlie dynamo as Vera D. I doubt whether he would get by with it. It is sound enough and ambitious but back of an ambition and soundness of idea must be a stirring human dynamo and that same is none other than my attractive Vera. Don't think I didn't gather his dependence on you that morning that he threw the new patient accross your capable and graceful shoulder. If I had you here I'd be having you write my next book, for you have the mind & the will and the delight in life and energy to make you capable of almost quite anything. For I noted that when I was with you anywhere—with and near you—I felt better for your being there, my girlie genius, just radiating energy—and good will and faith in the successful outcome of whatever task it was that was before us. And so I feel that your dear Dr. Lawton is just super-lucky. He's grabbing off a personality that can & could do wonders for itself and that can and will do wonders for him, even make him believe in himself. And that is going some as you probably know yourself deep down in that attractive personality of yours. But its so and you know it. And so luck to you Baby and to your Dr. Lawton, only I wish I had such a charming whirlwind attached to my humble little go cart. Would I go places? Id retire to my writing room, lie down and wait for you to bring the places to me. And as they come there you'd be along with smiles & good cheer and all the latest news. In fact my graceful girlie neice

Vera Dreiser.

refusing to even be complimented.—Oh, the hell with Lawton. Why didn't I draw my Vera D—. As for your songs[2] sweet—never mind that tricky son of God who wants to share the profits. Send me four of the best printed or copied copies. I know some one here who is a real judge and furthermore, if she likes them, can do something toward placing them and I'll take them to her and get her to move in the matter. Furthermore I'll write Deems Taylor[3] and he'll tell me what if any move to make.

Meanwhile here's love and best wishes for my pet neice. You were so nice to me dearie and I wont forget. Also here's love to Ed, your mother, Alfred, the Baby, even the car. And Luck to everything you choose to be interested in, from yours,

George Washington Dreiser

Your letter with Ed's song was darling.

1. Dr. Shailer Upton Lawton (1894–1966) was the psychiatrist with whom Vera Dreiser studied for her Ph.D. in psychology. She started her career in therapy working for him at the Lawton Foundation in New York City.

2. Both Vera and her husband, Alfred Scott, had sung professionally, and Vera had written songs of her own, one of which, "Afraid of You," published in 1938, was broadcast on New York radio stations in 1939. She had sung some of her songs at the family gathering when Dreiser was in New York.

3. Joseph Deems Taylor (1885–1966) composed operettas, comic operas, and operas. He was popular in his lifetime, having had many of his works produced at New York's Metropolitan Opera House, but his music has since been forgotten.

To Vera Dreiser [H-DPUP]

Aug 14–44

Vera Dear:

Your letter of last Thursday announcing your proposed visit to Los Angeles pleased me as much as anything could although, at the same time, it troubled me a little—First because Helen has been expecting the arrival of one of her mother's relations for a visit shortly & next because as you know, Marguerite[1] with whom I have arranged a literary working schedule which once she is here and has found a place to live in is going to require at least seven or eight hours of our regular working day for at least the next few months. And she is to arrive this coming week and start looking for a suitable working place for us as well as a residing place for her and her son.—No easy task in this overcrowded city which is difficult enough for those who know it and almost all but impossible for those who dont. I have advised Helen to help her since she knows more about the city than I do. How all that, together with my own daily work is to fit in with your short visit I don't know. For one thing I want to take the records of your songs over to Mrs. Goodman[2] in order to learn what she has to say about them. Next where, if anywhere, there is a movie under construction into which one or more of them might fit. However, in that connection, I want to say that placing anything—song, script, movie incident or idea with any of the principle companies or their agents or editors out here is a most difficult procedure. In the first place the movie company editorial offices are miles apart, eight to ten at least and next there is a considerable degree of race favoritism out here and the matter of making an appointment in order to place an idea is not always easy. For, as you can [word missing] for yourself it has taken me eighteen years in which to sell four of my books to four different movie companies. Sister Carrie, Jennie Gerhardt, An American Tragedy and My Gal Sal.[3] In between there have been almost endless talks or conferences between myself and this agent or editor or that or both but to no result. So that, as you can see, to anticipate swift results is more on the wishful rather than the real side of the picture. And hence going into business together as you so generously suggest, might not result in anything much more that a lot of hard work for you and me also and naturally I think you ought to know that in the first—not the last.

Your last letter is so gay and anticipatory that it seems rather dreadful on my part to lug in all this obstacle data at once and yet I truly feel that you ought to know. And if you come most certainly it would please me a lot to see and hear you. But I do feel that conditions being as they are right now, it might be best if your trip were delayed a few weeks by which time Helen would be free from relations and Mrs. Harris and myself might have solved our working routine so that there might be more time in which I could see more of you. Meantime I will have taken the songs to Mrs. Goodman and will have learned from her what she thinks and whether there is any immediate opening anywhere that she knows of.

If this sounds non welcoming and practical and unaffectionate blame circumstances and this generally crosspatch world for I would love to see you and feel the tang of your vivid personality. Here's with love & best wishes. Your worst of all uncles,

T.D

1. Marguerite Tjader had agreed to come to California, along with her young son Hillary Harris, to help Dreiser complete *The Bulwark*. See Dreiser to Marguerite Tjader, 5 July 1944.

2. Mrs. Mark Goodman. See Dreiser to Helen Richardson, 21 June 1938. n. 8.

3. Dreiser had a checkered history with filmmakers, leading him to be pessimistic about his niece's plans. He had sold the rights to *An American Tragedy* in 1926 to Famous Players Lasky for $90,000, but the contract was for a silent film that was never made. Then in 1931 he sold the sound rights to Paramount-Publix for $55,000. The contract included a clause promising to accept his "advice, suggestions, and criticisms." When the film was finished, Dreiser disliked it so much that he established a review committee of critics and writers to offer a judgment on the film that would allow him to file an injunction against the studio to prevent the film's distribution. He lost that case, but he again dealt with Paramount in 1932 when he sold the rights for *Jennie Gerhardt* (1933) for $25,000, unhappily signing a contract with no clause

allowing for author approval. In 1940 he sold the rights to *Sister Carrie* to RKO for $40,000, but the film was not made in his lifetime. (In 1952 Paramount released a version with Jennifer Jones as Carrie and Laurence Olivier as Hurstwood.) Finally, Dreiser wrote *My Gal Sal* (1942), basing it on his earlier sketch, "My Brother Paul," and incorporating into it several of Paul Dresser's songs. He sold it to 20th Century Fox for $50,000. See Dreiser to Yvette Szekely, 29 April 1942, nn. 1 and 2.

To Yvette Szekely [H-DPUP]

Dreiser had conceived of a project in which he would edit a series of articles by his friends which would consist of recollections of special events in their childhoods. He had not yet settled on a title for the group, though he eventually came to call it I Remember—I Remember.

Nov. 1–'44

Yvette Dear:

What I had in mind for you to do was a fifteen or eighteen hundred word sketch of your childhood—the formative years between five and eleven or twelve—the period in which all of us register our first impressions of this strange new world into which we come through no willing of our own. For then, for the first time we register totally strange figures moving about us—mother and father (maybe), brothers and sisters, strangers, the family doctor, cats and dogs to say nothing of birds and chickens, horses, cows, sheep, pigs, and those still stranger things—the sun, moon, stars, storms of wind or rain, or both—thunder, lightening, beautiful trees and flowers, the strange and unexplained moving traffic of life which as we live, and grow and for some unknown reason take for granted like houses, churches, schools, stores, dealers in this and that, police, the art of cooking, hunger and thirst—in sum a whole world of things through which the use and enjoyment and—or—difficulties of which, by degrees, we come to be what we are—craftsmen or doers of this or that, but still never knowing (any of us) how or why it all comes about.

The reason I wrote you about it was that one day it suddenly occurred to me what an interesting set of short articles,—a series of say six, all told, such a group would make:—six or seven *different people* from as different lands or cities or states or small town homes or farms,—the differing deductions and viewpoints the different writers of the same would present. And recalling your youth, the interesting things you told me, I decided to see if I couldnt stir up six or seven different individuals to *each do* one. And so I sat down and wrote to you because I know yours would be interesting and I might use yours as an illustration of what I meant—show in one or two instances to others.

Anyhow, Sweet, above is the idea. The general title for the entire six or seven might be—My *Native Heath* or My Natal Environment.[1] Maybe you could think of a better title. My idea is that I should get at least 200^{00} per article possibly 225^{00}. Each writer should or at least is free to sign his or her own name. If any do not wish to—(one has already refused) then each can use a pseudonym and I will appear merely as the originator of the idea—and-or—editor. What do you think, honey. Let me know. Personally I'm not feeling so well—(a bad cold is annoying me). Just now I'm all alone & how I wish you were here to look after me a little—to be close to me through the night & day. You have so much understanding and so much poetry of mind. I feel it always when I am near you. Only you are not near me. Love & all good things to you.

D

1. Louise Campbell and one or two others sent in their essays, but he didn't collect enough material before his death to bring the project to completion.

To Ruth Kennell [H-DPUP]

1015 N. Kings Road
Hollywood-46
Los Angeles, Calif

Nov. 28–44

Dear Ruth:

Thanks for your affectionate and informative letter and I note that you are still industrious in this matter of making right triumph over wrong, good over evil, wisdom over ignorance, liberality over greed etc. and as usual you'll never change. You have an eye single to perfection and you'll die working at the business of bringing them into being. As for myself while I fight for the cause of a better world, still I take occasional time off to brood over the possibility or impossibility of it. At the same time I contribute to the Red Cross, the 6th War loan, the Good Will association, the Russian Aid Society, and so save old papers, old clothing shirts, shoes—(just took a pair out to the garage for the old shoe box, in the hope that the collectors of material for Russia & the poor everywhere will arrive and pick them up). Their representatives are supposed to come every Tuesday a.m. And today is Tuesday.

Incidentally I preach and fight for the cause of Russia year in and year out,—to say nothing of the enslaved nations of Europe—the minor lands of which *once* I saw so much. But I'm a poor second to you, I know that, for I have always been able to feel your active and enduring humanity, and will die witnessing the same I am sure.

As for the long and very sweet letter you say you wrote me—nothing doing—It never arrived. If you'll look on the top shelf of the kitchen cupboard I think you'll find it. Meanwhile I know that you like me—(care a little) and always will. But that goes double, for I think of you plenty not only as working for a better day for everybody in Bridgeport but as once upon a time guiding and aiding me in Russia. Remember the night we left Moscow (laughing) for Kharkov leaving poor Dynamov[1] to stare after us?—and you laughed—you wretch! Well life will be as it will be and so I enter few complaints. I'd rather try to help where I can. By the way I have your article The Immortal Railroad[2] here beside me and will read it as soon as I finish this letter.

Incidentally if your thinking of a home in California why not try Los Angeles. Its grown & changed so enormously,—rapidly heading into a new kind of world city—artistic, vivid, crowded with all types of intelligence and ability. And as for me it interests me whether I will or not. So many esthetic and progressive things—radical and social things or movements are developing out here at one and the same time—and these I like to watch as I work. And if you were here I certainly would take time off to map out the new programs either for the magazines, the movies or the left wingers of whom I am one. And so we could see enough of each other to make it worthwhile. Anyhow there's the rudiment of an idea there.

Meanwhile this letter is drawing to a close. I have a bundle of mail—mostly believe it or not, papers, magazines, documents from Russia. Fortunately I have several pro-Russian friends who read Russian and I unload all this data on them. If you were here I'd turn it over to you. Anyhow here's to long life & better days and the wish that you show up here,—if for no more than a vacation. And so, with all good wishes—and the most pleasant of memories—

Affectionately
—D

1. The Russian critic and editor, Sergei Dinamov. (See Dreiser to Ruth Kennell, 24 February 1928, n. 4.) In the margin of the present letter Dreiser wrote: "By the way whatever became of Dynamov? I addressed several letters to him but never received a word in reply. Is he dead or in prison or what." Unbeknownst to Dreiser, Dinamov had been sent to prison for embezzlement; he was later killed in the war.

2. Unidentified.

1945

To Elizabeth Coakley [T-UCLA]

[Undated][1]

Dear Elizabeth:

You ask about story telling.

If a real life story presents enough drama, the proper emotions, etc. you may follow it as closely as you choose. Or you can bend it to your will or feeling. For instance, you may know or feel from your own knowledge of life that you can make it a better story—give it humor, drama, poignancy that it should have, or could have in real life. Such being the case any writer would be likely to do that. However, as you know, there are stories that need no altering. As they are, they seem to be better, more poignant, more dramatic or more humorous than the writer himself could possibly imagine. In that case it will be plenty to try to set it down as is. Portrait and landscape painters nearly always feel that nature outruns their skill but they will do the best they can. Rarely, if ever, do they feel wholly satisfied.

As to where a story begins . . . it should be easy to see where it must begin—with a man or woman sitting and thinking or saying something to someone else—or going somewhere with an intent which will presently appear. In the case of *ONE HUNDRED DOLLARS*[2] it could begin with the girl's dissatisfaction with her surroundings, and (most of all this) her loveless life—her dreams of a better one, or at best—the ideal solution for her. For myself I might begin it by saying:

> "Sometimes a great desire or necessity evokes its own cure—or, if not that, a pathetic shadow of itself—an apparition, say, which arrives, suggests what might be, provides a thrilling illusion of itself, then departs leaving not a wisp of itself behind. We call that drama, or on occasion, tragedy—albeit, it may be better in its effect than the mere dream, and again, lead to something better, later. Who is to say?"

The best thing is to begin anywhere, for presently the real beginning will disclose itself to you—the most natural.

But there are no rules for telling a story. The lovely thing you sent me[3] proves that. Real writers always have techniques of their own. You have. Your reactions to a given strong situation that has possibilities must be your guide. Instinctively you will select and put down what you think is worth while.

T. D.

1. As was her habit, Coakley typed the letters Dreiser had sent her and kept the originals as well. But in this case the original has been lost, and it was either undated or she had forgotten to include the date on her copy. The order of arrangement in her files and internal evidence suggest this was a late letter.

2. "One Hundred Dollars," a story Coakley was working on at the time. Dreiser often read her work and offered editorial suggestions.

3. A story called "Air Mail Special."

To Elizabeth Coakley [Hicks] [H-UCLA]

Dreiser remained on good terms with Coakley after her marriage and was an occasional family guest at her home until his death on 28 December 1945.

[19 January 1945]

Elizabeth Dear: I think of you so much these days,—And all because of your sensitive spirit;—your struggle with past ills and your own temperament—your desire to help your children through to a better life and the many obstacles you faced and struggled to overcome. And did at last. Even though, in so doing, you were again facing the possibility of having to sacrifice a great literary gift which you so well know you have.

What a dramatic and what a sad life!—for I saw with my own eyes the stories and sketches you struggled to perfect and the bitter want of reward that you reaped! And the patience and resignation and life philosophy with which you returned to your task to bring up three children and seek to support them by writing—and worse by day and night by labor in one or other of our great war plants! It all saddened me so much. And does to this hour, for I personally was never in any position to give you what you so richly deserved and which now (I sincerely hope) you finally have—a complete and final defense against a financial need that previously had so harried you—the accursed need of money—and that not for yourself but for your children. And all the while and justly seeking a little happiness for yourself.

God!

And how I hate the petty, greedy nature of a society that cannot to this hour be organized to do justly and fairly and lovingly by the struggling mothers of a money mad world! How despicable! And how truly sad! For through you I have seen a struggling mother drink to the dregs the cup of bitterness of those who would live a little and yet provide plentifully for those offspring that the God of this world has ordained are to be—and always through the love & the sacrifice of mothers.

Oh, Elizabeth! how deeply I respect you and how truly I pray for happiness for you to the end of your days in this world. For here was the cup

of happiness withheld from you and from it I drink to you—to your peace & strength & the fulfillment of all your dreams. For though you may not know it, of course, still I think of you all of the time & your new world almost as constantly. And I wish no least ill to befall you—only joy, always. And I do wish & hope that you may write more of the type of things that you are so tremendously able to express. Try, dear! Set yourself the task of expressing—at least a little—of the difficult world you have known. And know that I shall be wishing for and hoping for your success every hour of the day & year.

And you must know too how much I wish that I might see more of you, for minds and temperaments such as yours—how few! So with this, if not the sight of you—love & all good wishes—

D——

And if I can be of any service let me know. You will,—wont you.
My regard & respect to Mr. Hicks.[1]

1. Coakley married Robert Stanley Hicks in September 1944.

To Louise Campbell [H-DPUP]

Dreiser had been working hard to finish The Bulwark *and now enlisted Campbell's editorial skills one final time to prepare a manuscript for publication.*

1015 N. Kings Road
Hollywood-46

May 1–45

Dear Louise:

Forgive me for the long silence. I've been feeling pretty much down physically since I wrote you and worse slaving over the book.[1] However its done—actually completed!!—and with your permission I'll be sending it on to you for your reading and editing in about a week.[2] It will come parcel post and registered and I'll be deeply grateful if you will give it the once over, and indicate what if anything you feel might come out. Its about as long as *An American Tragedy* and about as tragic—not quite—I think, but nearly so. Anyhow you can tell me as to that and other things, for I know how good an editor you are. Incidentally you must name your editorial price and make it liberal to yourself. As for me truly I slaved over it and I'll be so glad to be rid of it. And in your turn maybe you will be too.

Today is May Day dear and I hope you find some way of enjoying it. As for me I have one more week to go on the book and so no *May Day* for me

Louise Campbell.

for I'll be thinking of you and be being glad that your still on Earth. Ours has been such a long and comforting friendship and one for which I've always been grateful. So with love and all good wishes I close and be thinking of you as you know.

Th. D.

I've never, as yet, been able to dispose of the *I Remember—I Remember*[3] series but still think I will sell it. Yours is the best.

1. *The Bulwark* was published posthumously in 1946 by Doubleday & Company.
2. Campbell eventually spent a good deal of time editing the manuscript, which she streamlined considerably—as did Donald B. Elder, Dreiser's editor at Doubleday.

3. See Dreiser to Yvette Szekely, 1 November 1944, n. 1. Campbell and a few others sent in their childhood reminiscences, but Dreiser never collected enough to complete *I Remember—I Remember*.

To Hazel Godwin [H-DPUP]

In the final months of his life Dreiser was beginning to forget such ordinary facts as the original publishers of The Financier *(Harpers) and* The Titan *(John Lane), but he remained at work on the last book of the trilogy,* The Stoic. *When he died on 28 December 1945, he had not fulfilled the hope expressed in this letter of completing the last chapters of the novel. He worked on the penultimate chapter the day before he died, and Helen Dreiser, heretofore having done practically no literary work for him, organized his notes for the conclusion of the book, published posthumously in 1947.*

July 15 [1945]

Hazel Dear:

That lovely oriental drawing you sent me arrived safely and I was intending each day to write you about it (thank you of course) also to take down your new address which was on the back when for some lunatic reason I mislaid it and have not as yet found it. Hence the reason for this old address which I hope brings this letter safely to you. Whether I hear from you or not (as so regularly I used to) I still think of our interesting days together—your rich love satiating temperament! And my happiness because of it and so today even when you do not write I feel close to you—as though you were not wholly separated from me.

Meanwhile I've been wanting to tell you that just recently—after about a year's steady work I finished the long-labored-over novel of mine, *The Bulwark*. The finally revised script of which—632 pages has gone off to my publishers—The Doubleday Doran Company who are to set it up and let me see proofs. Also, among other things I have just about finished the third volume of a trilogy that I once started back in the Thirties. It was to be called *A Trilogy of Desire* and still will be. Volume I was and remains The Financier—originally published by Liveright. Next came Vol II—*The Titan*—also published by Liveright. Lastly I mapped out Vol III to be called *The Stoic* and this last is within 3 short chapters of its end. When these are finished as I think they will be during the next two weeks then Vol. III goes to Doubleday Doran also. When it is set up and OKed by me all three volumes will be boxed in a single box and sold that way but under the general title of *A Trilogy of Desire*. When it comes out I'll be hoping that I can get you to read it—or them—and tell me what you think of them.

Hazel Godwin.

Incidentally although all this work seems to indicate that I must have been in fair health or even very good health the truth is that I have been feeling rather badly all the way through—and have worked constantly against a feeling of weariness bordering on exhaustion and yet I have so worked and at the same time thought of you much. Yet I must say your last two or three letters seem to indicate that you have been feeling that our correspondence is scarcely worth your time or mine and that we might as well stop writing when the truth is that whatever you get or fail to get out of my letters, I personally extract always intense satisfaction out of yours, for always you are so obviously frank and truthful. You say what you feel & in reading whatever you say I personally feel myself feeling close to you—that is, as though you were close at hand, and so extracting that old sense of human warmth and wisdom that so attracted me to you when you were here. And then I begin to wish that you would not stop writing or at least that I were still worthwhile enough for you to wish that you could be interested enough to write to me. For mentally you are so wise and generous and kind and I care so much for you as a person! However if you are reaching the place where you cannot feel the worthwhileness of it—I cannot do more or say more than I just have in the lines above. And yet how much I wish that I were able to bring you an enduring happiness. But if I cannot or do not and you feel it a labor—well.

Only please before you cease and disappear—write me one more letter. I would so much like to hear from you—coldly or warmly—just so I hear.

With love & good wishes.

—D

INDEX

Adams, Mrs. K. J., 331n2
Adams, Wayman, 210, 211n4
Addams, Jane, 48, 49n1, 85n5
Akins, Zoe, 160, 161n6
Albee, Edward, 171n4
Albee, Edward Franklin, 169, 171n4
Albert, Eddie, 348n6
Algonquin Round Table, 162n3, 196n9
Allen, Fred, 177, 178n2
Allen, Jerrard Grant, 116, 117n12
America First Committee, 352n1
American Academy of Arts and Letters, 352, 352n2, 355n10, 357, 361, 361n3, 362
American Civil Liberties Union, 230, 231n3
American Federation of Labor, 307n9
American League for Peace and Democracy, 270, 271n2
American Mercury, 151n4
American Socialist Party, 204n5
American Spectator, 86n1, 239, 240n6, 241n9, 243, 460
Amick, Robert, 68n4, 86, 88n7
Anderson, Hans Christian, 186
Anderson, Sherwood, 240n6, 247, 247n2, 359n2; *Winesburg, Ohio*, 247n2
Andrews, Ann, 124, 126n3
Anthony, Joseph, 195, 196n7
Apletin, Mikhail, 306, 307n5
Aragon, Louis, 270, 272n3, 275, 275n2, 279
Arbuckle, Roscoe ("Fatty"), 174, 176n1
Armour, Philip Danforth, 37, 39n1
Armour Institute of Technology, 38, 39n2, 39n4
Armstrong, Paul, 219
Armstrong, Rella Abell, 68n5, 219; Letter to, 219–20
Arnold, Matthew, 73, 74n4; "Dover Beach," 73, 74n4
Art Institute of Chicago, 61, 83n2
Aston, Winifred (Clemence Dane), 153n3; *Will Shakespeare*, 152, 153n3
Auerbach, Joseph S., 125, 127n8; "Essays and Miscellanies," 127n8
Authors' League of America, 97, 98, 98n1
Award of Merit Medal, 352n2, 357
Azaña, Manuel, 282, 282n5

Baker, May (Mae) Calvert, 285n1, 318; Letters to, 120–24, 128–33, 257–58
Balch, Earle H., 317, 318n2, 354, 355, 355n7, 356n2
Baldwin, Roger, 230, 231n3
Balzac, Honore De, 99n2; *Pere Goriot*, 97, 99n2
Barnum, Gertrude, 84, 85n10
Barrineau, Nancy, 25n8
Barry, Mary Elizabeth, 64n3
Barrymore, John, 125, 126n6
Bazalgette, Léon, 268, 269n1, 275, 276n6; *Henry Thoreau, Bachelor of Nature*, 269n1, 276n6
Beach, Lewis, 176n4; *The Goose Hangs High*, 175, 176n4
"Bear to the Left," 163, 164n1
Becker, Charles, 330, 331, 332n5
Beethoven, Ludwig van, 331
Belasco, David, 31n4, 331n2
Benchley, Robert, 169, 171n7
Benoit-Levy, Jean, 278n9; *La Maternelle*, 277, 278n9, 279, 281n3
Bercovici, Konrad, 206, 206n2
Bercovici, Rada, 206
Berkman, Alexander, 214n2, 230
Berlin, Irving, 171n8
Bernhardt, Carl, 119n6
Bernhardt, Sarah, 73, 74n3
Berry, Noah, 174, 176n2
Berry, Wallace, 174, 176n2
Bible House, 32, 33n2

Bigelow, Poultney, 96n1
Bigelow Homestead at Malden on the Hudson, 95, 96n1
Bingham, Alfred, 244n4
Biograph (film studio), 97, 99n3
Bissell, Harriet, 272, 286; Letters to, 272–76, 278–84, 286–97, 299–304
Bizet, George, 60n3; *Carmen*, 59, 60n3
Blaine, James Gillespie, 44, 45n2
Bland, James A., 45n4; "In the Evening by Moonlight," 45n4
Blaustein, Julian, 317, 317n2
Blech, Paul, 275, 276n2, 279
Bloom, Marion (Maritzer), 125, 127n13; Letters to, 153–54, 227–28
Blum, Jerome, 210, 210n2
Blum, Léon, 277, 278n11
Bohemian Magazine, 55n1, 246
Boni & Liveright, 127n9, 132, 133n1, 145, 164n5, 206n1, 231n6, 339n1, 352n1
Bonnet, Georges, 272n4, 277, 278n5, 279
Bookman, 47
Booth, Beatrice Wittmack: Letter to, 204–5
Booth, Jay Franklin, 103–4, 113, 192n2, 204
Botticelli, Sandro, 67, 68n1; "Primavera" ("Springtime"), 68n1
Boutnikoff, Ivan, 325, 326n2
Bowers, Claude, 180, 181n15, 277; *The Tragic Era*, 181n15
Boyd, Ernest, 159, 161n3, 240n6
Bradley, William A., 280, 281n9
Brady, Diamond Jim, 70n3
Brady, Mathew I., 240n3
Brahman, Lionel, 169, 171n3
Brandon, 3n2, 6, 7
Brecht, Bertolt, 359n2
Breen, H. M., 162, 163n9
Breen, Joseph, 292, 293n7
Brennan, Austin, 22, 24n3, 92, 103n2, 172, 173n1, 286
Brennan, Jay, 177, 178n3
Bridges, Calvin, 265n1, 291, 291n8
Brill, Abraham A., 187, 188nn1–2
Britton, Nan, 198n1
Broadway Magazine, 47
Brooks, Van Wyck, 269n1
Broun, Heywood, 195, 196n9
Brown, Grace, 157n5, 332n3
Browne, Maurice, 58, 92n9, 105n5, 127, 128n1, 208, 210; *Wings over Europe*, 210, 211n8
Brown's Mixture, 222n6
Bryan, William Jennings, 17–18n1, 19, 20, 40, 178–79, 180n3
Bryant, Louise, xxii, 204n5
Buchman, Frank N. D., 262n2
Buck, Pearl S., 285, 285n2
Bukharin, Nikolai, 198, 199n2
Bunyan, John, 305n2; *The Pilgrim's Progress*, 305n2
Burch, Arthur C., 248n1
Bureau de l'Association Internationale des Écrivains, 281n3
Burke, Claire, 116, 117n9, 162
Burke, Kenneth, 359n2
Burroughs, John, 28, 30n2
Bushnell, Belle, 80n4
Butterick Publishing Company, 48, 50, 92n10, 274n2
Bye, George T., 309n1

Cabell, James Branch, 240n6
Callicotte, Paul, 239, 240nn2–3
Calvert, May, *See* Baker, May Calvert
Cantor, Eddie, 269, 270n9
Campbell, Louise Heym, 138, 221, 227n2, 265n6; Letters to, 138–39, 205–6, 221–22, 231, 247, 250, 255, 313–14, 347–48, 372–74; *Letters to Louise: Theodore Dreiser's Letters to Louise Campbell*, 138; translation of *The Case of Clyde Griffiths*, 227n2, 255, 265, 265nn6–7, 267n4
Cape, Herbert Jonathan, 234, 235, 236n1
Caravan, 217, 217n1
Carnegie, Andrew, 111n4, 332n4
Carnegie Steel Company, 230
Carnovsky, Morris, 265n6
Carrel, Dr. Alexis, 257, 257n1; *Man the Unknown*, 257n1
Carroll, Lewis, 187n2; *Alice in Wonderland*, 187n2
Catholicism, 60n5, 120, 178–79, 180n2,

181n13, 197, 222n7, 261, 267, 268n1, 292, 293n7, 301, 305, 323n1
Cecil, Lord Robert, 270, 272n4, 277, 279
Celler, Emanuel, 316n1
Central Congregational Church in Chicago, 39n2
Central Musical Hall in Chicago, 39n3
Century, 47
Century-Appleton Co, 361
Century Company, xxi, 85n9, 88n11, 92n6
Century Illustrated Magazine, 31n4
Ce Soir, 272n3
Cezanne, Paul, 195n3
Chamberlain, Neville, 305
Chambrun, Jacques, 347n6, 359
Chaplin, Charlie, 349, 350n3, 359n2
Chaucer, Geoffrey, 188, 188n5; *The Canterbury Tales*, 188n5
Chekhov, Anton, 195n4
Chesterton, G. K., 102, 103n5
Chicago Athletic Club, 38
Chicago Daily News, 47, 56n3, 201n2
Chicago Evening Post, 66n1
Chicago Little Theater, 58, 59, 64n3, 70n6, 72n1, 77, 80n3, 82, 92n9, 105n5, 118, 128n1, 208
Chicago Post, 56
Chicago World's Fair of 1893 (World's Columbian Exposition), 40, 41n6, 42
Christ, 84, 95, 98, 274, 323n2
Christian Herald, 33n2
Christians (Christianity), 82, 103, 103n5, 135, 137, 204n6, 274
Christian Science, 171nn14–15, 261, 262n3, 354n2
Christian Science Monitor, 171
Churchill, Winston, 334n3
Cistercians, 61n5
Clair, René, 278n10; *Under the Roofs of Paris (Sous Les Toits de Paris)*, 277, 278n10, 279
Clark, Clara, 232, 250; Letters to, 232–33, 261–62, 304–05; *Philadelphia Rebel: The Education of a Bourgeoisie*, 232
Clark, Kenneth S., 315, 316n2, 324
Clark, Warner, 305n3
Clayburgh, Alma Lachenbruch, 244, 271, 273, 354, 355; Letter to, 244–45
Cleveland Plain Dealer, 9
Cliff-Dwellers' Club, 47n1
Coakley, Elizabeth Kearney [Hicks], 304, 305n1, 311; Letters to, 311–13, 317–19, 370–72; "Air Mail Special," 371n3; "One Hundred Dollars," 370, 371n2
Cochran, W. Bourne, 18, 18n4
Cohen, Harry, 290, 291n6
Cohen, Lester, 292, 293n5
Coleridge, Samuel, 161n4
Common Sense, 243, 244n4, 307n4
Commune, 276n2
Communism, xxvii, 196n5, 198, 218n1, 225, 231, 231n5, 239, 242, 269, 272n3, 281n1, 305, 307nn2–3, 319, 346n3
Congress of Industrial Organizations (CIO), 306, 307–8n9
Constable & Co., 195n1, 201, 202, 203, 271
Cooke, George Cram (Jig Cook), 126, 127n16
Coolidge, Calvin, 180n10, 299n3
Cosgrave, John O'Hara, 273, 274n2
Cosmopolitan [*Hearst's International-Cosmopolitan*], xx, 28, 34, 85n2, 126, 146n3, 215, 215n5, 216n4, 217n3, 351n1
Cotton & Finance, 74, 74n6
Covici-Friede, 215
Cowan, Bertha, 332
Cowley, Malcolm, 281n1
Craig, Calvert, 132, 133n2
Craig, Mrs. Jessie, 133n2
Craig, Virginia, 132, 133n2
Cram, Mildred, 350, 351n1; *Forever*, 350–51n1
Crane, Stephen, 332n5
Crowley, Aleister (Edward Alexander Crowley), 227, 228n1
Cubism, 61, 62nn3–4
Cudlipp, Anne Ericsson, 54
Cudlipp, Thelma Grosvenor [Whiteman], 52; Letters to, 52, 54–55, 251, 330–32, 339–40
Culver, Helen, 49n1
Czinner, Paul, 254n3

Dahlberg, Arthur C., 311, 313n2; *Jobs, Machines, and Capitalism*, 313n2

Damrosch, Walter, 354, 355n8
Darrow, Clarence, 93, 94n3, 173n7, 188, 316n1
Darwin, Charles, 19, 22n2
David, Jacques-Louis, 22n3
Davidson, John, 179, 180n13; "A Ballad of a Nun," 179, 180–81n13; "A New Ballad of Tannhauser," 179, 180–81n13
Davis, Hubert, 227; *The Symbolic Drawings of Hubert Davies for "An American Tragedy,"* 227n3
Davis, John W., 179, 180n10
Davis, Magdalen, 175
Debs, Eugene Victor, 244n5, 316n1
Deering, Charles, 38, 39n6
Deering, William, 39n6
Deeter, Jasper, 247n2, 265n6
Delineator, xix, xxxiii, 48, 49n1, 52, 54n3, 55n1, 70n5, 153n1, 213n1, 246
Dell, Floyd, xx, xxi, 56n3, 63, 64, 64n4, 65, 66n1, 89, 90nn3–4, 125, 195n2; "A Great Novel," 66n1; *Homecoming*, 66n1; *Love in Greenwich Village*, 66n1; "Mr. Dreiser and the Dodo," 90n3
Del Vayo, Julio Alvarez, 305, 307n3
De Merode, Cléo, 26, 27n1
DeMille, Henry, 5n1; *The Danger Signal*, 5, 5n1
Democratic Convention (1924), 178–80, 180n1
Demorest's, 34, 37n5
Dewey, George, 34, 37n4
Dewey, John, 111n4, 316n1
Dial, 216, 217n1
Dies, Martin, 306n1, 319, 320n3, 347
Dinamov, Sergei, 201, 202n4, 269, 369, 369n1
Direction, 272n2, 358, 359n2
Discipline of the Yearly Meeting of Friends, 321–22, 323n5, 324n5, 326, 328, 339n2
Divine, Reverend General Jealous (George Baker), 299, 300n1
Dodd, Mead, and Company, 37n6, 145
Dodge, Ben W., 47, 48n2
Dodge & Company, 47, 48n2, 49n2
Donnelly, Dorothy, 171n2; *Poppy*, 169, 171n2
Doran (publishing firm), 91
Dos Passos, John, 359n2
Dostoievsky, Feodor Mikhailovich, 186, 187n1
Doty, Douglas Z., 84, 85n9, 91
Doty, Duane, 38, 39n8
Doubleday & Company, 373nn1–2
Doubleday Doran Company, 374
Doubleday, Page & Co., xxi, 70n2, 74n3, 217
Douglas, George, 249, 249n2, 252
Douglas Aircraft, 337n1
Dreiser, Clara (sister, called Tillie or Claire), 22, 24n4
Dreiser, Edward Minerod (brother Ed Dresser), 19, 21n1, 22, 24n2, 116, 117n13, 125, 126n8, 154, 287, 329n1, 343n1, 354n5, 357n10, 362, 365
Dreiser, Emma Wilhelmine (sister Emma), xxv, 24n1, 116, 117n14, 149n2, 286
Dreiser, Theodore
Views on:
—Children, xxiii, 22, 52n1, 88n14, 93, 143, 276, 282n6, 324n6, 371
—Communism (connections to), xxvii, 196n5, 198, 218n1, 225, 231, 231n5, 239, 242, 269, 272n3, 281n1, 305, 307nn2–3, 319, 346n3
—Crime, 117n1, 167, 245, 248, 330, 331n2
—Drama and film: adapting *American Tragedy* to stage and film, 192, 206n2, 207, 217 218n1, 226, 227, 235, 255, 256n1, 265n6, 276n5, 292, 366, 366n3; adapting *The Financier*, 68, 219, 220n1, 304n4; adapting *The "Genius"* to drama, 144n1, 145, 146n1, 195n3, 280, 344; selling film rights to novels, 366n3; selling Paul Dresser's life story, 325n1; selling *Sister Carrie* to movies, 269, 270n10, 292, 299–300, 301–2n1, 303, 348n6, 366
—Germany, xxvii, 95, 207, 214, 217, 218n1, 244n6, 267, 269, 305–6, 306nn1–2, 307n2, 334n3
—God, xviii, xxviii, 12, 78, 84, 135, 137, 143, 323nn1–n2, 371
—Jews, 72, 80, 112, 117n1, 126n2, 160,

166, 202, 204n6, 247, 253, 277, 280, 358
—Politics, xviii, xxii, xxvi, xxvii, 40, 85n5, 200, 212, 230, 231n4, 240n4, 241n6, 244nn5–6, 267, 292, 308, 311, 332, 341
—Russia, xx, xxvi, xxvii, xxviii, 196–98, 200, 203, 244n6, 305, 306, 306–7n2, 307, 311, 319, 320, 341, 347, 350, 352n1, 368, 369
—Telepathy, 90n1, 167, 171, 186, 250n2, 295n1, 346, 246n1
Writings:
—*An Amateur Laborer*, 87, 88n11, 361n1
—*America Is Worth Saving*, 351, 352n1
—"Americans Favor U.S. Action to End Bombing Civilians, Dreiser Says," 281n6
—*An American Tragedy*, xx, xxi, xxvi, 138, 148, 274n2, 276, 277n2, 153, 154, 154n3, 157n5, 160, 146n5, 148, 149n2, 154, 157n5, 164, 173n7, 174–75, 182n2, 184n2, 189, 191n2, 192, 205, 206n2, 207, 217, 218n1, 226, 227n3, 232, 235, 240n1, 250n3, 255, 256n1, 265n6, 268n5, 292, 331n2, 332n3, 366, 366n3, 372
—"Baa! Baa! Black Sheep," 347, 348n4, 351n5
—*The Bad Girl*, 125, 126n7
—"Birth and Growth of a Popular Song," 36n2
—*The Blue Sphere*, 292
—*A Book About Myself*, 128, 136n5, 138, 139n1, 145, 146n2
—"The Born Thief," 116, 117n17
—*The Bulwark*, xx, xxv, xxix, 85n2, 87, 97, 106, 110, 113, 118, 125, 128–29, 135, 138, 145, 154, 228, 285, 319n2, 320n4, 321–22, 324, 324n6, 326, 327n1, 343, 344, 344n9, 346, 346n4, 356n2, 357, 358, 359n1, 372, 373n1, 374
—"Catalogue of an Exhibition of Paintings by Jerome Blum at the Anderson Galleries in New York, January 28th–February 9th" [Foreword], 210n2
—"Change," 327, 328n5
—"Chains," xxv, 138, 351
—*Chains, Lesser Novels, and Stories*, 352n1
—"Civilization—Where? What?" 306n1
—"The Complete Jingler," 52n1
—*The Color of a Great City*, 351, 352n1
—*Concerning Dives and Lazarus*, 310, 311n1
—*Dawn*, xi, xx, 3n3, 17n4, 39n3, 60n3, 105n2, 120, 130n2, 138, 139n2, 221, 222n4, 223, 235, 236n3, 351n3
—"The Dawn Is in the East," 306, 307n4
—"Democracy on the Offensive," 332
—Diaries, xvii, xxii, xxvi, 47n1, 58n6, 127n13, 154, 173n2, 195, 204n3, 204n7, 219
—*Dreiser Looks at Russia*, 202, 204n9, 206n1, 214–15n1, 245n1
—The Epic of Cowperwood, 86
—"Epitaph," 351, 352n1
—"Equity Between Nations," 271–72n2
—"Exordium," 34, 37n5
—"Fame Found in Quiet Nooks," 31n2
—*The Financier*, 68, 73–74, 86, 87, 91, 100n2, 138, 193n1, 206n5, 219, 304, 374
—"The Formula Called Man," 252, 257n2, 259n1, 294, 296n4, 357n3
—Foreword to George Sterling, *Lillith*, 180n11
—*A Gallery of Women*, xxv, 25n7, 55n1, 81n8, 145, 146, 148, 151n5, 200, 208, 212, 214n5, 336, 337n2; "Ellen Adams Wrynn" [Yvonne], 206n3; "Emanuela," 55n1; "Ernita," 200; "Olive Brand," 81n8; "Rella," 25n7; "Rona Murtha," 148, 149n4; "A True Patriarch," 21n6
—*The "Genius,"* xxi, xxiv, xxv, 21n6, 25n7, 54n1, 58, 64n4, 66n1, 87, 94n1, 98n1, 104, 104n1, 117nn3–4, 118, 127n8, 133n1, 135, 136n3, 139n3, 149n5, 190n2, 194, 280, 336, 337n3, 355n10; dramatization of, 144n1, 145, 146n1, 195n3, 344
—*The Girl in the Coffin*, 66n3, 68n3, 204n1
—"The Hand," 292, 293n4

—*The Hand of the Potter*, 115, 117n1, 118, 125, 126, 126n5, 127n8, 139n3, 142, 207, 208n3, 271, 272n9, 276
—*Hey Rub-A-Dub-Dub*, 192n2, 328n5
—"Hollywood, Now," 145
—*A Hoosier Holiday*, 58, 103, 106, 110, 113, 114 115n7, 116, 120, 128, 130nn1–2, 138, 192n2, 204
—*In the Dark*, 292
—Introduction to Albert Londres, *The Road to Buenos Ayres*, 195n1
—Introduction to H. G. Wells, *Tono-Bungay*, 225n3
—Introduction to Odin Gregory, *Caius Gracchus*, 173n3
—Introduction to *The Living Thoughts of Thoreau*, 274n1, 280, 291n1, 352n1
—Introduction to *The Songs of Paul Dresser*, 36n2
—"I Remember—I Remember," 367, 373, 374n3
—*Jennie Gerhardt*, xvii, xxiii, xxv, 24n3, 56, 66n1, 72, 75, 85n3, 87, 91, 93, 118, 119n1, 173n1, 248n5, 366, 366n3
—*Laughing Gas*, 118, 119n6, 292
—"A Leader of Young Mankind: Frank W. Gunsaulus," 39n2
—"A Literary Apprenticeship," 343, 344n9
—"The Mechanism Called Man," 257n2
—"Mirage" (working title for "An American Tragedy"), 145, 146n5
—*Moods, Cadenced and Declaimed*, 148, 149n5, 327, 328n4, 352n1
—*Moods, Philosophic and Emotional, Cadenced and Declaimed*, 352n1, 359
—*Newspaper Days*, xi, 128–29, 135, 136n5, 138, 139n2, 344n9
—*Notes on Life*, 257n2
—"Of One Who Dreamed," 41, 42n2
—"On the Banks of the Wabash," 34, 36n2
—Plays of the Natural and Supernatural, 58, 338, 339n1
—"The Rake," 78, 79n6, 87, 159, 331n2
—"Reflections," 25n8
—*The Reformer*, 118, 119n4
—"Resignation," 34, 37n5
—*Russian Diary*, 204n3, 204n7
—"Russia: The Great Experiment," 204n9
—"The Simpletons," 87, 88n13
—*Sister Carrie*, xix, xxi, xxv, 10n1, 12n3, 24n1, 47, 47n1, 48n2, 49n2, 56n1, 56n3, 70n2, 73, 74n3, 84, 87, 91–92n3, 125, 127n9, 135, 162n2, 170, 203, 205, 205n1, 269, 270n10, 292, 299, 300, 300n2, 348, 348n6, 354, 355n10, 366
—"The Soviet-Finnish Treaty and World Peace," 311n1
—"The Spring Recital," 58
—*The Stoic*, xxix, 86, 87, 88n5, 232, 236, 236n8, 237n3, 238, 263, 294, 296n3, 374
—*Tabloid*, 292
—"Temperaments, Artistic and Otherwise," 327, 328n6
—"Theodore Dreiser Condemns War," 310, 311n2
—"This Florida Scene," 191n4
—"This Madness," 58, 215, 215n5, 216n4
—"This Madness: The Book of Sidonie," 58, 146n3, 208, 209n1, 217
—"This Madness: The Story of Elizabeth," 85n2
—*The Titan*, xxi, xxiii, xxv, 58, 66n1, 68, 78, 82, 84, 85nn2–3, 86, 87, 88n4, 88n9, 89, 90n5, 90n8, 92n4, 93, 94n1, 94n4, 100n2, 147n1, 206n5, 209n1, 219, 237n3, 238, 346n1, 374
—"The Tithe of the Lord," 317, 317n1
—*Tragic America*, 231, 235, 236n3, 243, 244nn5–6
—*A Traveler at Forty*, xxi, 56, 57n6, 62n3, 66n1, 85n9, 87, 90n3, 117n12
—*The Trilogy of Desire*, 86, 88n6, 374
—*Twelve Men*, xxv, 21n6, 33n3, 36n2, 42n2, 94n5, 173n3, 187n3, 192n2, 361n2; "Culhane, The Solid Man," 187n3, 361n2; "My Brother Paul," 33n3, 36n2, 192n2, 361n2; "Peter," 94n5, 287n2; "A True Patriarch," 36n6, 192n2; "'Vanity, Vanity,' Saith the Preacher," 173n3; "W. L. S.," 42n2
—*Unworthy Characters*, 347
Dreiser, Helen Richardson. *See* Richardson, Helen Patges
Dreiser, John Paul, Jr. (brother Paul Dresser), xxviii, 1, 5, 5n1, 11, 22, 24n2, 32, 33n3, 36n2, 37n3, 126n8, 192n2,

228n3, 257, 324, 325n1, 329n1, 343n1, 356, 357n10, 360, 361nn1–2, 367; "Just Tell Them That You Saw Me," 360, 361n1; "My Gal Sal," xxviii, 324, 325n1, 325, 326n1, 326nn3, 343nn1–2, 348, 348n7, 360, 361n1, 366, 367n3; "On the Banks of the Wabash," 34, 36n2, 37n3, 324, 360, 361n1
Dreiser, Mai Skelly, 329n1
Dreiser, Marcus Romanus (brother Rome), 238n2, 269n5, 286, 347, 348n5
Dreiser, Mary Frances (sister Mame), xxv, 22, 24n3, 114, 116, 117n15, 161, 167, 168n7, 172, 173n1, 174, 238n2, 262, 266, 269nn5–6, 285, 286–87, 286n3, 329n1, 342, 343n1, 353–54, 356–57n9, 361n3, 362
Dreiser, Mary Theresa (sister), 22, 24n5
Dreiser, Sara Osborne White (first wife). *See* White, Sara Osborne
Dreiser, Sarah Schanab (mother), 154, 314, 314n2, 350, 360
Dreiser, Sylvia (sister), 24n5, 171, 171n14, 238n2, 261, 286, 342, 343n1, 353, 354, 357n10
Dreiser, Vera (niece), xvii, 354, 365nn1–2; Letters to, 362–67; "Afraid of You" (song), 365n2; *My Uncle Theodore*, 363
Dresser, Paul. *See* Dreiser, John Paul, Jr.
Du Bois, W. E. B., 85n5
DuChamp, Marcel, 61
Dudley, Dorothy, xvii, xviii, 234, 236n2; Letter to, 234–36; *Dreiser and the Land of the Free*, 234; *Forgotten Frontiers: Dreiser and the Land of the Free*, 234
Dudley, Katherine, 210, 210n3, 235, 236n9
Duncan, Isadora, xx, 111n1
Duneka, Frederick A., 91, 92n2
Durant, William James, 224, 225n2; *The Story of Philosophy*, 225n2
Dwan, Allan, 174, 176n2, 178n6
Dymow, Ossip, 126n2; "Nju," 124, 126n2

Eastman, Max, 127n16, 223
Ecclesiastes, 135, 136n2
Eisenberg, Emanuel, 319n4
Elder, Donald B., 373n2
Elias, Robert H., xv, xvii, xxxiii, 58; *Letters of Theodore Dreiser*, xi, 47n1
Ellison, Ralph, 381n1, 359n2
Ellsworth, W. W., 91, 92n6
Elser, Max, 194, 196n6
Emerson, Ralph Waldo, 290, 291n1
Epstein, Dr. Max, 208n4
Ernst, Morris L., 195, 196n8
Esherick, Wharton, 210, 211n5, 221, 247, 247n2, 256, 356
Esquire, 317, 329n3, 347, 350n1, 351n5
Eter, Dr. Paul, 207, 208n4
Ettinge, James A., 166, 166n4
Euripides, 58, 105n5; "The Trojan Women," 58, 70n6, 80n3, 105n5
Evans, Ernestine, 195n2
Evansville Courier, 41
Evening Sun, 93, 94n4
Ev'ry Month, xix, 11, 13, 17n1, 20, 21n5, 25n8, 28, 88n13

Fabri, Ralph, 222, 222n3, 356
Faithful, Starr, 283, 284n3
Falls, C. B., 352n1
Famous Players Lasky, 169, 171n9, 366n3
Farrell, James T., 241n6
Fawcett, Robert, 352n1
Ferguson, John Duncan, 206n3
Ficke, Arthur, 102, 103n7
Field, Marshall, 37, 38, 39n1
Fielding, Mildred, 120, 124n3
Fields, W. C. (Claude William Dukerfield), 168–69, 171n1
Fish, Mrs. Stuyvesant, 50, 51n1
Fisher, Libby, 280, 281n12
Fitzgerald, F. Scott, 332n5; *The Great Gatsby*, 332n5
Flynn, Errol, 349, 350n3
Ford, Henry, 289, 290n1
Ford, John, 117n13
Fort, Charles H., 175, 176n6, 237n2, 256, 256n3; *The Book of the Damned*, 175, 176n6; *Lo!* 176n6; *New Lands*, 176n6; *Wild Talents*, 176n6
Fortean Society, 176n6
Foster, Stephen, 352n2; "The Beautiful Shore," 351n2
Fox, George, 321–22, 323nn1–2, 338;

George Fox: An Autobiography, 323n1; *Journal*, 322, 323n1, 323n5
France, Anatole, 74n2; "Thais," 73, 74n2
Franco, Francisco, 281, 282n3, 305
Frank, Alice, 109, 111
Frank, Waldo, 116, 117n11
Frank Rehn Gallery, 252n1
Franks, Bobby, 173n7
Frapieé, Léon, 281n3
Freeman, Helen, 167, 168n6
Freeman, Mrs. Ross, 168n7
French League for the Rights of Man, 230
Freud, Sigmund, 187, 188nn1–2
Frick, Henry Clay, 230
Friede, Donald, 325, 326n3, 345, 346n3
Fuessle, Newton A., 147n3; *Gold Shod*, 147
Fuller, Henry Blake, 47, 47n1; *With the Procession*, 47n1
Futurist movement, 61, 62n2

Gaiter, David, 209, 210n1, 255
Gaither, David S., 209, 210n3
Gallagher, Leo, 243, 244n2, 343, 344n6
Garfield, John, 265n6
Garland, Hamlin, 111n4, 166n1, 345–46, 346n1; *Forty Years of Psychic Research*, 345, 346n1
Gauguin, Paul, 62n3
Gertz, Mitchell, 290, 291n5, 292
Gibson, Mary, 130, 130n3
Gide, Andre, 275, 276n4
Gilder, Richard Watson, 111n4
Gillette, Chester, 157n5, 332n3
Gillette-Brown case, 149nn2–3, 157n5
Gingrich, Arnold, 349, 350n1
Glass, Carter, 179, 180n8
Godwin, Hazel, 321, 328n4; Letters to, 321–24, 326–29, 332–39, 340–42, 344–47, 350–51, 360–61, 374–76
Golden, John, 277, 278n13
Goldman, Emma, 85n5, 111, Letters to, 212–14, 230–31; *Anarchism and Other Essays*, 214n4; *Living My Life*, 212, 231n4
Goldschmidt, Alfons, 265n7, 390n1
Goldschmidt, Lina, 207; Letters to, 207–8, 217–18, 226–27, 265n7
Gonled, Mr. and Mrs., 77, 79n1
Goodman, Lillian Rosedale, 269n8, 365–66
Goodman, Mark, 269n8
Goodrich, Elizabeth, 70, 70n6
Gorer, Geoffrey, 256n2; *Africa Dances: A Book about West African Negroes*, 256, 256nn2–3
Grand Street, 337n1
Gray, Charles N., 29, 31n5, 32, 34, 40, 73
Great Depression, xxvi, 205, 238, 243, 244n6, 251, 286
Greil, Dr. Cecile, 111–13, 111n2
Grey, Clifford, 178n1; *Vogues*, 178n1
Grey, Peter, 275n6
Griffin, Constance M., 47n1
Grigsby, Emilie, 92n3
Grimm, Jakob Ludwig Karl, 186
Grimm, Wilhelm Karl, 186
Groskopf, Samuel, 274, 275n7
Grosvenor, Anne, 251, 251n1
Grosvenor, Edwin, 251, 330
Guitteau, Maude, 172, 173n2
Gunn, Archie, 19, 21n4
Gunsaulus, Frank W., 37, 39nn2–4, 40

Haardt, Sara, 228n4
Hale, Ralph T., 114
Halton, Mary, 102, 103n2
Ham and Eggs Retirement Life Payments Association, 306, 307n8
Hammett, Dashiell, 281n1
Hapgood, Hutchens, 125, 126n8; "A Victorian in the Modern World," 126n8
Harcourt Brace, 268
Harding, Warren G., 197, 198n1, 211n4
Hardy, Thomas, 78; "I Look into My Glass," 78, 79n7
Harlan County miners strike, xxvii, 240n4, 277, 278n4
Harper, F. V., 319
Harper's, xxi, 82, 84, 87, 91, 92nn1–4, 94n4, 138, 355, 374
Harris, Frank, 140–41, 141n3, 141nn5–6, 212; *Contemporary Portraits, Second Series*, 141n5; *Contemporary Portraits: Fourth Series*, 212; "Dreiser vs. Harris," 141n5

Harris, Hillary, 357
Hartung, Gustave, 208n3
Harvey, Henry Blodgett, 234
Hauptman, Gerhart, 100n4, 106; "*Elga*," 100, 100n4; "*The Weavers*," 106
Havel, Hyppolyte, 212, 214n4; *Anarchism and Other Essays*, 214n4
Hayes, Arthur Garfield, 230, 231n2
Hays, William Harrison, 263, 292, 293n8, 299, 301
Hays Code, 263, 293n8, 300–301n2, 301
Haywood, William D. (Big Bill), 204n1
Hayworth, Rita, 324, 325n2
Hecht, Ben, 93, 94n2
Hedgerow Theatre, 211n5, 247, 247n2, 255, 265n6
Heinsberg, Emma, 95
Hellman, Lillian, 281n1
Hemingway, Ernest, 236n1, 281n1, 359n2
Henderson, Clayton W., 37nn2–3, 258n1
Henry, Arthur, 9, 9–10n1, 149n4, 161, 162n2, 162n4, 163, 246; *An Island Cabin*, 162n2
Herberman, Mrs., 102, 103n2
Heym, Mrs., 221; Letter to, 221
Hicks, Elias, 322, 323n2
Hicks, Robert Stanley, 372
Hines, Dixie, 118, 119n5
Hitchcock, Ripley, 84, 85n3, 89
Hitler, Adolf, 305, 306n2, 311
Hobbes, Halliwell, 169, 171n6
Hoffenstein, Samuel, 206n2
Holly, Flora Mai, 48, 49n2
Hollywood Ten, 205n1
Holman, Lilly, 247, 247n3
Home and Country, 27n3
Homestead Strike, 230
Hoover, Herbert, 180n2, 211n4
Hoover, J. Edgar, xxvii
Hopkins, Arthur, 125, 126, 126n5
House Un-American Activities Committee, 205n1, 319n3, 320n3
Howells, William Dean, xx, 37n6
Howley, Haviland & Co., 11, 87, 88n13
Howley, Patrick J., 17, 18n2
Hubbard, Arthur J., 184, 184nn1–2
Huebsch, Benjamin W., 194, 195n4
Hughes, Langston, 281n1, 359n2
Hughes, Rupert, 290, 291n2
Hull, Charles, 49n1
Hull, Cordell, 267, 268n2
Hull-House, 49n1
Hume, Arthur Carter, 266, 267n4, 274
Hume, Edna, 102, 103n2
Hume & Cameron (attorneys), 214
Hurst, Fannie, 248n5; *Back Street*, 248n5
Hussman, Lawrence E., 229n1
Hutchinson, Winfield, 23, 25n.9
Hylan, John F., 179, 180n5
Hyman, Belle Bushnell, 80n4, 85, 88n1
Hyman, Dorothy, 88nn1–2
Hyman, Elaine. *See* Markham, Kirah
Hyman, Harry S., 88n1, 95, 96n5
Hyman, Robert Bushnell, 88n2
Hynes, Captain William F., 242, 243, 243n1, 243n3

Ibsen, Henrik, 115n10; "Peer Gynt," 114, 115n10
Indiana University, 1, 3, 3n3, 5, 6, 124n3, 318, 319
Inness, George, 130, 130n5
Institute of Red Professors, 202n4
Insull, Samuel, 206n5
International Christian Hebrew Alliance, 204n6
Internationalist, 93, 94n1
International Newspaper Syndicate, 203
International Peace Campaign (Rassemblement Universal pour la Paix), 270–72
International Peace Mission, 300n1
International Workers of the World (IWW), 204n1
Iroki, xxvi, 228, 254n1, 265n3, 302n3
Ivan, Rosalind, 126n2

Jaeger, William, 262n2
James, William, 90n1
Jamin, George, 275, 276n5, 280
Jarmuth, Edith De Long, 80, 81n8, 113
Jessel, Eddie, 169
John Lane Co., xxi, 95, 96n4, 104n1, 117nn3–4, 119n7, 125, 127n8, 128, 133n1, 135, 136n3
Johns, Orrick, 172, 173n5

John Simon Guggenheim Memorial Foundation, 252
Johnson, Arthur John (Jack), 74, 74n8
Johnson, Charles Howard, 19, 21n4
Johnson, Margaret, 134; Letters to, 134–37, 139–44
Jones, H. C., 27, 27n3
Jones, J. Jefferson, 103, 104n1, 114, 115, 116, 117nn3–4, 125, 126
Jones, Jennifer, 367n3
Jones, Marjorie, 125, 127n12
Jones, Mary Harris ("Mother" Jones, "The Miner's Angel"), 74, 74n8
Jones, Rufus M., 323n1, 324n5
Joyce, James, 195n4

Kahn, Otto, 177, 178n4
Kahn, Roger Wolfe, 177, 178n4
Kalish, (Madame) Bertha, xx, 68, 68n6, 69, 72–73, 77, 80
Kallen, Horace, 206n2
Kandel, Aben, 301n7
Kandel, Libby (Fischer), 300, 301n7
Kaufman, Reginald Wright, 273, 275n3
Kazan, Elia, 265n6
Kearney, Patrick, 218n1, 226, 256, 256n1, 311
Keats, John, 63, 64n2, 73, 74n4; "Eve of St. Agnes," 63, 64n2, 73, 74n4; "Ode on a Grecian Urn," 63, 64n2; "Ode on Melancholy," 63, 64n2
Keith/Albee vaudeville circuit, 171n4
Kennedy, Benton, 249n1
Kennedy, Margaret, 254n3; *Escape Me Never*, 253, 254nn3–4
Kennell, Ruth Epperson, 200, 240n1; Letters to, 200–204, 214–16, 267–68, 298–99, 305–8, 310–11, 319–20, 368–69; *Adventures in Russia and Other Stories about Soviet Children*, 200; *That Boy Nikolka and Other Tales of Soviet Children*, 200; *Theodore Dreiser and the Soviet Union*, 200; *Vanya of the Streets*, 215n4, 216, 216n1
Kenton, Edna, xvii, xix, 47, 84, Letters to, 47–51, 56–57; "Some Incomes in Fiction," 56n3
Kertesz, Andrew, 265, 265n4
King James Bible, 327n1, 329n2
Kinnosuki, Adachi, 70, 70n5
Kiper, Miriam, 92
Kirkland, Alexander, 265n6
Knopf, Alfred A., 250, 250n2, 351n1
Kraft, Hy S., 205n1
Krog, Fritz, 55, 55n1
Krutch, Joseph Wood, 195n2
Kubitz, Estelle Bloom, 127n13, 128, 153, 154n2, 228, 228n5
Kummer, Clare (nèe Clare Rodman Bacher), 161, 162n4, 343; Letter to, 246; *Her Master's Voice*, 246n3
Kusell, Sallie: Letters to, 148–53, 189–91, 193
Kyllmann, Otto, 201, 202n3, 271, 276, 284

Ladies Home Journal, 138
Lardner, Ring, Jr., 183n4, 281n1; *You Know Me Al: A Busher's Letters*, 183n4
Lasky, Jesse L., 171n9
Laughton, Charles, 293n4
Laval, Pierre, 230, 231n1
Lawrence, D. H., 195n4
Lawrence, T. E., 236n1
Lawson, John Howard, 205nn1–2, 345, 346n3
Lawton, Dr. Shailer Upton, 363–64, 365n7
League of American Writers, xxi, 117n4, 270, 271n2, 307n3
Le Barbier, Charles, 112
Legros, Alphonse, 237n4; *Aged Spaniard*, 237n4
Lehr, Harry, 50, 51n1
Leigh, Frederick T., 91, 92n1
Lemon, Courtenay, 84, 85n7
Lengel, William C., 92n10, 246, 309, 318, 319n2 329, 329n3; "'The 'Genius' Himself," 329n3
Lenin, Vladimir, 202, 204n2, 226
Lenormand, Henri, 275, 276n3
Leopold, Nathan, 173n7
Leopold-Loeb case, 173, 173n7
Levinson, Leon, 202, 204n6
Levy, Louis, 125, 127n8
Lewis, Sinclair, 215n1
Libbey, Laura Jean, 69, 70n
Liberal Club, 84, 85n5, 98, 212

Liberty magazine, 246
Lieber, Hugh Gray, 352n1
Life on the Mississippi, 182
Light, Evelyn, 237n6, 238, 239
Light, James, 167
Lincoln, Robert Todd, 38, 39n8
Lippmann, Walter, 85n5
Liveright, Horace, 133n1, 136n5, 138, 139n1, 148, 149n5, 151, 152, 166, 176n6, 190, 203, 216, 358–59, 359n3, 374
Living Thoughts Library, 291n1, 352n1
Loeb, Richard, 173n7
Londres, Albert, 195n1; *The Road to Buenos Ayres*, 195n1
Long, John Luther, 31n4; *Madame Butterfly*, 31n4
Longfellow, Henry Wadsworth, 21n3, 44, 45n2; "Evangeline," 21n3
Longmans, Green and Co., 352n1
Longworth, Alice Roosevelt, 211n4
Loyalists (in Spain), 208n2, 267, 277, 281, 282, 282n3, 307
Lundberg, Ferdinand, 348n1; *America's Sixty Families*, 348n1

MacLeish, Archibald, 281n1
Madison, President James, 14n2
Mallon, Anna, 149n4
Mamoulian, Rouben, 211n8
Manhandled, 178, 178n6
Mann, Heinrich, 218, 218n2
Mann, Thomas, 218n2, 281n1
Manuel, Al, 345, 346n3
March, William, 346n5; *Company K*, 345–46, 346n5
Marden, Orison Swett, 33n2
Marinetti, F. T., 62n4
Maritzer, L. S., 153, 154n1
Markham, Kirah, xv, xvi, xvii, xix, xxi, xxv, xxviii, 211n5; Letters to, xxxiii, 58–119 124–28, 144–47, 208–11, 216–17, 238, 251–52, 254–55, 351–52, 361–62; (as Sidonie), 208–10, 217; (in *The Titan*), xxv, 90n8, 144, 163, 164n4, 168n4
Martin, Edward A., *In Defense of Marion*, 127n13
Marx, Karl, xxii, 226
Marxism, 218n1, 227n1, 305
Masken, Drei, 208n3
Masses, xx, 66n1, 92n9, 337n1
Masters, Edgar Lee, 102, 103n8, 115, 190, 234, 269, 283, 290, 343, 344n7; *Spoon River Anthology*, 103n8
Mathison, Edith Wynne, 77, 79n1
Matisse, Henri, 61, 62n3
Mature, Victor, 324, 325n2
McAdoo, William Gibbs, 178–79, 180n4
McAleer, John J., 257n2
McClure's, 52
McClure's Syndicate, 41
McCord, Donald, 286, 287n2
McCord, Peter, 93, 94n5, 287n2
McCormack, John, 168, 168n8; "The Bard of Armagh" (song), 168n8
McCormick, Anne O'Hare, 214, 215n2; *The Hammer & the Scythe*, 214, 215n2
McCoy, Esther, xvii, xxvi, 181, 293, 337n1, 343, 344n7; Letters to, 181–82, 185–88, 197–99, 236–37, 242–44, 248–50, 257, 258–60, 293, 296n2, 308–9; "The Death of Dreiser," 337n1; *Five California Architects*, 181
McKim, Charles F., 14n2
McNamara, James B., 315, 316n1
Mencken, H. L. (Henry Louis), xx, xxi, 85n5, 108n2, 116, 117n4, 117n8, 125, 126n5, 127n13, 139, 139n3, 141, 144, 145, 150, 151n4, 153, 160, 162, 168n3, 193, 193n3, 219, 219n9, 228, 228n4, 234–35, 236n2, 250, 250n3, 343, 344n7, 354, 355n10, 356
Mendel, Alfred O., 352n1
Messianic Judaism, 204n6
Metropolitan Magazine, 28, 36n2, 149n5, 162, 163n9
Metropolitan Syndicate, 196n6
Millay, Edna St Vincent, 268; "Euclid Alone Has Looked," 268
Miller, Kenneth Hayes, 52
Mitchell, S. Weir; *Hugh Wynne, Free Quaker*, 97, 99n2
Moffat, Stanley M., 354, 355n7, 356
Molineaux, Roland Burke, 330, 331n2; "The Man Inside," 331n2

Monahan, Margaret, 225n5
Monroe, Harriet, 234; *Poetry*, 234
Mooney, Thomas J., 239, 240nn1–2, 242
Moore, Marianne, 217n1
Moorhead, Dr. Thomas, 37n3
Mordell, Albert, 92n3, 95, 96n2, 96n4, 116; *The Shifting of Literary Values*, 96n2
Morgan, J. P., & Company, 298, 299nn2–3
Morris, Judson C., 129, 130n2
Morrow, Dwight, 298, 299n30
Morse, Theodore F., 17, 18n2, 19
Morse, Woolson, 19, 21n2
Mother Earth, 212, 214n2, 214n4
Motion Picture Association of America, 293n7
Mowatt, Anna Cora: *Fashion*, 163, 164n3
Muldoon, William, 187, 187n3, 361n2
"Music Master," 117n14
Mussolini, Benito, 305
Myrtil, Odette, 177, 178n5

Nathan, George Jean, 108n2, 160, 160n6, 240n6
Nation, 141, 190n2, 307n7
National Academy of Design, 61
National Committee for the Defense of Political Prisoners, xxvii, 240n4
Nationalist Socialist Party (Nazis), xxvii, 207, 218nn1–2, 267, 305, 306n1, 307n2, 307n6; Nazi-Soviet Pact, 305, 307n4, 304n7
Negrin, Juan, 305, 307n3
Nelson, Gertrude, 116, 117n14, 148, 149n2, 150, 163–64, 179, 286, 354
Newspaper Guild, 306, 307–8n9
New York Armory Show, 61, 62n2
New York Evening Mail, 117n9
New York Evening World, 181n15
New York Herald Tribune, 190n2; Paris Edition, 276, 279
New York Journal, 34
New York Society for the Suppression of Vice, xxi, xxiv, 117n4, 119n7, 136n3
New York Theater Guild, 100n4
New York World's Fair (1939–40), 295, 296n7
Nichols, Robert, 211n8; "Wings Over Europe," 211n8
Nobel Prize, 100n4, 257n1, 272n4, 285, 286n2
Nordfeldt, Bror Julius Olson, 80, 80n3, 114, 124, 126n1, 252, 252n3
Normandie, 270, 272, 277
Norris, Frank, 99n2; "Vandover and the Brute," 97, 99n2

O'Neill, Eugene, 85n5, 159, 161nn4–n5, 166, 240n6, 285, 285n2; *All God's Chillun Got Wings*, 161n5; *The Ancient Mariner*, 159, 161n4, 170; *The Emperor Jones*, 166–67, 168nn4–5, 170; *Strange Interlude*, 219, 220n2
Obenchain, Madalynne, 248, 248n1
Oglethorpe, James Edward, 108n1
Olivier, Lawrence, 301n2, 301n4, 348n6, 367n3
Olson, Culbert L., 240n1, 307n8
Oppenheim, James, 162, 162n6
Ordynski, Richard, 124, 126n4
Ornitz, Samuel, 239, 240n4, 242, 243n1
Osborne, Thomas Mott, 244
Ouija boards, 108, 108n2
Oxford Movement, 261, 262n2, 304n2

Parker, Dorothy, 281n1
Parks, Esther Schänäb (Helen's grandmother, Dreiser's aunt), 154
Pascelli, Eugenio (Pope Pius XII), 298, 299n4
Paterson Silk Strike, 66n3, 204n1
Patges, Myrtle (Helen Richardson's sister), 159, 161n1, 184n1, 343
Paul Dresser Memorial Committee, 257, 258n1
Pearl Harbor, 320
Pearson's Magazine, 140, 141n5
Peg-o-my-Heart, 162, 162n5
Pell, Arthur, 205, 206n1, 231n6, 359n3
People's World, 311n2
Permanent Court of International Justice, 168n2
Picabia, Francis, 61
Picasso, Pablo, 61, 62n3
Piscator, Erwin, 207, 217, 218n1, 226, 227nn1–2, 235, 255–56, 265n4, 265nn6–7, 266
Pittsburgh Dispatch, 331

Pizer, Donald, 92n3
Playter, Phyllis, 172, 173n4
Playwright's Club, 68, 68n4
Poe, Edgar Allen, 158
Pogany, William Andrew, 290, 291n3
Pola-Negri (Chalupec, Barbara Apollonia), 169, 171n10
Potter, Grace, 84, 85n6, 104, 105n4
Pound, Ezra, 62n4
Powys, Alyse Gregory, 158, 159n4, Letter To: 316–17
Powys, John Cowper, xx, 95, 96, 96nn3–4, 102, 103n7, 114, 116, 125, 139, 145, 158, 172, 173n4, 250, 271, 284, 316; *Weymouth Sands*, 250n4
Powys, Llewelyn, 158, 159nn3–4, 182, 271, 272nn6–7, 316–17; *Black Laughter*, 183; *Ebony and Ivory*, 317n1; *Love and Death*, 316–17n1
Powys [Grey], Marion, 102, 103n6, 116, 117n16, 271, 272n6, 273
Powys, Peter, 271, 272n6, 273
Powys, Theodore Francis, 271, 272n6, 284, 284n4
Pravda, 199n2, 583
Praxiteles, 165, 166n3
Production Code Administration, 293n7
Provincetown Players, 84, 113, 126, 127n16, 134, 167, 168n4
Provincetown Playhouse (Theatre), 161n4, 164n3
Puccini, Giacomo, 31n4
Putnam Publishing (G. P. Putnam & Son), 319n2, 320, 320n4, 343, 344n9, 354, 355, 356n2, 359

Quakers (Quakerism), xx, xxv, 85n2, 97, 128, 232, 262, 321–22, 323nn1–2, 323nn4–5, 324n6, 328n2, 338
Quintanilla, Louis, 207, 208n2

Random House, 355
Rauh, Ida, 126, 127n16
Reader's Digest, 347, 348n3
Recamier, Jeanne Francoise Julie Adelaide, 21–22, 22n3
Rector, Emma, xix, xxiii, 1; Letters to, 1–10
Rector, George (Rector's restaurant), 67, 68n2
Rector, Jesse, 5
Reed, Florence, 73, 74n5, 77
Reed, John, xxii, 57, 67n3, 85n5, 204n5; *The Paterson Strike Pageant*, 67n3
Reed, Thomas B., 45n2
Reedy, William Marion, 212, 214n3; "The Daughter of the Dream," 212, 214n3
Reicher, Emanuel, 100, 100n4
Reicher, Hedwiga, 100, 100n4
Reinhardt, Max, 171n3, 235, 236n6; *The Miracle*, 169, 171n3
Rejections, 216–17n1
Reswick, William, 201, 201n2, 202
Revell, Alexander H., 38, 39n5
Revolt, 328n5
Rice, Anne Estelle, 206n3
Rice, Edward; *Evangeline*, 21n3
Richards, Grant, 116, 117n12
Richardson, Helen Patges, xv, xvii, xx, xxi, xxvii, xxviii, 58, 88n5, 134, 144, 149n2, 151n3, 154, 155, 156n1, 157n5, 159n1, 166n5, 171n11, 176n1, 184nn1–2, 189, 195, 228n5, 231, 231n3, 237n1, 239–40, 241n8, 250, 253, 254, 259–60, 263, 265n2, 265n6, 270, 278n14, 286, 288, 292, 302, 311–13, 318, 326n5, 337, 342, 343n1, 243n3, 349, 350, 357n10, 358, 359, 361n3, 365, 366, 374; Letters to, 154–81, 182–84, 194–97, 262–67, 268–72, 276–78, 284–86, 325–26, 342–44, 355–57; *My Life with Dreiser*, 154, 157n5, 184n1
Richard III. *See* Shakespeare, William
Richelieu, Cardinal, 277, 278n6
Rivera, Diego, 194–95, 195n2, 196n5
RKO, 270n10, 300, 348n6, 367
Roberts, Charles George Douglas, 206, 206n2
Robeson, Paul, 168n4, 353
Robin, Joseph G. (Odin Gregory), 172, 173n3, 175, 194, 195n3; *Caius Gracchus*, 173n3
Rockefeller, John D., 143, 144n2
Rodick, Burleigh, 166, 168n1, 168n3; *The Doctrine of Necessity in International Law*, 168n3; *My Own New England*, 168n3
Rodman, Henrietta, 84, 85n6

Rogers, Robert, 13–14n1
Roosevelt, Franklin D., xxvii, 267, 268nn1–2, 270n9, 282, 282n6, 298, 310, 311, 320, 334n4
Roosevelt, Theodore, xix
Rosenthal, Dr., 152
Rosenthal, Elias, 113, 269n8
Rosenthal, Herman, 332n5
Rosenthal, Lillian, xxv, 269, 269–70n8
Rossett, Leo, 268, 269n2, 303, 304n3
Rossetti, Dante Gabriel, 29, 31n6, 79n8; "The Blessed Damozel," 78, 79n8; "The Stream's Secret," 29, 31n6
Rousseau, Jean Jacques, 338; *Confessions of Jean Jacques Rousseau*, 339n4
Ruddick, Dorothy, 88n1, 222n2
Russell, Lillian (born Helen Louis Leonard), 69, 70nn2–3
Russian Ballet, 201n2, 235, 236n4

Salmagundi Club, 28, 32
Sandison, George H., 33n2
Sanger, Margaret, 85n5, 111
Sappho, 12n3
Saturday Evening Post, xx, 52
Savo, Jimmy, 177, 178n2
Savoy, Bert (born Everett McKenzie), 177, 178n3
Schildkraut, Joseph, 235, 236n6
Schopenhauer, Arthur, 224, 225n4; *The World as Will and Idea*, 225n4
Scott, Alfred, 365n2
Scott, Howard, 146, 147n2, 255
Scottsboro Boys, xxvii, 240n4
Screen Actors Guild, 240n4
Scribner, Charles, 355
Scribners, 91, 355
Sebree, Milton Shubert, 243, 244n5
Selfridge, Harry, 38, 39n7
Sermon on the Mount, 329
Servai, Jean, 275, 276n5, 280
Seven Arts, xx, 47
Severance, Caroline M., 342n1
Severance Club, 340, 342n1
Shakespeare, William, 152, 161, 331; *Richard III*, 280, 281n10
Shay, Frank, 228, 229, 125, 126n8, 127n9
Sheffield, Justus, 112
Sherman, Stuart Pratt, 189, 190n2; *Cambridge History of American Literature*, 190n2; "Mr. Dreiser in Tragic Realism," 190n2
Shoup, John, 130n4
Shubert, Milton, 255, 265n6
Sidney, Sir Philip, 268; *My True Love Hath My Heart*, 268
Simon and Schuster, 203, 215, 320n4, 342, 343n2, 352n1, 356n2, 358, 359, 359n3
Simpson, Jeremiah ("Sockless Jerry"), 185, 186n1
Sinclair, Upton, 90n1, 281n1, 316n1
Smart Set, 47, 68n3, 117n9, 141, 153n1
Smith, Alfred Emanuel, 178–79, 180n2
Smith, Arthur Cosslett, 60n4; "The Monk and the Dancer," 59, 60n4
Smith, Edward H., 81n8, 140, 141n4; "Dreiser—After Twenty Years," 141n4
Smith, Harrison, 236n1
Smith, Harry Baile, 128
Smith, Lorna Dysart, 325, 326n4
Smith, Tom, 160, 161n9, 216
Smith's, 176n6
Society of Friends. *See* Quakers (Quakerism)
Sonntag, William Louis, Jr., 41, 42n2
South, Mary, 34, 37n3
Soviet Russia Today, 310, 311n1
Spanish Civil War, xxvii, 208n2, 282n6
Spencer, Herbert, 22n2, 111n4
Stalin, Joseph, 198, 199n2, 306, 307n3
Stanchfield, John B., 115, 125, 127n8
Standard Oil Company, 175
Stapp, John, 319n3
Starr, Ellen Gates, 49n1
St. Boniface Cemetery, 328, 329n1
Stedman, Edmund Clarence, 37n6
Stein, Gertrude, 61, 62n4
Steinbeck, John, 281n1
Sten, Anna, 247
Sterling, George, 179, 180n11; *Lillith*, 180n11
St. Joseph, 222, 222n7
St. Louis Dispatch, 25n9
St. Louis Globe-Democrat, 41, 94n5, 173, 173n6

St. Louis Mirror, 214n3
St. Louis Republic, 1, 3, 4, 11
Stone, William Joel, 17, 18n3
Stothart, Herbert P., 178n1
Stowe, Harriet Beecher, 17n1, 44; *Uncle Tom's Cabin*, 15, 17
St. Paul, 316; "First Corinthians," 316, 317n2
Strasberg, Lee, 265n6
Strindberg, (Johan) August, xxi, 195n4
Stuyvesant, Peter, 51n1
Success, 28, 33n2, 37
Sumner, John S., 115, 117n4, 136n3
Szekely, Suzanne, 325n3
Szekely, Yvette [Eastman], xv, xvii, 223, 241n11; Letters to, 223–25, 239–41, 252–54, 315–16, 324–25, 367–68; *Dearest Wilding: A Memoir*, 223

Taft, Owen: "Conscience," 101
Talmud, 274, 275n8
Tammany Hall, 178, 179
Tarkington, Booth, 99, 100n2, 176n6; "The Turmoil," 99, 100n2; "The Magnificent Ambersons," 100n2
Tatum, Anna P., xxv, 84, 85n2, 86, 89, 90n5, 324n6
Taylor, Joseph Deems, 364, 365n3
Taylor, Laurette, 160, 161n8, 162, 162n5
Taylor, William Desmond, 249n1
Tchicherin, Georgi, 198, 199n2
Technocracy Inc., 147n2, 311, 313n1
Thaw, Harry K., 330, 332n4
Thomas, Erwing R., 161n7
Thomas, Frank, 266n1, 286, 294, 296n5, 353
"Thomas Flyer," 161n7
Thompson, Dorothy, 214, 215n1; *The New Russia*, 214–15n1
Thompson, Fred, 178n1; *Vogues*, 177, 178n1
Thoreau, Henry David, 268, 273, 274n1, 277, 280, 289, 290n3, 304; *Journal*, 268; *The Living Thoughts of Thoreau*, 274n1, 278n12, 290n3, 291n1, 351, 352n1; *Voyage on the Concord & Merrimac Rivers*, 268; *Walden*, 507
Tillich, Paul, 359n2
Titzel, Mary Elizabeth, 63n3
Tjader, Marguerite [Harris], xvii, xxiv, xxvi, xxviii, 228, 229, 257n2, 259n1, 271n1, 361n3, 366n1; Letters to, 228–29, 357–59; *Birgitta of Sweden*, 228; *Borealis*, 228, 229n2; *Love That Will Not Let Me Go: My Time with Theodore Dreiser*, 228; *Mother Elizabeth*, 228; *Theodore Dreiser: A New Dimension*, 228
Tobey, Berkeley Greene, 92, 336, 337n1, 343, 345
Toledo Blade, 9n1
Tolstoy, Leo, 81n6, 204n3; "The Kreutzer Sonata," 80, 81n6
Tolstoy, Olga, 202, 204n3
Toronto Town Forum, 232, 233
Torrence, Ridgely, 175, 176n5
Towne, Charles Hanson, 152, 153n1
Transcendentalists, 182–83
Trappists, 59, 60n5
Trevis, 203, 204n7
Trotsky, Leon, 226
Turgenev, Ivan Sergeevich, 186, 187n1
Twentieth Century-Fox, 325n1, 326n3
Twilight Club, 111, 111n4, 112

Underwood, Oscar W., 179, 180n8

Van Doren, Carl, 141; "Contemporary American Novelists: Theodore Dreiser," 141n7
Van Gogh, Vincent, 62n3
Vanity Fair, 203, 204n9
Van Tassel, Sutphen, 89, 90n7
Van Vechten, Carl, 160, 161n6, 162, 291
Veblen, Thorstein, 80n3
Vermeer, Jan, 130, 130n5
Viereck, George Sylvester, 93, 94n1, 112
Volkenburg, Ellen Van (Nelly Van), 58, 128n1
Vollmoeller, Karl, 171n3; *The Miracle*, 171n3
Von Sabern, Henry, 312, 313n4

Walker, Maggie and Mark, 10
Wallace, Alfred Russel; *World of Life*, 90n1

Wanger, Walter, 290, 291n4, 292
Ward, Louis H., 240n3
Warfield, David, 116, 117n14
Warner Brothers, 225, 333
War Powers Act (1941), 334n4
Washington Square Players, 100, 100n4, 128
Watters, Sam, 345, 346n3
Watters, William, 292n2
Watts, Isaac, 309n2
Welles, Orson, 292, 293n3; *The Mercury Theatre on the Air*, 293n3
Wells, Herbert Gregory, 224, 225n3, 236n1; *Outline of History*, 225n3; *Tono-Bungay*, 225n3
West, Mae, 247, 248n4
White, Archibald Herndon, 21n6, 22
White, Ida, 54, 54n3
White, Richard Drace (brother-in-law), 31n3
White, Rose, 21n6, 23, 25n7, 31n3, 192n1
White, Sara Osborne (Mrs. Dreiser), xi, xv, xvi, xvii, xix, xxi, xxv, xxviii, xxix, 11, 58, 60n1, 97, 99, 100n3, 149, 151n1, 269n8, 285, 286n4, 337n4; Letter from, 192n2; Letters to, 11–45, 192
White, Stanford, 332n4
Whiteman, Paul, 179, 180n6
Whitman, Charles Symour, 330–31, 332n5, 339
Whitman, Walt, xxxiv, 63, 64n1, 158, 159n5; *Leaves of Grass*, "Ah Poverties, Wincings, and Sulky Retreats," "Camps of Green," "Crossing Brooklyn Ferry," "Out of the Cradle Endlessly Rocking," "A Noiseless Patient Spider," "The Prairie—Grass Dividing," "When I Heard the Learn'd Astronomer," 63, 64n1
Who's Who, 37n6
Wilde, Oscar, xxii, 140, 141n6, 285
Wilkinson, Louis Umfreville, 116, 125
Williams, Albert Rhys, 202, 204n5; *Through the Russian Revolution*, 204n5
Williams, William Carlos, 62n4, 281n1
Wilson, Woodrow, 143, 144n2
Winged Victory of Samothrace, 176n8
Wolff, Adolph, 118, 119n8
Wood, Junius, 201, 201nn1–2, 202
Woolcott, Alexander, 161, 162n3, 176n6
Woolley, Mary C., 316n1
Woolman, John, 322, 323n4, 338; *The Journal of John Woolman*, 323nn4–5
Woolwine, Thomas, 248, 249n1
Works Progress Administration, 251
Wright, Frank Lloyd, 119n2, 128
Wright, Frank Lloyd, Jr., 118, 119n2, 126, 127n14
Wright, Richard, 281n1, 359n2
Wright, Willard Huntington (Van Dine, S. S.), 116, 117n9, 125
Wuthering Heights, 300, 301n4
Wyler, William, 301n4

Yakey, William, 2, 3n3, 6, 7n1
Yerkes, Charles Tyson, 66n1, 206n5
Yewdale, Merton S., 125, 127n8

Zayre, Kathryn, 223